The Politics of Denial

WITHDRAWN

The Politics of Denial

Israel and the Palestinian Refugee Problem

Nur Masalha

CARL A. RUDISILL LIBRARY
LENOIR-RHYNE COLLEGE

LONDON • STERLING, VIRGINIA

First published 2003 by Pluto Press
345 Archway Road, London N6 5AA
and 22883 Quicksilver Drive, Sterling, VA 20166–2012, USA

www.plutobooks.com

Copyright © Nur Masalha 2003

The right of Nur Masalha to be identified as the author of this work has been asserted by him in accordance with the Copyright, Designs and Patents Act 1988.

British Library Cataloguing in Publication Data
A catalogue record for this book is available from the British Library

ISBN 0 7453 2121 6 hardback
ISBN 0 7453 2120 8 paperback

Library of Congress Cataloging in Publication Data
Masalha, Nur, 1957–
The politics of denial : Israel and the Palestinian refugee problem / Nur Masalha.— 1st ed.
p. cm.
ISBN 0–7453–2121–6 (cloth) — ISBN 0–7453–2120–8 (pbk.)
1. Refugees, Arab—Government policy—Israel. 2. Palestinian Arabs—Government policy—Israel. 3. Israel–Arab War, 1948–1949—Refugees. 4. Israel—Politics and government—20th century.
5. Israel—Ethnic relations. 6. Arab–Israeli conflict. I. Title.
DS113.7.M32 2003
325'.21'0899274—dc21

2003007464

DS
113.7
.M32
2003
Feb '05

10 9 8 7 6 5 4 3 2 1

Designed and produced for Pluto Press by
Chase Publishing Services, Sidmouth, EX10 9QG, England
Typeset from disk by Stanford DTP Services, Towcester, England
Printed and bound in the European Union by
Antony Rowe, Chippenham and Eastbourne, England

Contents

Acknowledgements

The support of MADAR – the Palestinian Centre for Israeli Studies (Ramallah, Palestine) – is gratefully acknowledged. At MADAR, I am particularly grateful to Muhsin Yusuf, the Centre's executive director, who encouraged me to undertake the project on the subject of Israel and the Palestinian refugee problem since 1948. Among the institutions that made this work possible by helping with source material were the School of Oriental and African Studies Library in London, the Public Records Office (Kew, London), 'Adalah (the Legal Centre for Arab Minority Rights in Israel), the Arab Association for Human Rights ('Arrabeh, Galilee), the National Committee for the Defence of Internally Displaced Palestinians in Israel, Badil Resource Centre in Bethlehem, the Israel State Archives (Jerusalem), the Central Zionist Archives (Jerusalem), the Histadrut Archives (Tel Aviv), Hashomer Hatza'ir Archives (Giva'at Haviva), the Jabotinsky Institute (Tel Aviv), the Hebrew University of Jerusalem Library. Many friends and colleagues have helped me greatly with ideas, discussions, criticism and material. Among them I would like to thank Michael Prior, As'ad Ghanem, Ilan Pappé, Naseer 'Aruri, Samih Farsoun, Peter Colvin, 'Abbas Shiblak, the late Israel Shahak, Michael Hayes, Tim Niblock, Michael Adams, Sari Hanafi, Farouq Mardam-Bey and Elias Sanbar. Of course, I alone am responsible for the deficiencies of this book. Finally, I owe a great debt to my partner, Dr Stephanie Cronin, for her invaluable moral and practical support, her useful comments and perceptive criticism while this research was being undertaken.

Introduction

The Palestinian refugee problem has been at the centre of the Arab–Israeli conflict since 1948. It was mainly the refugees themselves who opposed resettlement schemes in Arab countries. In the post-1948 period in general the Palestinians and the Arab states refused to discuss a general settlement of the Arab–Israeli conflict before Israel declared that it accepted the repatriation of the refugees, in accordance with UN General Assembly Resolution 194 (III) of December 1948. The resolution stated

> [that] the refugees wishing to return to their homes and live at peace with their neighbours should be permitted to do so at the earliest practicable date, and that compensation should be paid for the property of those choosing not to return and for loss or damage to property which, under principles of international law or in equity, should be made good by the governments or authorities responsible.

To Zionist Israelis, on the other hand, the Palestinian 'right of return' appears to entail nothing less than the reversal of Zionism and Israel's transformation into a bi-national state. The official Israeli position has always been that there can be no returning of the refugees to Israeli territories, and that the only solution to the problem is their resettlement in the Arab states or elsewhere.

Since 1949 Israel has consistently rejected a return of the 1948 refugees to their homes and villages; it has always refused to accept responsibility for the refugees and views them as the responsibility of the Arab countries in which they reside. The Zionist-Israelis did not want the refugees back under any condition. They did not want them to return because they needed their lands and their villages for Jewish immigrants. Nor did they want the repatriation of an Arab population that would question the Zionist-Jewish character of the state and undermine it demographically. Since 1948 all Israeli governments have even refused to discuss any possible return of refugees to the pre-1967 borders. Although Israel considered (between 1948 and 1956) some form of restitution of refugee property in lieu of repatriation, virtually all Israeli attempts to work out proposals on compensation were tied to a settlement of abandoned Jewish property in Iraq, and later in other Arab countries.

In moral (and perhaps even in legal) terms the issue of responsibility for the 1948 refugee exodus, which will be discussed in Chapter 1, has major ramifications for the refugee question, including the 'right of return', resettlement, compensation and restitution of property.[1] Since 1948 Israel has continued to propagate the myth that the Palestinian refugee exodus was a tactic of war on the part of the Arabs who initiated the war against the Jewish Yishuv in Palestine. In recent years the 'new historiography' of Israel/Palestine has revealed that this official myth was in fact invented by the Israeli government's Transfer Committee in its report of October 1948, which formulated the main line and arguments of Israeli propaganda in the following decades. It denied any Israeli culpability or responsibility for the Arab exodus – denied, in fact, its own members' roles in various areas and contexts. It also strongly advised against any return of the refugees and proposed that the government play a major role in promoting refugee resettlement in the Arab host countries. Israel has also argued that the Palestinian refugees constituted a 'population exchange' with those Jews who left the Arab world in the 1950s. Although Israel's case was as mendacious as it was misleading, Israeli spokesmen continued to propagate it at home and abroad and many of Israel's friends in the West continued to believe it. In his book, *The New Middle East* (1993), Shimon Peres rehashes many of the founding myths of Israel and repeats basic points of the Israeli propaganda for rejecting refugee return:

- the Palestinians fled from their villages and towns in 1948 under orders from their leaders (a myth that many researchers have exploded);
- the number of the 1948 refugees was 600,000[2] (an underestimate, equating them with the number of Jews who left Arab countries for Israel);
- the time has come to turn away from history and polemics and to seek a 'fair and reasonable solution to the refugee problem', i.e., one acceptable to Israelis.

According to Peres, the 'right of return' is an unacceptable 'maximalist claim; if accepted, it would wipe out the national character of the State of Israel, making the Jewish majority into a minority'.[3]

The principal aim of this work is to examine and analyse evolving Israeli policies towards the Palestinian refugees from 1948 to the present. Of course, any discussion of contemporary Israeli policies towards the Palestinian refugee problem must be anchored in their Zionist moorings and particularly linked to those policies that were instituted in the early years of the Israeli state. This work contains seven detailed chapters on the evolution of Israeli refugee policies since 1948. Structurally the book is organised around major themes and issues. Chapter 1 examines the road to *nakba* (the Palestinian catastrophe of 1948), the historical roots of the Palestinian refugee question and Israel's moral and legal responsibility towards the refugees. It also revisits the 1948 refugee exodus, with a discussion of the myths and realities surrounding the exodus. Chapter 2 focuses on Israel's 'New Historians' and explores the notion of 'shared responsibility' for the 1948 exodus put forward by some of these historians.

Chapter 3 discusses Israeli resettlement schemes since 1948. In the 1950s one key slogan coined by senior Israeli Foreign Ministry officials was: 'If You Can't Solve it, Dissolve it' (*Im Inkha Yakhol Leftor It Habe'aya-Mosseis Otah* in Hebrew),[4] meaning that if you cannot solve the Palestinian refugee problem, as a political problem, you can try to 'dissolve' the problem and disperse the refugees through economic means and employment projects. In other words, the problem of the Palestinian refugees could and should be solved by an economic approach, mainly through their integration into the economies of their actual countries of residence and/or through their dispersal throughout the interior of the Arab world. This preoccupation with the need to 'dissolve' the refugee problem stemmed from a variety of reasons including the deep fear of Arab 'return' and the determination to remove the problem from the heart of the Arab–Israeli conflict. The chapter explores the emphasis in the Israeli position on resettlement and rehabilitation in the Arab states, rather than repatriation and/or compensation. It also discusses numerous Israeli resettlement proposals and actual schemes put forward since 1948 and investigates the ideological, political, economic, diplomatic, public relations and psychological factors which motivated Israeli resettlement schemes in the 1950s.

Israeli approaches to compensation and restitution of property are discussed in Chapter 4, which focuses on the period between 1948 and 1956, and again in Chapter 7, which deals with the Israeli refugee policy from the Madrid peace conference of October 1991 to the final status negotiations at Taba of January 2001. Chapter 5 explores another dimension of Israeli refugee policies by focusing on those policies directed at the internally displaced, or the so-called 'Present Absentees' (*nifkadim nokhahim* in Hebrew). The term is a legal one, coined with Kafkaesque irony by Israel's legal bureaucracy in its 1950 Absentees' Property Law to describe those 'Israeli Arabs' who had been displaced from their homes and villages during the 1948–9 war and, unlike those Palestinians who became refugees in neighbouring Arab countries, became refugees inside the new state of Israel. Because they had not been in their 'regular place of residence' on an arbitrary date determined by the Israeli authorities – '27th Av, 5708: 1st September 1948' – their homes, fields and property were considered forfeit and made available to tens of thousands of migrants and settlers pouring into the country. Nearly one-quarter of the Palestinians remaining in Israel had thus become 'internal refugees'. Although historians and social scientists have devoted considerable attention to the question of the Palestinian refugees outside Israel, there has been little scholarly attention to the internally displaced and their struggles, and this fact is clearly demonstrated in this chapter, which also makes an attempt to address the general neglect of historical research on the 'Present Absentees'. Chapter 5 also provides an up-to-date discussion of the classical cases of Kafr Bir'im and Iqrit and assesses the impact of the Madrid and Oslo peace processes on the internal refugees and on their struggle to regain their rights.

Chapter 6 discusses the 1967 refugee exodus in the light of new revelations and the availability of new Hebrew documents. Chapter 7 analyses Israeli refugee policies during negotiations, with the main focus on the bilateral and multilateral negotiations in the period from the Madrid peace conference of October 1991 to the final status talks at Taba, Egypt, in January 2001. Although in theory the decade between 1991 and 2001 offered an opportunity to negotiate the Palestinian refugee issue with an intensity not witnessed for four decades, in reality (as this chapter will demonstrate), Israel's classical position on refugees remained largely unchanged throughout the negotiations.

Since the mass expulsions of 1948 a key element in Israel's refugee policies has always been the prevention of the return of Palestinian refugees – residing both inside and outside the borders of the Israeli state – to their ancestral villages and towns. In many ways the classic Israeli position against refugee repatriation to the pre-1967 borders has remained unchanged since 1948. Since then the successive policies adopted by the Jewish state – land, ethnic and demographic, legal and political, military and diplomatic – have been aimed at reinforcing the power and domination of Israel's ruling Jewish majority. This paramount objective has served until today as a guiding premise underlying successive Israeli policies towards Palestinian refugees, before and throughout the Israeli–Palestinian negotiations. However, methodologically the focus of the discussion within each chapter is on

- the conceptual filter through which Israeli governments have tended to view the refugee problem since 1948;
- the policies of these governments towards the refugee problem, highlighting in the process the evolution of these policies and the legal and political premises upon which these policies were based since 1948;
- the factors that have influenced and shaped the attitudes of Israeli governments towards the refugee problem;
- the historical context and particular conditions that have influenced and characterised Israeli policies.

This work is largely based on primary and archival sources (from the Israel State Archives, Jerusalem; the Central Zionist Archives, Jerusalem; the Histadrut Archives, Tel Aviv; Hashomer Hatza'ir Archives, Giva'at Haviva; Jabotinsky Archives, Tel Aviv; the Public Record Office, Kew, London). The Israel State Archives and the Central Zionist Archives in Jerusalem, in particular, contain a number of official files with extensive information pertaining to Israel's policies toward the refugees. A very large proportion of these files is open to researchers, although some Israel State Archives files remain classified. Although some of the material in Chapter 1 has already been published in my book *Expulsion of the Palestinians: The Concept of Transfer in Zionist Political Thought, 1882–1948* (1992), since the publication of this book in 1992 more archival evidence has been made available and this has been incorporated into this work. On the whole, the Hebrew press has been an important source for events since 1967. This was supplemented by secondary sources in Hebrew, Arabic and English.

NOTES

1. Don Peretz, *Palestinian Refugees and the Middle East Peace Process* (Washington, DC: United States Institute of Peace Press, 1993), p.6.

2. According to the UN Technical Committee on Refugees, the number of Palestinian refugees in August 1949 was '711,000', comprising about half of the total Palestinian population at that time (1.415 million).
3. Shimon Peres, *The New Middle East* (Dorset, England: Element Books, 1993), pp.188–9.
4. See 'Ezra Danin, *Tzioni Bekhol Tnai* [A Zionist in Every Condition], Vol.1 (Jerusalem: Kiddum, 1987), p.317.

1 The Palestinian *Nakba*: Zionism, 'Transfer' and the 1948 Exodus

Since the Palestinian refugee exodus of 1948 a controversy has raged concerning its causes and circumstances. Who was responsible for the dispersal of the refugees? The first United States ambassador to Israel, James McDonald, told of a conversation he had with the president of Israel, Chaim Weizmann, during which Weizmann spoke in 'messianic' terms about the 1948 Palestinian exodus as a 'miraculous simplification of Israel's tasks'. McDonald said that not one of Israel's 'big three' – Weizmann, Prime Minister David Ben-Gurion and Foreign Minister Moshe Sharett – and no responsible Zionist leader had anticipated such a 'miraculous clearing of the land'.[1] The available evidence (based on mountains of Israeli archival documents), however, shows that the big three had all enthusiastically endorsed the concept of 'transferring' the Palestinians in the 1937–48 period and had anticipated the mass flight of Palestinian refugees in 1948, referred to by Palestinians as the *nakba* (catastrophe).

Palestinian demography and the land issue were at the heart of the Zionist transfer mind-set and secret transfer plans of the 1930s and 1940s. In 1947 the indigenous Palestinians were the overwhelming majority in the country and owned much of the land. The Jewish community (mainly European settlers) was about a third of the total population and owned, after 50 years of land purchases, only 6 per cent of the land. In the 1930s and 1940s the general endorsement of transfer (in different forms: voluntary, agreed and compulsory) was designed to achieve two crucial objectives: (1) to clear the land for Jewish settlers and would-be immigrants, and (2) to establish an ethnocratic and fairly homogenous Jewish state. During the same period key leaders of Labour Zionism, such as Ben-Gurion, then chairman of the Jewish Agency, strongly believed that Zionism would not succeed in setting up a homogenous Jewish state and fulfilling its imperative of absorbing the expected influx of Jewish immigrants from Europe if the indigenous inhabitants were allowed to remain.

The 'nationalist socialist' ideology of Ben-Gurion and other leading figures of Labour Zionism, which from the 1930s into the 1970s dominated first the Yishuv (the pre-1948 Jewish community in Palestine) and then the state of Israel, was a form of integral 'tribal and *volkisch*' nationalism borrowed from central and eastern Europe. Labour Zionism rejected both Marxism and liberal forms of universalism, along with individual rights and class struggle. Instead, it gave precedence to the realisation of an 'organic nationalist' settler project: the establishment in Palestine of an ethnic settler state. In this project, socialism was deployed both as a useful 'mobilising myth' and an essential tool for collective (Jewish) control of the land. Although largely secular, Labour Zionism instrumentally emphasised Jewish religion and ethnicity, promoted the cult and myths of ancient history and biblical battles, revived a seemingly dead language, built up a powerful, Spartan army, surrounded its Yishuv with an 'Iron Wall' and waged a bitter struggle for political independence and territorial expansion throughout the land. Zionist 'nationalist socialists' repudiated liberal individualism and were suspicious of bourgeois liberal democracy.[2]

This illiberal, settler-colonial, Spartan legacy of Labour Zionism continued after the founding of the Israeli state in 1948. With no social perspectives or ideological directions beyond a *volkisch* nationalism based on abstract 'historical rights to the whole land of Israel', the mould set in the pre-state period did not change, and the Labour leadership was unable to cope with the consequences of the 1967 war. It continued with new settlements and territorial expansion, and tried to test the Zionist method of 'creating facts on the ground'. Unable to come to terms with Palestinian nationalism, Labour Zionism inevitably pursued its settler colonialism in the occupied territories.[3]

'Land redemption' (*geolat adama* in Hebrew), 'land conquest' (*kibbush adama*), settler colonisation, demographic transformation, the Judaisation of Palestine and Jewish statehood have been the permanent themes of political Zionism. Jewish nation-building, ever expanding settlements, territorial ambitions and the effective use of the myths/legends and epics of the Bible went hand in hand. Zionists claim that events described in the Old Testament establish the right of twentieth-century Jews to found an ethnic Jewish state in Palestine. Contrary to the archaeological and historical evidence, the view that the Bible provides Jews with a title-deed to the 'whole Land of Israel' and morally legitimises the creation of the state of Israel and its 'ethnic cleansing' policies towards the native Palestinians is still pervasive in Jewish Zionist circles.[4]

In modern times the 'Land of Israel' has been invested with far-reaching historical, geopolitical and ideological connotations in Israeli rhetoric and scholarship. The reconstruction of the past by Zionist authors has often reflected their own political and religious ideologies. Zionist authors and biblical scholars have based the historical claims of modern Zionism to *Eretz-Yisrael*, the land of Israel, on biblical (mythical) narratives. In his seminal work *The Invention of Ancient Israel: The Silencing of Palestinian History* (1996) Keith Whitelam has examined the political implications of the terminology of biblical scholarship chosen to represent this area and has shown how the naming of the land implied control and possession of it; how the terms '*Eretz-Yisrael*', 'the land of Israel' and Palestine have been invested with, or divested of, meaning in both Western and Israeli scholarship. Despite the fact that Western biblical scholarship has continually employed the term 'Palestine', Whitelam argues, the term has been divested of any real meaning in the face of the search for the ancient 'land of Israel'. Palestine has no intrinsic meaning of its own, no history of its own, but merely provides a background for the history of Israel. Commensurate with the lack of history is also the absence of the inhabitants of the land. The history of Palestine and its inhabitants in general is subsumed and silenced by the concern with, and in the search for, ancient Israel.[5]

THE 'EMPTY LAND'

The myth of 'a land without a people' is not just an infamous fragment of early Zionist propaganda: it is ubiquitous in much of the Israeli historiography of nation-building. A few weeks after the 1967 war, Israel's leading novelist, 'Amos 'Oz, drew attention to the deep-seated inclination among Israelis to see Palestine as a country without its indigenous inhabitants:

> When I was a child, some of my teachers taught me that after our Temple was destroyed and we were banished from our country, strangers came into what was our heritage and defiled it. The desert-born Arabs laid the land waste and let the terraces on the hillsides go to ruin. Their flocks destroyed the beautiful forests. When our first pioneers came to the land to rebuild it and to redeem it from desolation, they found an abandoned wasteland. True, a few backward, uncouth nomads wandered in it.

> Some of our first arrivals thought that, by right, the Arabs should return to the desert and give the land back to its owners, and, if not, that they (the Zionists) should 'arise and inherit,' like those who conquered Canaan in storm: 'A melody of blood and fire ... climb the mountain, crush the plain. All you see – inherit ... and conquer the land by the strength of your arm.' (Tchernichovsky, 'I Have a Tune')[6]

'Oz also drew attention to Na'omi Shemer's song 'Jerusalem of Gold', which encapsulated this deep-seated inclination among Israeli Jews to see Palestine as a country without its Arab inhabitants. The song 'Jerusalem of Gold', which came to be defined as a kind of 'national anthem of the Six Day War',[7] was commissioned by the municipality of Jewish Jerusalem, was written for a music festival held on the eve of the war,[8] and became a national hit after the Israeli seizure of Arab East Jerusalem, the West Bank, and Gaza Strip. It is the most popular song ever produced in Israel and in 1967 it swept the country like lightning, genuinely expressing Israeli national aspirations following the new conquests. Na'omi Shemer herself received the Israel Prize for her unique contribution to the Israeli song. The song contains the following passages:

> Jerusalem of Gold ...
> How did the water cisterns dry out, the market-place is empty,
> And no-one visits the Holy Mount [Al-Haram al-Sharif] in the Old City.
> And through the cave within the rock winds are whining,
> And no-one descends down to the Dead Sea en route for Jericho.
> .....
> Jerusalem of Gold ...
> We have returned to the water cisterns, to the market-place and the square.
> A shofar[9] sounds on the Holy Mount in the Old City.
> And in the caves within the rock a thousand suns do glow,
> We shall again descend to the Dead Sea en route for Jericho.[10]

The same myth of 'empty land' runs through state education in Israel and finds strong expression in children's literature. One such work for children contains the following excerpt:

> Joseph and some of his men thus crossed the land [Palestine] on foot, until they reached Galilee. They climbed mountains, beautiful but empty mountains, where nobody lived. ... Joseph said, 'We want to establish this Kibbutz and conquer this emptiness. We shall call this place Tel Hai [Living Hill]. ... The land is empty; its children have deserted it [the reference is, of course, to Jews]. They are dispersed and no longer tend it. No one protects or tends the land now.'[11]

In a similar vein, Israel's leading satirist, Dan Ben-Amotz, observed in 1982 that 'the Arabs do not exist in our textbooks [for children]. This is apparently in accordance with the Jewish-Zionist-socialist principles we have received. 'A-people-without-a-land-returns-to-a-land-without-people.'[12] These images and formulas of 'underpopulated and untended land' gave those who propounded them a simple and self-explanatory Zionism. These myths not only justified Zionist settlement but also helped to suppress conscience-pricking among Israeli Jews for the dispossession of the Palestinians before, during, and after 1948: if the 'land had been empty', then no Zionist wrongdoing had taken place.

Even in the 1990s, Israeli prime ministers such as Yitzhak Shamir and Binyamin Netanyahu were still propagating the myth of an underpopulated, desolate and inhospitable land to justify the Zionist colonisation of Palestine and its obliviousness to the fate of its native inhabitants.[13] In October 1991 Prime Minister Yitzhak Shamir, in his address to the Madrid Peace Conference, resorted to quoting from *Innocents Abroad* by Mark Twain. (Twain visited Palestine in 1867 and his description of its natives was either marked by invective or was humorously pejorative.) The aim of Shamir (who regarded the Madrid Conference as purely ceremonial and treated it as a propaganda platform) was to prove that Palestine was an empty territory, a kind of civilisational barrenness that (in Shamir's words) 'no one wanted'; 'A desolate country which sits in sackcloth and ashes – a silent, mournful expanse which not even imagination can grace with the pomp of life.'[14] Moreover, this (mythical) continuum between the ancient and the modern means this is a difficult land, one that resists agriculture and that can only be 'redeemed' and made to yield up its produce by the extraordinary effort of Jewish immigrants and Zionist pioneers. It mattered little that in reality most of Palestine, other than the Negev, was no desert but an intensely and successfully cultivated fertile land.

For the Zionist settler who is coming 'to redeem the land' the indigenous people earmarked for dispossession are usually invisible. They are simultaneously divested of their human and national reality and classed as a marginal nonentity. Furthermore, Zionism, like all European-settler, colonial movements, had to demonise and dehumanise the indigenous people in its path in order to legitimise their displacement and dispossession. Thus, the Palestinians were depicted as 'conniving', 'dishonest', 'lazy', 'treacherous', 'liars', 'murderous' and 'Nazis'. Indeed, Zionist historiography provides ample evidence suggesting that from the very beginning of the Yishuv in Palestine the attitude of most Zionist groups towards the native Arab population ranged from a mixture of indifference and patronising racial superiority to outright denial of its national rights, the goal being to uproot and transfer it to neighbouring countries. Leading figures such as Israel Zangwill, a prominent Anglo-Jewish writer, close lieutenant of Theodor Herzl (the founder of political Zionism) and advocate of the transfer solution, worked relentlessly to propagate the slogan that Palestine was 'a land without a people for a people without a land'. Another use of the same myth of an empty country was made in 1914 by Chaim Weizmann, later president of the World Zionist Congress and the first president of the state of Israel:

> In its initial stage, Zionism was conceived by its pioneers as a movement wholly depending on mechanical factors: there is a country which happens to be called Palestine, a country without a people, and, on the other hand, there exists the Jewish people, and it has no country. What else is necessary, then, than to fit the gem into the ring, to unite this people with this country? The owners of the country [the Ottoman Turks?] must, therefore, be persuaded and convinced that this marriage is advantageous, not only for the [Jewish] people and for the country, but also for themselves.[15]

DISPOSABLE PEOPLE

Neither Zangwill nor Weizmann intended these demographic assessments in a literal fashion. They did not mean that there were no people in Palestine, but that there were no people worth considering within the framework of the notions of European white supremacy that then held sway. In this connection, a comment by

Weizmann to Arthur Ruppin, head of the colonisation department of the Jewish Agency, is particularly revealing. When asked by Ruppin about the Palestinian Arabs and how he (Weizmann) obtained the Balfour Declaration in 1917 (promising 'the establishment in Palestine of a national home for the Jewish people'), Weizmann replied: 'The British told us that there are some hundred thousands negroes [*kushim* in Hebrew] and for those there is no value.'[16] In 1920, three years after the Zionist movement obtained the Balfour Declaration from the British, Zangwill himself spelled out the actual meaning of his myth ('a land without a people') with admirable clarity:

> If Lord Shaftesbury was literally inexact in describing Palestine as a country without a people, he was essentially correct, for there is no Arab people living in intimate fusion with the country, utilising its resources and stamping it with a characteristic impress; there is at best an Arab encampment.[17]

In this statement Zangwill hints at the fact that he was not the originator of the myth. The statement shows Lord Shaftesbury (1801–85; Anthony Ashley-Cooper before he became the Seventh Earl of Shaftesbury in 1851) to be Zangwill's source of the myth. The British Protestant Lord Shaftesbury espoused the Zionist idea nearly half a century before political Zionism was founded by Herzl. Shaftesbury coined the infamous phrase in 1853 during the Crimean War, when his Christian pro-Zionist interest in 'Jewish restoration to Palestine' coincided with what he saw as the beginning of the dissolution of the Ottoman Empire.[18] Yet, although not the originator of the myth of 'empty land', Zangwill was certainly its most effective propagandist.

Such pronouncements by Weizmann, Zangwill and other leading Zionists planted in the Zionist mind the racist notion of an empty territory – empty not necessarily in the sense of an actual absence of inhabitants, but rather in the sense of a 'civilisational barrenness' justifying Zionist colonisation and obliviousness to the fate of the native population and its eventual removal. Exemplifying once again the recurrent theme in certain Zionist writings of Palestinian 'cultural backwardness' as a justification for the population's removal, Zangwill continued:

> We cannot allow the Arabs to block so valuable a piece of historical reconstruction. ... And therefore we must gently persuade them

> to 'tick'. After all, they have all Arabia with its million square miles ... There is no particular reason for the Arabs to cling to these few kilometres. 'To fold their tents' and 'silently steal away' is their proverbial habit: let them exemplify it now.[19]

Driven by the same colonial mentality, Menahem Ussishkin, one of the leading figures of the Zionist Yishuv in the mandatory period, chairman of the Jewish National Fund and a member of the Jewish Agency Executive, had this to say in an address to journalists in Jerusalem in April 1930:

> We must continually raise the demand that our land be returned to our possession. ... If there are other inhabitants there, they must be transferred to some other place. We must take over the land. We have a greater and nobler ideal than preserving several hundred thousands of Arab *fellahin*.[20]

Thus, the idea that the Palestinian Arabs must find a place for themselves elsewhere was articulated early on. Indeed, the founder of the movement, Theodor Herzl, provided an early reference to transfer even before he formally outlined his theory of Zionist rebirth in his *Judenstat*. An 1895 entry in his diary provides in embryonic form many of the elements that were to be demonstrated repeatedly in the Zionist quest for solutions of the 'Arab problem' – the idea of dealing with state governments over the heads of the indigenous population, Jewish acquisition of property that would be inalienable, 'Hebrew land' and 'Hebrew labour' and the removal of the native population. Thus, contemplating the transition from a 'Society of Jews'[21] to statehood, he wrote on 12 June 1895:

> When we occupy the land, we shall bring immediate benefits to the state that receives us. We must expropriate gently the private property in the estates assigned to us.
>
> We shall try to spirit the penniless population across the border by procuring employment for it in the transit countries, while denying it any employment in our own country.
>
> The property owners will come over to our side. Both process of expropriation and removal of the poor must be carries out discreetly and circumspectly.[22]

Zagwill was one of the strongest early proponents of transferring the indigenous inhabitants of Palestine. In an April 1905 talk in Manchester in which he outlined the demographic realities, he went on to draw an obvious conclusion. Given that Palestine was 'already twice as thickly populated as the United States' and given that 'not 25 per cent of them [are] Jews',

> [We] must be prepared either to drive out by the sword the [Arab] tribes in possession as our forefathers did or to grapple with the problem of a large alien population, mostly Mohammedan and accustomed for centuries to despite us.[23]

Zangwill held firm to this idea in the years that followed, couching his arguments for transfer in pragmatic and geopolitical considerations. At one time he argued:

> If we wish to give a country to a people without a country, it is utter foolishness to allow it to be the country of two peoples. This can only cause trouble. The Jews will suffer and so will their neighbours. One of the two: a different place must be found either for the Jews or for their neighbours.[24]

In my previous works,[25] which are largely based on Hebrew and Israeli archival sources, I have dealt with the evolution of the theme of 'population transfer' – a euphemism denoting the organised removal of the Arab population of Palestine to neighbouring or distant countries. I have shown that this concept – delicately described by its proponents as 'population exchange', 'Arab return to Arabia', 'emigration', 'resettlement' and 'rehabilitation' of the Palestinians in Arab countries, etc. – was deeply rooted in mainstream Zionist thinking and in the Yishuv as a solution to Zionist land and political problems. Although the desire among Zionist leaders to 'solve' the 'Arab question' through transfer remained constant until 1948, the envisaged modalities of transfer changed over the years according to circumstances. From the mid-1930s onwards a series of specific plans, generally involving Transjordan, Syria and Iraq, were produced by the Yishuv's transfer committees and senior officials.

Denial of the existence of a Palestinian people has always been a key component of the Zionist 'transfer' discourse. The justifications used in defence of the transfer concept in the 1930s and 1940s formed the cornerstone of the subsequent argumentation for transfer, particularly in the proposals put forward after 1948 and in the wake of the 1967 conquest of the West Bank and Gaza. After 1967 Zionist territorial maximalists and proponents of ethnic cleansing continued to assert, often publicly, that there was nothing immoral about the idea. They asserted that the Palestinians were not a distinct people but merely 'Arabs', an 'Arab population', or an 'Arab community' that happened to reside in the land of Israel.

Closely linked to this idea of the non-existence of the Palestinians as a nation and their non-attachment to the particular soil of Palestine was the idea of their belonging to an Arab nation with vast territories and many countries. As Ben-Gurion put it in 1929, 'Jerusalem is not the same thing to the Arabs as it is to the Jews. The Arab people inhabit many great lands.'[26] Accordingly, if the Palestinians did not constitute a distinct, separate nation, had little attachment to Jerusalem, were not an integral part of the country and were without historical ties to it, then they could be transferred to other Arab countries without undue prejudice. Similarly, if the Palestinians were merely a marginal, local segment of a larger population of Arabs, then they were not a major party to the conflicts with Israel; therefore, Israeli efforts to deal over their heads were justified.

Despite their propaganda slogans of an underpopulated land, of Palestine's 'civilisational barrenness' and of their making 'the desert bloom', all of which were issued partly for external consumption, the Zionists from the outset were well aware that not only were there people on the land, but that they were there in large numbers. Zangwill, who had visited Palestine in 1897 and come face to face with the demographic reality of the country, himself acknowledged in a 1905 speech to a Zionist group in Manchester that 'Palestine proper had already its inhabitants. The pashalik [province] of Jerusalem is already twice as thickly populated as the United States, having fifty-two souls to the square mile, and not 25 per cent of them Jews.'[27] Abundant references to the Palestinian population in early Zionist texts show clearly that from the beginning of the Zionist settlement in Palestine the Palestinian Arabs were far from being an 'unseen' or 'hidden' presence.[28]

Thus, Yitzhak Epstein, an early settler leader who arrived in Palestine from Russia in 1886, warned not only of the moral implications of the Zionist colonisation but also of the political dangers inherent in the enterprise. In 1907, at a time when Zionist land purchases in Galilee were stirring opposition among Palestinian peasants forced off land sold by absentee landlords, Epstein wrote an article entitled 'The Hidden Question', in which he strongly criticised the methods by which Zionists had purchased Arab land. In his view these methods entailing dispossession of Arab farmers were bound to cause political confrontation in the future.[29] Reflected in the Zionist establishment's angry response to Epstein's article[30] are two principal features of mainstream Zionist thought: the belief that Jewish acquisition of land took precedence over moral considerations; and the advocacy of a physically separate, exclusionist and literally 'pure' Jewish Yishuv. 'If we want Hebrew redemption 100 per cent, then we must have a 100 per cent Hebrew settlement, a 100 per cent Hebrew farm, and a 100 per cent Hebrew port', declared David Ben-Gurion at a meeting of the Va'ad Leumi, the Yishuv's National Council, on 5 May 1936.[31]

Another leading liberal Russian Jewish thinker, Ahad Ha'Am (Asher Zvi Ginzberg), also warned of the moral implications of the Zionist colonisation and the political dangers inherent in the enterprise. Ahad Ha'Am, who visited Palestine in 1891, published a series of articles in the Hebrew periodical *Hamelitz* that were sharply critical of the ethnocentricity of political Zionism as well as the exploitation of the Palestinian peasantry by Zionist colonists.[32] Seeking to draw attention to the fact that Palestine was not an empty territory and that the presence of another people on the land posed problems, he observed that the Zionist 'pioneers' believed that

> the only language that the Arabs understand is that of force. ... [They] behave towards the Arabs with hostility and cruelty, trespass unjustly upon their boundaries, beat them shamefully without reason and even brag about it, and nobody stands to check this contemptible and dangerous tendency.

He cut to the heart of the matter when he ventured the opinion that the colonists' aggressive attitude towards the native peasants stemmed from their anger 'towards those who reminded them that there is still another people in the land of Israel that have been living there and does not intend to leave'.[33]

TRANSFER

Although the transfer idea has deep roots in early Zionism, it became central to Zionist strategy and action in the period 1936–48. Ben-Gurion, in particular, was an enthusiastic and committed advocate of the transfer 'solution'. The importance he attached not merely to transfer but 'forced transfer' (which was endorsed, together with partition, by the British Peel Commission) is seen in his diary entry for 12 July 1937:

> The compulsory transfer of Arabs from the valleys of the proposed Jewish state could give us something which we never had, even when we stood on our own feet during the days of the First and Second Temple – [a Galilee free of Arab population].[34]

Ben-Gurion was convinced that few, if any, Palestinians would 'voluntarily' transfer themselves to Transjordan. He also believed that, if the Zionists were determined in their effort to put pressure on the British Mandatory authorities to carry out 'compulsory transfer', the plan could be implemented:

> We have to stick to this conclusion in the same way we grabbed the Balfour Declaration, more than that, in the same way we grabbed Zionism itself. We have to insist upon this conclusion [and push it] with our full determination, power and conviction. ... We must uproot from our hearts the assumption that the thing is not possible. It can be done.

Ben-Gurion went as far as to write: '*We must prepare ourselves to carry out*' the transfer [emphasis in the original].[35]

A letter to his son, 'Amos, from London dated 5 October 1937, shows the extent to which transfer had become associated in his mind with expulsion. Ben-Gurion wrote:

> We must expel Arabs and take their places ... and, if we have to use force – not to dispossess the Arabs of the Negev and Transjordan, but to guarantee our own right to settle in those places – then we have force at our disposal.[36]

At the Twentieth Zionist Congress, held from 3 to 21 August 1937, Ben-Gurion emphasised that transfer of Arab villagers had been practised by the Yishuv all along:

> Was the transfer of the Arabs ethical, necessary and practicable? ... Transfer of Arabs had repeatedly taken place before in consequence of Jews settling in different districts.[37]

A year later, at the Jewish Agency Executive's transfer discussions of June 1938, Ben-Gurion put forward a 'line of actions' entitled 'The Zionist Mission of the Jewish State':

> The Hebrew State will discuss with the neighbouring Arab states the matter of voluntarily transferring Arab tenant farmers, workers and *fellahin* from the Jewish state to neighbouring states. For that purpose the Jewish state, or a special company ... will purchase lands in neighbouring states for the resettlement of all those workers and *fellahin*.[38]

Ben-Gurion returned to the transfer solution in his 'Lines for Zionist Policy' dated 15 October 1941 (several years after the partition solution was abandoned by the British mandatory government):

> We have to examine, first, if this transfer is practical, and secondly, if it is necessary. It is impossible to imagine general evacuation without compulsion, and brutal compulsion. ... The possibility of a large-scale transfer of a population by force was demonstrated, when the Greeks and the Turks were transferred [after the First World War]. In the present war [Second World War] the idea of transferring a population is gaining more sympathy as a practical and the most secure means of solving the dangerous and painful problem of national minorities. The war has already brought the resettlement of many people in eastern and southern Europe, and in the plans for post-war settlements the idea of a large-scale population transfer in central, eastern, and southern Europe increasingly occupies a respectable place.[39]

Ben-Gurion went on to suggest a Zionist-inspired campaign in England and the United States that would aim at 'influencing' Arab countries, especially Syria and Iraq, to 'collaborate' with the Jewish Yishuv in implementing the transfer of Palestinians in return for economic gains.[40]

Ben-Gurion entered the 1948 war with a mind-set and premeditation to expel Palestinians. On 19 December 1947 he advised that the Haganah, the Jewish pre-state army, 'adopt the method of aggressive defence; with every [Arab] attack we must be prepared to respond with a decisive blow: the destruction of the [Arab] place or the expulsion of the residents along with the seizure of the place'.[41]

In early February 1948 Ben-Gurion told Yosef Weitz:

> The war will give us the land. The concepts of 'ours' and 'not ours' are peace concepts, only, and in war they lose their whole meaning.[42]

At a meeting of the governing bodies of his own Mapai party on 7 February, Ben-Gurion spoke of 'major changes' that would occur in the composition of the population in the country. Ben-Gurion was referring to the Palestinian exodus, which he welcomed.[43]

In the pre-1948 period the transfer concept was embraced by the highest levels of Zionist leadership, representing almost the entire political spectrum. Nearly all the founding fathers of the Israeli state advocated transfer in one form or another, including Theodor Herzl, Leon Motzkin, Nahman Syrkin, Menahem Ussishkin, Chaim Weizmann, David Ben-Gurion, Yitzhak Tabenkin, Avraham Granovsky, Israel Zangwill, Yitzhak Ben-Tzvi, Pinhas Rutenberg, Aaron Aaronson, Zeev Jabotinsky and Berl Katznelson. Katznelson, who was one of the most popular and influential leaders of the Mapai party (later the ruling Labour party), had this to say in a debate at the World Convention of Ihud Po'alei Tzion (the highest forum of the dominant Zionist world labour movement), in August 1937:

> The matter of population transfer has provoked a debate among us: Is it permitted or forbidden? My conscience is absolutely clear in this respect. A remote neighbour is better than a close enemy. They [the Palestinians] will not lose from it. In the final analysis, this is a political and settlement reform for the benefit of both parties. I have long been of the opinion that this is the best of all solutions. ... I have always believed and still believe that they were destined to be transferred to Syria or Iraq.[44]

A year later, at the Jewish Agency Executive's discussions of June 1938, Katznelson declared himself in favour of maximum territory and the 'principle of compulsory transfer':

> What is a compulsory transfer? Compulsory transfer does not mean individual transfer. It means that once we resolved to transfer there should be a political body able to force this or that Arab who would not want to move out. Regarding the transfer of Arab individuals we are always doing this. But the question will be the transfer of a much greater quantity of Arabs through an agreement with the Arab states: this is called a compulsory transfer. ... We

> have here a war about principles, and in the same way that we must wage a war for maximum territory, there must also be here a war [for the transfer 'principle']. ... We must insist on the principle that it must be a large agreed transfer.[45]

In the early 1940s Katznelson found time to be engaged in polemics with the left-wing Hashomer Hatza'ir about the merits of transfer. He said to them: don't stigmatise the concept of transfer and rule it out beforehand.

> Has [kibbutz] Merhavya not been built on transfer? Were it not for many of these transfers neither Merhavya or [kibbutz] Mishmar Ha'emek or other socialist Kibbutzim would have been set up.[46]

Supporters of 'voluntary' transfer included Arthur Ruppin, a co-founder of Brit Shalom, a movement advocating bi-nationalism and equal rights for Arabs and Jews; moderate leaders of Mapai (later the Labour party) such as Moshe Shertok (later Sharett) and Eli'ezer Kaplan, Israel's first finance minister; and leaders of the Histadrut (Jewish Labour Federation of Palestine) such as Golda Meir and David Remez.

However, perhaps the most consistent, extreme and obsessive advocate of compulsory transfer was Yosef Weitz, director of the settlement department of the Jewish National Fund (JNF) and head of the Israeli government's official Transfer Committee of 1948. Weitz was at the centre of Zionist land-purchasing activities for decades. His intimate knowledge of and involvement in land purchase made him sharply aware of its limitations. As late as 1947, after half a century of tireless efforts, the collective holdings of the JNF – which constituted about half of the Yishuv total – amounted to a mere 3.5 per cent of the land area of Palestine. A summary of Weitz's political beliefs is provided by his diary entry for 20 December 1940:

> Amongst ourselves it must be clear that there is no room for both peoples in this country. No 'development' will bring us closer to our aim to be an independent people in this small country. After the Arabs are transferred, the country will be wide open for us; with the Arabs staying the country will remain narrow and restricted. ... There is no room for compromise on this point ... land purchasing ... will not bring about the state; ... The only way is to transfer the Arabs from here to neighbouring countries, all

> of them, except perhaps Bethlehem, Nazareth, and Old Jerusalem. Not a single village or a single tribe must be left. And the transfer must be done through their absorption in Iraq and Syria and even in Transjordan. For that goal, money will be found – even a lot of money. And only then will the country be able to absorb millions of Jews ... there is no other solutions.[47]

A countryside tour in the summer of 1941 took Weitz to a region in central Palestine. He recorded in his Diary seeing:

> large [Arab] villages crowded in population and surrounded by cultivated land growing olives, grapes, figs, sesame, and maize fields. ... Would we be able to maintain scattered [Jewish] settlements among these existing [Arab] villages that will always be larger than ours? And is there any possibility of buying their [land]? ... and once again I hear that voice inside me calling: *evacuate this country.* [emphasis in the original].[48]

Earlier in March 1941 Weitz wrote in his Diary after touring Jewish settlements in the Esdraelon Valley (Marj Ibn 'Amer):

> The complete evacuation of the country from its [Arab] inhabitants and handing it to the Jewish people is the answer.[49]

In April 1948 Weitz recorded in his Diary:

> I made a summary of a list of the Arab villages which in my opinion must be cleared out in order to complete Jewish regions. I also made a summary of the places that have land disputes and must be settled by military means.[50]

In 1930, against the background of the 1929 disturbances in Palestine, Chaim Weizmann, then President of both the World Zionist Organisation and the Jewish Agency Executive, actively began promoting ideas of Arab transfer in private discussions with British officials and ministers. In the same year Weizmann and Pinhas Rutenberg, who was chairman of the Yishuv's National Council and a member of the Jewish Agency Executive, presented Colonial Secretary Lord Passfield with an official, albeit secret, proposal for the transfer of Palestinian peasants to Transjordan. This scheme proposed that a loan of 1 million Palestinian pounds be raised from

Jewish financial sources for the resettlement operation. This proposal was rejected by Lord Passfield. However, the justification Weizmann used in its defence formed the cornerstone of subsequent Zionist argumentation. Weizmann asserted that there was nothing 'immoral' about the concept of transfer; that the 'transfer' of Greek and Turkish populations in the early 1920s provided a precedent for a similar measure for the Palestinians; and that the uprooting and transportation of Palestinians to Transjordan, Iraq, Syria, or any other part of the vast Arab world would merely constitute a relocation from one Arab district to another. Above all, for Weizmann and other leaders of the Jewish Agency, the transfer was a systematic procedure, requiring preparation, money and a great deal of organisation, which needed to be planned by strategic thinkers and technical experts.[51]

THE TRANSFER COMMITTEES

While the desire among the Zionist leadership to be rid of the 'Arab demographic problem' remained constant until 1948, the extent of the preoccupation with, and the envisaged modalities of, transfer changed over the years according to circumstances. Thus, the wishful and rather naive belief in Zionism's early years that the Palestinians could be 'spirited across the border', in Herzl's words, or that they would simply 'fold their tents and slip away', to use Zangwill's formulation, soon gave way to more realistic assessments. Between 1937 and 1948 extensive secret discussions of transfer were held in the Zionist movement's highest bodies, including the Zionist Agency Executive, the Twentieth Zionist Congress, the World Convention of Ihud Po'alei Tzion (the top forum of the dominant Zionist world labour movement), and various official and semi-official transfer committees.[52]

Many leading figures justified Arab removal politically and morally as the natural and logical continuation of Zionist colonisation in Palestine. There was a general endorsement of the ethical legitimacy of transfer; the differences centred on the question of compulsory transfer and whether such a course would be practicable (in the late 1930s/early 1940s) without the support of the colonial power, Britain.

From the mid-1930s onwards the transfer solution became central to the assessments of the Jewish Agency (then effectively the government of the Yishuv). The Jewish Agency produced a series of specific plans, generally involving Transjordan, Syria or Iraq. Some of these plans were drafted by three 'Transfer Committees'. The first two committees, set up by the Yishuv leadership, operated between 1937 and 1944; the third was officially appointed by the Israeli cabinet in August 1948.

By the late 1930s some of these transfer plans included proposals for agrarian legislation, citizenship restriction and various taxes designed to encourage Palestinians to transfer 'voluntarily'. However, in the 1930s and early 1940s Zionist transfer proposals and plans remained largely confined to private and secret talks with British (and occasionally American) senior officials. The Zionist leadership generally refrained from airing the highly sensitive proposals in public. (On one occasion, Weizmann, in a secret meeting with the Soviet ambassador to London, Ivan Maisky, on 30 January 1941, proposed transferring 1 million Palestinians to Iraq in order to settle Polish Jews in their place.) More important, however, during the Mandate period, for reasons of political expediency, the Zionists calculated that such proposals could not be effected without Britain's active support and even actual British implementation.

THE ORIGINS OF THE ROYAL (PEEL) COMMISSION'S TRANSFER RECOMMENDATION

The Zionist leadership was tireless in trying to shape the proposals of the Royal (Peel) Commission of 1937, which proposed a partition of Palestine between Jews and Arabs. It has generally escaped the attention of historians that the most significant transfer proposal submitted to the commission – the one destined to shape the outcome of its findings – was put forward by the Jewish Agency in a secret memorandum containing a specific paragraph on Arab transfer to Transjordan.

Given the demographic and land realities in Palestine at the time, whatever boundaries might be devised for partition would inevitably result in large numbers of Palestinian Arabs and even greater expanses of Arab-owned land becoming part of whatever Jewish state would be carved out. Thus, in Zionist strategy the notion of transfer was a natural concomitant of the partition idea. Evidence suggests that the proposal of Arab transfer that was ultimately made by the Royal Commission originated from, and had been secretly conveyed by, top Jewish Agency leaders, including Ben-Gurion, Moshe Shertok (later Sharett), and Weizmann. As early as the Jewish Agency Executive meeting in October 1936 Ben-Gurion had indicated his intention to raise the issue: 'if the Peel Commission and the London government accept [the idea of transfer to Transjordan], we will remove the land problem from the agenda.'[53] In March 1937, the Jewish Agency conveyed a confidential plan to the Royal Commission through Maurice Hexter, a member of the Jewish Agency Executive. Hexter explained that the aim of the plan was to solve the problem of land and Zionist colonisation in various districts, including the Hula and Baysan valley. Under the plan, the British government was to consider proposals submitted by Zionist settlement companies, which were engaged in the purchase of land for the collective use of the Jewish National Fund. The goal of the proposal, according to Hexter, was 'the herding together of the existing Arab villages and their concentration in order to evacuate territories for Jewish colonisation'. If the Arabs refused and put up an organised political resistance to evacuating their land, the government would intervene and 'force the people to exchange land and move from one place to another'. When Hexter was asked by one Peel commissioner whether the proposed evacuated land would be designated for Jewish settlements exclusively, he replied, 'our intention is [that they would be] only for Jews'.[54]

However, unquestionably the most significant proposal for transfer submitted to the Commission – the one destined to shape the outcome of its findings – was that put forward by the Jewish Agency in a May 1937 memorandum containing a specific paragraph on Palestinian transfer to Transjordan.[55] The impact of the memorandum, drafted jointly by Ben-Gurion and Pinhas Rutenberg, can be gauged from an entry in Sharett's political diary on 12 June 1937, almost a month before the publication of the Peel Commission's report. According to Moshe Shertok (later Moshe Sharett), the American general-consul in Jerusalem, George Wadsworth, had told him at a dinner that British officials had privately indicated that their government was inclined towards partition. Shertok went on:

> We talked about the question of partition in connection with Transjordan. Wadsworth said that it was known to him that the [British] government was very impressed by the proposal contained in the memorandum that we had submitted to the 'Royal Commission' concerning the transfer of Arabs from western *Eretz Yisrael* [i.e., Palestine] to Transjordan in order to evacuate the place for new Jewish settlers. They saw this proposal as a constructive plan indeed.[56]

Although by 1938 the Peel partition plan had been abandoned by the British government, the Jewish Agency's Transfer Committees continued to operate throughout the war period and Weizmann and Ben-Gurion continued to lobby behind the scenes for Western and Soviet endorsement of transfer.

THE 1948 EXODUS

The Zionist dream of de-Arabising Palestine and creating a clear Jewish majority finally came about during the 1948–9 war, when 750,000 Palestinians took up the road of exile. The events that led to the Palestinian exodus began on 29 November 1947, when the United Nation General Assembly passed resolution 191 endorsing the partition of Palestine into two states, Palestinian Arab and Jewish, with Jerusalem and Bethlehem consisting an international zone. Under the boundaries set out by the partition resolution, almost 45 per cent of the population of the Jewish state would be Palestinian Arab. This was a major preoccupation of the Yishuv leadership.

Within weeks of the UN partition resolution, the country was plunged in what soon became a full-scale civil war. By mid-December 1947, 'spontaneous and unorganised' Palestinian outbreaks of violence were being met with the full weight of Yishuv's armed forces, the Haganah, in what the British High Commissioner for Palestine called 'indiscriminate action against the Arabs' (Middle East Centre, St Antony's College Archives, Oxford, Cunningham Papers, 1/3/147, 'Weekly Intelligence Appreciation'. A three-day general strike started on 2 December in protest at the UN resolution). The Palestinians were completely unprepared for war, their leadership still in disarray and largely unarmed as a result of the 1936–9 rebellion. The Yishuv armed forces, the Haganah (to say nothing of the dissident Irgun Tzavi Leumi and Lehi groups), were fully armed and on the offensive. On 30 December a British Intelligence observer reported that the Haganah was moving fast to exploit Palestinian weaknesses and disorganisation, to render them 'completely powerless' so as to force them into flight. [A report by G. J. Jenkins, 30 December 1947, British Embassy, Cairo, PRO, FO 371/68366, E458.]

The unfolding of the war is beyond the scope of this study. Others have catalogued with meticulous detail the military strategy, the successive campaigns, and the various factors precipitating the exodus of Palestinian refugees. Note has been made of the failure of various Haganah commanders, in their attacks and evacuation orders, to distinguish between 'hostile' Arab villages and those that had concluded 'non-aggression' pacts with the Yishuv; the role of attacks on civilian targets in the months prior to and in the early phases of the war; the role of atrocities (such as Deir Yassin) and their seemingly judicious timing and placement so as to maximise their impact; and the impact of various forms of psychological warfare (see below).

There is plenty of evidence to suggest that as early as the beginning of 1948 Ben-Gurion's advisers counselled him to wage a total war against the Palestinians, and that he entered the 1948 war with the intention of expelling Palestinians.[57]

Plan Dalet

A straightforward document, Plan Dalet (*Tochnit Dalet*) is the Haganah plan of 1948 which, in many ways, was a blueprint for the expulsion of as many Palestinians as possible.[58] It constituted an ideological-strategic anchor and basis for the destruction of Arab localities and expulsion of their inhabitants by Jewish commanders. Formulated in early March 1948, its implementation began in early April in anticipation of Arab military operations. The essence of the plan (according to Benny Morris) 'was the clearing of hostile and potentially hostile forces out of the interior of the prospective territory of the Jewish State. ... As the Arab irregulars were based and quartered in the villages and as the militias of many villages were participating in the anti-Yishuv hostilities, the Haganah regarded most of the Arab villages as actively or potentially hostile.'[59] Morris goes on to explain that the plan

> constituted a strategic-ideological anchor and basis for expulsions by front, district, brigade and battalion commanders ... and it gave commanders, *post facto*, a formal, persuasive covering note to explain their actions.[60]

Morris goes further:

> In conformity with Tochnit Dalet (Plan D), the Haganah's master plan. ... The Haganah cleared various areas completely of Arab villages – the Jerusalem corridor, an area around Mishmar Ha'emek, and the coastal plain. But in most cases, expulsion orders were unnecessary; the inhabitants had already fled, out of fear or as a result of Jewish attack. In several areas, Israeli commanders

> successfully used psychological warfare ploys to obtain Arab evacuation (as in the Hula Valley, in Upper Galilee, in May).[61]

The general endorsement of the transfer solution and the attempt to promote it secretly by mainstream Labour leaders, some of whom played a decisive role in the 1948 war, highlight the ideological intent that made the 1948 refugee exodus possible. Ben-Gurion in particular emerges as both an obsessive advocate of compulsory transfer in the late 1930s and the great expeller of the Palestinians in 1948.[62] In 1948 there was no need for any cabinet decision to drive the Palestinians out. Ben-Gurion and senior Zionist military commanders, such as Yigal Allon, Moshe Carmel, Yigael Yadin, Moshe Dayan, Moshe Kalman and Yitzhak Rabin, played a key role in the expulsions. Israeli historian Benny Morris writes: 'Everyone, at every level of military and political decision-making, understood that [the objective was] a Jewish state without a large Arab minority.'[63] In 1948 the 'transfer' policy was based on an understanding between Ben-Gurion and his lieutenants rather than on a blueprint or a master plan. One of the hallmarks of Ben-Gurion's approach to expulsion in 1948 (according to Morris) was

> that the man knew what to say and what not to say in certain circumstances; what is allowed to be recorded on paper and what is preferable to convey orally or in hint.[64]

Ben-Gurion's admiring biographer Michael Bar-Zohar states:

> In internal discussions, in instructions to his men [in 1948] the Old Man [Ben-Gurion] demonstrated a clear position: It would be better that as few a number as possible of Arabs should remain in the territory of the [Jewish] state.[65]

With the 1948 war, the Zionists succeeded in many of their objectives. Above all, they created a vastly enlarged Jewish state (on 77 per cent of historic Palestine) in which the Palestinians were forcibly reduced to a small minority. The available evidence shows that the evacuation of some three-quarters of a million Palestinians in 1948 can only be ascribed to the culmination of Zionist expulsion policies and not to mythical orders issued by the Arab armies. Morris's *The Birth of the Palestinian Refugee Problem, 1947–1948* (1987) explodes many Israeli myths surrounding the 1948 exodus (see

Chapter 2). Morris assesses that of 330 villages whose experience he studied, a total of 282 (85 per cent) were depopulated as a result of direct Jewish attack.

LYDDA AND RAMLE

About 80 per cent of the Palestinians were driven out from the territory occupied by the Israelis in 1948–9, many by psychological warfare and/or military pressure. A very large number of Palestinians were expelled at gunpoint.[66] A major instance of 'outright expulsion' is the widely documented case of the twin towns of Lydda and Ramle in July 1948. More than 60,000 Palestinians were expelled, accounting for nearly 10 per cent of the total exodus. Ben-Gurion and three senior army officers were directly involved: Yigal Allon, Yitzhak Rabin and Moshe Dayan. Shortly before the capture of the towns, Ben-Gurion met with his army chiefs. Allon, commander of the Palmach, the Haganah's elite military force, asked Ben-Gurion, 'What shall we do with the Arabs?' Ben-Gurion answered (or according to one version, gestured with his hand), 'Expel them.' This was immediately communicated to the army headquarters and the expulsion implemented.[67] According to one version of Yitzhak Rabin's manuscript:

> We walked outside, Ben-Gurion accompanying us. Alon repeated his question: 'What is to be done with the population?' BG waved his hand in a gesture, which said: Drive them out! Alon and I held a consultation. I agreed that it was essential to drive the inhabitants out.[68]

Morris writes:

> At 13.30 hours on 12 July ... Lieutenant-Colonel Yitzhak Rabin, Operation Dani head of Operations, issued the following order: '1. The inhabitants of Lydda must be expelled quickly without attention to age. They should be directed to Beit Nabala ... Implement Immediately.' A similar order was issued at the same time to the Kiryati Brigade concerning the inhabitants of the neighbouring town of Ramle, occupied by Kiryati troops that morning. ... On 12 and 13 July, the Yiftah and Kiryati brigades carried out their orders, expelling the 50–60,000 remaining inhabitants of and refugees camped in and around the two towns.

> ... About noon on 13 July, Operation Dani HQ informed IDF General Staff/Operations: 'Lydda police fort has been captured. [The troops] are busy expelling the inhabitants [*oskim begeirush hatoshavim*].' Lydda's inhabitants were forced to walk eastwards to the Arab Legion lines; many of Ramle's inhabitants were ferried in trucks or buses. Clogging the roads ... the tens of thousands of refugees marched, gradually shedding their worldly goods along the way. It was a hot summer day. Arab chroniclers, such as Sheikh Muhammad Nimr al Khatib, claimed that hundreds of children died in the march, from dehydration and disease. One Israeli witness described the spoor: the refugee column 'to begin with [jettisoned] utensils and furniture and, in the end, bodies of men, women and children ...'[69]

The Secretary General of the Histadrut, Yosef Sprintzak, stated at a debate of the Mapai Centre on 24 July 1948, which was held against the background of the Ramle-Lydda expulsions:

> There is a feeling that *faits accomplis* are being created. ... The question is not whether the Arabs will return or not return. The question is whether the Arabs are [being or have been] expelled or not. ... This is important to our moral future. ... I want to know, who is creating the facts [of expulsion]? And the facts are being created on orders.[70]

Sprintzak added that there was 'a line of action ... of expropriating and of emptying the land of Arabs by force'.[71] Similar criticisms were made two months earlier by Aharon Cohen, the Director of the Arab Department of Mapam, who wrote in a memorandum dated 10 May 1948:

> There is reason to believe that what is being done ... is being done out of certain political objectives and not only out of military necessities, as they [Jewish leaders] claim sometimes. In fact, the 'transfer' of the Arabs from the boundaries of the Jewish state is being implemented ... the evacuation/clearing out of Arab villages is not always done out of military necessity. The complete destruction of villages is not always done because there are 'not sufficient forces to maintain garrison'.[72]

In the case of Nazareth, Ben-Gurion arrived only after its capture. On seeing so many Palestinians remaining *in situ*, he angrily asked the local commander, 'Why are there so many Arabs? Why didn't you expel them?'[73] Apparently the commander of the Seventh Brigade which had captured Nazareth, Ben Dunkelman, had received explicit orders from his superiors to drive out unarmed civilians who had formally surrendered. The following is Dunkelman's account:

> Two days after the second truce came into effect, the Seventh Brigade was ordered to withdraw from Nazareth. Avraham Yaffe, who had commanded the 13th battalion in the assault on the city, now reported to me [Dunkelman] with orders from Moshe Carmel [the army commander in Galilee] to take over from me as its military governor. I complied with the order, but only after Avraham had given me his word of honour that he would do nothing to harm or displace the Arab population. My demand may sound strange, but I had good reason to feel concerned on this subject. Only a few hour previously, Haim Laskov [of the high command] had come to me with astounding orders: Nazareth's civilian population was to be evacuated! I was shocked and horrified. I told him I would do nothing of the sort – in view of our promises to safeguard the city's people, such a move would be both superfluous and harmful. I reminded him that scarcely a day earlier, he and I, as representatives of the Israeli army, had signed the surrender document, in which we solemnly pledged to do nothing to harm the city or its population. When Haim saw that I refused to obey the order, he left.
>
> A scarce twelve hours later, Avraham Yaffe came to tell me that his battalion was relieving my brigade; I felt sure that this order had been given because of my defiance of the evacuation order. But although I was withdrawn from Nazareth, it seems that my disobedience did have some effect. It seems to have given the high command time for second thoughts, which led them to the conclusion that it would, indeed, be wrong to expel the inhabitants.[74]

The two episodes, Lydda–Ramle and Nazareth, occurred within days of one another. In both cases, orders had been issued for the forcible evacuation of the civilians. In both cases, the order was given personally by Ben-Gurion. The two descriptions, particularly when taken together, show that there were high-level directives for mass expulsion of the Palestinian population. The decision makers – in particular Ben-Gurion with his 'mute wave of hand' in the case of Lydda and Ramle – were eminently aware of the controversial nature of such a 'transfer' policy and were careful to leave no incriminating evidence about their personal and political responsibility.[75]

THE HAGANAH AND DEIR YASSIN

In the period between the mid-1930s and 1948 the Zionist leadership had embraced the concept of transfer while quietly pondering the question of whether there was a 'more humane way' of expelling the indigenous Palestinians. The 1948 war proved that engineering mass evacuation was not possible without perpetrating a large number of atrocities. Indeed, the most striking result of recent historical research is that the discourse has shifted away from the orthodox Zionist interpretation of the Deir Yassin massacre as 'exceptional'. The focus of study is no longer so much on the terrorism carried out by the Irgun and Lehi (Stern Gang) irregular forces before and during the 1948 war, but on the conduct of the mainstream Haganah/Palmach and Israel Defence Forces (IDF). At issue are the roles and involvement of the Haganah and the Israeli army in the numerous atrocities carried out in 1948. Sharif Kana'ana of Birzeit University places the massacre of Deir Yassin and the evacuation of Arab West Jerusalem in 1948 within the framework of what he terms the Zionists' 'maxi-massacre pattern' in their conquest of large Palestinian cities: Jewish attacks produced demoralisation and exodus; a nearby massacre would result in panic and further flight, greatly facilitating the occupation of the Arab city and its surrounding towns and villages.[76]

According to Israeli military historian Arieh Yitzhaki, about ten major massacres (of more than 50 victims each) and about 100 smaller massacres were committed by Jewish forces in 1948–9. Yitzhaki argues that these massacres, large and small, had a devastating impact on the Palestinian population by inducing and precipitating the Palestinian exodus. Yitzhaki suggests that in almost every village there were murders. Another Israeli historian, Uri Milstein, corroborates Yitzhaki's assessment and goes even further to suggest that each battle in 1948 ended with a massacre: 'In all Israel's wars, massacres were committed but I have no doubt that the War of Independence was the dirtiest of them all.'[77]

Deir Yassin was the site of the most notorious massacre of Palestinian civilians in 1948 – a massacre which became the single most important contributory factor to the 1948 exodus. On 9 April, between 120 and 254 unarmed villagers were murdered, including women, the elderly and children. (The number of those massacred at Deir Yassin is subject to dispute. The widely accepted death toll has been that reported in the *New York Times* of 13 April 1948: 254 persons.) There were also cases of rape and mutilation. Most Israeli writers today have no difficulty in acknowledging the occurrence of the Deir Yassin massacre and its effect, if not its intention, of precipitating the exodus. However, most of these writers take refuge in the fact that the massacre was committed by 'dissidents' of the Irgun (then commanded by Menahem Begin) and Lehi (then co-commanded by Yitzhak Shamir), thus exonerating Ben-Gurion's Haganah, the mainstream Zionist military force. Recently published Hebrew material, however, shows that:

- in January 1948, the *mukhtar* (village head man) of Deir Yassin and other village notables had reached a non-aggression agreement with the Haganah and the neighbouring Jewish settlements of Giva'at Shaul and Montefiori;
- the Irgun's assault on the village on 9 April had the full backing of the Haganah commander of Jerusalem, David Shaltiel. The latter not only chose to break his agreement with the villagers, but also provided rifles and ammunition for the Irgunists;
- the Haganah contributed to the assault on the village by providing artillery cover;
- a Haganah intelligence officer in Jerusalem, Meir Pa'il, was dispatched to Deir Yassin to assess the effectiveness and performance of the Irgun forces.[78]

Although the actual murders of the non-combatant villagers were carried out by the Irgun and Lehi, the Haganah must share responsibility for the slaughter.

More significantly, the recently published Israeli material shows that Deir Yassin was only one of many massacres carried out by Jewish forces (mainly the Haganah and the IDF) in 1948. Recent research proves that the Palestinians were less prone to evacuate their towns and villages in the second half of the war: hence the numerous massacres committed from June 1948 onwards, all of which were geared towards forcing mass evacuation.[79]

In 1948 al-Dawayma, situated in the western Hebron hills, was a very large village, with a population of some 3,500 people. Like Deir

Yassin, al-Dawayma was unarmed. It was captured on 29 October 1948 without a fight. The massacre of between 80 and 100 villagers was carried out at the end of October 1948, not in the heat of the battle but after the Israeli army had clearly emerged victorious in the war. The testimony of Israeli soldiers present during the atrocities establishes that IDF troops under Moshe Dayan entered the village and liquidated civilians, throwing their victims into pits. 'The children they killed by breaking their heads with sticks. There was not a house without dead.' The remaining Arabs were then shut up in houses 'without food and water' as the village was systematically razed.

> One commander ordered a sapper to put two old women in a certain house ... and blow up the house ... One soldier boasted that he had raped a woman and then shot her. One woman, with a newborn baby in her arms, was employed to clear the courtyard where the soldiers ate. She worked a day or two. In the end they shot her and her baby.

A variety of evidences indicates that the atrocities were committed in and around the village, including at the mosque and in a nearby cave, that houses with old people locked inside were blown up, and that there were several cases of the rape and shooting of women.[80]

CLEARING GALILEE

The evidence surrounding the Galilee expulsions shows clearly the existence of a *pattern* of actions characterised by a series of massacres designed to intimidate the population into flight. On 29–31 October 1948, the Israeli army, in a large military campaign named Operation Hiram, conquered the last significant Arab-held pocket of Galilee. According to new Israeli archival material uncovered by Morris, commanding officers issued expulsion directives: 'There was a central directive by Northern Command to clear the conquered pocket of its Arab inhabitants.'[81] Moreover the operation was 'characterised by a series of atrocities against the Arab civilian population'.[82] The new material uncovered by Morris, refers

> to the series of expulsions (from Iqrit, Kafr Bir'im, Tarbikha, al-Mansura, etc.) and to the massacres (at Majd al-Kurum, al-Bi'na, Deir al-Asad, Nahf, Safsaf, Jish, Sasa, Saliha, Ilabun [sic], and Huleh

> [sic]) carried out by [Operation Hiram commander] Carmel's troops, mostly after the end of the campaign.[83]

According to Morris,

> two things indicate that at least some officers in the field understood Carmel's orders as an authorisation to carry out murderous acts that would intimidate the population into flight. First there was *the pattern in the actions and their relative profusion* [emphasis by author] (the massacres were carried out by battalions of the three main brigades that participated in Operation Hiram-Golani, the Seventh, and Carmeli – as well as by second-line garrison battalions that replaced the assaulting brigades in the villages). Second was the absence of any punishment of the perpetrators. To the best of my knowledge, none of the soldiers or officers who carried out these war crimes was punished.[84]

On 6 November 1948, Yosef Nahmani, director of the Jewish National Fund office in eastern Galilee between 1935 and 1965, toured the newly conquered areas. He was accompanied by 'Emmanuel Fried of Israel's minority affairs ministry, who briefed him on 'the cruel acts of our soldiers', which Nahmani recorded in his diary:

> In Safsaf, after ... the inhabitants had raised a white flag, the [soldiers] collected and separated the men and women, tied the hands of fifty-sixty *fellahin* [peasants] and shot and killed them and buried them in a pit. Also, they raped several women ... At Eilabun and Farradiya the soldiers had been greeted with white flags and rich food, and afterwards had ordered the villagers to leave, with their women and children. When the [villagers] had begun to argue ... [the soldiers] had opened fire and after some thirty people were killed, had begun to lead the rest [towards Lebanon]. ... In Saliha, [where a white flag had been raised] ... they had killed about sixty-seventy men and women. Where did they come by such a measure of cruelty, like Nazis? ... Is there is no more humane way of expelling the inhabitants than such methods?[85]

The following is only a partial inventory of other IDF massacres committed in Galilee in 1948: Safsaf, Jish, Sa'sa', Saliha, 'Eilabun, Majd al-Kurum, Deir al-Asad, Nasr al-Din, 'Ayn Zaytun, Khisas, Kabri, al-Bi'na, Nahf, Hule.[86]

AL-MAJDAL

Moshe Dayan was not alone in supporting the expulsion of Israel's Arab minority. According to Morris: 'During the immediate post-1948 period, talk of "transferring" Israel's Arab minority was relatively common in Israel.'[87] Army Chief of Staff, Yigael Yadin, supported implicitly the 'transfer' of Israel's Arabs. In consultation with Ben-Gurion on 8 February 1950, he described the Israeli Arabs as 'a danger in time of war, as in time of peace'.[88] The head of the military government, Lieutenant Colonel Emmanuel Mor (Markovsky), stated in 1950 ('with probably only marginal exaggeration', according to Morris), that 'the entire nation [i.e., Jews] in Zion [i.e., Israel], without exception, does not want Arab neighbours.'[89] About the same time, in the summer of 1950, almost two years after the 1948 war, the remaining 2,700 inhabitants of the southern Arab town al-Majdal (now called Ashkelon) received expulsion orders and were transported to the border of the Gaza Strip over a period of a few weeks. The town, which on the eve of the war had 10,000 inhabitants, had been conquered by the Israeli army on 4 November 1948. From that time and throughout 1949 the Commanding Officer of the Southern Command, General Yigal Allon, had 'demanded ... that the town be emptied of its Arabs'.[90] A government 'Committee for Transferring Arabs' had decided in February 1949 in principle to remove the remaining 2,700 inhabitants of al-Majdal. A year later, in the spring of 1950, General Moshe Dayan, Allon's successor in the Southern Command, had decided to direct the clearing of al-Majdal's residents to Gaza. Authorisation for this action was given by Ben-Gurion on 19 June 1950.[91] A day earlier, on 18 June, Dayan had appeared before the Mapai Secretariat and stated that he supported the *total* transfer of all the Israeli Arabs out of the country.[92]

Some 700,000 Jews arrived in Israel between its proclamation as an independent state in May 1948 and the end of 1951. The state's leaders believed that al-Majdal and its lands were needed for rehousing and settling these new immigrants. Na'im Gila'adi, a newly arrived Iraqi Jew, was put together with other Iraqi immigrants in a *ma'abarah*, a transit camp, near al-Majdal. According to Gila'adi, several important figures in the Jewish Agency came to reassure them: 'Be patient: soon we shall drive the Arabs out of Majdal and you will be able to have their houses.' Gila'adi recalled many years later:

> For us this was a shock. Majdal was a nearby little town, and we knew nothing of its inhabitants. One night, five or six of us crossed the barbed wire that surrounded Majdal to go and speak to the inhabitants, to see who they were, and why they wanted to drive them out. Talking to them, we discovered that they were very peaceful people, very hospitably disposed towards us, and ready to behave as loyal citizens of the state that has just been founded. And it was those people they wanted to drive out to settle us in their houses![93]

THE NEGEV

The Negev was an early focus of expulsion activities. According to the 1947 UN Partition Plan, the Negev had been included in the areas allotted to the Palestinian Arab state. After its occupation, Prime Minister Ben-Gurion in particular had been anxious to populate the Negev with Jews. In November 1949 some 500 Arab Bedouin families (2,000 people) from the Beer Sheba area were forced across the border into the West Bank. Jordan complained about this expulsion.[94] A further expulsion of 700–1,000 persons of the 'Azazme or Djahalin tribes to Jordan took place in May 1950.[95] On 2 September 1950 the Israeli Army rounded up hundreds of 'Azazme tribesmen (a United Nations Truce Supervision Organisation (UNTSO) complaint spoke of 4,000) from the Negev 'and drove them ... into Egyptian territory'.[96] A week later further expulsion of the 'Azazme tribesmen was carried out. UNTSO chief of staff Major-General William Riley put the total number of Bedouin at Qusayma in Sinai in mid-September 1950 at 6,200, the majority having been recently expelled by the Israeli army from the Negev. Riley also wrote that the Israeli army killed 13 Bedouin during these expulsion operations.[97] (The Israelis claimed that the 'Azazme tribesmen were crossing back and forth continually between the Negev and Sinai.) In September 1952 the Israeli army expelled some 850 members of the Al-Sani' tribe from the northern Negev to the West Bank. 'Subsequently,' Morris writes, 'several thousand more 'Azazme and other bedouin tribesmen were expelled to Sinai.'[98]

An Israel Foreign Ministry report stated that during 1949–53 'Israel expelled all told "close" to 17,000 Negev bedouin, not all of them alleged infiltrators.'[99] The Arabs of the Negev had been reduced through expulsion and flight from 65,000–95,000, at the end of the British Mandate, to 13,000 by 1951.[100] In fact, the remaining Arabs of the Negev were not granted Israeli identity cards until 1952, a situation which made it easier for the Israeli army to push them out. A year later, in 1953, it was reported in the United Nations that 7,000 Arab Bedouin, approximately half of them from the 'Azazme tribe, had been forcibly expelled from the Negev.[101]

ERASING VILLAGES

In August 1948 a *de facto* 'Transfer Committee' was officially (though secretly) appointed by the Israeli cabinet to plan the Palestinian refugees' organised resettlement in the Arab states. The three-member committee was composed of: 'Ezra Danin, a former senior Haganah intelligence officer and a senior foreign ministry adviser on Arab affairs since July 1948; Zalman Lifschitz, the prime minister's adviser on land matters; and Yosef Weitz, head of the Jewish National Fund's land settlement department, as head of the committee. The main Israeli propaganda lines regarding the Palestinian refugees and some of the myths of 1948 were concocted by members of this official Transfer Committee. Besides doing everything possible to reduce the Palestinian population in Israel, Weitz and his colleagues sought in October 1948 to amplify and consolidate the demographic transformation of Palestine by:

- preventing Palestinian refugees from returning to their homes and villages;
- destroying Arab villages;
- settling Jews in Arab villages and towns and distributing Arab lands among Jewish settlements;
- extricating Jews from Iraq and Syria;
- seeking ways to ensure the absorption of Palestinian refugees in Arab countries and launching a propaganda campaign to discourage Arab return.

Apparently, Prime Minister Ben-Gurion approved of these proposals, although he recommended that all the Palestinian refugees be resettled in one Arab country, preferably Iraq, rather than be dispersed among the neighbouring states. Ben-Gurion was also set against refugee resettlement in neighbouring Transjordan.

An abundance of archival documents shows a strong correlation between the Zionist transfer solution and the 1948 Palestinian *nakba*. By the end of the 1948 war, hundreds of villages had been completely depopulated and their houses blown up or bulldozed. The main objective was to prevent the return of refugees to their homes, but the destruction also helped to perpetuate the Zionist myth that Palestine was virtually empty territory before the Jews entered. An exhaustive study by a team of Palestinian field researchers and academics under the direction of Walid Khalidi details the destruction of 418 villages falling inside the 1949 armistice lines. The study gives the circumstances of each village's occupation and depopulation, and a description of what remains. Khalidi's team visited all except 14 sites, made comprehensive reports and took photographs. The result is both a monumental study of the *nakba* and a kind of memoriam. It is an acknowledgement of the enormous suffering of hundreds of thousands of Palestinian refugees.[102]

Of the 418 depopulated villages,[103] 293 (70 per cent) were totally destroyed, and 90 (22 per cent) were largely destroyed. Seven survived, including 'Ayn Karim (west of Jerusalem), but were taken by Israeli settlers. While an observant traveller can still see some evidence of these villages, in the main all that is left is a scattering of stones and rubble.

LEGALISING EXPROPRIATION

Israel created a system of laws to legalise and support its massive seizure of refugee property. The Absentees' Property Law, first promulgated in 1948, stated that any Arab who left his normal residence between 29 November 1947 and 1 September 1948 to go to areas outside Palestine, or to areas within Palestine that were occupied by Arab military forces, would be considered an 'absentee', his land and property subject to confiscation (see also Chapters 3 and 4). Violent confrontations with border 'infiltrators', often refugees in search of food and property, became the norm throughout the early 1950s. Jews, many of them new immigrants from Arab countries, were settled in homes and neighbourhoods belonging to Palestinian refugees. Subsequent policies adopted by the Jewish state – military and diplomatic, legal and political – were aimed at consolidating the power and ethnic domination of Israel's Jewish majority. A key element in this effort was the prevention of the return of Palestinian refugees – residing inside and outside the borders of the new state – to their ancestral homes and properties. This objective has served until today as a guiding premise underlying subsequent Israeli policy concerning Palestinian refugees.

The outcome of the 1948 war left Israel in control of over 5 million acres of Palestinian land. After the war the Israeli state took over the land of three-quarters of a million refugees, who were barred from returning, while the remaining Palestinian minority were subjected to laws and regulations that effectively deprived it of most of its land. The entire massive drive to take over Palestinian (refugee and non-refugee) land has been conducted according to strict legality. Between 1948 and the early 1990s, Israel enacted some 30 statutes that transferred land from private Arab to state (Jewish) ownership. At the United Nations Israel denied the right of the Palestinian refugees to return to their homes and villages, opposing in particular UN General Assembly Resolution 194 of December 1948.

RESPONSIBILITY AND REDRESS

The 1948 Palestinian catastrophe was the culmination of over half a century of often secret Zionist plans and, ultimately, brute force. The extensive evidence shows a strong correlation between transfer discussions, their practical application in 1948 and the Palestinian *nakba*. The primary responsibility for the displacement and dispossession of three-quarters of a million Palestinian refugees in 1948 lies with the Zionist-Jewish leadership, not least David Ben-Gurion.

Since the late 1980s the work of several Israeli 'new historians', such as Benny Morris, Simha Flapan, Tom Segev, Ilan Pappé and Avi Shlaim (see Chapter 2), has contributed to demolishing some of the long-held Israeli and Western misconceptions surrounding Israel's birth. Containing remarkable revelations based on Hebrew archival material, their studies throw new light on the conduct of the Labour Zionist founding fathers of the Israeli state.

At the same time the Israeli establishment has done everything it can to crush these early buds of Israeli self-awareness and recognition of Israel's role in the Palestinian catastrophe. Departments of Middle Eastern studies in Israeli universities and mainstream academics in Israel have continued to erase the Palestinian *nakba* as a historical event.

The moral responsibility for the 1948 Palestinian catastrophe has, of course, major ramifications for the refugee question, including the issues of compensation, restitution of property and the 'right of return'. The Palestinian refugee problem has remained at the centre of the Arab–Israeli conflict since 1948. It was mainly the refugees themselves who opposed schemes to resettle them in Arab countries. In general, Palestinians and Arabs refused to discuss an overall solution of the Arab–Israeli conflict before Israel declared that it accepted the repatriation of refugees, in accordance with UN General Assembly Resolution 194 (III) of December 1948. The resolution states that: 'the refugees wishing to return to their homes and live at peace with their neighbours should be permitted to do so at the earliest practicable date.' To Zionist Israelis, on the other hand, the Palestinian right of return appears to entail nothing less than the reversal of Zionism. The official Israeli position has always been that there can be no return of the refugees to Israeli territories, and that the only solution to the problem is their resettlement in the Arab states or elsewhere. Since 1949 Israel has consistently rejected a return of the 1948 refugees to their homes and villages; it has always refused to accept responsibility for the refugees and views them as the responsibility of the Arab countries in which they reside.

A comprehensive and durable settlement of the Arab–Israeli conflict will depend on addressing the refugee problem seriously. For over five decades, the right of return (some would say the 'dream of return') has been central to the Palestinians' struggle against dispossession and expulsion from their ancestral homeland and to their struggle for national reconstitution. Only by understanding the centrality of the *nakba* that befell the Palestinian people in 1948 is it possible to understand the Palestinians' sense of the right of return. The wrong done to the Palestinians can only be righted through an acknowledgement of their right to return to their homeland and/or their right to restitution of property.

The Palestinian refugees should be given a free choice between repatriation and/or compensation, in line with the international consensus enshrined in UN Resolution 194. The trauma of the *nakba* remains central to present-day Palestinian society (in the same way that the Holocaust has been central to Israeli and Jewish society). Today, the aspirations and hopes of millions of Palestinian refugees (in the diaspora, in the West Bank and Gaza and even some 250,000 'internal refugees' in Israel) are linked to the catastrophe of 1948. Any genuine reconciliation between the two peoples (peace between peoples as opposed to a political settlement achieved by leaders) can only begin when Israel takes responsibility for having created the Palestinian refugee problem.

NOTES

1. James MacDonald, *My Mission in Israel, 1948–1951* (London: Gollancz, 1951), pp.160–1.
2. Zeev Sternhell, *The Founding Myths of Israel: Nationalism, Socialism and the Making of the Jewish State* (Princeton: Princeton University Press, 1998).
3. Ibid.
4. The archaeological findings blatantly contradict the biblical picture. Professor Zeev Hertzog an Israeli archaeologist (of Tel Aviv University), has written recently: following decades of intensive excavations in Palestine/Israel, archaeologists have found that the patriarch's acts are legendary; that the Israelites did not sojourn in Egypt or wander in the desert; they did not conquer the land of Canaan in a military campaign, and did not pass it on to the twelve tribes. Neither is there any evidence of the empire of David and Solomon. The united monarchy under David and Solomon, which the Bible describes as a regional power, was at most a small tribal kingdom. See Zeev Hertzog, in *Haaretz*, 29 October 1999. See also Hugh Harcourt, 'In Search of the Emperor's New Clothes', in Tomis Kapitan (ed.), *Philosophical Perspectives on the Israeli–Palestinian Conflict* (New York: M.E Sharpe, 1997), p.289; Thomas Thompson, *The Early History of the Israelite People* (Leiden, Netherlands: E.J. Brill, 1992); Michael Prior, 'Zionism and the Bible', in Naim Ateek and Michael Prior, *Holy Land Hollow Jubilee: God, Justice and the Palestinians* (London: Melisende, 1999), p.70. The link between Israeli territorial conquests and the Old Testament is also reflected in the propagandistic claim of David Ben-Gurion, Israel's first and secular Prime Minister, that the Bible is the 'Jews' sacrosanct title-deed to Palestine ... with a genealogy of 3,500 years'. David Ben-Gurion, *The Rebirth and Destiny of Israel* (New York: The Philosophical Library, 1954), p.100.
5. Keith W. Whitelam, *The Invention of Ancient Israel: The Silencing of Palestinian History* (London: Routledge, 1996), pp.40–5.
6. Amos Oz, 'The Meaning of Homeland', *New Outlook* 31, no.1 (January 1988), p.22, reproducing an article originally published in *Davar* in 1967.
7. Cited from the back cover of 'Jerusalem of Gold', Fontana Record, SRF, 67572, MGF 27572.
8. Tamar Avidar, 'Na'omi Updated her Jerusalem [of Gold]', *Ma'ariv*, 11 June 1967, p.5.
9. The Shofar is a horn used on Jewish high holidays to commemorate events of major significance.
10. Translated from Hebrew, Fontana Records, in Uri Davis and Norton Mezvinsky (eds), *Documents from Israel 1967–1973* (London: Ithaca Press, 1975), p.220.
11. Yehuda Gurvitz and Shmuel Navon (eds), *What Story Will I Tell My Children?* (Tel Aviv: Amihah, 1953), pp.128, 132, 134, cited in Fouzi El-Asmar, 'The Portrayal of Arabs in Hebrew Children's Literature', *Journal of Palestine Studies* 16, no.1 (Autumn 1986), p.83.

12. Dan Ben-Amotz, *Seporei Abu-Nimr* [The Stories of Abu-Nimr] (Tel Aviv: Zmora-Bitan, 1982), p.155.
13. Binyamin Netanyahu, *A Place among the Nations* (London: Bantam Press, 1993), pp.39–40.
14. For excerpts of Shamir's address, see *Journal of Palestine Studies* 21, no.2 (Winter 1992), pp.128–31.
15. Chaim Weizmann, speech delivered at a meeting of the French Zionist Federation, Paris, 28 March 1914, reproduced in Barnet Litvinoff (ed.) *The Letters and Papers of Chaim Weizmann*, Vol. 1, series B, paper 24 (Jerusalem: Israel University Press, 1983), pp.115–16.
16. See Yosef Heller, *The Struggle for the State: Zionist Policy, 1936–48* (Jerusalem: Zalman Shazar Centre, 1984), p.140 (Hebrew).
17. Israel Zangwill, *The Voice of Jerusalem* (London, William Heinemann, 1920), p.104.
18. Adam M. Garfinke, 'On the Origin, Meaning, Use and Abuse of a Phrase', *Middle Eastern Studies* 27, no.4 (October 1991), pp.539–50.
19. Zangwill, *The Voice of Jerusalem*, p.93.
20. *Doar Hayom* (Jerusalem), 28 April 1930.
21. 'Society of Jews' was the name used by Herzl in his book *Judenstat* to designate the political organisation that he envisaged as the future representative of the Zionist movement.
22. Rephael Patai (ed.), *The Complete Diaries of Theodor Herzl*, Vol.1 (New York: Herzl Press and T. Yoseloff, 1960), pp.88–9.
23. Israel Zangwill, *Speeches, Articles and Letters* (London: Soncino Press, 1937), p.210.
24. Cited in Yosef Gorny, *Zionism and the Arabs, 1882–1948* (Oxford: Clarendon Press, 1987), p.271; Yosef Nedava, 'Tochniyot Helufei Ochlosin Lepetron Be'ayat *Eretz Yisrael'* [Population Exchange Plans for the Solution of the Problem of the Arabs of the Land of Israel], *Gesher* 24, nos1–2 (Spring–Summer 1978), p.153; Yosef Nedava, 'Yisrael Zangwill Vehabe'ayah Ha'arvit' [Israel Zangwill and the Arab Problem], *Haumah*, no.14 (October 1965), pp.209–16.
25. Nur Masalha, *Expulsion of the Palestinians: The Concept of 'Transfer' in Zionist Political Thought, 1882–1948* (Washington, DC: Institute for Palestine Studies, 1992); *A Land without a People: Israel, Transfer and the Palestinians, 1949–1996* (London: Faber and Faber, 1997); *Imperial Israel and the Palestinians: The Politics of Expansion, 1967–2000* (London: Pluto Press, 2000).
26. Shabtai Teveth, *Ben-Gurion and the Palestinian Arabs* (Oxford: Oxford University Press, 1985), p.39.
27. Zangwill, *Speeches, Articles and Letters*, p.210.
28. A reference to a well-known essay, Yitzhak Epstein, 'The Hidden Question', *Hashiloah* (1907), pp.193–206.
29. Epstein, 'The Hidden Question', pp.193–206.
30. Gorny, *Zionism and the Arabs*, pp.49–50.
31. David Ben-Gurion, *Zichronot* [Memoirs], Vol.3 (Tel Aviv: 'Am 'Oved, 1971–1972), p.163.
32. Ahad Ha'Am, 'Emet Meeretz Yisrael' [The Truth from the Land of Israel], in *Complete Works*, (Jerusalem, 1961), pp.27–9.

33. Ibid. Ahad Ha'Am wrote in 1913 that 'Apart from the political danger, I can't put up with the idea that our brethren are morally capable of behaving in such a way to men of another people ... If this be the 'Messiah,' I do not wish to see him coming.' Ahad Ha'Am quoted by Hans Kohn, in 'Zion and the National Idea', in Michael Selzer (ed.), *Zionism Reconsidered: The Rejection of Jewish Normalcy* (London: Macmillan, 1970), p.196.
34. David Ben-Gurion, *Zichronot* [Memoirs], Vol. 4 (Tel Aviv: 'Am 'Oved, 1974), pp.297–9.
35. Ibid.
36. Cited in Teveth, *Ben-Gurion and the Palestinian Arabs*, p.189. The above quote in the English translation of Teveth's book is quoted from Ben-Gurion's handwritten letter, and also found in the typewritten copy, both of which are to be found in Ben-Gurion's Archives in Sde Boker. In the Hebrew version of Teveth's book, however, four words have been added making it read, 'We do not want and do not need to expel Arabs and take their place.' Shabtai Teveth, *Ben-Gurion and the Palestinian Arabs* (Jerusalem, 1985), p.314 (Hebrew). These additional four words (together with the previous two-and-a-half lines) are in fact crossed out in Ben-Gurion's handwritten letter. In the published edition of this letter, apparently the editor omitted this sentence. See David Ben-Gurion, *Michtavim el-Pola Ve el-Hayeladim* [Letters to Pola and the Children] (Tel Aviv, 'Am 'Oved, 1968), p.213. In an article in *Alpayim*, Benny Morris wrote that 'between 1937 and the 1970s, someone – presumably not Ben-Gurion himself – 'vandalised' the original letter' by crossing out several lines of it. He added that the Archives of the Israel Defence Force had, with the aid of modern technology, managed to decipher these crossed-out words. Benny Morris, 'Mabat Hadash 'Al Mismachim Tzioniyim Merkaziyim', *Alpayim* 12 (1996), pp.76–7, note 4. Morris, in a subsequent article, somewhat modified slightly this statement, suggesting that these lines had been crossed out 'by Ben-Gurion or someone else, subsequently'. Benny Morris, 'Refabricating 1948', *Journal of Palestine Studies* 27 no.2 (Winter 1998), p.84.
37. As reported in the *New Judea* 13, nos11–112,(August–September 1937), p.220.
38. Protocol of the Jewish Agency Executive meeting of 7 June 1938, in Jerusalem, confidential, Vol.28, no.51, Central Zionist Archives (CZA), Jerusalem.
39. David Ben-Gurion, 'Lines for Zionist Policy', 15 October 1941, quoted in Masalha, *Expulsion of the Palestinians*, pp.128–9, and note no.9, p.166.
40. Ibid.
41. David Ben-Gurion, *Yoman Hamilhamah* [War Diary], Vol.1 (Tel Aviv: Misrad Habitahon, 1982), p.58.
42. Ben-Gurion, *Yoman Hamilhamah*, Vol.1, entry dated 6 February 1948, p.211.
43. Tom Segev, *1949: The First Israelis* (New York: The Free Press, 1986), p.25.
44. *'Al Darchei Mediniyutenu: Mo'atzah 'Olamit Shel Ihud Po'alei Tzion (c.s.)-Din Vehesbon Male, 21 July–7 August* [1938], [A Full Report about the

World Convention of Ihud Po'alei Tzion, C.S.] (Tel Aviv: Central Office of Hitahdut Po'alie Tzion Press, 1938).
45. Protocol of the Jewish Agency Executive meeting of 12 June 1938, Vol.28, no.53, Central Zionist Archives, Jerusalem.
46. Cited in Gorny, *Zionism and the Arabs*, p.304. Katznelson's support for Arab transfer is also found in his writings. See Berl Katznelson, *Ketavim* [Writings] (Tel Aviv: Mapai Publications, 1949), Vol.12, pp.241, 244. See also Anita Shapira, *Berl: The Biography of a Socialist Zionist* (Cambridge: Cambridge University Press, 1984), p.335.
47. Weitz Diary, A246/7, entry dated 20 December 1940, pp.1090–91, CZA, Jerusalem.
48. Ibid., entry dated 17 July 1941, p.1204, CZA.
49. Ibid., entry dated 20 March 1941, p.1127.
50. Ibid., entry dated 18 April 1948, p.2358, CZA.
51. Masalha, *Expulsion of the Palestinians*, pp.30–8.
52. Ibid., pp.49–124.
53. Ibid., p.55.
54. Moshe Sharett, *Yoman Medini* [Political Diary], Vol.2 (Te Aviv: 'Am 'Oved, 1971), pp.16–17.
55. David Ben-Gurion, *Zichronot* [Memoirs], Vol.4 (Tel Aviv: 'Am 'Oved, 1974), pp.173, 175, 207.
56. Sharett, *Yoman Medini*, Vol.2, pp.187–8.
57. Simha Flapan, *The Birth of Israel: Myths and Realities* (New York: Pantheon Books, 1987), p.90.
58. Walid Khalidi, 'Plan Dalet: Master Plan for the Conquest of Palestine', *Journal of Palestine Studies* 18, no.1 (Autumn 1988), pp.4–19.
59. Benny Morris, *The Birth of the Palestinian Refugee Problem, 1947–1949* (Cambridge: Cambridge University Press, 1987), p.62.
60. Ibid., p.63.
61. Ibid., p.21.
62. See my *Expulsion of the Palestinians* and the work of several Israeli revisionist historians, including Morris, *The Birth of the Palestinian Refugee Problem*; Simha Flapan, *The Birth of Israel: Myths and Realities* (New York: Pantheon Books, 1987); Tom Segev, *1949: The First Israelis* (New York: Free Press, 1986); Ilan Pappé, *The Making of the Arab–Israeli Conflict, 1947–1951* (London: I. B. Tauris, 1992); Eugene L. Rogan and Avi Shlaim (eds), *The War for Palestine: Rewriting the History of 1948* (Cambridge: Cambridge University Press, 2001); and Avi Shlaim, *Collusion Across the Jordan* (Oxford: Oxford University Press, 1996).
63. Benny Morris, *1948 and After: Israel and the Palestinians* (Oxford: Clarendon Press, 1990), p.22.
64. Benny Morris, 'The New Historiography and the Old Propagandists', *Haaretz*, 9 May 1989).
65. Michael Bar-Zohar, *Ben-Gurion*, Vol.2 (Tel Aviv: 'Am 'Oved, 1977), p.703 (Hebrew).
66. Examples of 'outright expulsions' include the towns of Lydda and Ramle in July; the expulsion of the town of al-Faluja and remaining inhabitants of the towns of Beisan and of al-Majdal (in 1950); the expulsion of the villages of Safsaf, Sa'sa', al-Mansura, Tarbikha, Nabi

Rubin, Kafr Bir'im, Suruh, Iqrit, Farradiya, Kafr 'Inan, al-Qudayriya, 'Arab al-Shamalina, Zangariya, 'Arab al-Suyyad, al-Bassa, al-Ghabisiya, Danna, Nuris, al-Tantura, Qisarya, Khirbet al-Sarkas, al-Dumayra, 'Arab al-Fuqara, 'Arab al-Nufay'at, Miska, Tabsar (Khirbet 'Azzun), Zarnuqa, al-Qubayba, Yibna, Zakariya, Najd, Sumsum, 'Iraq al-Manshiya, al-Dawayma, Deir Yassin and al-Majdal.

67. Benny Morris, 'Operation Dani and the Palestinian Exodus from Lydda and Ramle in 1948', *Middle East Journal* 40, no.1 (Winter 1986), p.91.
68. Cited in Peretz Kidron, 'Truth Whereby Nations Live', in Edward Said and Christopher Hitchens (eds) *Blaming the Victims: Spurious Scholarship and the Palestinians Question*, (London and New York: Verso, 1988), pp.91–2.
69. Morris, *1948 and After*, p.2.
70. Quoted in ibid., p.42
71. Ibid., pp.42–3.
72. Aharon Cohen, memorandum entitled 'Our Arab Policy During the War', in Giva'at Haviva, Hashomer Hatza'ir Archives, 10.10.95 (4).
73. Michael Bar-Zohar, *Ben-Gurion*, Vol. 2 (Tel Aviv: 'Am 'Oved, 1977), p.776 (Hebrew).
74. Cited in Kidron, 'Truth Whereby Nations Live', pp.86–7.
75. Ibid, pp.92–3.
76. Sharif Kana'ana, *Still on Vacation! The Eviction of the Palestinians in 1948* (Ramallah: SHAML (Palestinian Diaspora and Refugee Centre), 1992), p.108.
77. See Guy Erlich 'Not only Deir Yassin', *Ha'ir*, 6 May 1992 (Hebrew).
78. For further details, see Nur-eldeen Masalha, 'On Recent Hebrew and Israeli Sources for the Palestinian Exodus, 1947–49', *Journal of Palestine Studies* 18, no.1 (Autumn 1988), pp.122–3.
79. There are widely documented massacres at Lydda, Khirbet Nasir al-Din, 'Ayn Zaytun, 'Eilabun, Sa'sa', Jish, al-Dawayma, al-Tira (near Haifa), Safsaf, Sha'ib, Saliha and Hule.
80. Masalha, 'On Recent Hebrew and Israeli Sources for the Palestinian Exodus', pp. 127–30. See also Morris, *The Birth of the Palestinian Refugee Problem*, pp. 222–3, and Walid Khalidi, *Deir Yassin: Friday, 9 April 1948* (Beirut: Institute for Palestine Studies, 1999) (Arabic).
81. Benny Morris, 'Operation Hiram Revisited: A Correction', *Journal of Palestine Studies* 28, no. 2 (Winter 1999), p.70.
82. Benny Morris, 'Falsifying the Record: A Fresh Look at Zionist Documentation of 1948', *Journal of Palestine Studies* 24, no. 3 (Spring 1995), p.55.
83. Morris, 'Operation Hiram Revisited', p.73.
84. Ibid.
85. Nahmani Diary, 6 November 1948, Hashomer Archive, Kfar Gila'adi, quoted in ibid.
86. Morris, *The Birth of the Palestinian Refugee Problem*, pp.229–30; Guy Erlich in *Ha'ir*, 6 May 1992; '*Al-Hamishmar*, 3 March 1978; *Jerusalem Post*, 28 February 1978; Nafez Nazzal, *The Palestinian Exodus from Galilee 1948* (Beirut: Institute for Palestine Studies, 1978). Nasr al-Din, 12 April: a Haganah force 'captured the village of Khirbet Nasir ad Din ... some

non-combatants were apparently killed and some houses destroyed.' In *The Palestinian Exodus from Galilee, 1948*, by Nazzal, we find the following: 'Zionists attacked the village of Nasr-ed Din (with 90 Arab inhabitants) and destroyed all its houses, killing some of its inhabitants, including women and children, and expelling all the rest' (p.29). In the final days before Jewish conquest of Arab Tiberias on 16–18 April, Yosef Nahmani recorded in his diary the Haganah's rejection of all negotiations with the local Arab inhabitants and its attack on the neighbouring village of Nasr al-Din, in which a number of Arab civilians, including children, were massacred.

'Ayn Zaytun, 3–4 May: A few days before the conquest of Safad, some 37 young men were rounded up from the neighbouring village of 'Ayn Zaytun after its occupation by the Haganah. They were among the 70 Arab detainees massacred by two Palmach 3th Battalion soldiers, on battalion commander Moshe Kalman's orders, on 3 or 4 May in the gully between 'Ayn Zaytun and Safad.

Al-Tantura, 22–23 May: In the case of al-Tantura, the large-scale massacre was well-planned ahead. Al-Tantura (population 1,500) and about four coastal villages south of Haifa were targeted by the Israelis for expulsion. They refused to surrender. On 9 May, local Haganah Intelligence and Arab experts held a meeting in Netanya to find the best way to 'expel or subdue' these coastal villages. The meeting had been 'preceded by a Haganah effort to obtain the village's surrender without a battle; the village elders refused, rejecting the Haganah terms which included the surrender of arms.' Recently an Israeli researcher, Teddy Katz, using oral history (taped testimonies of both Arab and Jewish witnesses) uncovers the al-Tantura blood-bath, in which more than 200 Tantura villagers, mostly unarmed young men, had been shot dead after the village had surrendered following the onslaught of the Haganah troops.

Lydda, 11–12 July: On 11–12 dozens of unarmed civilians who were detained in a mosque and church premises of the town were gunned down. One official Israeli source put the casualty figures at 250 dead and many injured. It is likely, however, that somewhere between 250 and 400 Arabs were killed in the large-scale IDF massacre at Lydda and estimated 350 more died in the subsequent expulsion and forced march of the townspeople. Tel Gezer (in the south): A soldier of the IDF Kiryati Brigade testified that his colleagues got hold of a number of Arab men and two Arab women, a young one and an old one. All the men were murdered; the young woman was raped; the old woman was murdered.

Khisas, 12 December 1947: 12 Arab villagers were murdered in cold blood in a Haganah raid. Asdud (in the south), end August 1948: IDF Giva'ati Brigade soldiers murdered ten Arab *fellahin* in cold blood.

Qisarya (Caesarea), February 1948: The Fourth Battalion of the Palmach forces, under the command of Yosef Tabenkin, conquered Qisarya. According to Uri Milstein, all those who did not escape from the village were murdered. Kabri, 20 May 1948: On 20 May the Carmeli Brigade conquered the village. One of the Israeli soldiers,

Yehuda Rashef, got hold of a few youngsters who did not escape, probably seven, ordered them to fill up some ditches and then lined them up and fired at them with a machine gun. A few died. Abu Shusha, 14 May 1948: evidence of a large-scale massacre.

87. Benny Morris, *Israel's Border Wars, 1949–1956* (Oxford: Clarendon Press, 1993), note 160, p.164.
88. Cited in ibid., p.164.
89. Ibid.
90. Cited in Morris, *1948 and After*, p. 257.
91. Ibid., pp. 258–9.
92. Cited by Yehuda Litani in *Hadashot*, 7 December 1990.
93. Quoted in Ilan Halevi, *A History of the Jews* (London: Zed Books, 1987), pp. 203–4.
94. Morris, *Israel's Border Wars*, p.154.
95. Ibid.
96. Ibid., p.155.
97. Ibid., pp.155–6.
98. Ibid., p.157.
99. Ibid.
100. Cited in Penny Maddrell, *The Beduin of the Negev* (London: The Minority Rights Group, Report no.81, 1990), p.6
101. Cited in Christina Jones, *The Untempered Wind: Forty Years in Palestine* (London: Longman, 1975), p.218.
102. Walid Khalidi (ed.) *All That Remains: The Palestinian Villages Occupied and Depopulated by Israel in 1948* (Washington, DC: Institute for Palestine Studies, 1992).
103. There is an apparent inconsistency in the determination of the number of Palestinian localities depopulated and destroyed in 1948. *The Destroyed Arab Villages* (1975), a study conducted by the late Israel Shahak in the 1970s, lists 385 villages destroyed in 1948. Cited in *Internally Displaced Palestinians in Israel on the Eve of the Peace Settlement: The National Committee for Defence of the Rights of the Internally Displaced in Israel*, Badil Resource Centre (available on the internet at http://www.badil.org/Press/2000/manifesto.htm). Morris lists 369 villages and towns, and gives the date and circumstances of their depopulation, relying mostly on Israeli archival and non-archival sources. Morris, *The Birth of the Palestinian Refugee Problem*, pp.xiv–xviii. Khalidi's figure of 418 is based on the villages or hamlets (only) which are listed in the Palestine Index Gazetteer of 1945 falling inside the 1949 Armistice Lines. Khalidi's figure of 418 amounts to half the total number of Palestinian villages in Mandated Palestine. More recently Palestinian researcher Salman Abu-Sitta provided an updated register of 531 villages. Abu-Sitta's register includes the localities listed by Morris and Khalidi, and adds those of the tribes in the Beer Sheba District. Salman Abu-Sitta, *Palestinian Right to Return: Sacred, Legal and Possible* (London: The Palestinian Return Centre, second edition, May 1999), p.12. While Abu-Sitta adds to the list of destroyed villages, Khalidi's account is the most meticulous and comprehensive.

2 Israel's 'New Historians' and the *Nakba:* A Critique of Zionist Discourse

Much of the rewriting of the history of 1948 has been a combined effort undertaken by several Israeli and Palestinian scholars, with minor contributions from outsiders. This revisionist historiography, critically acclaimed by the early 1990s, was initiated by a small group of Israeli historians and researchers in the immediate period following the 1982 Israeli invasion of Lebanon. Stimulated partly by the shattering of the Zionist national consensus, historical revisionism was given a huge boost by the opening of Israeli archives and the discovery of an astonishing array of new documents.[1] Since then, major works on 1948 have also been contributed by Palestinian authors, including Walid Khalidi, Rashid Khalidi, Sharif Kana'ana and myself.[2] The 1948 *nakba* is central to Palestinian memory and the society of today. However, although the issue of the 1948 exodus is a critical turning point in the Palestinians' history, only a small number of Palestinian historians and academics have investigated its actual roots and causes.[3] This is rather ironical since the debate over the causes and circumstance of the exodus is also reflected in the array of proposed solutions to the refugee problem.

In a number of articles I published between 1988 and 1991 I was in fact the first Arab historian to provide a critical assessment of the Israeli 'new historiography' of the refugee exodus and to draw attention to the significance of this new scholarly phenomenon.[4] Central to this 'new historiography' are the debates on the 1948 Palestinian refugee exodus (expulsion versus flight), the impact of the British mandate on Palestinian Arab and Jewish (Yishuv) societies, the Zionist–Hashemite alliance of the 1930s and 1940s, the regional balance of power in 1948, the questionable nature of Zionist acceptance of the 1947 UN partition resolution, and the new revelations about early peace negotiations between Israeli and Arab leaders. In 1948, while Arab leaders were in league against each other and had little interest in assisting the Palestinians, the Israelis were consolidating their new conquests far beyond the Jewish state's boundaries as envisaged by the UN. The picture that emerges from the 1948 war, for example, as Israeli 'new historian' Avi Shlaim has shown, is not the mythical one (still repeated by Israeli orthodox historians and spokespersons) of Israel standing alone against the combined might of the entire Arab world. It is rather one of convergence between the interests of Israel and those of Hashemite Transjordan against other members of the bickering Arab coalition, and especially against the Palestinians.[5]

The rise in Israel of an influential, though controversial, 'new historiography' was a remarkable phenomenon. On the whole, the terms of the debate on the early history of the Israeli state and the birth of the Palestinian refugee question have been transformed by the works of the Israeli 'new historians', including Benny Morris, Simha Flapan, Tom Segev, Ilan Pappé and Avi Shlaim. Containing remarkable revelations based on Hebrew and archival material, these works closely scrutinised the conduct of the (Labour Zionist) founding fathers of the Israeli state, thus contributing to the demolition of some of the long-held misconceptions surrounding Israel's birth. Several foundational myths surrounding 1948 have been examined and discredited as being part of an Israeli disinformation campaign. Most of these highly innovative works appeared in the late 1980s and early 1990s, sparking an internal debate within Israel as well as a keen interest worldwide. It also soon became apparent that the Israeli 'new historiography' was part of the much wider phenomenon of the development of new critical perspectives, encompassing several disciplines within the social sciences, with contributions from a long list of authors, most of whom held teaching positions in Israeli universities. These Israeli authors are not a monolithic group; they range from the liberal Zionist to the 'post-Zionist', from the good old-fashioned positivist historian to the 'post-modernist' relativist.[6]

The Palestinian *nakba*, however, has become central to the new Israeli discourse on 1948 only among some of contributors to the Israeli 'new historiography'. Ilan Pappé, for instance, provides a critical assessment of the 'old and new' Israeli historiography of the refugee exodus by noting – in contrast to Benny Morris – that expulsion was a dominant feature of the Palestinian *nakba* and experience in 1948.[7] Pappé had this to say in a recent article entitled: 'Demons of the Nakbah':

> For a short while at the end of the 1980s, several academics, including myself, caught public attention by publishing scholarly

books that challenged the accepted Israeli version of the 1948 War. In these books, we accused Israel of expelling the indigenous population and of destroying the Palestinian villages and neighbourhoods. Although our early works were hesitant and cautious, and mine were not even translated into Hebrew, it was still possible to gather from them that the Jewish State was built on the ruins of the indigenous people of Palestine, whose livelihood, houses, cultures and land had been systematically destroyed.[8]

A liberal Zionist interpretation of the phenomenon, however, is found in *Palestinian Refugees and the Middle East Peace Process* (1993) by Don Peretz, a leading American Jewish expert on the Palestinian refugee problem, who concluded that the Israeli 'revisionist' historians highlighted the issue of Israel's 'shared accountability for the [refugee] flight'.[9] Peretz also believes that the issue of moral responsibility for the 1948 refugee exodus has major ramifications for the refugee question, including the 'right of return', compensation and restitution of property.[10]

By the mid-1990s the great history debate in Israel, remorselessly aired in the Hebrew media, had divided generations and driven the old guard of establishment academics to a better defence of their turf against the encroachments of the 'new historians'. The latter were described as 'self-hating Jews', and subjected to relentless abuse and personal attacks, often resembling witch-hunts. They were accused of rewriting the history of Zionism in the image of its enemies and dedicating themselves to the destruction of the state of Israel by sapping its legitimacy. The old guard turned to the Israeli media to mobilise public opinion against the 'traitors' by manipulating public fears and apprehensions.[11] The attacks on them involved not only many orthodox historians and partisans of labour Zionism (Shabtai Teveth, Anita Shapira, Shlomo Aharonson, Itamar Rabinowich, Efraim Karsh, Yoav Gelber) but also some popular writers and journalists (Aharon Megged, Hanoch Bar-Tov, David Bar-Ilan).[12] Karsh, in particular, responded by waging a bitter campaign against the 'new historians', which was designed (in the words of Benny Morris) to 'refabricate 1948'.[13] Karsh and other orthodox academics accused the 'new historians' of destroying the foundations of the state of Israel and threatening its legitimacy. The old guard, themselves responsible for the foundational myths, demanded a return to a 'committed' (Zionist) scholarship; on the contrary, their opponents (especially Benny Morris) argued, it was precisely because

Israel had come of age, was strong enough and its right to exist now recognised by its Arab enemies, that a new, 'non-ideological' history was born.[14]

Ideological (Zionist) mobilisation has always presented Israeli social scientists and historians with professional and ethical dilemmas. Faced with the competing demands of their professions and the requirements of the Zionist-Jewish state – a state created on the ruins of Palestinian society – many Israeli academics have opted for 'committed' (Zionist) scholarship and 'official' versions of events. It is hardly surprising, therefore, that both academic and political establishments reacted to the 'new historiography' with dismay. They did everything they could to stifle these early signs of Israeli self-awareness and the recognition of Israel's role in the Palestinian catastrophe. Departments of Middle Eastern Studies at Israeli universities and mainstream academics in Israel have continued to erase the Palestinian *nakba* as a historical event, discouraging new scholars and academics from challenging the overall denial and suppression of the Palestinian catastrophe which took place in the world outside their ivory towers.[15]

A CRITIQUE OF BENNY MORRIS

Benny Morris spent the mid-1980s investigating what led to the creation of the Palestinian refugee problem, publishing *The Birth of the Palestinian Refugee Problem, 1947–1949* in 1987. Since then he has come to be seen in the West as the ultimate authority on the Palestinian exodus of 1948. Indeed, his work has contributed to demolishing some of the long-held (at least in Israel and the West) misconceptions surrounding Israel's birth. His subsequent collection of essays, *1948 and After: Israel and the Palestinians* (1990), revisits the ground covered in *The Birth of the Palestinian Refugee Problem*, bringing to light new material he discovered himself or which became available only after the completion of the first book.

Morris's work belongs to the Israeli 'new historiography'. Despite his passionate Zionism and, worse, his recent conversion to the right-wing cause in Israel,[16] his real contribution to the new scholarship and to the creation of a phenomenon of considerable political and scholarly significance has been widely acknowledged. Morris himself does not like the term 'revisionist' historiography, in part because it 'conjures up' images of the Revisionist Movement in Zionism of Zeev Jabotinsky, and thus causes 'confusion'. He further eschews the term because 'Israel's old historians, by and large, were not really historians, and did not produce real history. In reality they were chroniclers, and often apologetic.'[17] Morris examines this 'old' – orthodox and official – historiography in the opening essay of *1948 and After*, referring to the historians who produced it over three decades after 1948 as 'less candid', 'deceitful' and 'misleading'.[18] As examples, he cites the accounts provided by Lieutenant-Colonel (ret.) Elhanan Orren, a former officer at the Israel Defence Force (IDF) History Branch, in his *Baderech el Ha'ir* (On the Road to the City), a detailed account of Operation Dani, published by the IDF Press in 1976, and *Toldot Milhemet Hakomemiyut* (History of the War of Independence), produced by the General Staff/History Branch, as well as Ben-Gurion's own 'histories' *Medinat Yisrael Hamehudeshet* and *Behilahem Yisrael*.[19]

Two remarks are in order here: first, having myself examined many of the 'old' and official Hebrew chronicles, it is quite clear to me that Morris does not always live up to his claim of using this material in a critical manner and this casts doubts on his conclusions. For instance, in *The Birth of the Palestinian Refugee Problem*, Morris quotes uncritically the 'major political conclusions' Ben-Gurion drew from the Arab departure from Haifa and makes little effort to reconcile the 'deceitfulness' of such a chronicle with uncritical reliance on it. Also, generally speaking, having based himself predominantly, and frequently uncritically, on official Israeli archival and non-archival material, Morris's description and analysis of such a controversial subject as the Palestinian exodus have serious shortcomings. Second, Morris's description of the works by the 'new' Israeli historians – while ignoring the recent works by non-Zionist scholars on 1948 – gives rise to the impression that these discourses are basically the outcome of a debate among Zionists which, unfortunately, has little to do with the Palestinians themselves.

Morris's central thesis, as first expounded in *The Birth of the Palestinian Refugee Problem*, is summed up in the following passage from *1948 and After*:

> what occurred in 1948 lies somewhere in between the Jewish 'robber state' [i.e., a state which had 'systematically and forcefully expelled the Arab population'] and the 'Arab orders' explanations. While from the mid-1930s most of the Yishuv's leaders, including Ben-Gurion, wanted to establish a Jewish state without an Arab minority, or with as small an Arab minority as possible, and

> supported a 'transfer solution' to this minority problem, the Yishuv did not enter the 1948 War with a master plan for expelling the Arabs, nor did its political or military leaders ever adopt such a master plan. What happened was largely haphazard and a result of the war. There were Haganah/IDF expulsions of Arab communities, some of them at the initiative or with the *post facto* approval of the cabinet or the defense minister, and most with General Staff sanction – such as the expulsions from Miska and Ad Dumeira in April; from Zarnuqa, Al Qubeiba, and Huj in May; from Lydda and Ramle in July; from the Lebanese border area (Kafr Bir'im, Iqrit, Al Mansura, Tarbikha, Suruh, and Nabi Rubin) in early November. But there was no grand design, no blanket policy of expulsion.[20]

In other words, only in 'smaller part' were Haganah/IDF expulsions carried out and these were impromptu, ad hoc measures dictated by the military circumstances, a conclusion that deflects serious responsibility for the 1948 exodus from the Zionist leadership. But can his claim that there was no transfer design and expulsion policy in 1948 be sustained? Does the fact that there was no 'master plan' for expelling the Palestinians absolve the Zionist leadership of responsibility, given, *inter alia*, its campaign of psychological warfare (documented by Morris and others) designed to precipitate Arab evacuation? How can Morris be so categorical in stating that there was no Israeli expulsion policy when his own work rests on carefully released partial documentation and when many of the Israeli files and documents relating to the subject are still classified and remain closed to researchers? Is it inconceivable that such a 'transfer' policy was based on an understanding between Ben-Gurion and his lieutenants rather than on a blueprint? Morris himself writes in an article in *Haaretz* (entitled: 'The New Historiography and the Old Propagandists', 9 May 1989) in which he discusses the transfer notion and Ben-Gurion's role in 1948:

> One of the hallmarks of Ben-Gurion's greatness was that the man knew what to say and what not to say in certain circumstances; what is allowed to be recorded on paper and what is preferable to convey orally or in hint.

Ben-Gurion's admiring biographer Michael Bar-Zohar states:

> In internal discussions, in instructions to his men [in 1948] the Old Man [Ben-Gurion] demonstrated a clear position: It would be better that as few a number as possible of Arabs should remain in the territory of the [Jewish] state.[21]

Morris claims (in *1948 and After*, p.16) that it 'was the Arab contention ... that the Yishuv had always intended forcible 'transfer'. Is it merely an 'Arab contention', or perhaps, a figment of Arab imagination? Yet the evidence Morris adduces points to a completely different picture. In his 9 May 1989 article in *Haaretz*, Morris traces 'the growth of the transfer idea in Ben-Gurion's thinking' from the second half of the 1930s. 'There is no doubt', Morris writes,

> that from the moment [the Peel proposal was submitted] ... the problem of the Arab minority, supposed to reside in that [prospective Jewish] state, began to preoccupy the Yishuv's leadership obsessively. They were justified in seeing the future minority as a great danger to the prospective Jewish state – a fifth political, or even military, column. The transfer idea ... was viewed by the majority of the Yishuv leaders in those days as the best solution to the problem.

In *The Birth of the Palestinian Refugee Problem* (p.25) Morris shows that Ben-Gurion advocated 'compulsory' transfer in 1937. In his *Haaretz* article he writes of the 'growth of the transfer idea in Ben-Gurion's thinking' and that in November 1947, a few days before the UN General Assembly's partition resolution, a consensus emerged at the meeting of the Jewish Agency Executive in favour of giving as many Arabs in the Jewish state as possible citizenship of the prospective Arab state rather than of the Jewish state where they would be living. According to Morris, Ben-Gurion explained the rationale in the following terms:

> If a war breaks out between the Jewish state and the Palestine Arab state, the Arab minority in the Jewish state would be a 'Fifth Column': hence, it was preferable that they be citizens of the Palestine Arab state so that, if the War breaks out and, if hostile, they 'would be expelled' to the Arab state. And if they were citizens of the Jewish state 'it would (only) be possible to imprison them'.

Does not this show that the Yishuv's leaders entered the 1948 war at least with a transfer desire or mind-set?

Morris argues that a new approach emerged in 1948 among the ruling Mapai Party leaders, presided over by Ben-Gurion, in support of a transfer 'solution' to the 'Arab demographic problem':

> Ben-Gurion understood ... that war changed everything; a different set of 'rules' had come to apply. Land could and would be conquered and retained; there would be demographic changes. This approach emerged explicitly in Ben-Gurion's address at the meeting of the Mapai Council on 7 February: Western Jerusalem's Arab districts had been evacuated and a similar, permanent demographic change could be expected in much of the country as the war spread.[22]

Other prominent Mapai leaders such as Eliahu Lulu (Hacarmeli), a Jerusalem branch leader, and Shlomo Lavi, an influential Kibbutz movement leader, echoed the same approach. In an internal debate at the Mapai Centre on 24 July 1948, held against the background of the expulsion of the Palestinian towns of Lydda and Ramle, Shlomo Lavi stated that 'the ... transfer of Arabs out of the country in my eyes is one of the most just, moral and correct things that can be done. I have thought this ... for many years.'[23] Lavi's views were backed by another prominent Mapai leader, Avraham Katznelson: there is nothing 'more moral, from the viewpoint of universal human ethics, than the emptying of the Jewish State of the Arabs and their transfer elsewhere ... This requires [the use of] force.'[24] Contrary to what Morris claims, there was nothing new about this approach of 'forcible transfer', nor did it emerge out of the blue merely as a result of the outbreak of hostilities in 1948.

The Yishuv's leaders pursued transfer schemes from the mid-1930s onwards almost obsessively. Transfer Committees were set up by the Jewish Agency between 1937 and 1942 and a number of transfer schemes were formulated in secret. A thorough discussion of these schemes is found in my book *Expulsion of the Palestinians: The Concept of 'Transfer' in Zionist Political Thought, 1882–1948* (1992). Shortly after the publication of the Peel Commission report, which endorsed the transfer idea, Ben-Gurion wrote in his diary (12 July 1937): 'The Compulsory transfer of the Arabs from the valleys of the proposed Jewish state could give us something which we never had ... a Galilee free of Arab population.'[25] Already in 1937 he believed that the

Zionists could rid themselves of 'old habits' and put pressure on the Mandatory authorities to carry out forced removal. 'We have to stick to this conclusion', Ben-Gurion wrote,

> in the same way we grabbed the Balfour Declaration, more than that, in the same way we grabbed Zionism itself. We have to insist upon this conclusion [and push it] with full determination, power and conviction. ... We must uproot from out hearts the assumption that the thing is not possible. It can be done.

Ben-Gurion went on to note: 'We must prepare ourselves to carry out' the transfer.[26] Ben-Gurion was also convinced that few, if any, of the Palestinians would be willing to transfer themselves 'voluntarily', in which case the 'compulsory' provisions would have to be put into effect. In an important letter to his 16-year-old son Amos, dated 5 October 1937, Ben-Gurion wrote: 'We must expel Arabs and take their places ... and if we have to use force – not to dispossess the Arabs of the Negev and Transjordan, but to guarantee our own right to settle those places – then we have force at our disposal.'[27] It is explicit in this letter that the transfer had become clearly associated with expulsion in Ben-Gurion's thinking. In reflecting on such expulsion and the eventual enlargement of, and breaking through, the Peel partition borders, Ben-Gurion used the language of force, increasingly counting on Zionist armed strength. He also predicted a decisive war in which the Palestinian Arabs aided by neighbouring Arab states would be defeated by the Haganah.[28] From the mid-1930s onwards he repeatedly stated his advocacy of transfer.

The debates of the World Convention of Ihud Po'alei Tzion – the highest political forum of the dominant Zionist world labour movement – and the Zurich 20th Congress in August 1937 revealed a Zionist consensus in support of transfer. Eliahu Lulu, for instance, had this to say at the debate of Ihud Po'alei Tzion convention:

> This transfer, even if it were to be carried out through compulsion – all moral enterprises are carried out through compulsion – will be justified in all senses. And if we negate all right to transfer, we would need to negate everything we have done until now: the transfer from Emek Hefer [Wadi al-Hawarith] to Beit Shean, from the Sharon [coastal plain] to Ephraem Mountains, etc ... the transfer ... is a just, logical, moral, and humane programme in all senses.[29]

During the same debate, Shlomo Lavi expressed a similar view: 'The demand that the Arabs should move and evacuate the place for us, because they have sufficient place to move to ... in itself is very just and very moral.'[30] There were, of course, Zionist leaders who supported 'voluntary' transfer, but to suggest as Morris does that the notion of 'forcible transfer' is merely an 'Arab contention' or that it was only in 1948 that Mapai leaders such as Ben-Gurion adopted the radical new approach of using force to transform Palestine's demographic reality is a misrepresentation of the facts, of which Morris must be aware.

Is Morris's conclusion that a Zionist transfer/expulsion policy was never formulated borne out of the evidence he adduces in *The Birth of the Palestinian Refugee Problem* and in *1948 and After*? In *The Birth of the Palestinian Refugee Problem* Morris describes how the Yishuv military establishment, presided over by Ben-Gurion, formulated in early March 1948 and began implementing in early April Plan Dalet (*Tochnit Dalet*) in anticipation of Arab military operations. According to Morris, the

> essence of the plan was the clearing of hostile and potentially hostile forces out of the interior of the prospective territory of the Jewish State. ... As the Arab irregulars were based and quartered in the villages, and as the militias of many villages were participating in the anti-Yishuv hostilities, the Haganah regarded most of the Arab villages as actively or potentially hostile.[31]

Morris goes on to explain that Plan Dalet 'constituted a strategic-ideological anchor and basis for expulsions by front, district, brigade and battalion commanders (who in each case argued military necessity) and it gave commanders, *post facto*, a formal, persuasive covering note to explain their actions'.[32] In *1948 and After*, Morris states:

> In conformity with Tochnit Dalet (Plan D), the Haganah's master plan ... The Haganah cleared various areas completely of Arab villages – the Jerusalem corridor, an area around Mishmar Haemek, and the coastal plain. But in most cases, expulsion orders were unnecessary; the inhabitants had already fled, out of fear or as a result of Jewish attack. In several areas, Israeli commanders successfully used psychological warfare ploys to obtain Arab evacuation (as in the Hula Valley, in Upper Galilee, in May).[33]

He further notes: 'if the denial of the right of return ... was a form of 'expulsion', then a great many villagers – who had waited near their villages for the battle to die down before trying to return home – can be considered 'expelees'.[34]

Plan Dalet is a straightforward document (now accessible both in Hebrew and English), which has generated a great deal of historiographical debate among Israeli and Palestinian historians. Yet, contrary to Morris's conclusion, Plan Dalet has been described by another leading Israeli 'new historian', Ilan Pappé, as

> a master plan for the expulsion of as many Palestinians as possible. Moreover, the plan legitimized, a *priori*, some of the more horrendous atrocities committed by Jewish soldiers. In some cases, particularly in the north, in the area under the command of Moshe Carmel, the order 'to destroy,' meant also to kill off the local population. Hence, those responsible for the Deir Yassin massacre could have legitimized their action by referring to Plan D, as almost every village in the vicinity of Jerusalem was considered as an enemy base.[35]

However, even if, for the sake of argument, we were to accept that Plan Dalet was not a political blueprint or a 'master plan' for a blanket expulsion of the Arab population, and even if the plan 'was governed by military considerations', how can Morris square his own explanations with his conclusion that there existed no Haganah/IDF 'plan' or policy decision to expel Arabs from the prospective Jewish state?

Furthermore, in the context of 'decision-making' and 'transfer' policy, Morris shows in his essay 'Yosef Weitz and the Transfer Committees, 1948–49', how Weitz – the Jewish National Fund executive in charge of land acquisition and its distribution among Jewish settlements and an ardent advocate of mass Arab transfer since the 1930s (he was on the Jewish Agency's Transfer Committees between 1937 and 1942)

> was well placed [in 1948] to shape and influence decision-making regarding the Arab population on the national level and to oversee the implementation of policy on the local level.[36]

From early 1948, Weitz began to exploit the conditions of war to expel Arab villagers and tenant-farmers, some of whom cultivated lands owned by Jewish institutions. He personally supervised many local evictions during the early months of the war, frequently with the assistance of local Haganah commanders.[37] Moreover, Morris explains:

> Everyone, at every level of military and political decision-making, understood that a Jewish state without a large Arab minority would be stronger and more viable both militarily and politically. The tendency of local military commanders to 'nudge' Palestinians into flight increased as the war went on. Jewish atrocities – far more widespread than the old histories have let on (there were massacres of Arabs at Ad Dawayima, Eilaboun, Jish, Safsaf, Majd al Kurum, Hule (in Lebanon), Saliha, and Sasa, besides Deir Yassin and Lydda and other places) – also contributed significantly to the exodus.[38]

I cannot see how the above explanation regarding 'decision-making' can be reconciled with Morris's denial of a transfer policy. Does it matter in the end whether such a policy was actually formulated, or whether it was just *de facto* and clearly understood at every level of military and political decision-making?

On the basis of the revelations, documentation, and factual findings brought to light by Morris, other Israeli 'new historians' and myself (in *Expulsion of the Palestinians: The Concept of 'Transfer' in Zionist Political Thought, 1882–1948*), the traditional Palestinian contention that there was a Zionist consensus on the question of finding a 'solution' to the 'Arab demographic problem' – the Palestinian Arabs, even in 1947, still constituted two-thirds of the population of Palestine – through 'transfer'/expulsion of Arabs to areas outside the prospective Jewish state, and barring their return to their villages and towns, is corroborated. Zionist parties of all shades of opinion – with the exception of muted, internal criticism from a few members of the Mapam and Mapai parties – were in basic agreement about the need and desirability of utilising the 1948 war to establish an enlarged Jewish state with as small an Arab population as possible. Yosef Sprintzak, the relatively liberal secretary-general of the Histadrut, a critic of the forcible transfer policy, had this to say at the 24 July 1948 meeting at the Mapai Centre, some ten days after the Lydda–Ramle expulsion:

> There is a feeling that *faits accomplis* are being created. ... The question is not whether the Arabs will return or not return. The question is whether the Arabs are [being or have been] expelled

> or not. ... This is important to our moral future. ... I want to know, who is creating the facts? And the facts are being created on orders. ... [there appears to be] a line of action ... of expropriation and of emptying the land of Arabs by force.[39]

It is difficult, using Morris's own evidence and other evidence produced by Palestinian historians and Israeli 'new historians', not to see on the part of the leaders of mainstream labour Zionism a *de facto*, forcible, transfer policy in 1948.

Morris's analysis of the Palestinian catastrophe is also flawed by his treatment of the Palestinian exodus largely in an historical and political vacuum, without any intrinsic connection with Zionism. Although he does refer to the Zionist consensus emerging from the mid-1930s in support of transferring the Arab population, he sees no connection between this and the expulsions of 1948. This brings us to the explanatory framework underlying Morris's work: the Zionist leadership's ideological-political disposition for transferring/expelling Arabs resulted from the 'security' threat (the 'fifth column') the Arab population posed to the Jewish state. The facts presented earlier, on the other hand, show that the 'voluntary/compulsory' transfer of the indigenous Arabs was prefigured in the Zionist ideology a long time before the 1948 war broke out and advocated 'obsessively' by the Zionist leadership from the mid-1930s onwards. Consequently, the resistance of the indigenous Arab population to Zionism before and in 1948 emanated from precisely the Zionist goal of establishing a Jewish state that would, at best, marginalise the Palestinians as a small, dependent minority in their own homeland, and, at worst, eradicate and 'transfer' them. The 'security' threat posed by the 'transferred' inhabitants of the Palestinians towns and villages resulted from the Zionist movement's ideological premises and political agenda, namely the establishment of an ethnocratic, exclusionist Jewish state.

From the perspective of Morris's 'new' historiography, there was no inherent link between the 'transfer' of the Palestinians and the acquisition of their lands on the one hand and Zionism's long-advocated imperative of accommodating millions of Jewish immigrants in the Jewish state on the other. The nearest he comes to hinting at such a connection is the following:

> The war afforded the Yishuv a historic opportunity to enlarge the Jewish state's borders and, as things turned out, to create a state

> without a very large Arab minority. The war would solve the Yishuv's problem of lack of land, which was necessary to properly absorb and settle the expected influx of Jewish immigrants.[40]

Would Zionism have succeeded in fulfilling its imperative of absorbing the large influx of Jewish immigrants while allowing the indigenous population to remain *in situ?* If not, could the Zionist objective of 'transferring' the Arabs from Palestine have been carried out 'voluntarily' and peacefully, without Palestinian resistance or the destruction of their society in 1948?

Morris's findings constitute a landmark and are a major contribution to our knowledge because they show that the evacuation of hundreds of thousands of Palestinians was a result of direct attacks, fear of attacks, intimidation, psychological warfare (e.g., the whispering campaign) and sometimes outright expulsions ordered by the Haganah/IDF leadership. Yet, a wider explanatory and theoretical framework within which the Palestinian catastrophe can be properly understood must be sought elsewhere.

Morris's work reflects a nuanced Israeli view of the 1948 events. However, his historiography is a typical example of the narrative of victor: triumphalist, well-organised, well-written and comprehensive. His narrative remains anchored to its (ideological) Zionist moorings, which also provide the wider context for Israel's politics of denial. As Morris made clear in an interview with the Hebrew daily *Yedi'ot Aharonot* in November 2001 (and in his article in the *Guardian* of 21 February 2002) he firmly believes that Arabs started the 1948 war and, therefore, have only themselves to blame for the creation of the Palestinian refugee problem.[41] In a recent article, entitled: 'Peace? No Chance', Morris had this to say:

> My conclusion, which angered many Israelis and undermined Zionist historiography, was that most of the refugees were a product of Zionist military action and, in smaller measure, of Israeli expulsion orders and Arab leaders' urgings or orders to move out. Critics of Israel subsequently latched on those findings that highlighted Israeli responsibility while ignoring the fact the problem was a direct consequence of the war that the Palestinians – and in their wake, the surrounding Arab states – had launched. ... I had explained that the creation of the problem was 'almost inevitable', given the Zionist aim of creating a Jewish state in a land largely populated by Arabs and given Arab resistance to the Zionist enterprise.[42]

It is important to note that similar views were expressed by Morris in the early 1990s and were discussed in my 1991 critique of Morris.[43] Moreover, despite the mountains of evidence about Israel's culpability, even from some of its 'revisionist historians', Morris suggests that Israel should continue with its pre-emptive strategy of refusing to accept any moral and legal responsibility for the creation of the refugee problem.

Morris is aware of the fact that the range of proposed solutions to the refugee problem would reflect the debate over the causes and circumstance of the 1948 exodus. While acknowledging the connection between the creation of Israel and the birth of the Palestinian refugee problem, he clearly believes that a Zionist offensive strategy is the best form of defence; he blames the victims, denying any major Zionist wrongdoing or any historical injustice; he also denies Palestinian 'right of return', and restitution of refugee property and Israel's moral responsibility or culpability for the creation of the refugee problem. For Morris, Israel should never atone and the Palestinian refugees should never gain restitutions.[44]

1948 was both the year of Palestinian catastrophe and the year of Israel's 'independence', of the triumph of the Zionist colonial project and rise of Israel. Moreover, history and historiography ought not to be written, exclusively or mainly, by the victors. They should be used as tools for initiating dialogue and cooperation across the national divide. The Palestinians still need a 'new *nakba* historiography' and the rewriting of their own history: one that does attempt to determine objectively the events in the most critical academic fashion; but they also need a critical *nakba* history that re-examines their nationalist perspective and narrative of the marginalised and of the victim. This should be the role of progressive historians, Palestinian, Israeli and others. Interpreting the history of the Holocaust has been a common endeavour towards which many Israelis, Germans, Europeans and Americans have contributed. It is in the interest of Israeli 'new historians' not to be carried away by triumphalism, but rather to concentrate on the task of expanding our common knowledge.

NOTES

1. Benny Morris, *The Birth of the Palestinian Refugee Problem, 1947–1949* (Cambridge: Cambridge University Press, 1987); see also Benny Morris, 'The New Historiography: Israel Confronts its Past', *Tikkun* 6

(November–December 1988), pp.14–23; Simha Flapan, *The Birth of Israel: Myths and Realities* (New York: Pantheon Books, 1987); Tom Segev, *1949: The First Israelis* (New York: The Free Press, 1986); Avi Shlaim, *Collusion Across the Jordan* (Oxford: Oxford University Press, 1996); Avi Shlaim, *The Politics of Partition: King Abdullah, the Zionists and Palestine, 1921–1951* (Oxford: Oxford University Press, 1990); Ilan Pappé, *The Making of the Arab–Israeli Conflict, 1947–1951* (London: I. B. Tauris, 1992); Eugene L. Rogan and Avi Shlaim (eds), *The War for Palestine: Rewriting the History of 1948* (Cambridge: Cambridge University Press, 2001).

2. Nur Masalha, *Expulsion of the Palestinians*, pp.173–99; Walid Khalidi (ed.) *All That Remains: The Palestinian Villages Occupied and Depopulated by Israel in 1948* (Washington, DC: Institute for Palestine Studies, 1992); Walid Khalidi, 'Plan Dalet: Master Plan for the Conquest of Palestine', *Journal of Palestine Studies* 18, no.1 (Autumn 1988), pp.4–19; Rashid Khalidi, 'The Palestinians and 1948: The Underlying Causes of Failure', in Rogan and Shlaim, *The War for Palestine*, pp.12–36; Sharif Kana'ana, *Still on Vacation! The Eviction of the Palestinians in 1948* (Ramallah: Palestinian Diaspora and Refugee Centre-Shaml, 1992); Erskine Childers, 'The Other Exodus', *The Spectator*, 12 May 1961.
3. These include 'Arif al-'Arif, Walid Khalidi, Elias Shoufani, Nafez Nazzal, Rashid Khalid, Sharif Kana'ana, Elias Sanbar, and myself.
4. Nur-Eldeen Masalha, 'On Recent Hebrew and Israeli Sources for the Palestinian Exodus 1948–49', *Journal of Palestine Studies* 18, no.1 (Autumn 1988), pp.121–37; Nur Masalha and F. Vivekananda, 'Israeli Revisionist Historiography of the Birth of Israel and its Palestinian Exodus of 1948', *Scandinavian Journal of Development Alternatives* 9, no.1 (March 1990), pp.71–9; Nur Masalha 'A Critique of Benny Morris', *Journal of Palestine Studies* 21, no.1 (Autumn 1991), pp.90–97.
5. Avi Shlaim, 'Israel and the Arab Coalition in 1948', in Rogan and Shlaim, *The War for Palestine*, pp.79–103.
6. See Masalha, 'A Critique of Benny Morris,' pp.90–97; Nur Masalha, '"1948 and After" Revisited', *Journal of Palestine Studies* 24, no.4 (Summer 1995), pp.90–95; Ilan Pappé, 'Critique and Agenda', *History and Memory* 7, no.1 (1995), pp.60–90; Baruch Kimmerling, 'Between Celebration of Independence and Commemoration of Al-Nakbah: The Controversy Over the Roots of the Israeli State', *Middle East Studies Association Bulletin* 32, No.1 (1998), pp.15–19; Rogan and Shlaim (eds), *The War for Palestine: Rewriting the History of 1948*; Neil Caplan, 'The "New Historians"', *Journal of Palestine Studies* 24, no.4 (Summer 1995), pp.96–103; Nur Masalha, Review of *Fabricating Israeli History: The 'New Historians'*, by Efraim Karsh, in *British Journal of Middle Eastern Studies* 26, no.2 (1999), pp.346–50.
7. Ilan Pappé, 'Were They Expelled? The History, Historiography and Relevance of the Palestinian Refugee Problem', in Ghada Karmi and Eugene Cotran (eds), *The Palestinian Exodus, 1948–1988* (Reading: Ithaca Press, 1999), pp.37–61.
8. 'Demons of the Nakbah', *Al-Ahram Weekly Online*, no.586, 16–22 May 2002; Ilan Pappé, 'Critique and Agenda', *History and Memory* 7, no.1 (1995), pp.60–90. See also Baruch Kimmerling, 'Between Celebration of Independence and Commemoration of Al-Nakbah: The Controversy

Over the Roots of the Israeli State', *Middle East Studies Association Bulletin* 32, no.1 (1998), pp.15–19

9. Don Peretz, *Palestinian Refugees and the Middle East Peace Process*, (Washington, DC: United States Institute of Peace Press, 1993), p.6.
10. Ibid., p.6.
11. Baruch Kimmerling, 'Shaking the Foundations', *Index on Censorship* 24, no.3 (May/June 1995), pp.47–52; Baruch Kimmerling, 'Between Celebration of Independence and Commemoration of Al-Nakbah: The Controversy Over the Roots of the Israeli State', *Middle East Studies Association Bulletin* 32, no.1 (1998), pp.15–19.
12. Attacks on the 'new historians' are also found in Anita Shapira, 'Politics and Collective Memory: The Debate over the "New Historians" in Israel', *History and Memory* 7, no.1 (1995), pp.9–10; Itamar Rabinovich, *The Road Not Taken: Early Arab-Israeli Negotiations* (New York and Oxford: Oxford University Press, 1991); Yoav Gelber, *Palestine 1948: War, Escape and the Emergence of the Palestinian Refugee Problem* (Brighton: Sussex Academic Press, 2001). A debate between the old guard and the 'new historians' is found in a major collection of articles in Hebrew entitled: *Ben Hazon Le-Revizyah: Meah Shnot Historiyografyah Tziyonit* [Between Vision and Revision: A Hundred Years of Historiography of Zionism] Yehi'am Weitz (ed.) (Jerusalem: Zalman Shazar Centre, 1997). See Masalha, 'Critique of Benny Morris', pp.90–97; Nur Masalha, '"1948 and After" Revisited', *Journal of Palestine Studies* 24, no.4 (Summer 1995), pp.90–95; Rogan and Shlaim (eds), *The War for Palestine: Rewriting the History of 1948*; Neil Caplan, 'The "New Historians"', *Journal of Palestine Studies* 24, no.4 (Summer 1995), pp.96–103; Nur Masalha, Review of *Fabricating Israeli History: The 'New Historians'*, by Efraim Karsh, in *British Journal of Middle Eastern Studies* 26, no.2 (1999), pp.346–50.
13. See Benny Morris, 'Refabricating 1948', *Journal of Palestine Studies* 27 (1998), pp.81–95.
14. Kimmerling, 'Shaking the Foundations', pp.47–52.
15. Ilan Pappé, 'Demons of the Nakbah', *Al-Ahram Weekly Online*, no.586, 16–22 May 2002.
16. Benny Morris, '"The Arabs Are Responsible": Post Zionist Historian Benny Morris Clarifies His Thesis', interview with *Yedi'ot Aharonot*, 23 November 2001; Benny Morris, 'Peace? No Chance', the *Guardian*, 21 February 2002.
17. Morris, *The Birth of the Palestinian Refugee Problem*, p.6.
18. Benny Morris, *1948 and After: Israel and the Palestinians* (Oxford: Clarendon Press, 1990), p.3.
19. Ibid, pp.2–5.
20. Ibid., p.17.
21. Bar-Zohar, *Ben-Gurion*, Vol. 2, p.703.
22. Morris, *1948 and After*, p.40.
23. Ibid., p.43.
24. Ibid., pp.43–4.
25. David Ben-Gurion, *Zichronot* [Memoirs], Vol. 4 (Tel Aviv: 'Am 'Oved, 1974), pp.297–9.
26. Ibid., p.299.

27. Shabtai Teveth, *Ben-Gurion and the Palestinian Arabs* (Oxford: Oxford University Press, 1985), p.189). For further discussion of the original Hebrew version of this quote, see Chapter 1, note 36.
28. Ibid.
29. *'Al Darchei Mediniyotenu: Mo'atzah 'Olamit Shel Ihud Po'alei Tzion (c.s), Din Vehesbon Male 21 July–7 August* (1937) [A Full Report about the World Convention of Ihud Po'alei Tzion] (Tel Aviv, 1938), p.122 (Hebrew).
30. Ibid., p.100.
31. Morris, *The Birth of the Palestinian Refugee Problem*, p.62.
32. Ibid., p.63.
33. Ibid., p.21.
34. Ibid, p.343, note 7.
35. Pappé, *The Making of the Arab–Israeli Conflict*, p.94.
36. Morris, *1948 and After*, p.91.
37. Ibid., pp.92–8.
38. Ibid., p.22.
39. Ibid., pp.42–3.
40. Ibid., pp.39–40.
41. Benny Morris, 'The Arabs Are Responsible': Post Zionist Historian Benny Morris Clarifies His Thesis', interview with *Yedi'ot Aharonot*, 23 November 2001; Benny Morris, 'Peace? No Chance', the *Guardian*, 21 February 2002.
42. Benny Morris, 'Peace? No Chance,' the *Guardian*, 21 February 2002.
43. Benny Morris, 'Transfer Tzioni' [Zionist Transfer], *Svivot* 31 (1993), pp.67–75; Masalha, 'A Critique of Benny Morris', pp.90–97.
44. For further discussion of 'atonement' and 'restitution', see Naseer Aruri, 'Will Israel ever Atone? Will the Palestinians gain Restitutions?' at: http://www.tari.org/will_israel_ever_atone.htm (accessed on 28 December 2002).

3 'If You Can't Solve it, Dissolve it': Israeli Resettlement Schemes since 1948

Since 1948 Israel has consistently denied any moral responsibility for the creation of the Palestinian refugee problem. Always maintaining that the responsibility for the creation and non-solution of the problem lies with neighbouring countries, Israel has never been short on plans to resettle the refugees in the Arab countries. Except for one limited offer in mid-1949 to take back '100,000' of the refugees to be settled in places of Israel's choosing[1] (an offer which was made under intense American pressure, but on certain conditions which were not acceptable to the Americans or the Arabs – and were soon retracted), Israel has made no significant proposal to repatriate the 1948 refugees. The Israeli position towards the refugees has always emphasised their resettlement and rehabilitation in the Arabs states, rather than repatriation and/or compensation. In the 1950s there were several Israeli proposals and plans to resettle the Palestinian refugees in the host Arab states: between 1948 and the late 1980s around 20 official Israeli plans dealing with the Palestinian refugees – first with the 1948 refugees and later those of 1967 – were put forward by Israel; from 1967 to 1987, the start of the first Palestinian *intifada* (uprising) in the occupied territories, no less than a dozen Israeli proposals and schemes were suggested to deal with the refugee camps in the West Bank and the Gaza Strip.[2]

Israeli resettlement proposals and actual schemes were motivated by political, diplomatic, military and psychological considerations and reflected a long-standing and consistent policy aimed at:

- preventing Palestinian refugee return;
- 'dissolving' the refugee question and removing this critical problem from the heart of the Arab–Israeli conflict;
- reducing both international humanitarian, UN and Western diplomatic pressures on Israel;

- breaking up the collective identify of the refugees and their perceived militancy;[3]
- removing the refugee camps in the West Bank and Gaza that posed a security threat to Israel's control of the occupied territories: the visible reminder which the refugee camps provided of the dispossession of 1948 constituted a thorny problem for the Israeli government, especially after 1967. As a focal point of Palestinian national identity and militant resistance, the camps, as perceived by the occupation authorities, required constant army surveillance. Faced with this hostile and resentful population, the Israeli army sought to break up the camps' concentrations in an attempt to quell Palestinian resistance in the Strip and the West Bank;[4]
- (after June 1967) facilitating and consolidating political and administrative control over the West Bank and Gaza Strip.

Also at least two Arab regimes considered (rather half-heartedly) similar resettlement plans for short periods of time: in 1949 the Syrian dictator Husni al-Za'im accepted a plan to resettle 300,000 refugees in the al-Jazira region of north-east Syria;[5] in 1954, against the background of escalating Israeli 'retaliatory' attacks against the Gaza Strip, the Egyptian government – fearing a potentially explosive situation in the Strip and the consequences of provoking the Israelis into a war for which Egypt still was unprepared – considered a United States–UNRWA plan to resettle the Gaza refugees in Sinai. Husni al-Za'im's military dictatorship lasted only four-and-a-half months, and the Egyptians were forced to discard the Sinai scheme following strong protests, when details of the scheme leaked from the refugees, which culminated in two days of demonstrations and rioting in Gaza and the besieging of Egyptian government buildings and the burning of Egyptian vehicles.[6] However, as this chapter will show, Israel has been by far the most persistent advocate and practitioner of refugee resettlement schemes which it perceived as the only secure way of preventing refugee return and of ensuring the removal of the Palestine refugee problem from the heart of Arab–Israeli conflict. This chapter will discuss various Israeli resettlement schemes within their historical contexts from 1948 to the present.

While the Arab states and the Palestinians have traditionally demanded that the Palestinian refugees be given a free choice between repatriation or compensation, by contrast the official Israeli position has always been that there can be no returning of the refugees to Israeli territories, and that the only solution to the problem is their resettlement in the Arab states or elsewhere. Since 1949 all Israeli governments have consistently refused to discuss any possible return of refugees to the pre-1967 borders.

Almost exactly the same points were reiterated in a background paper published by the Israeli government on the refugee issue in October 1994.[7] Another statement of the traditional Israeli position on the issue was voiced by Yossi Beilin, then Deputy Foreign Minister, after the fourth meeting of the Multilateral Committee on Refugees/Refugee Working Group, held in Tunis in October 1993: 'the leaders of the 1948 refugees know full well that these refugees will not be able to return to residence in Israel.'[8]

In the 1950s one key slogan coined by senior Israeli Foreign Ministry officials was: *'If You Can't Solve it, Dissolve it'* (in Hebrew: *'im inkha yakhol leftor it habe'aya-moseis otah'*),[9] meaning if you cannot solve the Palestinian refugee problem by political means, you can try to 'dissolve' the problem and disperse the refugees through economic means and employment projects. These officials argued that the problem of the 1948 Palestinian refugees should be solved by an economic approach, mainly through their integration into the economies of their actual countries of residence and/or their dispersal throughout the interior of the Arab world. This preoccupation with the need to 'dissolve' the refugee problem stemmed from a variety of reasons including the deep fear of Arab 'return'.

A combination of Zionist-ideological, political, economic, diplomatic, public relations and psychological factors motivated Israeli resettlement schemes in the 1950s. Moreover, proponents of the active approach to resettlement schemes encompassed both hawkish and dovish members of the Israeli establishment. Foreign Minister Moshe Sharett (a man with a dovish reputation who, under intense American pressure, agreed in 1949 to allow the return of 100,000 refugees as part of an overall settlement of the Arab–Israeli conflict, but soon changed his mind and retracted the offer[10]), and his senior Foreign Ministry officials as well as hawkish Jewish National Fund executives (such as Yosef Weitz and Yosef Nahmani), all advocated an active approach to resettlement schemes. In the 1950s, in particular, the Palestinian refugee problem was a major 'diplomatic headache' for the Israeli Foreign Ministry, particularly in its dealing with United States and United Nations officials. The United States had supported the UN General Assembly Resolution

194 (III) of 11 December 1948, the essence of which was a call for repatriation and/or compensation to the refugees. The US had also suggested in 1949 that Israel allow the return of one-third of the refugees (assumed to be some 250,000) while the US would cover the costs of resettling the other two-thirds in Arab states.[11] For primarily diplomatic and public relations and political reasons, senior Foreign Ministry officials saw the urgency of actively pursuing secret resettlement schemes. The same preoccupation led Israeli ministers and officials to attempt to promote a variety of secret resettlement and employment projects, one of which was what they termed the 'Libyan Operation': a secret plan to transfer Palestinians from refugee camps in Jordan (including the West Bank), the Gaza Strip and Lebanon and their resettlement permanently in Libya and other parts of North Africa, away from Israel and the 1949 ceasefire lines.

The refugees themselves have traditionally demanded repatriation and refused resettlement. Among the Palestinians the word 'refugee' is synonymous with 'returnee' (*'a'aid'*). The belief in return is strongly held. Refugee feelings concerning the 'dream of return' are intense. The yearning for Palestine permeates the whole refugee community, and is strongly felt by younger refugees, for whom home exists only in the imagination. In the early 1950s the Palestinian refugees themselves clung stubbornly to the 'right of return' that was enshrined in UN General Assembly Resolution 194, passed on 11 December 1948 and reaffirmed almost yearly by the General Assembly. The resolution stated that 'the refugees wishing to return to their homes and live at peace with their neighbours should be permitted to do so at the earliest practicable date.' The refugees themselves believed they would eventually return to their homes and villages in what had became Israel. Moreover, many of the refugees camped either along, or within a short distance of, Israel's borders, in southern Lebanon, in the West Bank and the Gaza Strip, creating a major 'infiltration' problem for Israel. Although there is no possibility of arriving at a reliable estimate of the number of returnees/'infiltrators', the actual use of the term 'infiltrator' by the Israeli authorities expressed both their unwillingness to permit the return of the refugees to their homes and villages and their marked anxiety regarding the possibility of increasing numbers of Palestinians returning to Israeli territories and may have contributed to exaggerating the number of those who actually succeeded in doing so.[12] In the Gaza Strip, moreover, the population trebled from 80,000 in 1947 to nearly 240,000 at the end of the 1948 war, creating a massive humanitarian problem of tens of thousands of destitute refugees crammed into a tiny area. In 1956 of the then 300,000 inhabitants of the Gaza Strip, 215,000 were listed as refugees, occupying eight vast camps. The Strip had nearly one-fourth of the total of about 900,000 refugees from historic Palestine.

Between 1949 and 1956 refugees continued to cross the armistice lines, 'infiltrating' back to their villages either to collect possessions and pick up unharvested crops or, in some cases, to raid Israeli settlements adjacent to Gaza and the West Bank.[13] The first Israeli objective was to prevent the return of the Palestinian refugees (or 'infiltrators' in Israeli terminology), to their homes and villages.[14] To combat this persistent 'infiltration' by refugees, the Israelis carried out 'retaliatory' attacks against Palestinian civilian targets in general and refugee camps in the Gaza Strip in particular. These attacks resulted in many civilian deaths. According to the Israeli historian Benny Morris,

> Israel's defensive anti-infiltration measures resulted in the death of several thousand mostly unarmed Arabs during 1949–56, the vast majority between 1949 and 1952. ... Thus, upward of 2,700 Arab infiltrators, and perhaps as many as 5,000, were killed by the IDF, police and civilians along Israel's borders between 1949 and 1956. To judge from the available documentation, the vast majority of those killed were unarmed 'economic' and social infiltrators.[15]

One major reason for the insistence with which Israel prosecuted its 'retaliatory' policy during these days, according to former Israeli journalist Livia Rokach

> was the desire of the Zionist ruling establishment to exercise permanent pressure on the Arab states to remove the Palestinian refugees from the 1948 war from the proximity of the armistice lines and to disperse them throughout the interior of the Arab world. This was not due, in the early fifties, to military considerations.[16]

Also thousands of Palestinian refugees who had managed to return to their villages and homes were expelled by the Israeli army across the border in the early years of the state.

EARLY PROPOSALS (AUGUST 1948–50)

(i) The Israeli Cabinet Transfer Committee's Recommendations

The Israeli Cabinet Transfer Committee of 1948 recommended that all the Palestinian refugees be resettled in Iraq.[17]

(ii) Resettlement in Iraq

One of the Transfer Committee's initiatives was to invite Dr Joseph Schechtman, a right-wing Zionist Revisionist leader, an expert on 'population transfer' and a contributor to *Encyclopaedia Britannica* on the same issue, to join its efforts. Schechtman, who for three decades had been a close associate of Vladimir Jabotinsky (the founder of the Zionist Revisionist Movement), and who had written a book called *European Population Transfers, 1939–1945* (published by Oxford University Press, in 1946) would soon after 1948 become the single most influential propagator of the Zionist myth of 'voluntary' exodus in 1948.[18] Schechtman had settled in New York in 1941. He had served as a research fellow in the Institute of Jewish Affairs, 1941–3, as Director of the Research Bureau on Population Movements, which he had helped to establish, and as consultant for the United States Office of Strategic Services in Washington DC, specialising in population movement, 1944–5. With this background in mind, members of the Transfer Committee met Schechtman during his visit to Israel in September 1948 and hired him to carry out research and advise them on the question of the Palestinian refugees' resettlement in Arab states.

In August 1948, at a session of the Zionist Actions Committee, the New York-based Schechtman had been elected as a Revisionist representative on the Executive of the Jewish Agency and the World Zionist Organisation, which for the first time included all Zionist parties. More important, at some time in early 1948 he worked out his own plan entitled 'The Case for Arab–Jewish Exchange of Population', and submitted it in 1948 in the form of a 'study' to Eliyahu Epstein (Elath), Israel's ambassador to Washington, who later forwarded it to the Israeli Cabinet Secretary, Zeev Sharef, and to the head of the Transfer Committee, Yosef Weitz.[19]

Schechtman wanted formal Israeli government acknowledgement of the research he was carrying out for the Israeli Cabinet's Transfer Committee. In mid-October 1948 he asked Arthur Lourie of the Israeli United Nations Office in New York whether Foreign Minister Sharett

> could send him (Schechtman) a note stating that you [Sharett] are glad to learn that he has been in touch with friends in Israel who are interested in this matter of resettlement of Arabs, particularly in Iraq, and that you could be pleased if he would continue with his investigations. On the basis of such a letter, Schechtman would approach men like [former U.S. President Herbert] Hoover with a view of interesting them further in this work.[20]

Two weeks later, on 27 October 1948, Schechtman received a cable from Cabinet Secretary Sharef: 'Approve your proposal collect material discussed. Danin [and] Lifschitz will refund expenses five hundred dollars.'[21] Schechtman's urgent assignment on behalf of the Israeli government and its Transfer Committee included the collection of material and the carrying out of further 'study' on Palestinians' resettlement in Iraq. On 17 December Sharett himself wrote to Schechtman from Paris telling him how 'glad' he was to hear that he was pursuing his 'studies with regard to the resettlement possibilities of Palestinian Arab refugees. Now that Mr [Zalman] Lifshitz [sic] is in the United States I am sure that you two got together and pooled your knowledge on the subject.'[22]

Outlining his 'compulsory' plan, Schechtman explained that his 'study' ('The Case for Arab–Jewish Exchange of Population') was not merely a descriptive and historical explanation of the facts; rather he believed 'that many important conclusions for the future can and must be drawn from the experience of past transfer and that the underlying idea of any transfer scheme is basically a preventive one'. If a problem of an ethnic minority cannot be solved within the existing territorial frame, then 'timely recourse must be taken to the essentially preventive devise of transfer'. According to Schechtman, 'the case of Palestine seems to offer a classic case for quick, decisive transfer action as the only constructive possibility of breaking the present deadlock' and 'no constructive solution can be arrived at without a large-scale [Arab] transfer.'[23] 'The only workable solution is an organised exchange of population between Palestine and the Arab states mainly to Iraq of Palestine Arabs', and the transfer to Israel of the Jewish communities in Arab countries.[24]

Schechtman's scheme called for the 'compulsory' transfer of Palestinian refugees and non-refugees to, and their resettlement in, Iraq and cited the Eliahu Ben-Horin plan of Arab transfer to Iraq of 1943 as justification.[25] Ben-Horin was another New York-based Zionist Revisionist publicist and a close associate of Vladimir

Jabotinsky. He was also an advisor to the American Zionist Emergency Council. More important, in late 1943 Ben-Horin met Herbert Hoover, the former US President and a Zionist sympathiser, who agreed to join the Zionist campaign in support of Ben-Horin's plan. Both men appealed to the US administration to support the Zionist drive and 'dictate' Palestinian evacuation to, and resettlement in, Iraq. Two years later, on 19 November 1945, the so-called 'Hoover-plan' – in fact, a repackaging of Ben-Horin's initiative – was launched in the *New York World-Telegram*.[26] Schechtman's plan of early 1948, which was directly inspired by the 'Ben-Horin–Hoover plan' of 1945, was supplemented by a brief additional section written in the wake of the refugee exodus of the spring of 1948. In this addition to his plan, he observed 'unmistakable indications to the effect that the Israeli Government begins earnestly to weigh an Arab–Jewish exchange of population as the most thorough and constructive means of solving the problem of an Arab minority in the Jewish state'. As evidence of transfer discussions in Israeli government circles, he cited remarks by Arthur Lourie, the head of the Israeli United Nations Office and the representative at the Lake Success talks in New York, in an interview that appeared in the *New York Times* of 20 July 1948.[27] In the Spring of 1948 Schechtman had written to Israel's ambassador to Washington, Eliyahu Epstein, saying that the Arab flow out of the area of the Jewish state 'only strengthens the case for the organised Arab transfer' to Iraq.[28]

In his plan, Schechtman maintained that, although it was evident that the Palestine Arab leaders would never agree to any plan of this kind, 'which provoked on their part limitless indignation',[29] 'once uprooted, they [the Arabs] would probably be responsive to any plan of their resettlement in Iraq, with full compensation by the state of Israel for their property left behind.'[30] The working of the transfer/resettlement scheme would be underpinned by an interstate treaty between the governments of Israel and Iraq and possibly other Arab states. These treaties 'would provide a compulsory, but not all-inclusive, ethnic sorting out. As a rule, every Arab in the Jewish State and every Jew in Iraq would be subject to transfer; no specific option to this effect would be necessary.'[31] For Schechtman 'the equality of numbers on both sides' of the so-called exchange of population 'in this particular case was of no importance whatsoever, since the prospective Palestine Arab transferees in Iraq' would be resettled 'not on land vacated by the Jewish evacuees', but on land provided by the Iraqi state. As a result 'the amount of land ... would be sufficient in Palestine where millions of dunums[32] would be left behind by the departing Arabs.'[33]

In December 1948 Zalman Lifschitz arrived in the United States to lobby for the Israeli drive to resettle the refugees in Iraq. On the initiative of the Israeli ambassador to the United States, Eliyahu Epstein, a meeting was held in mid-December in the ambassador's office in Washington, in which Epstein, Schechtman, Lifschitz, Edward Norman, a New York-based Jewish millionaire who had devoted much of his fortune to supporting the Jewish Yishuv in Palestine and had been secretly lobbying for his plan to transfer the Palestinians to Iraq between 1934 and 1948,[34] and Elish'a Friedman, a New York economics consultant and member of the Ben-Horin–Hoover team which was active from the middle to the late 1940s in the attempt to remove the Palestinians to Iraq. Epstein had been in close contact with Schechtman throughout 1948 and had received a copy of the manuscript of Schechtman's plan in early May 1948. On 18 May, three days after the proclamation of the State of Israel, Epstein had written from Washington to Schechtman in New York telling him that he had read his manuscript 'with great interest and found it to be an important and constructive contribution to the subject of Jewish–Arab exchange of population'.

> The events in Palestine are developing meanwhile in such a way that if not your conjectures, at least certain of your conclusions will have to be modified in view of the Arab flow out of the area of our State. Certain problems, however, in the exchange of population will remain, especially in view of the necessity of a transfer within possibly a very short time of the Jews living in the Arab countries to Israel.[35]

Epstein and Schechtman had also met in New York in mid-June 1948 to discuss the subject. In mid-December 1948 Lifschitz told the gathering in the Israeli ambassador's office in Washington about the activities of the official Transfer Committee and suggested that Schechtman, Norman and Friedman

> might be of very great help in this matter, in two directions in particular. The first that he [Lifschitz] mentioned was in the presentation of ideas and supporting data, on which a plan to be adopted by the Government of Israel might be based. The second

> was to mobilise the leaders of public opinion in this country to speak out in support of such a plan as soon as the Government of Israel would make public announcement of it. It was agreed that the three of us who were present who are American citizens would be considered a sort of advisory committee, with myself as chairman, working in close cooperation with Mr Epstein. It is our purpose now to produce a more or less detailed plan, which presumably will be forwarded to you [Sharett] for your consideration and possible presentation eventually to your government.[36]

Like Eliahu Ben-Horin, Edward Norman and former US President Hoover, Schechtman appealed to the US administration and the White House to support the Israeli drive and 'dictate' Palestinian resettlement in Iraq. A revised version of his 'study' of 1948, in which he outlined his plan for the removal of virtually all the Palestinians to Iraq, appeared in Chapter III of Schechtman's book *Population Transfers in Asia*, published in March 1949.[37] At the same time the actual research carried out by Schechtman on behalf of the Israeli government and its Transfer Committee in late 1948 and early 1949 appeared in his propagandistic work *The Arab Refugee Problem* (1952).[38] In his letter to Hoover dated 9 April 1949 Schechtman wrote:

> I take the liberty of sending you the enclosed copy of my study 'Population Transfers in Asia' whose chapter on the Arab–Jewish population transfer owes so much to the inspiration provided by your plan for the resettlement of Arabs from Palestine in Iraq, published in 1945 ... Recent events in the Middle East have pushed this idea into the foreground of public attention, and have impelled me to publish this study of the transfer issue against the background of similar transfer movements elsewhere in Asia. ... As one of the world's elder statesmen who helped originate the transfer idea as a way out of the Palestine conflict, and from whom public hopes to receive further wise guidance in this issue, you will – I sincerely hope – be interested in this book of mine.[39]

In the event, however, only a small proportion of the Palestinian refugees ended up in Iraq. The participation of the Iraqi army in the 1948 Arab–Israeli war played a role in the transfer of a number of Palestinian refugees to Iraq. This was especially so with some residents from the Jenin area, where the Iraqi army fought during the war and, likewise, many residents from the al-Karmel villages of Ijzim, Jaba' and 'Ayn al-Ghazal. Overall the number of refugees who actually reached Iraq during the 1948–9 period was estimated at 3,000.[40] There are no accurate statistics on the refugees in Iraq. However, by 1996 their total number was estimated at 45,000, mostly concentrated in and around the capital Baghdad.[41] In reality this constitutes a tiny number among the Palestinian communities living outside historic Palestine. Indeed, Iraq does not belong to the main regions with Palestinian refugee concentrations (Jordan, Syria, Lebanon and the occupied territories).

(iii) The 1949 '100,000 Offer' and the Gaza Scheme

Early in 1949 'Ezra Danin, the senior Foreign Ministry official dealing with the refugee resettlement issue and a member of the official Transfer Committee, was sent by the Foreign Ministry to England to discreetly lobby for 'initiatives that would assist as many refugees as possible to be absorbed and strike roots in various Arab countries'.[42] Before his departure to England Danin visited Weitz on 23 January 1949 in Jerusalem and expressed the opinion that 'a propaganda [campaign] must be conducted among the Arabs [refugees] that they demand their resettlement in the Arab states.'[43] The main motive for the involvement of Danin, Weitz and other colleagues in refugee resettlement projects outside Palestine stemmed from the fear of refugee return. In his letter to Cabinet Secretary Zeev Sharef, from London on 6 May 1949, Danin wrote about a letter he had received from Weitz in which the latter complained about the lack of 'planning and direction' on the question of refugee resettlement; 'at times' Weitz 'sees a nightmarish picture of long convoys of returning refugees and there is no one to help'.[44]

About the same time the US suggested that Israel allow the return of one-third of the refugees (assumed to be some 250,000). On 27 July 1949 Foreign Minister Sharett informed members of the Transfer Committee (Weitz, Danin and Lifschitz) that the US government was putting strong pressure on Israel to agree to the return of a quarter of a million refugees. As a result, Sharett explained, the Israeli government was considering putting forward a counter proposal to allow '100,000' refugees back, including those 30,000 refugees who (according to Israel) had already 'infiltrated' back to their villages, on condition that the Arab states agreed to full peace with Israel and resettled the remainder of the refugees. Weitz replied to Sharett that he saw a 'big disaster' in the proposal to allow '100,000' refugees to return.[45] A document distributed to Israeli ministries in May 1953 estimated that '23,000 infiltrators' who had returned to Israeli territories had been allowed to remain. On the whole the anxiety displayed by the Israeli leadership regarding the possibility of increasing numbers of Palestinians returning to their homes and villages may have contributed to exaggerating the number of those who actually succeeded in doing so. A document distributed to Israeli ministries in May 1953 estimated that '23,000 infiltrators' had returned to Israeli territories without permission. However, according to a 1987 study by Charles Kamen, this estimate is probably an exaggeration.[46] Weitz had also expressed his extreme apprehensions in a letter to Sharett on 28 May 1949:

> Infiltration of the refugees across all the borders, from the north, the south and the east, is no longer an isolated phenomenon but a common occurrence which is increasing all the time. Every day our people meet acquaintances who were formerly absent now walking about in complete freedom and also returning step by step to their villages. I fear that by the time you finished discussing the subject of the refugees in Lausanne and elsewhere the problem will have solved itself to some degree. Refugees are returning! Nor does our government offer any policy to prevent the infiltration. There appears to be no authority, neither civil nor military. The reins have been loosed, and the Arab in his cunning has already sensed this and knows to draw the conclusion he wishes.[47]

The Israeli government, however, soon changed its mind and retracted the '100,000 offer'.[48]

In early-mid-1949 Israel also put forward another plan to the Americans and British: the Gaza Strip – the small coastal strip of Palestine, occupied by the Egyptian army since May 1948, and which had 200,000–250,000 refugees and 100,000 locals – would be transferred to Israeli sovereignty along with its relatively large local and refugee populations. While gaining territorial and strategic advantages by taking over the Strip, Israel presented the whole plan as part of its readiness to contribute to refugee repatriation. However, in 1949 the Israeli leaders were mainly thinking in terms of 'more territory' and 'fewer Arabs' in the Jewish state; they were very concerned about enlarging Israel's Palestinian minority and, judging by the treatment of the 'internally displaced persons' by the Israeli authorities (see Chapter 4), it is very doubtful whether they would have allowed the refugee population of the Strip to return to their original villages. Initially the relatively moderate Foreign Minister Sharett, while mindful of the price, thought that Israel would gain a 'strategic peace of real estate', and

> could portray the absorption of 100,000 refugees as a major contribution ... to the solution of the refugee problem as a whole and to free itself once and for all of UN pressure in this regard.[49]

It is interesting that David Ben-Gurion was more open to the Gaza scheme. He saw in Gaza good agricultural and fishing opportunities, the possibility of a territorial barrier with Egypt and a reduced threat from Transjordan.[50] Sharett, however, remained hesitant; he opposed having to 'swallow [an additional] 150,000' Arabs in the Jewish state and argued against the incorporation of and joint Israeli–Egyptian condominium over the Strip. If Israel became responsible, the Strip's refugees would have to be allowed to return to their original homes in Israel, he argued.[51] Zalman Lifschitz of the official Transfer Committee also opposed Israeli incorporation of the Gaza Strip, though he wanted to annex the West Bank towns of Qalqilya and Tulkarm (then under Transjordanian control), which had only '20,000 Arabs'.[52]

Interestingly, in most American and British readings of the 'Gaza plan', the refugees of the Strip, after the take-over by Israel, would be allowed to return to their original homes, villages and towns in Israel. In a revised version of the plan, Israel was expected to give either Egypt or Transjordan (or both) 'territorial compensation' for the Strip, probably in the southern Negev region. Although real hope of its acceptance by Egypt and actual implementation were always very slim, discussion of the plan continued through the summer, with the Americans and the UN Palestine Conciliation Commission hoping that Israel would be induced to agree to a substantial repatriation, and the Arab states would agree to plan refugee resettlement in the Arab countries. However, given the realities of Egyptian–Israeli relations in 1949 and the lack of any positive Egyptian response, the 'Gaza plan' was a mirage, with little chance of being accepted either by the Egyptians or the residents of the Gaza Strip.[53]

In 1949 Danin travelled to England under the cover of fundraising for the United Jewish Appeal, a cover that also enabled him to meet Jewish financiers. Like many leading Zionists who had argued in the 1930s and 1940s that the Palestinians should be treated as an economic problem to be bought out of their lands, relocated and resettled outside Palestine, Danin believed that money would 'dissolve' the refugee problem.[54] 'My main efforts were directed at finding big contracting companies, carrying out various schemes in the Middle East, and seeking ways to persuade them to employ mainly Palestinian refugees', Danin later recorded.[55] Throughout the spring of 1949 Danin sought partners for the Israeli projects of refugee resettlement. He was also joined in London by Teddy Kollek, then an aid to Prime Minister Ben-Gurion.[56] Danin found a collaborator in Marcus Sieff, a Zionist Jewish businessman, who began approaching British firms, construction and oil companies, on behalf of Danin, to employ Palestinian refugees.[57] Among the big projects that interested Danin were the laying down of the 'Aramco' oil pipeline from Saudi Arabia to Lebanon and the building of the Latakiya port in Syria, within which Danin believed thousands of refugees could find work and, consequently, be integrated into Syria. On the advice of his Jewish partners in Britain, Danin approached Scottish Quakers, who were on the management of a large firm involved in the Middle East, and put forward to them an 'original proposal': for every 10 piasters per day the company would pay a worker, the Israelis would be prepared to add 5 piasters provided that the company chose its employees from the refugees.[58] It was also 'during these days that we coined the saying with regard to the solution of the Palestinian refugee problem: "If you cannot solve it – dissolve it"', Danin wrote.[59]

To begin promoting these schemes, Danin requested 50,000 Israeli lira be initially allocated by the Israeli government.[60] In early July 1950 Finance Minister Eli'ezer Kaplan placed only 1,000 Israeli lira at the disposal of Danin in connection with the proposal of 'exchanging properties of Jews in Iraq with the properties of present (not absentee) Arabs'. By 'present Arabs' Kaplan meant Israeli Arab citizens, as opposed to 'absentee Arabs', the Israeli term for Palestinian refugees. In a letter to Danin dated 7 July, Kaplan wrote: 'I herein authorise you to begin the implementation of the project of exchanging the property of Arabs present in Israel with the property of Jews from Iraq.' Kaplan asked Danin to deduct 2 per cent of the value of the properties exchanged, to be set aside as a fund required to carry out these activities.[61]

These initial efforts by Danin ended in vain, according to his account, partly because of the delays he encountered and the financial difficulties the Israeli government faced in those days. Prime Minister Ben-Gurion told Danin and his colleagues that he could not spare money for these projects. Furthermore the talks with the people of 'Aramco' had no success, and the Arabs had refused to discuss his plans.[62] More crucially, however, the Middle East peace conference, convened by the UN Palestine Conciliation Commission at Lausanne in August 1949, following Israel's rejection of Palestinian and Arab demands that a general return of refugees be allowed within a political solution of the Arab–Israeli conflict. The Palestinian refugees simply demanded to return to their homes and villages and they showed little interested in Israeli employment and resettlement schemes in the Arab states.

RESETTLEMENT IN LIBYA, 1950–8

While the idea of relocating Palestinian refugees from Jordan to, and their organised resettlement in, North Africa was being put forward by senior Israeli diplomats to the French authorities in October 1948,[63] the proposal of resettling refugees in Libya and Somalia was raised by Israeli Foreign Ministry officials in March 1950. On 24 March the Director of the Foreign Ministry International Organisations Division, Ezekiel Gordon, sent a memo to the Foreign Ministry Director General entitled 'The Resettlement of Arab Refugees in Italian-held Somalia and Libya'. Gordon explained that the Italian representative on the UN Trusteeship Council had stated that his government's policy was to encourage immigration of Arab farmers to Somalia, who would not be foreigners in that country. In Gordon's opinion the Italian representative's statements about resettling the Palestinian refugees deserved serious consideration and they should investigate the feasibility of this scheme by approaching the Italians directly. 'I would also like to draw your attention to the possibility of settling Arab refugees in Cyrenaica and Tripoli who would occupy the place of the 17,000–18,000 Jews who had emigrated from there to Israel since its establishment', Gordon wrote.[64] Three weeks later, in reference to Gordon's memo, Yehoshu'a Palmon, the Prime Minister's Advisor on Arab Affairs, wrote a letter to the Foreign Ministry Director General expressing the view that Israel should not pay individual compensation for the properties of those refugees who would be resettled in Libya and Italian-held Somalia, but would rather pay a certain sum, all of which was to be used for a collective resettlement of those refugees in Arab countries, including Libya.[65]

The Libyan scheme was conceived as a combined operation that would include the resettlement of Palestinian refugees in Libya and the inducement of Palestinians to emigrate from Israel to Libya while exchanging their properties in Israel with those of North African Jews who would be encouraged to emigrate to Israel. In the context of the Israeli scheme for resettling Palestinian refugees in Libya two points are relevant. First, there was a growing tendency among Israeli ministers and officials to link the fate of the Palestinian refugees to that of the Jewish communities in Arab countries. Second, the Israelis wanted to exploit the fact that the Sanusi monarchy, set up in Libya in 1951, was heavily dependent on and under indirect control of Britain and the United States.

On 13 March 1952 Moshe Sasson, a senior official of the Foreign Ministry Middle East Department and the son of the Israeli ambassador to Turkey Eliyahu Sasson (Moshe Sasson later became Israeli ambassador to Egypt, 1981–8), wrote a highly secret letter to Foreign Minister Moshe Sharett outlining 'A Combined Proposal for the Resettlement of Arab Refugees in Libya, the Rescue of Jewish Property [in Libya] and the Emigration of Arabs from Israel to Libya'.[66] Moshe Sasson explained that there were still 3,500 Jews 'lingering' in Libya who did not feel in a hurry to immigrate to Israel. Most of these Jews owned property. According to Sasson, a modest estimate of their real estate property was £6 million sterling.

Sasson cited the names of two Palestinians, one living in Israel and the other a refugee in Lebanon, who would collaborate in carrying out this scheme and who would be able to persuade certain groups of Palestinian refugees in neighbouring Arab countries to immigrate to and settle permanently in Libya. (It is hard to establish the truth about this claim of the willingness on the part of the two Palestinians mentioned to collaborate in such a scheme.)

In his 1952 proposal, Sasson asserted that 'poor Libya would willingly receive intellectual and technical Arab [human] resources, which have a much higher level than those existing in Libya':

> the success of this small scale resettlement in Libya depends on the agreement, in principle, of Britain and the local Libyan authorities and the ensuring of means for its financing, on the one hand, and the advance planning and organisation, on the other. Diplomatic activity at high levels in London ... and negotiation with UN institutions on the permanent resettlement of the refugees (in order to finance the resettlement of those [refugees] who would emigrate from [neighbouring] Arab countries [to Libya] – would ensure one side of the coin, and the JNF [Jewish

> National Fund] (which agrees to be in charge of the exchange of properties between Israeli Arabs and Libyan Jews) would ensure the other side of the coin. The JNF is prepared to undertake the carrying out of this task only after the Foreign Ministry empowers it solely to talk to elements concerned in Israel in order to begin implementation.[67]

Sasson believed that 'the political and propagandistic reward that would stem from the emigration of Arabs from Israel, after they had been living there and the lesson for the refugees, who are still demanding to return, is great.' Sasson suggested that if

> the proposal as a whole, or in part, were to be approved, we [the Foreign Ministry Middle East Department] would be able to work out a detailed plan which would be implemented in stages. It is worth emphasising here that the first stage would be directed towards the emigration of three to four Arabs from Israel and a similar number of refugees from [neighbouring] Arab countries [to Libya].

Sasson concluded his letter to Foreign Minister Sharett by pointing out that Prime Minister Ben-Gurion's Advisor for Arab Affairs, Yehoshu'a Palmon, 'approves of the plan and would be prepared to assist in its implementation'.

Although Sharett's formal response to this specific proposal from one of his senior officials in the Foreign Ministry is not known, it is most likely that he approved of it. Sharett, who stood at the centre of Israel's foreign diplomacy, had always advocated an active approach towards resettling the refugees in the Arab states. He also provided strong encouragement for his senior officials to pursue the Libyan scheme, both during his short premiership (1954–November 1955), as well as during his last six months in office as Foreign Minister until his resignation in June 1956.

Finance Minister Levi Eshkol – like Prime Minister Sharett – was heavily involved in the Libyan plan and other Israeli resettlement schemes of the 1950s. Eshkol had become head of the Land Settlement Department of the Jewish Agency and in this capacity had coordinated the settlement of the masses of new immigrants arriving from Arab countries in Israel, mostly resettled on land and property belonging to Palestinian refugees. Eshkol also planned the construction of hundreds of new Jewish agricultural settlements throughout the country. From 1950 to 1952 he served as treasurer of the Jewish Agency. In 1951 he became Minister of Agriculture and Development, and in June of that year he became Finance Minister, a post in which he was responsible for the implementation of the 1952 reparations agreement with West Germany. This agreement obliged Germany to pay to the State of Israel, over a period of 12 to 14 years and in kind, the counter-value of $845,000,000. Of this amount, $110,000,000 was to be turned over by Israel to the Conference on Jewish Material Claims against Germany, representing 23 Jewish organisations.[68] Eshkol directed reparations funds mainly to the development of Israeli industry.

The Libyan plan was formally approved in a meeting held on 13 May 1954 with the participation of Prime Minister Sharett, Finance Minister Levi Eshkol, Agriculture Minister Peretz Naftali, Director General of the Finance Ministry Pinhas Sapir, Shmuel Divon, the Prime Minister's advisor on Arab affairs, and Yosef Weitz of the Jewish National Fund. 'As to the question of exchanging properties of the Arabs here [in Israel] with the properties of Jews in other countries, to which [Arab[farmers would emigrate – a positive answer was given', by the participants, who concluded that 'this way is desirable.'[69] According to Weitz, Sharett, who did not ask many questions, said that 'the matter is respectable and serious and must be carried out.' The participants also approved Weitz's proposal that Yoav Tzuckerman, of the JNF, and Weitz should travel to 'North Africa to investigate the possibility of the exchange of properties of Jews in Tunisia, Algeria, etc.',[70] presumably with those of Palestinian refugees and Israeli Palestinian citizens who would be offered financial incentives for departing to North Africa. A second meeting for detailed discussions of these proposals, with the participation of 'Ezra Danin, of the Foreign Ministry, was set for the Monday of the following week. Either at this second meeting of mid-May 1954 or shortly afterwards Sharett entrusted Danin with the task of coordinating the Libyan scheme.[71]

Weitz, like Danin, was a key player in the Israeli schemes for refugee resettlement in North Africa, which was largely under French and British domination. On 25 October 1954 Weitz was granted an audience with Prime Minister Sharett, and both discussed the 'question of the Arab refugees outside Israel'. Weitz told Sharett:

> We have not been assisted by the means proven by us since the new return to Zion [the beginning of the Zionist movement], i.e.

> recruiting envoys among the Arabs themselves who would carry out work at our instruction. It is possible ... that we missed the hour and that the conditions created in recent years in the political world surrounding us have blocked that way for us. However we are not absolved from checking it again. The investigation must be carried out by the men of the veteran group [Danin, Tzuckerman, Palmon etc.], who are well-versed in the customs of negotiation with the Arabs. The purpose is to find out whether there is still now a possibility for that. Should it become clear that this exists – a detailed plan of action would be worked out.[72]

Six days later, on the afternoon of 1 November, a meeting was held at the Prime Minister's home in Jerusalem, which was attended by Sharett, Weitz, Danin, Teddy Kollek, the Director General of the Prime Minister's Office, Shmuel Divon, advisor to the Prime Minister on Arab affairs and Gide'on Raphael, advisor on Middle Eastern affairs in the Foreign Ministry. The meeting was called by the Prime Minister to discuss a proposal by Weitz and Danin to set up a 'special committee for dealing with the Arab refugee affair'. During the discussion Weitz and Danin emphasised that 'only when the subject is exhausted [investigated thoroughly] would it be possible to know whether there is a place for the desired solution.'[73] Weitz recorded in his diary: 'It was also pointed out that the special committee would carry out its work in the underground also towards internal [Israel people]', a matter which echoed the strictly confidential activities which had surrounded similar Israeli projects in the early 1950s. At the meeting it was agreed that Weitz and Danin would present Sharett with one page of general outlines regarding the special committee and that the Prime Minister would consult other colleagues and inform Weitz of his reply.[74]

Two weeks later, on 13 November, Weitz consulted Yoav Tzuckerman on the matter of the 'special committee for the question of the refugees and the company for the purchase of urban properties from Arabs' in Israel, who presumably would also be encouraged to emigrate to North Africa. The two men also thought that a need would arise for them to travel to France to meet Yehoshu'a Palmon, who at the time was carrying out investigations regarding the scheme of resettling refugees in Libya.[75]

In fact, it took Prime Minister Sharett several months to decide on the appointment of the 'special committee' or the 'refugee committee'. On the morning of 5 May 1955 Weitz met Sharett. Weitz recorded:

> As for my travel [to France and North Africa] it was agreed that Tzuckerman, Palmon and I constitute a committee which would discuss the possibility of finding a solution to the problem of Arab refugees outside the country. The decision to take action must be the responsibility of the three of us, and he [Sharett] should be informed about it. We have to collect material in connection with the exchange of properties of Jews in North Africa with Arab properties here [in Israel], and perhaps there is a possibility of combining these properties with the resettlement of refugees [in North Africa]. He [Sharett] promised to inform Palmon and [Eliyahu] Sasson [then Israel's ambassador to Italy].[76]

Six days later, on 11 May, Weitz talked to Finance Minister Eshkol, who agreed to put at Weitz's disposal 10,000 Israeli lira, as the latter had suggested, for the purpose of carrying out initial investigations on the North African–Libyan resettlement scheme.[77]

On the evening of 25 May 1955 Yehoshu'a Palmon arrived in Paris from London to meet Weitz and Tzuckerman, who were already in France. The three men talked into the late hours about the refugee problem. They continued their discussion the next morning and discussed the 'means of resettling part of the refugees in the Jordan valley and Sinai and the exchange of [Arab] properties in Israel with properties of Jews in North Africa'. It was also decided that Weitz and Tzuckerman should meet Israel's ambassador to Rome, Eliyahu Sasson, before their departure for North Africa.[78]

Weitz and Tzuckerman flew from France to Tunisia on 2 June 1955. On the same day, after their arrival in Tunis, they talked to a few local Zionist functionaries and the Jewish Agency envoy on their aim to meet Tunisian Jews who were planning to immigrate to Israel and were 'prepared to exchange their mainly agricultural properties with [Arab] properties in Israel'.[79] In early June Weitz toured the environs of the Tunisian capital, accompanied by two Zionist functionaries, visiting farming estates belonging to Jews. Most of the farming was dry, and some of the owners of these properties were prepared to transfer them to the control of the Jewish Agency.[80] Weitz arrived back in Israel on 28 June 1955,[81] after spending nearly five weeks in France, Tunisia and Algeria investigating the feasibility of the combined scheme for resettling Palestinian refugees and Israeli-

Palestinians in Libya and North Africa, while encouraging North African Jews to immigrate to Israel.

The special 'refugee committee', in charge of the secret activities aimed at promoting the North African resettlement schemes, held a meeting in Jerusalem on the afternoon of 6 November 1955. Its member Yehoshu'a Palmon said that Sharett, then back as Foreign Minister, had recently told US Secretary of State John Foster Dulles about Israeli intentions to deal directly with the Palestinian refugees and arrange for them compensation and resettlement, provided the United States would make the necessary funds available to the Israeli government. According to Palmon, it sounded as if Dulles agreed to Sharett's proposal, which would be further discussed between the two men during Sharett's visit to the United States due to take place in the next few days. Sharett requested data from the 'refugee committee' on the subject in preparation for his forthcoming meeting with Dulles.[82] Once again the 'refugee committee' member Weitz met Sharett on 18 January 1956 in Jerusalem to discuss the project of resettling 'tens of thousands' of refugees in Libya. One of the possibilities, Weitz explained to Sharett, was 'the resettlement of refugees in Libya. In order to carry out this possibility one million Israeli lira is required as a first step and therefore the government should [firmly] decided: yes or no', on the question of financial allocation. Sharett replied that he 'agrees with this with his heart and soul', but Finance Minister Levi Eshkol's financial reservations should first be overcome. Sharett also told Weitz that he intended to arrange a meeting for discussing the financial issue, in which Prime Minister Ben-Gurion, Eshkol and some members of the 'refugee committee' would take part.[83] Sharett's 'promised meeting' was held on the morning of 27 February 1956 in Jerusalem and was attended by Ben-Gurion, Eshkol, Sharett, Weitz, and Palmon. Weitz explained that 'it was necessary to set up a fund of five million Israeli lira (£1 million sterling) to be used for the purpose of resettling refugees permanently. Eshkol suggested that Israel should ask the US government to increase its foreign aid grant to Israel by US$5 million, and this extra sum would be allocated exclusively for refugee resettlement schemes. In the end the leading members of the Israeli Cabinet agreed to approve in principle the resettlement projects of the 'refugee committee' and to meet again and consult when the detailed finances were worked out and requested.[84]

Two days later the special 'refugee committee' met with the participation of Palmon, Tzuckerman, Danin, and Weitz. Palmon said that Teddy Kollek had told him about the possibility of receiving US$5 million from a US government grant or even from Jews abroad to begin practical work on the refugee resettlement project. At this meeting the committee decided to bring to Foreign Minister Sharett the following summary:

- 'It is necessary to secure a fund of at least one million pounds sterling for the initial action';
- 'the action must be carried out by a non-governmental committee, which would be appointed by the Foreign Minister. We propose the four of us [as members], in addition to Teddy Kollek';
- 'the committee would be authorised to implement actions, after bringing them for the approval of the Foreign Minister only';
- 'we are recommending that the committee be subordinate to the JNF and it should appear as such to the Arabs and others';
- 'the first amount [required] for starting the negotiation should be immediately fixed at 50,000 Israeli lira. This amount would be made available by the JNF at the expense of the [government] treasury';
- 'the action would be in three directions: a) the rehabilitation of one of the villages of the Hebron mountain [in the West Bank]. We are talking about 'Ajur [village]; b) the purchase of lands from owners who live in villages situated in the Jordanian border region [the West Bank], and whose lands are located in Israel; c) the resettlement of one village in Libya.'[85]

The resettlement of one village in Libya was supposed to be the beginning of an operation to transfer and resettle tens of thousands of Palestinian refugees in that country.

More discussions on the refugee resettlement scheme followed. On the morning of 21 May 1956 a meeting was held in the Foreign Ministry's office in Jerusalem, which was attended by Sharett, Eshkol, Weitz, Danin, Palmon, Kollek, Tzuckerman, Divon, and Reuven Shiloah, Israeli Minister Plenipotentiary in Washington. Sharett opened the discussion by saying that they had already been discussing the subject for two years without getting into action:

> Now since the action has been approved by the Prime Minister [Ben-Gurion] and there is money, it is necessary to begin work – which is investigating the possibilities of working with those who

> have political and organisational capability among Arab refugees to solve the refugee problem [through resettlement schemes].[86]

Eshkol, on the other hand, described the financial situation of the state of Israel as 'catastrophic' – a situation which made it very difficult to allocate funds for such resettlement projects. Teddy Kollek suggested putting pressure on the Americans to increase their grant aid by US$5 million, which would be devoted to refugee resettlement. Sharett thought that Israel should aim at getting half of the amount suggested by Kollek from the Americans. However, when Weitz asked for US$1 million to be immediately allocated by the Israeli government to begin work on the project, Eshkol accepted this and it was decided to bring the matter before the government for formal approval. Following this, the discussion moved on to the methods by which the 'new committee' in charge of the refugee resettlement scheme would work, after being officially appointed by the Foreign Minister.[87] The new 'refugee committee', which was officially appointed by Sharett on 30 May 1956, was headed by Weitz and included Palmon, Tzuckerman, Danin, and Kollek. Divon was also asked by Sharett to participate in the committee's meetings. In his letter of appointment, Sharett wrote to Weitz that the role of the committee was:

- to investigate practical possibilities regarding liquidating the claims of Arab refugees from Israel, individually and collectively, whether by payment of compensation for their lands, or by arrangement of their resettlement in other countries, or by both means;
- to submit plans for these resettlements;
- to implement the same plans which the government would approve through the Foreign Ministry.[88]

Weitz, Danin, Tzuckerman, Palmon, Divon, Eliyahu Sasson, Israel's ambassador to Italy (Libya's former colonial ruler), and (to some extent) Kollek, worked together for several years until 1958 to bring the Libyan–North African plan to fruition. Their efforts included numerous hours of secret meetings to raise money for the purchase of Libyan agricultural land from Italian colonial settlers who had returned to Italy. This land, situated in the provinces of Tripoli and Cyrenaica, was to be provided to Palestinian refugees who agreed to farm it with the help of Libyan workers. Danin wrote in his autobiography:

> The initial investigation I carried out revealed [the area] in question was sandy land [occupied by former Italian settlers], and it seemed to me that it would be possible to grow on it peanuts on a large scale, and especially at that time since the Chinese had stopped exporting peanuts to Europe and a big shortage of this commodity had been created.[89]

Danin added that he conceived this project before the discovery of oil in Libya and envisaged the possibility of resettling permanently thousands of refugees within the scheme. According to Danin, a secret agreement was reached with ministers in the Libyan government to the effect that prospective Palestinian settlers in Libya would be allowed one Palestinian worker with his family for every five Libyan workers they employed. In the initial stage of this project Danin and his team envisaged the transfer of 300 Palestinian agricultural experts and their families from Jordan to Libya. These candidates would be refugees who had abandoned properties in Israel. Also according to Danin, a secret tacit agreement was reached with the Jordanian authorities that these Palestinian candidates would be allowed to leave the country via Syria, and a similar tacit agreement was reached with the Lebanese authorities to allow prospective Palestinian settlers to pass through Lebanon and sail through its ports to Libya.[90] Danin wrote in his autobiography:

> This whole operation involved enormous efforts of persuasion of people in Jordan, Libya and Lebanon and obtaining their consent. Within the framework of the operation English Jews, who did not have Jewish names, were persuaded to act for the promotion of the project in Libya. At an advanced stage of the dealings we registered a limited company for development and construction, with the help of a Jewish lawyer from Geneva. The financing was supposed to come from two sources: from the country [Israel] and rich Jews in the USA, including those who had oil business in Libya. We arranged with an insurance company that all the [Palestinian] settlers in Libya would be given life insurance; we would pay the premium, while the company would put at our disposal an advance payment from the amounts to which the insured would be entitled in the future. The candidates for

> resettlement in Libya undertook to give up their claims for compensation from the government of Israel in the future.[91]

It is hard to establish the truth about these claims of secret tacit agreements with the Jordanian and Lebanese authorities in connection with the Libyan scheme. What is clear, however, is that Danin, Palmon, Weitz, and other colleagues exerted a great deal of effort in promoting this plan. Moreover, from Danin's explanations it seems that those Palestinian refugees in Jordan who had agreed to become candidates for the Libyan scheme did not know that the whole project was orchestrated by senior Israeli officials with the assistance of Zionist Jews from England (such as British Zionist author Jon Kimche[92]), Switzerland and other Western countries. On Sunday 17 June 1956 the new 'refugee committee' met in Jerusalem with the participation of Danin, Weitz, Kollek, Tzuckerman, and Shmuel Divon, to discuss the Libyan project. Palmon reported on his dealings with Arab collaborators in London and gave

> details on his conversation with the [Arab?] envoy who will go out there [to Libya] in order to arrange that permission be given to a number of [Palestinian] families [in Libya] to bring relatives and relatives of relatives to settle there, in such a way that they would join 75–100 [Palestinian] clans [expected to settle in Libya].[93]

According to Weitz's diary, Palmon reported that it was

> possible to obtain from the Prime Minister there [in Libya] permission for four to five Palestinian families, who settled in Libya and occupy posts in the government, to bring their relatives and the relatives of their relatives to settle there. In this way resettlement of former Palestinian Arabs would be established there ... and this is an opening for the development of Palestinian resettlement in Libya.[94]

Shortly before Sharett's resignation as Foreign Minister he met Finance Minister Eshkol and the head of the 'refugee committee', Weitz, on 21 June 1956. At this meeting Weitz's proposal to allocate US$1 million dollars for the Libyan scheme was approved in principle,[95] although a formal approval by the Israeli government was still required. In early July Golda Meir (a Mapai leader who subsequently became Prime Minister) succeeded Sharett as Foreign Minister and, according to Danin, 'she encouraged us and even obtained the consent of David Ben-Gurion for the continuation of this exceptionally extraordinary and dangerous experiment [the Libyan project], although he [Ben-Gurion] doubted its feasibility.'[96] Ben-Gurion did approve of the Libyan project, although he had a great deal of scepticism about its practicability. Eminently a realist, Ben-Gurion believed that there was a limit to what Israel could do in terms of resettling Palestinian refugees in Arab countries. Furthermore, when Weitz came to see the Prime Minister on 4 October 1956 and asked him why the government was not doing enough to implement the proposals submitted by the 'refugee committee', Ben-Gurion replied that the money needed for such a project was not available because much of the government's budget was spent on the purchase of weapons.[97] This meeting took place on the eve of the tripartite Israeli–British–French attack on Egypt and the remark of Ben-Gurion, who was also Defence Minister, about the money spent on weapons seems to point to his preoccupation with the impending 1956 war.

The prospects for the Libyan scheme succeeding were dimmed by political developments in the Middle East between 1954 and 1958. However, according to Danin, what really aborted the plan was sudden and unsuspected publicity. The revelations about the plan and its source of financing occurred in 1958 while Danin and Palmon were in Italy seeking to register the transfer of the first 100,000 dunums from the control of former Italian settlers in the Tripoli region to Zionist control.[98] At that time, the operation, which until then had been kept strictly confidential, was leaked to an Israeli journalist, who treated it as a journalistic scoop and passed it to the *Sunday Times* in London, and to *Ma'ariv* and *Lamerhav* in Israel. The whole operation collapsed as a result of this leak. Danin wrote: 'our men in Libya were immediately persecuted by the men of the Mufti [Haj Amin al-Husayni], and some of them were detained and tortured.' In summing up his efforts Danin wrote that, although the actual implementation of the project – the transfer of Palestinian refugees from Jordan and their resettlement in Libya – had not been tested, there was no certainty that it would have succeeded even had the whole operation remained confidential and the leakage to the press not occurred.[99] One might also add that, judging by the fact that those very few Israeli Arab citizens who were enticed to Libya then insisted on returning to Israel,[100] this scheme was doomed to failure as far as persuading a substantial number of Israeli-Palestinians to leave for Libya was concerned.

The collapse of the Libyan project did not bring an end to the efforts by Israeli Foreign Ministry officials to try to 'dissolve' the refugee problem and disperse the refugees throughout the interior of the Arab world through economic means, employment projects and resettlement schemes. Moreover, the Libyan scheme would resurface ten years later, after the Israeli occupation of the West Bank and the Gaza Strip, in conversations and correspondence between Danin, then retired from the Foreign Ministry, and Yitzhak Rabin, then Israel's ambassador to Washington. Rabin and Danin appear to have discussed in 1968 the idea of 'infiltrating' skilled Palestinians – refugees and otherwise – from the West Bank and Gaza to Libya, who would then attract Palestinian refugee emigration to that country, resulting in the thinning-out of the teeming refugee camps in the Gaza Strip and the West Bank.[101]

DURING THE 1956–7 OCCUPATION OF THE GAZA STRIP AND SINAI

On 29 October 1956 the Israelis invaded the Gaza Strip and Sinai, as part of the tripartite attack on Egypt, holding both areas for four months before strong international, and especially US–Soviet, pressure eventually forced them to evacuate both areas. Originally, the Israelis had every intention of staying in what their government considered to be an integral part of the Land of Israel. Foreign Minister Golda Meir told a Mapai Party rally on 10 November 1956 that 'the Gaza Strip is an integral part of Israel.'[102] However, when the Israeli army captured the Gaza Strip in early November 1956, Prime Minister Ben-Gurion was clearly disappointed about the demographic outcome of the war: the vast majority of the refugees and other residents in the Strip stayed put.[103] Of the then 300,000 inhabitants of the Gaza Strip, 215,000 were listed as refugees, occupying eight vast refugee camps. The Strip had nearly one-fourth of the total of about 900,000 Arab refugees from historic Palestine.

During the short-lived occupation of 1956–7 a secret committee composed of senior Israeli officials was set up by Ben-Gurion to consider proposals for resettling elsewhere hundreds of thousands of refugees from the Gaza Strip. Little is known about the ideas put forward by this committee, which was headed by 'Ezra Danin, who, at the same time, was deeply involved in the Libyan resettlement scheme. In a letter dated 10 December 1956 to Eliyahu Sasson, Israel's ambassador to Italy (who was at the time involved in the scheme of purchasing the lands of former Italian settlers in Libya for resettlement of Palestinian refugees in that country), Danin explained that the Prime Minister had appointed the committee and that Finance Minister Levi Eshkol had approved the allocation of financial resources for the work to be carried out by the committee whose members would be Haim Gvati (Director-General of the Ministry of Agriculture and later Minister of Agriculture), Yitzhak Levi (Secretary General of the Prime Minister's Office), Yitzhak 'Elam (Director-General of the Ministry of Labour), Shmuel Divon (Ben-Gurion's advisor on Arab affairs), and Ra'anan Weitz (Yosef Weitz's son, Director-General of the Jewish Agency's Land Settlement Department).[104] It is not clear whether there was any direct link between this committee and Danin's Libyan scheme. Only patchy information is available about the Israeli intention to relocate and resettle Palestinian refugees from the Gaza Strip during this short period. Yosef Nahmani, the Jewish National Fund's senior executive in Galilee, wrote to his senior colleague Yosef Weitz (who was also a member of the Israeli team of senior officials working on the Libyan resettlement plan), on 22 December 1956:

> You certainly know that a committee headed by 'Ezra Danin is considering proposals to resettle the refugees of Gaza. If Gaza remains in Israeli hands together with its refugees this would put a great burden on the economic development and security of Israel. ... Your absence denies the Jewish National Fund representation on the committee.[105]

The official Israeli position had always been that there could be no return of the Palestinian refugees to Israeli territory, and that the only solution to the problem lay in their resettlement in the Arab states or elsewhere. If Israel intended to annex the Gaza Strip late in 1956, the official Israeli reasoning was that a solution had to be found to the critical refugee problem. Indeed, the idea of relocating the refugees residing in the Strip to the Sinai Peninsula was raised in internal debates. For instance, on 23 December 1956 Premier Ben-Gurion cut short a cabinet session in Jerusalem in order to have a lunch meeting with President Yitzhak Ben-Tzvi and his wife Rahel Yanait. The latter was a prominent Mapai leader, who subsequently joined the Whole Land of Israel Movement advocating the annexation of the West Bank and the Gaza Strip to Israel. The conversation at the presidential residence in Jerusalem on 23 December, which focused on the future of the Gaza Strip and the Sinai Peninsula, contained the following exchange between the Prime Minister and Rahel Yanait.

> Ben-Gurion: 'We will hold on to Gaza. However we have no need of the 300 thousand refugees, it would be better for UNRWA to deal with them.'
> Rahel Yanait: 'You should propose a constructive settlement.'
> Ben-Gurion: 'These things are abstracts. Would you suggest the resettlement of the refugees of Gaza in Israel?'
> Rahel Yanait: 'We would settle them in El 'Arish [in Sinai].'
> Ben-Gurion: 'Do you know that in 1920 an expedition went to investigate whether or not El 'Arish was suitable for [Jewish] settlement and the conclusion was negative. How would we settle them in El 'Arish if the land is not suitable?'
> Rahel Yanait: 'But things have changed since. Today there are new and modern methods for discovering water and improving the soil.' (see note 106)

Rahel Yanait and the President were also trying to persuade Ben-Gurion not to yield to US President Eisenhower's pressure and evacuate the Sinai Peninsula. An implied threat by the United States of economic sanctions against Israel had already forced Premier Ben-Gurion to agree to withdraw from Sinai when a United Nations force moved into the Suez Canal zone. Ben-Gurion, on the other hand, replied to Ben-Tzvi and Rahel Yanait that Israel could not fight two superpowers – the United States and the Soviet Union – and therefore would be forced to evacuate Sinai. However, he still regarded Gaza as part of the Jewish 'homeland' and wanted, he said, to hold on to the Gaza Strip.[106] Judging by his past record before and during 1948 and his previous vigorous advocacy of Palestinian population transfer to Transjordan and Iraq, it seems that Ben-Gurion's scepticism towards Yanait's argument in favour of relocating the refugees from the Gaza Strip to Sinai had more to do with political realism and the need to evacuate Sinai in the face of strong US–Soviet pressure, than with any fundamental rejection of the idea of resettling Palestinian refugees in Sinai.

The same idea of resettling the refugees residing in the Gaza Strip was frequently raised by top officials of the Foreign Ministry, which at the time was headed by Golda Meir. In his personal diary entry for 20 November 1956, former Foreign Minister Moshe Sharett cited a cable sent to him in India by Walter Eytan, Director General of the Foreign Ministry. Eytan explained in his cable that 'the problem of the refugees [in Gaza] is very pressing ... there is a need now for more far-reaching actions with the aim of ensuring the future.' In response Sharett – who was at the time bitter about having been manoeuvred out of office by Ben-Gurion and had opposed the occupation of Gaza largely because of the hundreds of thousands of refugees in it – recorded in the same entry of his diary his amazement at the content of Eytan's cable: 'What is far-reaching action – the transfer of the refugees to Iraq or their resettlement in Israel? The two solutions are impractical'; neither Iraq nor Israel was prepared to accept them.[107] Eytan did not explain what he meant by 'far-reaching actions', and it seems that in Jerusalem Ben-Gurion and Golda Meir were determined to keep Sharett in the dark, mainly because of his known opposition to the 1956 war. Sharett, on the other hand, felt deceived and humiliated for not being informed about the impending attack on Egypt, and this might also explain his amazement at the suggestion of 'far-reaching actions' in connection with the refugees in Gaza.

About the same time, another senior official of the Foreign Ministry and Minister plenipotentiary to the Scandinavian countries, Haim Yahil (later to be Director General of the Foreign Ministry, 1960–64), wrote a secret letter from Stockholm to Walter Eytan in Jerusalem. He strongly advocated the annexation of the Gaza Strip to Israel. Yahil at the same time totally rejected a proposal put forward in *Haaretz* on 22 November 1956 by Eli'ezer Livneh, a Mapai colleague and member of the First and Second Knessets of 1949–55, calling for the annexation of the Gaza Strip to Israel together with all its Palestinian residents, including the refugees. Describing Livneh's proposal as totally impractical, Yahil instead suggested that the refugees in the Strip be divided into three groups: the first group would be resettled in Sinai; the second in Israel, outside the Gaza Strip; and the third in the Strip itself. No specific figures were mentioned in Yahil's proposal as to how many refugees should be included in each category.[108] A month later, Yahil returned to the same proposal in another secret letter to Eytan, dated 26 December. After the annexation of the Gaza Strip to Israel, Yahil explained, Israel would then absorb some of the refugees residing in the Strip 'and the rest of them would be resettled in Sinai or some other Arab country through the payment of compensation on our part'. No less important, for Yahil,

> a solution to the refugee problem is necessary not only for political reasons – as our contribution to a resettlement – and humanitarian reasons, but also for [Jewish] settlement reasons. Here the incorporation of Gaza to Israel would be secure and durable only if certain Jewish settlement would be also in this area, and how could we carry out [Jewish] settlement in the area when it is full of refugee camps.[109]

In private and internal discussions, senior officials of the Foreign Ministry and the Prime Minister's Office, including members of the committee set up to deal with the Palestinian refugees in the occupied Gaza Strip, emerged as the strongest advocates of encouraging the refugees to emigrate from the Gaza Strip to countries overseas. The same officials also realised that neither Egypt nor Syria and Iraq had any intention of opening their borders to the masses of refugees in Gaza. There were three men at the centre of these discussions: 'Ezra Danin, a senior advisor on Arab affairs at the Foreign Ministry and head of the Gaza Strip's refugee committee; Shmuel Divon, a member of the same refugee committee and Ben-Gurion's advisor on Arab affairs; and Ya'acov Hertzog, the son of the Chief Rabbi of Israel and a brother of Haim Hertzog, who later became President of Israel, 1983–93.

During the 1956–7 occupation of Gaza, Ya'acov Hertzog, in his official capacity as Israel's Minister plenipotentiary in Washington, as well as other officials of the Foreign Ministry in Jerusalem and the Israeli embassy in Washington, were involved in the efforts to encourage the emigration of refugees from Gaza to countries overseas, including the United States and Latin American countries. It is also inconceivable that Ya'acov Hertzog's boss in the Washington embassy, Abba Eban, Israel's ambassador to Washington (later to be Foreign Minister), was not privy to these official efforts, which were presided over by Walter Eytan and his boss, Foreign Minister Golda Meir. Gershon Avner, Director of the Foreign Ministry's US Division, wrote a secret letter to Hertzog dated 24 January 1957, telling him about 'a new attempt to deal with the problem of the refugees': the 'rehabilitation' of Gaza's refugees through 'the Intergovernmental Committee for European Migration (ICEM)'.[110] Avner had been the Director of the Foreign Ministry's West Europe Division between

1948 and 1952. (He later became Secretary to the Israeli Cabinet, 1974–7[111]). In December 1951 the ICEM had been set up on the initiative of the United States, at a meeting in Brussels in which 16 nations took part, to be 'responsible for the movement of migrants, including refugees, for whom arrangements could be made with the governments of the countries concerned'. In his letter to Hertzog, Avner explained that 'Ezra Danin was enthusiastic about this plan which fits in with Israel's effort to move a number of refugees to resettle permanently, in the hope that this example would activate others [refugees to emigrate].'

Avner added:

> As is known, we are prepared to pay compensation to refugees exploiting this possibility. Assuming that it is possible to reach an agreement with the ICEM, there will be a need for a gentle whispering activity initially in order to move a number of families to take this road, but it is still early [to know whether this would work].

The key to success, according to Avner, was to secure the support of the US representative on the ICEM and his government's influence on this organisation. Avner also suggested that the Israeli embassy in Washington should discuss exploiting these ideas to the full.[112] At this stage the Israeli government was still insisting that under no circumstances could it agree to the return of Egypt to the Gaza Strip.

A few weeks later Moshe Bartur, Director of the Economic Division of the Foreign Ministry (and later to become ambassador to the UN Europe Bureau), wrote a strictly secret memorandum dated 10 February 1957 (copies were sent to three officials of the Ministry: Y. Hertzog; Arthur Lourie, Deputy Director General of the Foreign Ministry and a member of the Israeli delegation to the UN General Assembly; and Yosef Teko'ah, later to be ambassador to the UN), suggesting the following:

> Since we are determined to stay in the Strip in one way or another, we have in fact taken responsibility for the 200,000 refugees. It cannot be assumed that we would be able to cause their departure except through an orderly process of resettlement in and outside Israel. For the sake of that we need the assistance of the UN and USA.

In order to achieve this aim, Bartur went on, the Israeli administration in the Strip should assume joint responsibility with UNRWA for the refugees in Gaza (an Israeli–UN 'condominium', in his words) and set up an international committee, the composition of which would remain private, for working out a final solution to the problem through resettlement. Bartur did not specify how many refugees would be resettled in the Gaza Strip after its annexation by Israel or how many of them would be resettled overseas.[113]

By March 1957, Israel, under intense international pressure, was preparing to withdraw from Gaza. Reporting to the Knesset on 7 March, Ben-Gurion stressed that under any administration 'the Gaza Strip would be a source of trouble as long as the refugees had not been resettled elsewhere.'[114] By this stage, the United Nations agreed to station an emergency force (UNEF) between Israel and Egypt in the Gaza Strip.

On 12 March 1957, shortly before Israel was forced to evacuate the Strip, the US Division of the Foreign Ministry received an undated memorandum addressed to Ya'acov Hertzog from Yehuda Harry Levine, a counsellor at the Israeli embassy in Washington who was also in charge of information, suggesting that a unilateral, practical, and dramatic measure should be undertaken by Israel that would demonstrate that the Arab leaders were deliberately preventing a solution to the Palestinian refugee problem. Israeli official claims had always been that the refugee problem was not created by Israel; that most Arab countries intentionally left the refugees in the squalor of miserable refugee camps so they could use them as a political and propaganda weapon in their struggle with Israel. The Oxford-educated Levine, who had been Director of the English Propaganda Department of the Jewish National Fund and subsequently became Director of the Information Department of the Foreign Ministry and ambassador to Denmark, explained that he had just met the editor of *Harper*'s magazine, John Fisher, who had expressed an opinion in favour of a similar proposal. According to Levine, Fisher assumed that for the first time since 1948 the refugees in Gaza were now free of pressure from Arab leaders, and consequently, as a first step and gesture of goodwill, Israel should offer compensation to a number of refugees in Gaza (he mentioned 5,000 people) that would enable their relocation to and resettlement in other countries, with the UN's assistance.[115] In May 1949, during the last stage of the Palestinian refugee exodus, *Harper*'s magazine had published an article by Eliahu Ben-Horin, a Zionist Revisionist publicist and advocate of Arab population transfer since the early 1940s, entitled 'From Palestine to Israel'. The then editor of *Harper's* noted that in an earlier article in the magazine's December 1944 issue, Ben-Horin had advocated a plan that at the time 'looked far-fetched ... that the Arabs of Palestine be transferred to Iraq and resettled there. Now, with thousands of Arab refugees from Palestine facing a dismal future, the transfer idea appears to be a likely bet ... in view of the sound character of Mr. Ben-Horin's earlier judgements and prophecies, we feel we can bank on his word about present-day Israel: "It works."'[116]

Two days later, on 14 March 1957, another senior Israeli official, Hanan Bar-On (later to become Consul General in Ethiopia), wrote a secret letter to Ya'acov Hertzog and Shmuel Divon containing the following:

> Following through our conversation, the outlines of the plan for encouraging emigration of refugees from the [Gaza] Strip are as follows:
>
> - the setting-up of an organisation in the United States or Latin America, whose aim is to encourage the emigration of refugees to countries of the world, including countries of the American continent, without becoming involved in the political problems of the Middle East;
> - the organisation must be based first of all on the leaders of Arab migrants in Latin America and the United States; however, this could also include in it other elements, such as Christian clergy and perhaps even Jewish factors who are not publicly known as distinguished sympathisers of Israel (Lessing Rosenwald?);[117]
> - the organisation should operate on a scale similar to that of HIAS [the Hebrew Sheltering and Immigrant Aid Society] and the JOINT [American Jewish Joint Distribution Committees] in the years before the Second World War; that is to say, it should not only try to concern itself with the matter of financing emigration as such, but first of all conduct negotiations with governments and various bodies in the world to find absorption places in various countries. The proposed body should operate as a political body based on humanitarian principles, without pretending to represent the refugees or any other Middle Eastern community. In addition to this the body should work in order to bring about

the emigration of refugees without religious distinction, in spite of the fact that most of the activists of the organisation would, undoubtedly, naturally be Christians;

- Notwithstanding that the financing of the first steps of such an organisation would, undoubtedly, have to come from our own sources, it is possible to assume that it would be possible when the time comes to finance the lion's share of the organisational expenditures with the help of various fund-raising appeals. Clearly this could not include the actual costs of rehabilitating the refugees in their new countries of residence, but perhaps it would be possible to find solutions for this in the framework of UNRWA;
- Despite the fact that the proposed organisation should be based first of all on Arab elements, the action of organising and guidance must, undoubtedly, be made by Israeli and Jewish bodies and personalities jointly, of course with adequate camouflage and concealment.

In summing up the outlines of his proposed plan, Bar-On wrote:

> The above are only a few initial thoughts, and it is possible, no doubt, to find impractical flaws in them, but it seems to me that the central idea, that is to say, the setting up of an organisation which would attempt by various means to persuade governments to open their borders for emigration, even if limited, is likely to give us not insignificant advantages in the sphere of our dealing with the refugee problem in general and the Arab refugees in particular.[118]

In the same month in which Israel was forced to evacuate the Gaza Strip, Danin, the head of the official committee set up to consider the resettlement of the Gaza refugees, complained in a letter to David Shaltiel, Israel's ambassador to Brazil, that 'it was possible to operate a great deal in Gaza, but we did not receive permission and money for it.'[119] Perhaps, because the 1956–7 occupation was short-lived and uncertain, the Israeli goal of dispersing the refugees under their control through relocation and resettlement schemes was not prosecuted vigorously. After the withdrawal from Sinai and the Gaza Strip, Danin and other Foreign Ministry officials were back dealing with the Libyan scheme. The Israeli goal of dispersing and resettling the hundreds of thousands of refugees residing in the Strip

CARL A. RUDISILL LIBRARY
LENOIR-RHYNE COLLEGE

(constituting over three-quarters of the Strip's population) indeed would remain constant for many years to come.

It is clear that these official, though secret, Israeli schemes of the 1950s ended in failure. However, they are significant in the sense of showing how the Israelis wanted to remove the refugee problem from the centre of the Arab–Israeli conflict and remove the possibility of Palestinian return in the future. These schemes also constituted a background against which other Israeli schemes were attempted by the governments of Eshkol and Golda Meir in the aftermath of the conquest of the West Bank and Gaza Strip in June 1967. Faced with what they termed a 'demographic problem' and the existence of hundreds of thousands of refugees in the occupied territories, the governments of Eshkol and Meir (both were involved in the schemes of the 1950s) operated a plan (see below) between the summer of 1967 and 1970 that was aimed at the thinning-out of the population of the refugee camps, particularly in Gaza.

RESETTLEMENT SCHEMES SINCE 1967

Since 1967 official Israeli attitudes towards the Palestinian refugees have remained tied to the classical position established soon after 1948, with Labour showing only marginally more flexibility on the issue than the Likud.[120] After 1967 Israeli resettlement schemes in the West Bank and Gaza Strip were viewed by many of their advocates as a method of facilitating and consolidating Israeli control over the newly acquired territories. However, these schemes were not universally backed by all factions within the ruling Labour coalition and there was a marked hesitancy (for a variety of reasons which will be explained below) towards refugee resettlement schemes within the borders of the territories occupied by Israel in 1967, especially within the biggest faction of Mapai which publicly advocated international cooperation to solve the refugee problem. Moreover, while influential right-wing factions within the government, such Rafi (Israel Workers List) and the Mifdal (National Religious Party), called publicly for the encouragement of emigration of refugees from the West Bank and Gaza as a solution to the problem,[121] the dovish Mapam party supported resettlement schemes as a genuine attempt to improve the living conditions of refugees, without, as its leaders suggested, undermining the refugees' basic rights to the return of property in Israel and the obtaining of humanitarian assistance from the United Nations Relief and Works Agency (UNRWA).[122]

After the 1967 war Israel was confronted with a major problem, finding itself in control of about 600,000 refugees in the West Bank and Gaza Strip. By 1984 two-thirds of the 650,00 inhabitants of the Gaza Strip were registered with the UNRWA as refugees. By 1990 37 per cent, or 817,000, of the total registered Palestinian refugee population were living under Israeli occupation in the West Bank and Gaza Strip; 41 per cent of the 817,000 (339,000), lived in the refugee camps of the West Bank and Gaza.[123] After 1967 Israeli leaders realised that the refugee communities in the West Bank and the Gaza Strip presented in more than one way the most serious problem for Israel. The refugee camps were (and still are) the most overcrowded parts of the West Bank and Gaza and were therefore the most difficult parts to control. Furthermore, because the refugees did not accept their sojourn in the territories as an indefinite one, Israeli leaders saw a greater long-term challenge from the refugees than from the indigenous population. Against this backdrop the Israeli attempts to encourage the emigration and resettlement elsewhere of Palestinian refugees living under occupation were inevitable. However, as emigration of refugees from the West Bank and Gaza Strip did not meet the expectations of the Israeli authorities, Israeli resettlement schemes in these areas still reflected a continuity of policy, aimed at dispersing refugees in an attempt to remove them from the centre of the Arab–Israeli conflict and weaken their collective identity and perceived militancy.

During the early years of occupation, a wide-ranging debate on the future of Palestinian refugees under Israeli control was conducted openly in the Knesset. Furthermore, Israeli (official and semi-official) proposals to solve the refugee problem ranged over a wide area: opposition to any form of resettlement of refugees in the West Bank and Gaza; the wholesale transfer of refugees from the Gaza Strip camps and resettlement in West Bank villages and towns and in north Sinai; improvements to the living and housing conditions in refugee camps combined with the permanent resettlement of refugees where they lived, while encouraging their full and permanent integration into the general life of the West Bank and Gaza; voluntary and partial resettlement schemes backed by financial inducements; compulsory resettlement schemes designed and forcibly implemented by the Israeli army as a counter-insurgency measure.[124] In essence, the range of proposals and plans put forward reflected a continuation of pre-1967 policy, although the main thrust of Israel's resettlement effort was directed towards the Gaza Strip – a region which (according to the original proposals of the Allon Plan) was supposed to be annexed to Israel.

In the early days of occupation, encouragement of Palestinian emigration particularly from the densely populated refugee camps of the Gaza Strip by the Israeli authorities was reported early on in the foreign press. The *New York Times* of 26 August 1967 reported that each day for the last two weeks some 500 residents had left the Gaza Strip, adding that 'any reduction in Gaza area's population is a benefit to everyone in Israel's view.' Several months later, The *Observer* (London) reported on 17 December 1967:

> The opportunity of reprisals on security grounds has been taken to hasten the departure of more people from the West Bank and the Gaza Strip and to prevent the return of those who had fled. The Israeli authorities believe that whatever the eventual political status of the Gaza Strip, the refugees there should be moved elsewhere.[125]

The *Observer* of 28 January 1968 also reported: 'It is estimated that between 30,00 and 35,000 people have left the [Gaza] Strip as a result of the measures taken by the Israeli authorities.' Ironically most of these people were forced into exile by Israel for the second time.

(i) The Israeli Cabinet Discussions of 15–19 June 1967

Within a fortnight after the seizure of the West Bank and the Gaza Strip, the Israeli Cabinet headed by Prime Minister Levi Eshkol convened for a number of secret meetings, held between 15 and 19 June 1967, to discuss, *inter alia,* what to do with the Palestinian refugee communities under Israeli control. In the 1950s Eshkol had been personally involved in several Israeli schemes designed to resettle Palestinian refugees in Arab countries. The official transcript of the June 1967 meetings remains secret. However, according to private diaries kept by Ya'acov Hertzog, who was at the time Director General of the Prime Minister's Office, both Finance Minister Pinhas Sapir and Foreign Minister Abba Eban called at these meetings for the relocation and resettlement of the Palestinian refugees residing in the West Bank and Gaza in neighbouring Arab countries. These discussions at cabinet level were revealed for the first time in June 1987 by the Israeli researcher Meir Avidan,[126] and were also reported by the Israeli journalists Yossi Melman and Dan Raviv in February

1988.[127] Relying on Avidan' research, Melman and Raviv pointed out that at these meetings that

> sentiment seemed to favour Deputy Prime Minister Yigal Allon's proposal that Palestinian refugees be transported to the Sinai Desert and that Palestinians should be persuaded to move abroad.

According to Hertzog's notes, Allon complained at the meeting of 15 June: 'We do not do enough among the Arabs to encourage emigration.'[128] At the same meeting Menahem Begin, then minister without portfolio and later Prime Minister (1977–83), recommended the demolition of the refugee camps and the resettlement of their residents in El 'Arish in Sinai, which had been captured from Egypt.[129] Begin's proposal was also supported by the Labour leader and Minister of Transport Moshe Carmel at the discussions of 17–19 June 1967.[130]

Avidan also revealed that the ministerial defence committee decided on 15 June 1967 to adopt the following policy line regarding the Palestinian refugees under Israeli control:

> Israel will demand from the Arab countries and the superpowers to start preparing an elementary plan to solve the refugee problem, which would include the resettlement of refugees in Iraq, Syria, (Egypt?), Algeria, Morocco, Jordan, and other countries (in the presentation of this demand emphasis will be made on the fact of population exchange, i.e., that the resettlement of the Palestinian refugees in Arab countries will come in exchange for the Jews who left Arab countries for Israel.[131]

In fact, about the same time, a special ministerial committee was set up to look into ways of solving the refugee problem.[132] In the same context Yosef Weitz, former head of the Jewish National Fund's Settlement Department, recorded in his diary: 'instructions were given by the [Eshkol government] to [a group] of experts to work out a plan' for relocating the Gaza refugees to the West Bank and the East Bank (in Jordan) and resettling them there.[133] In July 1967 Prime Minister Eshkol appointed Ra'anan Weitz, then director of the Jewish Agency's Rural Settlement Department, to head a team of 120 advisors, Arabists and technical experts (including several senior professors from the Hebrew University of Jerusalem), who were entrusted with the task of working out various practical solutions to the problem of Palestinian refugees in the West Bank and the Gaza Strip.[134] During the short-lived occupation of 1956–7 Ra'anan Weitz (himself a Labour Party man), had served on a secret committee composed of senior Israeli officials, which had been set up by the Israeli government to consider proposals for resettling elsewhere hundreds of thousands of refugees from the Gaza Strip. Two years later, in 1969, Weitz submitted a detailed plan to the Israeli government for the transfer of 50,000 refugees from the Gaza Strip and their resettlement in El 'Arish in north Sinai. However, this plan, which was designed to contribute to other efforts aimed at the thinning-out of the teeming refugee camps in Gaza, never reached the stage of implementation, possibly because of the difficulties the Israeli authorities had encountered in their previous attempts to relocate large numbers of Gaza refugees to Sinai.[135]

Within the ruling Labour coalition members of the right-wing Rafi faction were among the leading figures opposing refugee resettlement within the borders of the territories occupied by Israel in 1967; voluntary emigration of refugees was seen as a solution to the problem. Rafi argued that a solution to the territories' refugee problem should be carried out through an 'exchange of population' between Sephardic Jews who had emigrated to Israel from Arab countries and Palestinian refugees residing in the West Bank and Gaza.[136] Further evidence as to the kind of solution the leaders of Rafi had in mind during those days was provided by Defence Minister Moshe Dayan, who, a few weeks after the Cabinet discussions of June 1967, stated publicly that the refugees should be encouraged to move across the Jordan River to Jordan and resettled there.[137] In the following year Dayan, while reviewing the political situation in the occupied territories at a meeting of the Secretariat of his party Rafi, talked about 'encouraging the transfer of the Gaza Strip refugees to Jordan'.[138] However, this policy line seemed to have been abandoned several years later, primarily because there was no evidence to suggest that either Jordan or any other Arab country was prepared to accept such a course of action. Dayan himself, writing eleven years later in his book *Living with the Bible*, explained that 'all the proposals put forward by Israel to transfer them [the refugees] to other countries and rehabilitate them there [in Arab countries], were rejected by their Arab leaders.'[139]

(ii) Resettlement in the Jordan Valley

Yosef Weitz, former head of the Jewish National Fund's Land Department and a leading Zionist proponent of 'transfer' with experience in dealing with the 'Arab problem' spanning four decades, realised immediately after the war that the 'Arab problem' had acquired a new quality. On 29 September 1967 he published an article in *Davar* in which he quoted his 1940 proposal to transfer all the Palestinians, and urged the public to consider the notion in the wake of the new conquests. The article was based on a six-page memorandum written by Weitz 12 days earlier,[140] and possibly submitted to the Israeli government for consideration.

> Amongst ourselves it must be clear that there is no room for both peoples in this country. ... With Arab transferring the country will be wide-open for us. And with the Arabs staying the country will be narrow and restricted ... the only solution is the Land of Israel, or at least the Western Land of Israel [i.e., the whole of Palestine], without Arabs. The Zionist work ... must come all simultaneously in the manner of redemption (here is the meaning of the Messianic idea); the only way is to transfer the Arabs from here to neighbouring countries, all of them, except perhaps Bethlehem, Nazareth, and old Jerusalem. Not a single village or a single tribe must be left. And the transfer must be done through their absorption in Iraq and Syria and even in Transjordan. For that goal money will be found and even a lot of money. And only then will the country be able to absorb millions of Jews. ... There is no other solution.[141]

From this perspective, Weitz explained in his *Davar* article, a solution of 'transfer' was advocated in the early 1940s and was supported by Berl Katznelson,[142] Yitzhak Volcani[143] and Menahem Ussishkin,[144] and 'investigations were undertaken to put this concept into effect.'[145] Weitz argued that 'any suggestion for the settlement of the liberated territories (the West Bank and Gaza Strip) must be subjected necessarily to a definite policy which addresses and solves three fundamental problems rendered more acute' by the June war: regional security, the demographic problem and the 'resettlement of the refugees'.

> [As to] the demographic problem, there are some who assume that non-Jewish population, even in high percentage, can be more effectively under our surveillance if it is within our boundaries, and there are some who assume the contrary. ... The author of this article tends to support the second assumption and has an additional argument to support his position: the need to sustain the character of the state, which will henceforth and obviously in the near future be Jewish, by the majority of its inhabitants, with a non-Jewish minority limited to 15%.[146]

Early on, Israeli leaders realised that the refugee communities in the West Bank and Gaza[147] in more than one way presented the most serious problem for Israel. The refugee camps were (and still are) the most overcrowded parts of the territories, and are therefore the most difficult parts to control. In addition, because the refugees did not accept their sojourn in the territories as an indefinite one, Israeli leaders saw a greater long-term challenge from the refugees than from the indigenous population. In his *Davar* article, Weitz referred to a memorandum drawn up by 'Ezra Danin, Zalman Lifschitz and himself (all members of the Israeli government Transfer Committee of 1948) called 'Memorandum On Settlement of the Arab Refugees', and dated October 1948, 'the composition of which was preceded by investigations, surveys and research based on data considered reliable at the time'.[148] In 1967 Weitz believed that 'the logical and possible way of rehabilitating the refugees in the Arab countries is blocked by their rulers, and will be blocked for a long time to come; with no alternative the way leads, at least initially', to the West Bank side of the Jordan Valley. In this region the arable lands could be increased by means of desalination and some of the refugees could be settled there. However, for Weitz, the solution for too many residents in the territories' refugee camps remained transfer. Although willing to cede some of the heavily populated regions of the territories to Jordan, Weitz argued that forestalling the Arab 'demographic problem ... should consider as an essential action towards the solution of the refugee problem making financial assistance available to families who are prepared to emigrate to countries outside the Arab world. Every financial investment in these [transfer] activities will be of great blessing to our state today and in the future.'[149]

It should be pointed out that not everyone in Israel was satisfied merely with financial incentives and encouragement of the kind proposed by Weitz. An opinion poll carried out three weeks after the

1967 victory showed 28 per cent of the Israeli Jewish electorate in favour of expelling the Palestinian citizens of Israel, and 22 per cent favouring expulsion of Palestinians from the occupied territories.[150]

In a way Weitz's practical and usually discreet approach to Arab transfer activities characterised the pragmatism of Labour Zionism and its handling of this very prickly and explosive issue. Although in 1940 he had advocated 'total' Arab removal from the whole of Palestine, in 1967 he opted for 'partial' transfer. It is likely that four decades of immersion in the attempts to implement secret plans of Arab transfer taught Weitz to take pragmatic constraints into consideration, including opposition among the Palestinians themselves, rejection from Arab states as well as the sensitivity of Western public opinion. All these factors rendered the transfer task exceedingly difficult.

RESETTLEMENT IN SOUTH AMERICA

As noted earlier, General Moshe Dayan was against the resettlement of refugees within the borders of the territories occupied by Israel in 1967; voluntary emigration was seen by him as a solution to the problem. Dayan was the most typical exponent of Israeli post-1967 expansionism and the *de facto* integration of the West Bank and the Gaza Strip into Israel. He was appointed Defence Minister on the eve of the 1967 war and retained his pivotal post until 1974. During this period he presided over a policy of 'creeping annexation', a process by which Israeli administration, jurisdiction and law were gradually imposed on the occupied territories, in ever-expanding areas, yet without a comprehensive act of legal annexation. That process of *de facto* annexation was generally seen in the actual transformation of the physical and demographic realities in these areas. Dayan also instituted a secret policy discreetly designed to thin out the refugee population of the West Bank and the Gaza Strip, beginning with the inhabitants of the refugee camps.

It seems that one of the products of the Cabinet discussions of June 1967 was the institution of a voluntary and secret project, which later became known as the 'Moshe Dayan plan', and was revealed for the first time in June 1985 by Ra'anan Weitz, who for many years headed the rural settlement department of the Jewish Agency with responsibility for settling Jews in certain areas in the West Bank. According to Ra'anan Weitz, shortly after the 1967 war Dayan worked out a secret plan for encouraging Palestinian emigration from the

West Bank and Gaza to South America. Under this scheme, each Arab family which agreed to cooperate would receive sums ranging from US$3,000 to $5,000. However, in the end, according to Weitz, the project ended in failure: scores of Arab families from the West Bank which accepted the Israeli proposals and travelled to Latin America did not succeed in establishing themselves there and after a certain period returned to their homes on the West Bank.[151]

The same plan was also referred to in public by the Likud Minister of Industry and Trade, Ariel Sharon, in November 1987.[152] According to an Israeli newspaper report, the scheme began with the formation of a highly secret unit composed of representatives of the Prime Minister's Office, the Ministry of Defence, the Israeli army and the Shabak, Israel's internal secret service. This secret unit was also called the 'Eshkol unit' named after Prime Minister Eshkol, during whose tenure of office it was set up. The unit was charged with encouraging the emigration of Palestinians, refugees and non-refugees, from the occupied territories to South America and other destinations. It functioned in the utmost secrecy for three years from the office of the Israeli military governor in Gaza city on 'Omar al-Mukhtar Street, one of the main streets in the city. The unit provided the emigrants with one-way tickets to various south American countries, mainly Paraguay, through a Tel Aviv-based travel agency, and promised to give further financial assistance to get them established once they had arrived.[153] Apparently, the military authorities in the Gaza Strip worked hard to find individual Palestinians, particularly among the residents of refugee camps, who were disappointed with their lot and might be candidates for the secret programme. The clandestine activities of the unit also included the purchase through intermediaries of land in Paraguay, Brazil and even in pre-Qaddafi Libya for carrying out the emigration and resettlement scheme.[154]

The secret operation continued for about three years, from 1967 until mid-1970. During this period the semi-official unit managed, according to an Israeli newspaper report, to arrange for the emigration of about 1,000 Palestinians.[155] However, in May 1970 the scheme came to an end as a result of a sudden development. In desperation a refugee from the Jabalya refugee camp in the Gaza Strip, the 21-year-old Talal Ibn Dimassi, who agreed to emigrate to Paraguay and was promised financial assistance and received none, went to the Israeli consulate in Asunción on 4 May 1970 and demanded to see the Israeli ambassador. When his request was denied, he pulled out a pistol and shot the ambassador's secretary dead.[156] The incident led to the collapse of the Dayan scheme.

RESETTLEMENT AS A COUNTER-INSURGENCY MEASURE

After the 1967 conquests the visible reminder which the eight large refugee camps in the Gaza Strip provided of the dispossession of 1948 constituted a major and thorny problem for the Israel army. As a focal point of growing Palestinian nationalism and militant resistance, the camps, as perceived by the occupation authorities, required constant army surveillance. Failing to encourage the emigration of a large number of the Gaza Strip's refugee population to Latin America and faced with this hostile and resentful population, the Israeli army sought to break up their concentration in an attempt to quell Palestinian resistance in the Strip.[157] By 1970, with the escalation of armed resistance in the Strip, the Israeli government began to discuss openly the need to 'thin out' Gaza's refugee camps. In 1969 the Israeli army had already embarked on a new programme to do this by coercion. The programme, which began with road-widening operations in the Strip's refugee camps, ploughing 50m-wide roads through the camps, continued throughout the 1970s. Because the refugees resisted resettlement, the road-widening operation was presented as a limited security operation to facilitate army patrols, but later developed into fully-fledged resettlement projects. The forced resettlement activities of the Israeli army in and around the Gaza Strip, under Defence Minister Dayan, were initially closely associated with General Ariel Sharon, the IDF Commander of the Southern Front (end of 1969–71). The main objective of Sharon, according to his biographer 'Uzi Benziman, was to create a 'security belt' around the heavily populated Gaza Strip:

> Sharon's plan called for the isolation of the Gaza Strip from the Sinai peninsula, severing the continuity of the Palestinian population within Gaza by introducing Jewish settlements in its midst, and thinning out the population of the refugee camps.[158]

In the late 1960s and early 1970s the Israeli army's resettlement activities in the Gaza Strip took on a combination of military/security and political dimensions. Like the Malayan 'New Villages', the 'Strategic Hamlets' in Vietnam, the 'Aldeamentos' in Angola and the 'Douars' in Algeria, the Israeli army's policy of forced refugee resettlement in the Gaza Strip was carried out within a colonial framework of counter-insurgency strategy and, more specifically, in response to the rise of the Palestinian guerrilla (*fedayeen*) organisations and the escalation of Palestinian armed resistance in the Strip. Within the context of this counter-insurgency strategy resettlement schemes were perceived as being a part of 'civic-action' projects designed to improve refugee material conditions as a requirement for the success of Israeli pacification policies.[159] In *Armed Struggle in Palestine* (1978), Bard O'Neill remarked on the importance of these 'civic action' resettlement projects as another device sought by colonial regimes or governments to sever the links between insurgents and population:

> Resettlement ... may be necessary if the government is to sever the links between the insurgents and the populace, particularly when terror and/or guerrilla attacks persist and are attributed, at least partially, to support rendered the insurgents by portions of the population. Civic action and political organization are extremely important during resettlement; indeed, they are often viewed as concomitant to that technique. The Briggs plan for moving the Chinese squatters in Malaya, the Kitchener resettlement scheme during the Boer War, and the relocation program during the Mau Mau uprising are examples where transporting segments of the population was instrumental in denying insurgents support of the population.[160]

By July 1971, Israeli army dissatisfaction with the security situation in the Gaza Strip resulted in a military scheme to relocate and resettle forcibly a large number of refugees outside the large incident-prone camps such as Jabalya. Other aspects of the plan included the construction of new roads inside the camps and the installation of electric lighting to facilitate policing. Following the second stage, which involved building new housing outside the camps and providing electricity and water, the Israeli army hoped that a series of small camps would be more manageable. It was the resettlement aspect, however, which caused the greatest furore among the refugees. Resettlement actually began in July with movement of some 100 families from Jabalya to El 'Arish in north Sinai. Although the official reason given by the Israeli army was the need to decrease the camp's population and to make way for new patrol roads, the local refugees remained opposed and a wave of protests and strikes began.

Israeli promises that choice of new housing or compensation would be given along with employment opportunities proved unpersuasive. After weeks of protest by the refugees, which had attracted widespread coverage in the Israeli press and strong criticism of General Sharon's heavy-handed activities in the Strip and north Sinai, the Jabalya resettlement scheme was halted, pending further deliberations by the Israeli government.[161]

About the same time a special cabinet committee composed of Yigal Allon, Yisrael Galili and other senior ministers arrived in the Gaza Strip for a briefing from General Sharon on his activities in the Strip and north Sinai. Sharon typically recommended to the committee members, *inter alia*, the establishment of Jewish settlements in the Strip and the total elimination of the refugee camps there and resettlement of their residents:

> I put a third proposal in front of them, essentially the same proposal I made in person to Levi Eshkol after the Six Day War – which he had rejected. I told them – Yigal Allon, Israel Galili and the others – just as I had told Eshkol, that I believed it was time to solve the Palestinian refugee problem and that I was prepared to do it. The essence of my plan was to get rid of the Palestinian refugee camps altogether. Despite the UN subsidies the refugees received and despite the powerful economic and educational uplift the camps experienced after 1967, these places still bred the most serious problems for us and always would. It would be to our great advantage to eliminate them once and for all, and in my view such a thing was quite feasible. Specifically, of the approximately 160,000 Palestinians in the camps, I believed we should resettle 70,000 in the established towns of the district, devoting the necessary resources to build new housing for them and integrate them into the normal life of these places. Another 70,000 refugees I believed we should settle in the same way in the cities and towns of Samaria and Judea. ... I recommended that we take twenty to thirty thousand Gaza refugees, families that had never had any contact with the PLO ... and settle them inside the pre-1967 boundaries of Israel. We would settle them in Nazareth, Acre, Ramle, and other places, according to the local ability to absorb them. We would have essentially nothing to lose by this gesture and everything to gain. (I did not, by the way, believe that these people deserved to come back by right. ... They had remained

> refugees because of the inhumanity of the Arab states in refusing to resettle and absorb them.[162]

Sharon was basically repeating the traditional Israeli position towards the Palestinian refugee problem: the refugees had no right to return to their villages and towns in Israel, with the exception of the suggestion he made that Israel should undertake a gesture of goodwill by resettling up to 30,000 refugees in Israel and this should be part of a wider plan for total elimination of the Gaza refugee camps. Some of the camps' residents would also be encouraged by financial incentives to emigrate to and settle in Arab countries. Sharon wrote:

> it was the obligation of the Arab world to absorb the Arab refugees. And since the Jewish as well as the Arab refugees had left all their property behind, any compensation had to be reciprocal. But though Israel's position on this was absolutely fair, I proposed that we go a step beyond it. ... I believed we could agree to pay the legitimate claims of Arab refugee families once they had permanently settled in other countries. I had no doubt whatsoever that we could establish a long-term fund for that purpose, that however large a sum we would need for this could be raised from a variety of sources, including the immensely supportive overseas Jewish communities ... the elimination of the camps would be neither easy nor quick; it would take, as I envisioned it, ten years or so.[163]

Sharon's activities in the Gaza Strip and northern Sinai, which had included the forcible eviction of 6,000 to 20,000 Bedouin farmers from their lands in the Rafah salient between 1969 and 1971,[164] had already won for him a reputation for brutality and had generated a great deal of public criticism and adverse coverage in the Israeli press. Consequently, it was unlikely that the Labour coalition government, which then included the dovish Mapam Party, would have sanctioned the implementation of Sharon's plan for the total, forcible elimination of the Gaza Strip refugee camps. In fact, Sharon complained many years later that he had not been able to persuade the Israeli ministers to approve of his 1971 plan for the total elimination of the refugee camps. The same members of the special Cabinet committee, according to Sharon, however, 'approved wholeheartedly' his proposals 'to widen the camps' streets' (which in practice amounted to thinning out the population of the camps) and to establish Jewish settlement in the midst of the Palestinian population in the densely populated Strip.[165]

In 1971 the Israeli army, in an attempt to fight the escalating Palestinian resistance in the Strip, planned to relocate one-third of the refugees to new places in the Strip and in north Sinai. This was confirmed by General Shlomo Gazit, former army coordinator for the occupied territories, who stated in an interview in 1971 'the intention to evacuate one-third of the Strip's refugee population, about 60–70,000 to new places in the Strip'.[166] In the same year the Israeli army began systematically destroying homes in refugee camps, and forcibly removing thousands of Gaza residents to El 'Arish in north Sinai; other refugees were evacuated to unoccupied refugee camps in the West Bank or small camps in Gaza. The demolition of camp shelters by road-widening operations continued through the 1970s at a slow pace. In all, road-widening operations in Gaza resulted in the demolition of 10,000 shelters between 1967 and 1984.[167] During the same period thousands of Gaza refugees were forcibly relocated to Israeli-established resettlement projects as part of Israel's policy of thinning out the crowded refugee camps.[168] The plight of some of these relocated refugees has continued to the present day. Today there are about 5,000 of these, who were first made refugees in 1948, and who had been forcibly moved by the Israeli army and placed on the Egyptian side of the Sinai border with the Gaza Strip in a resettlement project called the Canada Camp (named after the Canadian contingent of UNEF who camped there after the 1956 war). The 5,000 residents of this camp have been left in limbo since Israel withdrew from Sinai in April 1982. Because they are not Egyptian citizens, the Egyptian government expected them to be moved back to the Strip. Although agreement between Israel and Egypt was already reached in the mid-1980s on the terms of their relocation back to the Strip, it still awaits implementation.[169]

RESETTLEMENT THROUGH SOCIAL AND ECONOMIC INTEGRATION IN THE WEST BANK AND GAZA

(i) Proposals of Mapam and Israeli Academics

Since 1967 moderate and pragmatic Israelis have been calling for the rehabilitation of the refugees through their integration into the general life of the West Bank and Gaza Strip. The pragmatists, like many other Israelis, believed that the refugee camps in the West Bank and Gaza were perpetuated, to a large extent, by the existence and activities of UNRWA. Therefore getting rid of UNRWA, or at least drastically reducing its size and altering its functions in the West Bank and Gaza, would be the first step in the direction of 'solving' the refugee problem. In December 1969 and August 1972 the 'peace proposals' of Mapam, a left-wing Zionist party and a partner in the ruling Labour coalition, called for the integration of refugees in the general life of the occupied territories, through the construction of housing projects, the adoption of new socio-economic policies designed to improve living conditions in refugee camps and provision of employment.[170] Mapam's proposals were inspired by plans drafted by two teams which consisted of university professors, engineers, sociologists, economists and technical experts on water and electricity. The plans involved the evacuation of refugee camps, beginning with the Rafah camp in the Gaza Strip and the evacuation of 2,400 of the 6,000 families which lived in the camp. The two teams suggested offering economic incentives to the camp residents – for example, housing at a token price in urban regions and the improvement of public services in the new locations.

In January 1968 and again in March 1969 resettlement projects had been developed by one team consisting of Professor Michael Bruno (as chairman), Dr Yoram Ben-Porat, Dr Eytan Berglass, Professor Haim Ben-Shahar, Professor Nadav Halevy, Professor Giora Hanoch, 'Ezra Segen, and Vicky Plasger. The second team consisted of social scientists with close links to the Labour establishment, headed by Dr Rivka Bar-Yosef, whose members included economist Dr Yoram Ben-Porat, social anthropologist Professor 'Emanuel Marx and historian Professor Shimon Shamir, later to become ambassador to Egypt and Jordan. During the early 1970s Shamir, Marx and Ben-Porath conducted extensive research on the Jalazun refugee camp, near Ramallah, and other refugee camps in the West Bank. They subsequently recommended to the Israeli government that, because 'the Palestinian refugee problem was a major obstacle to peace' in the Middle East, the Israeli authorities should speed up the processes causing the refugee camps to become working-class neighbourhoods 'by taking over responsibility for the refugee from UNRWA, and by facilitating the full incorporation of the camps into the urban fabric' of West Bank towns.[171] In fact, similar, though not identical, proposals were made in the Galili Document of the late 1960s, entitled: 'Rehabilitation of Refugees and Development in the West

Bank and the Gaza Strip'. In his document Labour cabinet minister Yisrael Galili suggested the allocation of funds for a four-year plan for rehabilitation of refugees, including the setting-up of new housing projects outside the camps, the renovation of existing camps and the integration of their residents with neighbouring towns.[172] Apparently a secret trust fund was set up by another Labour cabinet minister, Shimon Peres, in May 1970 for the same purpose of economic development and refugee resettlement.[173] However, writing two decades later, Professor 'Emanuel Marx remarked somewhat critically: 'The Israeli government discussed and rejected our recommendations, on the grounds that the refugee problem should be solved in the framework of peace with the Arab states.'[174]

The slightly different proposals of Mapam were unveiled by a leading Knesset Member of the left-wing Zionist party, Dov Zakin (who was also a member of Kibbutz Lahavot Habashan) in *New Outlook* of November–December 1972. Zakin's outlines included:

- *Dissolution of the camps*. This dissolution of the camps can be accomplished gradually by offering economic incentives to the camp residents, principally (a) housing at a symbolic price in urban regions and close to new places of employment which are to be created and (b) improvement of the public services in the towns (health, education, welfare). The housing which must be dispersed in urban settlements must not have the characteristics of 'housing for refugees'. Evacuation of the camp at the rate of 4,000 to 5,000 families per annum would solve the problem within about eight years. At the same time it will be necessary to deal with those groups whose livelihood depends on the existence of the camps, such as shopkeepers and the UNRWA staff. It will also be necessary to prevent the settling of other population groups in the camps.
- *Construction*. The construction of housing to solve the housing problem of the camp inhabitants will be a powerful lever to boost economic activity and employment. Various estimates show that the very activity of building an apartment for a family creates jobs for 3–4 wage-earners (heads of families) for one year. It is assumed that local and Israeli labour and raw materials will be used in the implementation of the construction programme.
- *Limitation of agriculture*. Economic analyses show that in the development of the occupied territories and in the plans for

the rehabilitation of the refugees agriculture will play only a small part in the additional employment.

- *Industrialisation*. In the long run the development of the territories and the rehabilitation of the refugees will have to be achieved through industrialisation.
- *Investment and Financing*. The most desirable form of development of industries will be through private initiative, using local labour as far as possible, with the Israeli factor providing a helping and guiding hand when needed but not to achieve economic or political domination. To supplement private financing funds should be made available in the form of loans on easy terms to provide entrepreneurs from Israeli public sources or international funds. The Government should guarantee financial investments in the territories.[175]

The cost of one plan which involved the gradual rehabilitation of the camp inhabitants, including creating employment and providing housing, was estimated at 50 million Israeli lira per annum in the first four years and about 80 million per annum in the following four years. The investment involved in the resettlement of a refugee family, including housing, was estimated at an average of 20,000 to 25,000 Israeli lira.[176] With regard to the provision of incentives, the team's programme explained that

> The incentives are meant to hasten the process of evacuating the camps as part of the general change. Caution must be observed to prevent the impression among the refugees that the evacuation policy will liquidate their status as refugees or undermine its two basic principles – the right to the return of property and to draw food rations and other UNRWA amenities. The supply of housing or any other assistance was not to be linked to the matter of compensation for property in Israel or with giving up the refugee ration cards.

(ii) Likud's Schemes

In 1975 the election platform of the Likud, then in opposition, proposed settling the Palestinian refugee problem on the basis of an 'exchange' of people and property between Palestinian refugees and Jewish immigrants from Arab countries.[177] In 1982 the Likud government of Menahem Begin appointed a ministerial committee headed by Mordechai Ben-Porat (an Iraqi Jew and minister without portfolio) to look into the refugee question. In December of the same year the Israeli authorities issued an order making building or adding to the camp shelters an offence. Penalties for violators involved paying heavy fines or imprisonment besides the removal of the building at the expense of the contravenor.[178] A year later, on 20 November 1983, Ben-Porat, who was later to become head of the World Organisation of Jews from Arab Countries (WOJAC), unveiled by far the largest and most ambitious resettlement scheme to be put forward by Israel after 1967. Ben-Porat, reiterating the classical Israeli position of rejecting refugee repatriation or compensation for lost property, came up with a detailed plan to integrate the refugees in the West Bank and Gaza in neighbouring towns through the dismantlement of 28 refugee camps. His resettlement project involving resettling 30,000 refugee families (about 250,000 people; nearly a quarter of all refugees in the West Bank and Gaza) over a period of five years, put the cost of the project at $2 million, to be raised from the United States and European countries.[179] Speaking at a press conference, Ben-Porat described the Likud government's intention to erase the camps as 'humanitarian and voluntary' and talked about foreign aid to finance his scheme, but failed to indicate how the scheme would be implemented in practice.[180] The Ben-Porat programme involved removing refugee camps in the occupied territories and the resettlement of their inhabitants, on a 'voluntary' basis, in new housing in neighbouring towns and cities in the occupied territories. Although the full details of the scheme were never fully disclosed by the Likud government, Israeli sources did reveal many of its basic elements:

- the plan to be carried out in phases over a five-year period;
- new houses for camp residents to be built in five stages: 5 per cent of the population would be housed during the first year, 15 per cent during the second year, 25 per cent during the third year, and 30 per cent during each of the fourth and fifth years;
- land and financial aid to be given under the motto 'build your own home' in accordance with an overall plan;
- an independent municipal status to be given to the new housing settlement;
- the overall coordination of the project with UNRWA to be ensured, incorporating UNRWA's educational and social

services into existing governmental institutions in the West Bank and Gaza;[181]

- proposed locations for resettlement were to be: the Fasayel area in Jordan Valley as a priority; and two refugee camps near Jerusalem (Qalandia and Shu'afat) to be among the first refugee camps to be cleared.[182] Another location for resettlement was to be the Jericho area, where relocated refugees would occupy three empty camps whose former residents were driven out across the river to Jordan during the 1967 war.[183]

In 1983 Ben-Porat stated that the ambitious Likud resettlement and 'rehabilitation' project in the West Bank and Gaza would be an example and a model for the resettlement of other Palestinian refugee communities in the Middle East.[184] However, nothing came out of this project, partly because of Israel's protracted military involvement in Lebanon and partly because of the widespread opposition of the Palestinian refugees themselves.[185] When Israeli efforts to secure American and European funds failed, the plan completely disappeared from official Israeli policy.[186]

The eruption of the Palestinian *intifada* (uprising) in 1987 saw yet another series of Israeli proposals focusing on refugee resettlement schemes in the Arab countries. During a visit to the US in 1989 Prime Minister Yitzhak Shamir called for the convening of an international conference to solve the refugee issue. Israel, he said, would contribute expertise and ideas to resettlement projects, and the United States, the Arab countries, and the international community, could fund them. Shamir's ideas echoed similar ideas raised by Yitzhak Rabin, then Minister of Defence in the National Unity Government, who proposed dismantling refugee camps because they posed a security threat to Israel's control of the West Bank and Gaza. Likud Moshe Arens, who succeeded Rabin in the Defence Ministry, also called on the US government to head a campaign to raise $2 billion for resettling the refugees.[187] Although nothing came out of these proposals, they reflected the well-known and rigid positions that had been reiterated by Israel consistently since 1948.

EPILOGUE

The Israeli position towards the 1948 refugees has always emphasised their resettlement and rehabilitation in the Arabs states, rather than repatriation and/or compensation. Israel has always maintained that there can be no return of the refugees to Israeli territories, and that the only solution to the problem was their resettlement in the Arab states or elsewhere. Israel has not wanted the refugees back under any condition. It has not wanted them to return because it has needed their lands and their villages for Jewish immigrants. Nor has it wanted the repatriation of a large Palestinian population that would question the Zionist-Jewish character of the state and undermine it demographically. Israel did, however, consider in the 1950s some form of restitution of refugee property in lieu of repatriation, although all attempts to work out policy on compensation were tied to a settlement of abandoned Jewish property in Arab states.

In the 1950s the Israeli Foreign Ministry attempted to 'dissolve' the refugee problem and disperse the Palestinian refugees through Western-sponsored employment projects and resettlement schemes in neighbouring Arab countries. While the desire among Israeli leaders to resettle the refugees in the Arab states or elsewhere, or, stated baldly, to be rid of the 'Palestinian refugee problem', remained a constant until the present day, the envisaged modalities of resettlement changed over the years according to circumstances. Realistic assessments during the 1950s and after 1967 necessitated strategies and planning that produced a series of specific resettlement schemes, generally involving a few Arab states – such as Iraq, Syria, pre-Qaddafi Libya, El 'Arish in Sinai, the West Bank and Gaza Strip, and various Latin American countries. This preoccupation with the need to thin out the refugee camps and resettle their residents stemmed from a variety of reasons including the fear of refugee return and the determination to remove the refugee problem from the centre of the Arab–Israeli conflict.

During the early 1950s and the short-lived occupation of the Gaza in 1956–7, and especially in the aftermath of the 1967 conquests of the West Bank and Gaza, the Israeli authorities drafted a range of proposals and plans designed to encourage the resettlement of Palestinian refugees. During this period several Israeli ministers and senior officials, who realised that neither Egypt nor Syria nor Iraq had any intention of opening their borders for the masses of refugees in the West Bank and Gaza, suggested in internal debates and secret correspondence that Israel should encourage the refugees under its control to emigrate to countries overseas, particularly Latin America. Several emigration and resettlement projects were attempted by the Labour government in the aftermath of the June 1967 war. Although the official, though largely secret, resettlement schemes of the 1950s and 1960s ended in failure, they are significant in the sense of showing how successive Israeli governments wanted to remove both the refugee question from the heart of the Arab–Israeli conflict and the possibility of refugee return in the future. The practical (and usually discreet) approach to resettlement plans and activities characterised the pragmatism of Labour Zionism.

To sum up, although since 1948 Israel has put forward many plans for resettling the refugees in the Arab states, the fact that no such resettlement has taken place is due to several factors including:

- the refugees' desire for repatriation, their determination to return to their homes and their traditional rejection of resettlement in the Arab states;
- the emergence of the refugees' own powerful diaspora nationalism, furthermore, precluded accepting resettlement outside their traditional homeland;[188]
- the unwillingness of the host Arab states (with the exception of Jordan) to absorb the refugees; historically the Arab states held Israel responsible for creating the refugee problem and demanded publicly that the refugees be repatriated to their homes and lands;
- the growth in Palestinian nationalism since the mid-1960s and the emergence of the PLO as a national organisation dedicated to regaining Palestinian rights;[189] the development of a powerful Palestinian nationalism militated against any idea of resettling the refugees outside mandatory Palestine.[190]

Over the years the Israelis became more realistic in their attitudes towards refugee resettlement schemes. For instance, on 7 December 1976, Deputy Prime Minister Yigal Allon explained at a political discussion in Jerusalem that the failure to carry out the resettlement of the Gaza refugees in Sinai had brought him to the conclusion there was a need to give up most of the Gaza Strip.[191] It is also likely that several decades of immersion in the attempts to implement plans of refugee resettlement have taught Israeli government officials to take pragmatic constraints into consideration, including opposition among the refugees themselves, rejection from Arab states as well as the sensitivity of Western public opinion. All these constraints rendered the refugee resettlement task exceedingly difficult.

NOTES

1. Benny Morris, *The Birth of the Palestinian Refugee Problem, 1947–1949* (Cambridge: Cambridge University Press, 1987), pp.275–85.
2. Elia Zureik, *Palestinian Refugees and the Peace Process* (Washington DC: Institute for Palestine Studies, 1996), p.68; Nawaf Al-Zaru, 'Israeli Plans to Liquidate the Palestinian Camps', *Samid al-Iqtisadi*, no.83 (1991), pp.134–42 (Arabic).
3. Norma Masriyeh Hazboun, *Israeli Resettlement Schemes for Palestinian Refugees in the West Bank and Gaza Strip since 1967* (Ramallah, Palestinian Diaspora and Refugee Centre-Shaml, 1996) at: http://www.shaml.org/publications/monos/mono4.htm (accessed on 1 December 2001).
4. Richard Locke and Antony Stewart, *Bantustan Gaza* (London: Zed Book, 1985), p.58; Bard E. O'Neill, *Armed Struggle in Palestine: A Political Military Analysis* (Boulder: Colorado, Westview Press, 1978), pp.96–7.
5. Avi Shlaim, 'Husni Zaim and the Plan to Resettle Palestinian Refugees in Syria', *Middle East Focus* 9, no.2 (Fall 1986), pp.26–31. The al-Jazira plan was also enthusiastically supported by George McGhee, special assistant to the US Secretary of State. For an extensive discussion of Zionist proposals to 'transfer' Palestinians to the al-Jazira region in the late 1930s and early 1940s, see Nur Masalha, *Expulsion of the Palestinians: The Concept of 'Transfer' in Zionist Political Thought, 1882–1948* (Washington DC: Institute for Palestine Studies, 1992), pp.130–41.
6. Michael Palumbo, *Imperial Israel* (London: Bloomsbury, updated edition, 1992), p.28; Paul Cossali and Clive Robson, *Stateless in Gaza* (London: Zed Books, 1986), pp.13–15. Quoted in *New Outlook* 4, no.9 (December 1961), p.9.
7. Cited in Elia Zureik, *Palestinian Refugees and the Peace Process*, pp.70–1.
8. Quoted in *al-Sharq al-Awsat* (London), 16 October 1993. For an Israeli perspective on the final status solution to the refugee problem, see also Shlomo Gazit, *The Palestinian Refugee Problem* (Tel Aviv: Tel Aviv University, The Jaffee Centre for Strategic Studies, 1995).
9. See 'Ezra Danin, *Tzioni Bekhol Tnai* [A Zionist in Every Condition], Vol.1 (Jerusalem: Kiddum, 1987), p.317.
10. For further discussion of the '100 thousand' offer see Varda Schiffer, 'The 1949 Israeli Offer to Repatriate 100,000 Palestinian Refugees', *Middle East Focus* 9, no.2 (Fall 1986), pp.14–20; Morris, *The Birth of the Palestinian Refugee Problem*, pp. 275–85; Muhammad Abu-Masara, 'Be'ayat Haplitim Bamdiniyut Hayisraelit Bashanim 1948–49', [The Refugee Problem in Israeli Policy in 1948–49], *International Problems, Society and Politics* 28, no.53 (1989), pp.48–53.
11. Gazit, *The Palestinian Refugee Problem*, p.11.
12. Charles S. Kamen, 'After the Catastrophe I: The Arabs in Israel, 1948–51', *Middle Eastern Studies* 23, no. 4 (October 1987), pp.462–3.
13. On Arab refugee 'infiltration', see Benny Morris, *Israel's Border Wars, 1949–1956* (Oxford: Clarendon Press, 1993), pp.28–68.
14. Segev, *1949: The First Israelis*, p.52.
15. Morris, *Israel's Border Wars*, pp.135–7.

16. Livia Rokach, 'Israel State Terrorism: An Analysis of the Sharett Diaries', *Journal of Palestine Studies* 9, no.3 (Spring 1980), p.21.
17. Benny Morris, 'Yosef Weitz and the Transfer Committees, 1948–49', *Middle Eastern Studies* 22, no.4 (October 1986), pp.549–50.
18. Simha Flapan, *The Birth of Israel: Myths and Realities* (New York: Pantheon books, 1987), p.107; Joseph Schechtman, *The Arab Refugee Problem* (New York: Philosophical Library, 1952); Joseph Schechtman, *European Population Transfers 1939–1945* (New York: Oxford University Press, 1946); Joseph Schechtman, *Population Transfers in Asia* (New York: Hallsby Press, 1949); Joseph Schechtman, *Post-War Population Transfers in Europe, 1945–1955* (Liverpool, Charles Birchall and Sons, 1962).
19. I first came across the manuscript of Schechtman's 'study' in Weitz's Papers, at the Institute for Settlement Studies, Rehovot, in 1989. In 1993 I saw a copy of the same manuscript in Weitz's Papers, in the Central Zionist Archives in Jerusalem.
20. From Arthur Lourie, Consulate General of Israel, New York, to Moshe Shertok (later Sharett), Foreign Minister, letter dated 15 October 1948, in Israel State Archives (ISA), Foreign Ministry, 2402/15.
21. From Joseph B. Schechtman to 'Ezra Danin, Israeli Ministry of Foreign Affairs, letter dated 7 December 1948, in Jabotinsky Institute, Schechtman's Papers, file F. 2/10/227.
22. Moshe Shertok, Paris, to Dr Schechtman, New York, letter dated 17 December 1948, Foreign Ministry, 2402/15.
23. Joseph Schechtman, 'The Case for Arab-Jewish Exchange of Population', manuscript (in Weitz's Papers, Institute for Settlement Study, Rehovot), pp.75–6.
24. Ibid., p.103.
25. For further discussion of Ben-Horin's plan of transfer to Iraq, 1943–8, see Masalha, *Expulsion of the Palestinians*, pp.161–5; Eliahu Ben-Horin, *The Middle East: Crossroads of History* (New York: W. W. Norton & Company, 1943), pp.224–37.
26. Masalha, *Expulsion of the Palestinians*, pp.162–4.
27. Schechtman, 'The Case for Arab-Jewish Exchange of Population', p.156.
28. Joseph Schechtman, New York, to Eliyahu Epstein, Washington DC, letter dated 20 May 1948, in Jabotinsky Institute, Schechtman's Papers, F. 2/10/227.
29. Schechtman, 'The Case for Arab-Jewish Exchange of Population', pp.103–4.
30. Ibid., p.158.
31. Ibid., pp.160–1.
32. One dunum equals 1,000 square metres.
33. Schechtman, 'The Case for Arab-Jewish Exchange of Population', p.163.
34. For further discussion of Norman's plan, see Masalha, *Expulsion of the Palestinians*, pp.141–55; Moshe Shertok, Paris, to Edward Norman, letter dated 17 December 1948, Foreign Ministry 2402/15.
35. Epstein to Schechtman, letter dated 18 May 1948, in Jabotinsky Institute, Schechtman's Papers, F. 1/10/227.
36. Edward Norman, to Foreign Minister Moshe Shertok, letter dated 24 December 1948, Foreign Ministry, 2402/15.

37. Joseph Schechtman, *Population Transfers in Asia*, pp.84–145.
38. Joseph Schechtman, *The Arab Refugee Problem*, (New York: Philosophical Library, 1952).
39. Schechtman's letter to Hoover, dated 9 April 1949, in Jabotinsky Institute, Schechtman's Papers, file F. 1/11/227.
40. Labib Qudsiyyah, *Al-Lajiun al-Filastiniyun fi al-'Iraq* [The Palestinian Refugees in Iraq], Monograph no.7 (Ramallah, Palestine: Palestinian Diaspora and Refugee Centre-Shaml, 1997) at: http://www.shaml.org/arabic/publications/monos/a_m007.htm (accessed on 1 December 2001).
41. Ibid.
42. Danin, *Tzioni Bekhol Tnai*, Vol.1, p.317.
43. Yosef Weitz, *Yomani Veigrotai Labanim* [My Diary and Letters to the Children] (Tel Aviv: Massada, 1965), Vol. 4, entry for 23 January 1949, p.7.
44. Danin, *Tzioni Bekhol Tnai*, Vol.1, p.319; Benny Morris, *1948 and After: Israel and the Palestinians* (Oxford: Clarendon Press, 1990), p.138, citing Danin's letter to Weitz from London dated 26 April 1949.
45. Weitz, *Yomani Veigrotai Labanim*, Vol. 4, entry for 27 July 1949, p.42.
46. Quoted in Kamen, 'After the Catastrophe I', p.462.
47. Ibid., p.463.
48. Schiffer, 'The 1949 Israeli Offer to Repatriate 100,000 Palestinian Refugees', pp.14–20; Morris, *The Birth of the Palestinian Refugee Problem*, pp. 275–85; Abu-Masara, 'Be'ayat Haplitim Bamdiniyut Hayisraelit Bashanim 1948–49', pp.48–53.
49. Morris, *The Birth of the Palestinian Refugee Problem*, pp.266–7.
50. Ben-Gurion's diary, 26 June 1949, cited in Avi Shlaim, *Collusion Across the Jordan, King Abdullah, the Zionist Movement, and the Partition of Palestine* (Oxford: Clarendon Press; Toronto: Columbia University Press, 1988), p.471.
51. Morris, *The Birth of the Palestinian Refugee Problem*, p.268.
52. Ibid.
53. Ibid, pp.266–70.
54. Danin, *Tzioni Bekhol Tnai*, Vol.1, p.317.
55. Ibid.
56. Ibid.
57. Morris, *1948 and After*, pp.139–40.
58. Danin, *Tzioni Bekhol Tnai*, Vol.1, p.317.
59. Ibid.
60. Ibid., p.318.
61. Kaplan's latter dated 7 July 1950, no.1613710/18998, in ISA, Foreign Ministry, 2402/16. A copy of the letter was also sent to Sharett.
62. Danin, *Tzioni Bekhol Tnai*, Vol.1, p.318.
63. Weitz, *Yomani Veigrotai Labanim*, Vol.6, appendix 21, p.526.
64. See Gordon's memo, dated 24 March 1950, in ISA, Foreign Ministry, 2402/15.
65. See Palmon's letter, dated 17 April 1950, no.12246/89, in ISA, Foreign Ministry, 2402/15.

66. From M. Sasson, Foreign Ministry Middle East Department, to Foreign Minister, Most Secret letter, dated 13 March 1952, in Israel State Archives (ISA), Foreign Ministry, 2402/5. Copies of the letter were also sent to Foreign Ministry Director General (Walter Eytan), Prime Minister's advisor for Arab affairs (Yehoshu'a Palmon), and Israel's ambassador to Turkey (Eliyahu Sasson).
67. Ibid.
68. *New Encyclopedia of Zionism and Israel*, Vol.1 (London and Toronto: Associated University Presses, 1994), p.468.
69. Weitz, *Yomani Veigrotai Labanim*, Vol.4, entry for 13 May 1954, p.285.
70. Ibid.
71. Danin, *Tzioni Bekhol Tnai*, Vol.1, p.323.
72. Weitz, *Yomani Veigrotai Labanim*, Vol.4, entry for 25 October 1954, p.270.
73. Ibid., entry for 1 November 1954, p.270.
74. Ibid.
75. Ibid., entry for 13 November 1954, p.272; Danin, *Tzioni Bekhol Tnai*, Vol.1, p.323. Two days earlier, on 11 November, two Jews, one a lawyer from Haifa and the other from Tunisia, came to see Weitz and told him that they had brought to Finance Minister Eshkol a plan concerning the setting-up of a company abroad with the capital of half a million dollars for the purchase of Jewish properties in Tunisia and Morocco and its exchange with Arab properties in Israel. See ibid., entry for 11 November 1954, p.271.
76. Weitz, *Yomani Veigrotai Labanim*, Vol.4, entry for 5 May 1955, p.294.
77. Ibid., entry for 11 May 1955, p.295.
78. Ibid., appendix 8, entries for 25 and 26 May 1955, p.375.
79. Ibid., appendix 8, entry for 2 June 1955, p.377.
80. Ibid., entry 5 June 1955, p.377.
81. Ibid., entry for 28 June 1955, p.295.
82. Ibid., entry for 6 November 1955, pp.303–4.
83. Ibid., entry for 18 January 1956, p.311; Sharett, *Yoman Ishi*, Vol.5, entry for 18 January 1956, p.1335.
84. Weitz, *Yomani Veigrotai Labanim*, Vol.4, entry for 27 February 1956, p.313.
85. Ibid., entry for 29 February 1956, p.314.
86. Ibid., entry for 21 May 1956, pp.322–3.
87. Ibid.
88. Sharett's letter to Weitz, dated 30 May 1956, no. 27/5/56, in CZA, Weitz's papers, A246/819.
89. Danin, *Tzioni Bekhol Tnai*, Vol.1, p.323.
90. Ibid., p.324.
91. Ibid.
92. In his letter to Eliyahu Sasson, dated 17 November 1957, Danin wrote that Jon Kimche had suggested that he meet a top man from the Shell oil company, who determined the politics of the company in the Persian Gulf and controlled millions of pounds sterling. Apparently this contact with the man from Shell was in connection with Danin's search for large employment projects for the refugees aimed at economically 'dissolving' the refugee problem. See ibid., p.253.

93. Undated strictly secret note, signed by Yosef Weitz, in Weitz's Papers, III, General A. The Arabs, in the Institute for Settlement Study, Rehovot.
94. Weitz, *Yomani Veigrotai Labanim*, Vol.4, entry for 17 June 1956, pp.324–5.
95. Ibid., Vol. 6, appendix 21, p.528.
96. Danin, *Tzioni Bekhol Tnai*, Vol.1, pp.324–5; Weitz, *Yomani Veigrotai Labanim*, Vol.4, entry for 10 July 1956, p.325.
97. Weitz, *Yomani Veigrotai Labanim*, Vol.4, entry for 4 October 1956, p.336.
98. Danin, *Tzioni Bekhol Tnai*, Vol.1, p.324;
99. Ibid., p.325.
100. Ibid.
101. Ibid., pp.346–7, citing his letter to Rabin, Israel's ambassador to Washington, dated 20 July 1969.
102. Cited in the *New York Times*, 11 November 1956.
103. Michael Bar-Zohar, *Mool Hamarah Haakhzarit: Yisrael Berega'a Haemet* [Facing a Cruel Mirror: Israel's Moment of Truth], (Tel Aviv: Yedi'ot Aharonot Books, 1990), p.27.
104. Danin, *Tzioni Bekhol Tnai*, Vol. 1, pp.328–9.
105. Yosef Weitz (ed.), *Yosef Nahmani: Ish Hagalil* [Yosef Nahmani: Man of Galilee], (Ramat Gan: Massada, 1969), p.139.
106. Quoted in Yosef Carmel, *Yitzhak Ben-Tzvi: Metokh Yoman Bevet Hanasi* [Diary of Yitzhak Ben-Tzvi's bodyguard] (Ramat Gan: Massada, 1967), p.92.
107. Moshe Sharett, *Yoman Ishi* [Personal Diary], Vol.7, entry for 20 November 1956 (Tel Aviv: Sifriyat Ma'ariv, 1978), p.1866.
108. ISA, Foreign Ministry, 3085/16, from Israel's Minister to Stockholm, Haim Yahil, to Foreign Ministry's Director General, Walter Eytan, secret and personal letter no. ST/101, dated 28 November 1956.
109. ISA, Foreign Ministry, 3085/16, from Haim Yahil, Stockholm, to Walter Eytan, secret letter, dated 26 December 1956.
110. ISA, Foreign Ministry, 3085/16, G. Avner, to Y. Hertzog, Israel's Minister to Washington, secret letter dated 24 January 1957. Abba Eban is also brother-in-law of Haim Hertzog.
111. Avner also served as ambassador to Norway, 1962–3; ambassador to Canada, 1963–7; President of Haifa University, 1977–81.
112. Avner to Hertzog, letter dated 24 January 1957, ibid.
113. ISA, Foreign Ministry, 2448/8.
114. David Ben-Gurion, *Israel: A Personal History* (New York: Funk & Wagnalls, 1971), p.534.
115. ISA, Foreign Ministry, 3085/16, from Y. H. Levine, to Y. Hertzog, memo no. YHL/114.
116. Central Zionist Archives (CZA) (Jerusalem), A 300/54, Ben-Horin's file.
117. Lessing Rosenwald was an American non-Zionist Jewish merchant and philanthropist. In 1943 he led the foundation of the American Council for Judaism and was its first president. Before 1948 the Council was against the establishment of a Jewish state in Palestine. It is not clear whether Rosenwald would have been interested in cooperating with an Israeli plan of transferring Palestinian refugees from the Gaza Strip to the USA or Latin America. His younger brother William, a financier,

served as chairman of the National United Jewish Appeal campaign, and vice-chairman of the Joint Distribution Committee, American Jewish Committee, and United HIAS Service. Although generally non-Zionists, the Rosenwalds contributed modestly to Jewish educational and agricultural institutions in Palestine.

118. ISA, Foreign Ministry, 3085/16, Hanan Bar-On, to Ya'acov Hertzog and Shmuel Divon, personal and secret letter, dated 14 March 1957. HIAS is the international migration agency of the organised American Jewish community. It assists Jewish migrants and works with various agencies to increase Jewish immigration opportunities.
119. Danin, *Tzioni Bekhol Tnai*, Vol.1, p.251, citing a letter to Shaltiel dated 21 March 1957.
120. Zureik, *Palestinian Refugees and the Peace Process*, p.65.
121. The *Jerusalem Post*, 6 December 1987.
122. Dov Zakin, 'Rehabilitation of the Refugees', *New Outlook* 15, no.9 (November–December 1972), pp.59–67.
123. Emanuel Marx, 'Palestinian Refugee Camps in the West Bank and the Gaza Strip', *Middle Eastern Studies* 28, no.2 (April 1992), p.281.
124. Hazboun, *Israeli Resettlement Schemes for Palestinian Refugees in the West Bank and Gaza Strip*, pp.1–22.
125. The *Observer*, 17 December 1967.
126. See articles by Meir Avidan in *Davar*, 2, 5 and 19 June 1987.
127. Yossi Melman and Dan Raviv, 'Expelling Palestinians', *Washington Post*, 7 February 1988; The *Guardian Weekly*, 21 February 1988; *Davar*, 19 February 1988, pp.10–11.
128. Melman and Raviv, 'Expelling Palestinians', *Washington Post*, 7 February 1988; Avidan, in *Davar*, 2 June 1987.
129. Avidan, in *Davar*, 2 June 1987.
130. Ibid.
131. Ibid.
132. Cited by Shimon Ballas, in *Haumah*, no.2 (November 1967), p.216.
133. Weitz, *Yomani Veigrotai Labanim*, Vol.6, appendix 21, p.529.
134. Yuval Elitzur, in *Ma'ariv*, 4 August 1967.
135. See 'Amir Shapira, in *'Al-Hamishmar*, 12 May 1972, supplement; *Davar*, 25 July 1972; Dani Tzedoki, in *Davar*, 31 August 1972.
136. *Haaretz*, 13 November 1992.
137. Ballas, in *Haumah*, p.216
138. Cited in Tzvi Shiloah, *Ashmat Yerushalayim* [The Guilt of Jerusalem] (Tel Aviv: Karni Publishing House, 1989), p.36.
139. Moshe Dayan, *Lihyot 'Im Hatanakh* [Living with the Bible] (Jerusalem: 'Edanim Press, 1978), p.143.
140. See Weitz's memorandum: 'The Problem: The Refugees', dated 17 September 1967, in Weitz's Papers, The Institute for Settlement Studies, Rehovot; *Davar*, 29 September 1967.
141. This quote is found in the manuscript of Weitz's Diary in the Central Zionist Archives (Jerusalem) A246/7, entry for 20 December 1940, pp.1090–1. The quote in the article in *Davar* is a slightly edited version of the entry in the diary. The *Davar* article is entitled: 'A Solution to the Refugee Problem: An Israeli State with a Small Arab Minority'.

142. Katznelson was the founder and the leading ideologue of Mapai, the hard-core political component of the Labour Party.
143. Volcani was for many years a director of the Jewish National Fund and a member of the Executive Committee of the Histadrut.
144. Ussishkin was a key leader of the Zionist movement and the Jewish National Fund Board of Directors, the Chairmanship of the latter resting in his hands for nearly 20 years (1923–41).
145. Weitz hints here at the Jewish Agency Transfer Committees and schemes before 1948 and his own investigations in preparation for carrying out the transfer solution. See Masalha, *Expulsion of the Palestinians*, pp.49–199.
146. In fact the figure 15 per cent was referred to for the first time in 1948 in the recommendations of the Israeli Government Transfer Committee – of which Weitz was a member, submitted to Prime Minister Ben-Gurion, on 26 October 1948. According to these recommendations the Arabs should not exceed 15 per cent of the population of the mixed cities such as Haifa.
147. The number of the refugees on the West Bank registered with the United Nations Relief and Works Agency (UNRWA) in 1984 was 357,000. In the Gaza Strip an estimated two-thirds of the 700,000 inhabitants are refugees.
148. The Memorandum was not designed for publication but drafted for Ben-Gurion by the then Transfer Committee.
149. *Davar*, 29 September 1967.
150. Israeli Institute of Applied Social Research, 'Israeli and Palestinian public opinion,' p.154, cited in D. McDowall, *Palestine and Israel: The Uprising and Beyond* (London, I.B. Tauris, 1989), p.197. Dr Ya'acov Cohen of the Hebrew University's Hillel institution wrote an article in *Davar* on 4 October 1967 (p.14), about the 'dangerous nationalistic atmosphere which has been created in the wake of the 1967 war and asked "isn't it a fact that many Jews in Israel would welcome the emigration of the Israeli Arabs to Arab countries?"'
151. *Ma'ariv*, 2 June 1985, p.2; Mordechai Nisan, *Hamedinah Hayehudit Vehabe'ayah Ha'arvit* [The Jewish State and the Arab Problem] (Jerusalem: Rubin Press, 1987), pp.119 and 200.
152. Melman and Raviv, 'Expelling Palestinians'; Melman and Raviv, in *Davar*, 19 February 1988.
153. Ibid.
154. Ibid.
155. Melman and Raviv, in *Davar*, 19 February 1988.
156. Ibid.
157. Locke and Stewart, *Bantustan Gaza*, p.58; O'Neill, *Armed Struggle in Palestine*, pp.96–7.
158. Uzi Benziman, *Sharon: An Israeli Caesar* (London: Robson Books, 1987), p.119.
159. Haboun, *Israeli Resettlement Schemes for Palestinian Refugees*, p.15.
160. O'Neill, *Armed Struggle in Palestine*, p.31.
161. Ibid., pp.96–7.
162. Ariel Sharon, *Warrior: The Autobiography of Ariel Sharon* (London: Macdonald, 1989), pp. 258–59.

163. Ibid., pp.258–60.
164. Moshe Negbi, *Kevalim Shel Tzedek* [added title: Justice Under Occupation] (Jerusalem: Cana Publishing House, 1981), p.30.
165. Sharon, *Warrior*, p.260.
166. *Al-Quds*, 22 August 1971; *The Times*, 22 July 1971.
167. 'Palestine Refugees Today,' UNRWA *newsletter*, no.108 (October 1984), cited in Locke and Stewart, *Bantustan Gaza*, pp.59 and 62.
168. For further discussion of Israeli resettlement projects in the Gaza Strip, see Norma Masriyeh, 'Refugee Resettlement: The Gaza Strip Experience', *Israel-Palestine Journal* 11, no. 4 (Autumn 1995), pp.59–64; Norma Masriyeh, 'The Resettlement of Palestinian Refugees in the Gaza Strip' (unpublished Ph.D. dissertation, University of Leeds, 1994); Nawwaf Zaru, 'The Israeli Projects to Eliminate Palestinian Refugee Camps', *Samid al-Iqtisadi*, no.83 (January–March 1991) (Arabic).
169. Locke and Stewart, *Bantustan Gaza*, pp.58–9; Deborah Pugh in the *Guardian*, 4 January 1993; Ann M. Lesch, 'Gaza: Forgotten Corner of Palestine', *Journal of Palestine Studies* 15, no.1 (Autumn 1985), pp.53–4.
170. Hazboun, *Israeli Resettlement Schemes for Palestinian Refugees*, p.3.
171. Marx, 'Palestinian Refugee Camps in the West Bank and the Gaza Strip', p.282.
172. See *Davar*, 16 August 1973.
173. The *Observer*, 1 August 1971; the *Jerusalem Post*, 22 September 1971.
174. Marx, 'Palestinian Refugee Camps in the West Bank and the Gaza Strip', p.282.
175. Dov Zakin, 'Rehabilitation of the Refugees', *New Outlook* 15, no.9 (November–December 1972), pp.62–3.
176. Ibid., pp.63–4.
177. Zureik, *Palestinian Refugees and the Peace Process*, p.69; Al-Zaru, 'Israeli Plans to Liquidate the Palestinian Camps'.
178. *Al-Fajr*, 2 December 1983 (English).
179. Zureik, *Palestinian Refugees and the Peace Process*, p.69.
180. Locke and Stewart, *Bantustan Gaza*, p.58.
181. Zureik, *Palestinian Refugees and the Peace Process*, pp.69–70; Zvit Steinboim, *The Palestinian Refugees: Portrait and Possible Solutions* (Tel Aviv: Tel Aviv University, 1993) (Hebrew).
182. *Al-'Awdah*, December 1983 and *al-Huriyya*, October 1985, cited in Hazboun, *Israeli Resettlement Schemes for Palestinian Refugees*, p.6
183. *Al-Bayadir al-Siyasi*, November 1983.
184. Jerusalem Post, 21 November 1983, cited in Hazboun, *Israeli Resettlement Schemes for Palestinian Refugees*, p.6
185. Zureik, *Palestinian Refugees and the Peace Process*, p.69.
186. Milton Viorst, *UNRWA and Peace in the Middle East* (Washington DC: The Middle East Institute, 1984).
187. Zureik, *Palestinian Refugees and the Peace Process*, p.70.
188. Benjamin N. Schiff, *Refugees unto the Third Generation: UN Aid to Palestinians* (New York: Syracuse University Press, 1995), p.5.
189. Zureik, *Palestinian Refugees and the Peace Process*.
190. Schiff, *Refugees Unto the Third Generation*, p.5.
191. See Yosef Harif in *Ma'ariv*, 8 December 1976, p.1.

4 Israeli Approaches to Restitution of Property and Compensation (1948–56)

INTRODUCTION

The creation of Israel in 1948 led to the eviction and displacement of over 750,000 Palestinian refugees and the subsequent loss of an enormous amount of land and other property belonging to the refugees. In the post-1948 period Israel displayed more flexibility on the question of compensation for loss of refugee land and other property than it did on the question of the 'right of return'. This flexibility also went hand-in-hand with Israel's economic approach to the refugee question: to try to solve the problem mainly through the integration of the refugees into the economies of various Arab countries and through the initiation of various organised resettlement schemes. While Israel's obligation to compensate Palestinian refugees for land and other property owned by them was affirmed in paragraph 11 of United Nations General Assembly Resolution 194 (III) of December 1948, successive Israeli governments not only denied the Palestinian refugees their rights over their property, but also adopted the attitude that they were only prepared 'to consider a measure of compensation', and that only if the necessary funds became available. Although the Israelis took possession of the refugee lands and other property and exploited them as if they were their rightful owners, they began to argue that they, alone, could not be expected to pay for them. This line of thinking is found in the following statement made by the Israeli representative at the UN before the Ad Hoc Political Committee in 1954:

> My Government reaffirms its willingness to consider a measure of compensation for abandoned Arab lands. ... The first, quite simply, is money – the ability to pay. It will be understood that such a financial operation does not depend on us, and – with the best will in the world – it would be premature to make specific proposals until we have found means of making the necessary sums available.

In a similar vein, the pragmatic Prime Minister Moshe Sharett, in a speech at the annual Mapai conference on 21 August 1954, reminded his listeners that Israel had some obligation to compensate Arab refugees for land and other property 'formerly' owned by them. He stated that it was not necessary to budget immediately for such compensation, and it was inconceivable that Israel should make payments while the Arab states maintained their economic boycott of Israel. He declared, nevertheless, that the obligation still existed.[1]

After 1948 and throughout the early to mid-1950s Israel consistently resisted any outside mediation (i.e., with proposals) on the Palestinian refugees, and was only ever willing to accept limited third-party mediation under duress.[2] Israel also rejected American mediation and specific Anglo-American proposals for solving the refugee problem. These proposals were put forward within the framework of 'Operation Alpha', a secret plan launched at the end of 1954 by senior American and British officials who embarked on a joint effort to convince Israeli and Egyptian leaders to consider a 'comprehensive settlement' (in British Foreign Office terminology) of the Palestine question through secret negotiations. The joint plan of the two Western powers sought to promote ideas for the financing of Palestinian refugee compensation, an issue which was considered by the Alpha planners as an essential element for the success of their project. However, in his lengthy letter to Secretary of State John Foster Dulles of 4 May 1955, Prime Minister Moshe Sharett was most emphatic: he went on to 'make it clear beyond any possibility of misunderstanding' that there could be 'no question for us of cession of territory or the return of Arab refugees'. At the same time Israel announced that it was ready to proceed with payment of compensation for Arab refugee lands – 'provided Egypt lifted the Suez Canal blockade and the Arab States discontinued their threats and reprisals against foreign firms, aviation companies, etc. operations in Israel'.[3]

Israel's largely instrumental emphasis on compensation was also designed to de-emphasise the territorial aspect of the 1947 UN partition resolution with its provision for a two-state solution, Palestinian Arab and Israeli Jewish. In the 1950s the United Nations resolutions, especially the 1947 partition resolution and the December 1948 resolution on the refugees, became central to the Arab position on any settlement of the Arab–Israeli dispute. Predictably, however, any reference to the territorial dimension of the 1947 partition as a factor that had to be taken into account in any settlement was found upsetting by Israeli spokespersons. Often with the aim of seeking to counter the territorial issue involved in the 1947 partition resolution Israeli spokesmen tended to focus on the question of compensation for Palestinian refugees. This was the case in November 1955 when Israeli diplomats countered the Guildhall speech by British Prime Minister Anthony Eden by waging a campaign in the US and Britain designed also to undermine the Alpha plan.[4] Delivered in public on 9 November, Eden's speech was clearly linked to the joint American–British efforts within the framework of 'Operation Alpha'. It referred to the 'tragic problem of the refugees' and proposed the bridging of the Arab and Israeli positions on the basis of an 'even-handed compromise' between the 1947 United Nations partition resolution (which was the Arab position) and the then territorial status quo (which was the Israeli position). However, the very reference to the 1947 partition resolution with its territorial implications – a resolution which Israel, after its 1948 conquests, considered as null and void – in combination with the Palestinian refugee problem, aroused great anger and fear in Israel and brought repeated attacks by Israeli spokespersons on the Guildhall speech and the entire British policy in the Middle East.[5]

Back in 1948 Israel took over the land and other property of Palestinian refugees through a variety of mechanisms, legal, technical and bureaucratic. As early as March the Haganah established the Committee for Arab Properties in the Villages to control land abandoned by refugees. According to one estimate, in the aftermath of the 1948 war the new Israeli state absorbed about 15 million dunums (one dunum equals 1,000 square metres)[6] that it claimed did not belong to individual refugees. While in 1951 the UN Conciliation Commission for Palestine – established under UN Resolution 194 – placed a general estimate of the amount of land left behind by Palestinian refugees at some 16,324,000 dunums, Yosef Weitz of the Jewish National Fund (JNF), estimated the refugees' losses in 1948 at only 3,175,000 dunums.[7] Of course, the huge discrepancy between these two estimates derives from the lands collectively owned by Palestinian refugees, which are not included in the Israeli figure.[8] In addition to the land collectively owned by the Palestinian refugees, over 3 million dunums of individually owned refugee land were taken over under various legal pretexts by Israel's Custodian of Enemy Property, an office soon replaced by the Custodian of Absentees' Property, under the Absentees' Property Law enacted by the Knesset in 1950. This land included the property of the internal refugees ('Present Absentees' or *nifkadim nokhahim*') who remained inside the borders of the new state of Israel, but were displaced and not allowed to return to their homes and villages.[9] Two years later, in March 1950, with the adoption of the Absentees' Property Law, the Israeli government transferred the property of the refugees from Palestinian to Jewish ownership by a legal device and by virtue of a government payment to the Custodian of Absentees' Property. The Israeli government could thus claim that the property had been acquired legally (i.e. by payment) rather than through confiscation, although no compensation went to the legal owners. The government also adopted a series of laws and regulations to validate the transfer of property owned by internal and external refugees.[10] It is not clear whether the appointment of a Custodian of Absentees' Property by the Israeli authorities was merely designed to give the world the impression that the interests of the refugees were being safeguarded as required by international law. However, all studies of the Israeli Absentees' Property Law of 1950 show that the powers given to the Custodian of Absentees' Property were not merely those of administration but of such a nature that the office should be more properly described as 'liquidator of Arab property'.

Indeed, subsequently the Custodian of Absentees' Property was allowed to transfer the land it held to a new agency called the Development Authority. In March 1953 the Custodian disposed all of its refugee property to the Development Authority, to be utilised as a land reservoir for the development of Israel's Jewish majority.[11] Other refugee land fell under the control of the Jewish National Fund (JNF): in June 1953 the state and the Development Authority agreed to sell over 2,300,000 dunums of the land under their control to the JNF, which by its charter held the land in perpetuity for the Jewish people and was forbidden to transfer it. Finally, the Israeli Lands law of July 1960 enabled the state, the Development Authority and the JNF to transfer their land to a new agency: Israel Lands Authority. By 1960 all refugees' land had ended up in the hands of the Israel Lands Authority. To make sure that these lands remain in Jewish hands for ever, the Knesset enacted the Basic Law of 1960: The Law of Israel Lands. Article 1 of this law establishes that the *ownership of Israel's lands is not transferable through selling*, or any other way.[12]

An illustration of the huge benefits which Israel derived from Palestinian refugee property was given by Don Peretz in his 1954 Ph.D. 'Israel and the Arab Refugees', Volume II, Chapters VIII and IX.

The source of his information was stated to be Israeli publications and statements:

> Abandoned property was one of the greatest contributions toward making Israel a viable state. The extent of its area and the fact that most of the regions along the border were absentee property made it strategically significant. Of the 370 new Jewish Settlements established between 1948 and the beginning of 1953, 350 were on absentee property. In 1954, more than one-third of Israel's Jewish population lived on absentee property, and nearly a third of the new immigrants (250,000 people) settled in urban areas abandoned by Arabs. They left whole cities like Jaffa, Acre, Lydda, Ramle, Beisan, Majdal; 388 towns and villages;[13] and large parts of 94 other cities and towns, containing nearly a quarter of all the building in Israel. 10,000 shops, businesses and stores were left in Jewish hands. At the end of the Mandate, citrus holdings in the area of Israel totalled about 240,000 dunums of which half were Arab owned. Most of the Arab groves were taken by the Israeli Custodian of Absentee Property. But only 34,000 dunums were cultivated by the end of 1953. In 1951–52, former Arab groves produced one and a quarter of a million boxes of fruit, of which 400,000 were exported. Arab fruit sent abroad provided nearly 10 per cent of the country's foreign currency earnings from exports in 1951. In 1949, the olive produce from abandoned Arab groves was Israel's third largest export ranking after citrus and diamonds. The relative economic importance of Arab property was largest from 1948 until 1953 during the period of greatest immigration and need.[14]

In 1951, abandoned cultivable land included nearly 95 per cent of all Israel's olive groves, 40,000 dunums of vineyards, and at least 10,000 dunums of other orchards excluding citrus. 20,000 dunums of absentee property were leased by the Custodian in 1952 for individual industrial purposes. A third of Israel's stone production was supplied by 52 Arab quarries under his jurisdiction.[15]

This great Palestinian refugee wealth the Israelis continued to exploit from year to year under the pretext that it was 'abandoned property'. The major wave of Jewish immigration in the early 1950s saw over 200,000 people obtain housing by moving to abandoned Palestinian villages and homes. By 1954, nearly one-third of Israel's Jewish population was living on 'absentee property' and one-third of the new immigrants (250,000) had settled in urban areas left by Palestinian refugees.[16] These urban and rural properties would not have been presumed 'abandoned' had the Israelis complied with Resolution 194 of the UN General Assembly and allowed the refugees to return to their homes.

ISRAELI COMPENSATION PROPOSALS, OCTOBER 1948–56

The idea of restitution of Jewish property in Germany was central to the Reparations Agreement between Israel and the Federal Republic of Germany of September 1952.[17] In theory, that agreement could have serve as a model for settlement between Israel and the Palestinians. In reality, however, the Israeli government rejected the principle of 'restitution' of Palestinian refugee property, accepting only some measure of responsibility for compensating the refugees for their individually owned properties. It ruled out explicitly:

- restitution of properties – i.e., returning the properties to their rightful owners;[18]
- compensating the refugees for their collectively owned properties.

Moreover Israel's view was that compensation should be paid on a collective, rather than an individual, basis – the Arab states' preference – to the United Nations Relief and Works Agency's (UNRWA's) refugee integration fund, and that payment should be used specifically for the purpose of resettling the refugees in host Arab countries.

As early as October 1948 the official Transfer Committee had recommended that the 'resettlement [costs should come out of] the value of the immovable goods [that is, lands, houses abandoned] in the country (after reparations [for war damages to the Zionist Yishuv] are deducted), the Arab states will give land, the rest [will come from] the UN and international institutions.'[19] The committee had also attempted to work out the financial value of abandoned Arab property, but was unable to reach any conclusions without further study.[20] The same ideas were echoed by Foreign Minister Moshe Sharett at a press conference in March 1949, one month before the opening of the Lausanne peace conference. Sharett pointed out that Israel would expect to be compensated for its own losses during the 1948 war and that compensation to Palestinian refugees would only be part of a general settlement of the Arab–Israeli conflict:

> To help finance resettlement projects in neighbouring countries Israel is prepared to pay compensation for land abandoned in Israel by Arabs who have fled. This again can only be arranged as part of a general peace settlement. For when peace is negotiated the payment of compensation by Israel for land abandoned by Arabs will not be the only financial item discussed. Israel will claim damages from the aggressor States for losses sustained as a result of their aggression and the crushing burden of war expenditures inflicted upon its population.[21]

While accepting the principle of compensation for refugee land, the head of the Israeli delegation to the UN, Walter Eytan, made it clear that Israel did not accept restitution of the lands and properties involved.[22]

Several months later, in October 1949, the Israeli cabinet Transfer Committee was reconstituted as the Compensation Committee with the addition of a number of technical advisors and submitted its recommendations six months later. It recommended that in the context of an overall settlement of the Arab–Israeli conflict Israel should make a single, global payment of compensation for rural refugee property, for undamaged urban property, and for bank accounts. At the same time the Compensation Committee advised against the payment of compensation for the Arab share of state land and against making individual restitution payments for individual refugees, for two main reasons (according to the committee): first, this would take years to arbitrate, and second, and perhaps more important, this would require that refugee owners of property be allowed to return to Israel to take part in the evaluation of their assets. This prospect was considered entirely undesirable.[23] Prime Minister Ben-Gurion, in particular, ruled out the idea of personally compensating each refugee; Israel would not enter into individual claims of compensation.[24]

The Israeli cabinet meeting of 4 November 1951 discussed refugee compensation against the background of a forthcoming report by the UN Conciliation Commission for Palestine. At the meeting in November Foreign Minister Moshe Sharett revealed that the estimate of the value of immovable 'abandoned refugee property' by the Conciliation Commission for Palestine was $1 billion ($6 billion at 1997 prices, although without adding interest on these), according to articles published in *Haaretz* in April 1997 by Israeli journalist Yossi Melman, based on unpublished Israeli state archival sources.[25] Apparently the proposals of the Conciliation Commission for

Palestine were rejected by the Israeli cabinet – with the exception of one recommendation: the release of £1 million in bank accounts belonging to refugees, mostly held in Barclays Bank. In return Israel received five times that amount of money from Britain (£5 million) – the amount of money deposited by Jews in bank accounts during the mandatory period.[26] In 1953 the Israeli government made another attempt to work out a policy on compensation by appointing in June a new committee that also included senior government officials. The committee's recommendations were submitted in December 1953 suggesting that Israel should contribute $100 million, on account of the overall compensation bill, to an international fund which would be created in order to initiate collective resettlement projects in Arab countries.

This willingness on the part of Israel to contribute a share towards the financial cost of compensation was encouraged by the anticipated increase in foreign currency liquidity as a result of the Reparations Agreement with the Federal Republic of Germany, signed earlier in September 1952.[27] It would seem, however, that the Agreement precluded the possibility of diverting German reparations to the Palestinian refugees in host Arab countries as a means of Israel's meeting its compensation requirements. The preamble of the Agreement indicates that the purpose of the Agreement was to assist Israel in resettling Jewish immigrants. Article V, Paragraph E laid down the requirement that German goods sent to Israel may not be re-exported to a third party unless they have been subject to further fabrication in Israel. Paragraph F of that same article provides a penalty against Israel for any goods re-exported to a third country. These provisions appeared mutually advantageous from the point of view of Israel and Germany. However, the existence of the Reparations Agreement would not appear to prevent Israel, by agreement, from setting up a procedure whereby once funds were received from Germany into the general treasury they could immediately be earmarked for, or turned over to, an international body settling compensation claims of Palestinian refugees. Interestingly, however, in February 1955 a US State Department paper on Palestinian refugee compensation suggested that the Reparations Agreement might well serve as a model for agreement between Israel and one or more of the host Arab states whereby Israeli goods could be turned over to the host Arab state concerned in part-payment of refugee compensation. If such a procedure were used, it would have to be based on the host Arab governments agreeing to compensate individual Palestinian refugees directly or in kind. Such an agreement might advantageously be used in the case of Jordan where Jordan might receive goods in return for making land available to the Arab refugee instead of cash, the State Department paper stated.[28]

About the time when the Reparations Agreement was signed, various Israeli estimates of the global value of total movable and immovable Palestinian refugee property were close to US$350 million.[29] Although this figure was close to the United Nations Refugee Office estimate of £120 million, it was only about 16 per cent of the global valuation of Palestinian property losses arrived at in two detailed Palestinian studies.[30] During the early 1950s the Israeli government signalled its willingness to contribute to any international fund established to resettle Palestinian refugees in Arab countries or elsewhere collectively. However, at the same time, Israel was prepared to shoulder only a share of the total financial costs of resettling the refugees.

Moreover, gradually all Israeli attempts to work out proposals on compensation for Palestinian refugee property were tied to a settlement of abandoned Jewish property in Iraq, and later in other Arab countries.[31] Also, although the question of compensation for Palestinian refugee property in Israel did figure in the Israeli–Palestinian permanent status negotiations in 2000–January 2001, especially at Taba, when Labour Yossi Beilin, in his private 'Non-Paper', suggested that, in lieu of repatriation and restitution of property, a fund for compensating refugees should be established to which both the international community and Israel would be required to contribute (see Chapter 6), in reality, since the mid-1950s all Israeli governments have refused to admit any major responsibility for monetary compensation to the Palestinian refugees.[32]

NOTES

1. For further discussion of Sharett's views on compensation, see Gabriel Sheffer, *Moshe Sharett: Biography of a Political Moderate* (Oxford: Clarendon Press, 1996), p.811.
2. Neil Caplan, *Futile Diplomacy*, Vol. 4: *Operation Alpha and the Failure of Anglo-American Coercive Diplomacy in the Arab-Israeli Conflict, 1954–1956* (London: Frank Cass, 1997), p.117.
3. Cited in ibid, p.117; Sharett to Dulles, 4 May 1955, in Lawson to USSD, 5 May 1955, *FRUS 1955–1957*, XIV, pp.170–74 (D87).
4. Caplan, *Futile Diplomacy*, Vol. 4, p.188.
5. Ibid., pp.179–83, 188.

6. Sabri Jiryis, 'The Legal Structure for the Expropriation and Absorption of Arab Lands in Israel', *Journal of Palestine Studies* 2, no.4 (Summer 1973), p.83.
7. Joseph Weitz, 'Land Ownership', in *Israel Pocket Library: Immigration and Settlement* (Jerusalem: Keter Books, 1973), p.108.
8. Jiryis, 'The Legal Structure for the Expropriation and Absorption of Arab Lands in Israel', p.89; Michael R. Fischbach, 'Settling Historical Land Claims in the Wake of Arab–Israeli Peace', *Journal of Palestine Studies* 27, no.1 (Autumn 1997), p.40.
9. Simha Flapan, *The Birth of Israel: Myths and Realities* (New York: Pantheon Books, 1987), p.106. For further discussion on the 'Present Absentees', see Chapter 5.
10. Terry Rempel, 'The Ottowa Process: Workshop on Compensation and Palestinian Refugees', *Journal of Palestine Studies* 29, no.1 (Autumn 1991), p.38.
11. Flapan, *The Birth of Israel*, pp.106–7.
12. Usama Halabi, 'The Impact of the Jewishness of the State of Israel on the Status and Rights of the Arab Citizens in Israel', in Nur Masalha (ed.), *The Palestinians in Israel: Is Israel the State of all its Citizens and 'Absentees'?* (Nazareth: Galilee Centre for Social Research, 1993), p.21.
13. A more accurate figure of the depopulated Palestinian villages was given in *All That Remains: Depopulated and Destroyed Arab Villages* (Washington DC: Institute for Palestine Studies, 1992), which documents in detail the destruction of 418 villages..
14. Don Peretz, Israel and the Arab Refugees, Ph.D. Thesis, Vol.II, Chapter VIII, pp.231–3.
15. Ibid.
16. Ian Lustick, *Arabs in the Jewish State: Israel's Control of a National Minority* (Austin: University of Texas Press, 1980), p.5; Donna Arzt, *Refugees into Citizens: Palestinians and the End of the Arab–Israeli Conflict* (New York: Council on Foreign Relations Inc, 1997), p.17; Flapan, *The Birth of Israel*, p.107.
17. Ronald W. Zweig, 'Restitution of Property and Refugee Rehabilitation: Two Case Studies', *Journal of Refugee Studies* 6, no.1 (1993), p.61.
18. Flapan, *The Birth of Israel*, pp.106–7.
19. Benny Morris, 'Yosef Weitz and the Transfer Committees, 1984–1949', *Middle Eastern Studies*, 22, no.4 (October 1986), p.550.
20. Zweig, 'Restitution of Property and Refugee Rehabilitation', p.61; Benny Morris, *The Birth of the Palestinian Refugee Problem 1947–1949* (Cambridge: Cambridge University Press), p.259.
21. UN General Assembly, Report by the Special Political Committee, 23 November 1967, A/6115, p.13.
22. Ibid.
23. Zweig, 'Restitution of Property and Refugee Rehabilitation', p.61.
24. Shlomo Gazit, *The Palestinian Refugee Problem*, Final Status Issues-Israel-Palestinians, Study no.2 (Tel Aviv: Tel Aviv University, The Jaffee Centre for Strategic Studies, 1995), p.11.

25. Yossi Melman, 'The 1948 Refugees Abandoned Property in the Country Worth Six Billion Dollars', *Haaretz*, 18 April 1997, p.1; Yossi Melman, 'Dunum Plus Dunum Worth a Billion', *Haaretz*, 20 April 1997, p.36.
26. Ibid.
27. Zweig, 'Restitution of Property and Refugee Rehabilitation', pp.59 and 62.
28. Alpha: Compensation, US State Department, (possible date) 18 February 1955, in PRO FO371/115866, VR1076/35.
29. Zweig, 'Restitution of Property and Refugee Rehabilitation', pp.61–2.
30. The estimate produced by Sami Hadawi and Atef Kubursi is £743 million, while Yusif Sayigh's estimate is £756.7 million. For further discussion, see Sami Hadawi, *Palestinian Rights and Losses in 1948: A Comprehensive Study* (London: Saqi Books, 1988), pp.186–9; Yusif A. Sayigh, *The Israeli Economy* (Beirut: PLO Research Centre, 1966), pp.92–133 (Arabic).
31. Zweig, 'Restitution of Property and Refugee Rehabilitation', p.62.
32. Gazit, *The Palestinian Refugee Problem*, p.10.

5 The 'Present Absentees' and their Legal Struggle: Evolving Israeli Policies Towards the Internally Displaced (1948–2003)

According to 'Adalah (the Legal Centre for Arab Minority Rights in Israel), nearly one-quarter of the Palestinian residents remaining in Israel had been displaced from their homes and villages during the 1948 war and had become 'internal refugees' in Israel or internally displaced persons.[1] Israeli Jewish authors, on the other hand, have suggested much more conservative estimates of the internal refugees.[2] Clearly, therefore, there are no precise statistics on the internal refugees. Moreover although official Israeli, Palestinian and international organisations have devoted considerable attention to the question of how many Palestinian refugees were outside Israel after 1948, there was very little public concern regarding the number of those Palestinians who became refugees in Israel. The Israeli population censuses which were carried out in 1948 and in 1961 did not include questions designed to distinguish between Israeli Arabs who had become internally displaced and those who had not. This lack of attention to the internal refugees was deliberate. Its is also consistent with the general neglect suffered by the Palestinian citizens of Israel. Another reason for the lack of official Israeli statistics was the unwillingness on the part of official quarters to draw attention to the existence of the internal refugees and their difficult situation by providing a means of identifying them. The identification of their problem would have served as a reminder that the Palestinian refugee problem created in 1948 also existed within Israel, although its scope, in comparison with the wider Palestinian refugee problem (those 750,000 Palestinian refugees who in 1948 were driven out from the would-be Jewish state and their descendants), was limited, and its nature was unique.[3] In 1988 Israeli-Palestinian sociologist Majid al-Haj, of Haifa University, put the figure at 200,000;[4] however most estimates today are between 220,000 and

250,000,[5] originating from some 60 displaced communities inside Israel, who were dispossessed by the Israeli army in 1948–9 and were not allowed to return to their homes.

In 1950 the internally displaced Palestinians in Israel were considered as 'Present Absentees' (*nifkadim nokhahim* [6]) under the Absentees' Property Law (which will be discussed below). Acquiring the paradoxical title of 'present absentees', the internally displaced had their property and homes taken by the state, making them refugees within their own country. Most of them were forced to leave their villages under military orders during the 1948–9 war, locking their doors, taking their keys and land deeds, and planning to return as soon as the Israeli army allowed. Internal movements of the Palestinian population during 1948–9 continued for many months and in 1950 Palestinians were still being expelled by Israeli forces from localities where they had managed to hang on for two years.[7] Other evictions carried out in the post-1948–9 period were designed to break up areas of Arab concentration under the pretext of security needs.[8] The internal refugees are 'present absentees' because most of them have never left the country, remaining through the 1948–9 war and the years following.[9] Subject to unjust laws which were passed to gain Arab land for the state (especially the Absentees' Property Law of 1950), they are considered 'absentees' because they left their original villages, regardless of the reason. Although the internally displaced Palestinians were eventually accorded Israeli citizenship under the 1952 Israeli Nationality Law, as 'present absentees' they have been systematically prevented from returning to their homes and lands or regaining their property. Successive policies adopted by the Jewish state – military and diplomatic, legal and political – were aimed at consolidating the power and domination of Israel's Jewish majority. A key element in this effort was to prevent the return of Palestinian refugees – residing inside and outside the borders of the state of Israel – to their ancestral homes and properties. This objective has served until today as a guiding premise underlying Israeli policy concerning the internal refugees.

The internally displaced have found themselves in a unique situation. Despite their historic, geographic, cultural and national ties with the Palestinian people, they are internal refugees in their own homeland and their special situation is shared with the Palestinian national minority in Israel. They hold Israeli citizenship, a fact which distinguishes them from all other Palestinian refugee communities in the region. In addition, the 'internal refugees' have been conspicuous by their long absence from the international agenda and the denial of international refugee aid to them: UNRWA's operations in Israel were discontinued in July 1952. Sharing common memories of their towns and villages of origins, they have formed a distinct group among the Israeli-Palestinians: 'a minority within the minority'. Forming a separate social category which was very noticeable in the Arab villages and towns, the Arabic word for 'refugee', *laji*, became common among the Arabs in Israel when referring to the 'internally displaced'.[10] The vast majority of them are Muslim (about 90 per cent) and the remainder are Christians; the Druze are not represented among the internally displaced refugees since no Druze permanently left their villages.[11] The internally displaced differ from the Palestinian 'external refugees' in another respect: they came exclusively from rural agricultural areas, whereas the 'external refugees' originated from both urban and rural populations.[12]

In terms of their geographical distribution, the overwhelming majority of the internally displaced originated from, and currently live (like most of the Palestinians in Israel) in the northern part of the country, in the Palestine mandatory government districts of Safad, Acre, Haifa, Baysan and Tiberias.[13] A study carried out by Charles Kamen in the mid-1980s found that a substantial number of the residents of villages in the northern part of the country which had been completely destroyed, such as al-Mujaydil, al-Damun, al-Birwa, Iqrit, Kafr Bir'im, al-Ruways, Haditha, Ma'lul, al-Muftakhara, al-Mansura and Qumiya, remained in Israel.[14] To this list one should add other villages such as Hittin, Nimrin, al-Shajara, 'Arab al-Khisas, 'Arab al-Baqqara, al-Kabri, al-Zib, al-Bassa, 'Amqa, al-Shaykh Dawud, al-Ghabisiya, al-Farradiya, al-Manshiya, Mi'ar, al-Nahr, Suhmata, Tarbikha, Umm al-Faraj, and Saffuriya. The latter's former residents, for instance, currently occupy a whole quarter in Nazareth. Apparently, the internally displaced are currently residing in around 80 villages and towns and their movements caused the Arab populations of various localities in Israel to increase or decrease. Most of them had found temporary places of asylum in, and were eventually absorbed into, the remaining nearby Arab localities, situated on average between 3 and 16 kilometres from their original place of residence.[15] In his study Charles Kamem found that half of the inhabitants of Judyada are refugees: one-third of the population of Majd al-Kurum; almost one-third of that of Rama and Jish; one-fourth of the population of Nazareth,[16] Kafr Yassif and Yafa (near Nazareth) are refugees.[17] Also a few of the internally displaced today live in the most impoverished and overcrowded neighbourhoods of what are now 'mixed towns' – the previously Arab towns of Jaffa, Acre, Lydda and Ramle.[18] It should be pointed out that the desire among many of the internally displaced to return to their 'original' homes and 'personal territory' is not just based on nostalgia for the past or yearning for the 'lost paradise', but rather on existential and day-to-day problems, including the pressing need for housing among the internal refugees and their descendants and the ever shrinking surface areas available to Arab villages and towns in Israel.[19]

UNDER THE MILITARY ADMINISTRATION, 1948–66

The internally displaced were subjected to a repressive military administration for some 18 years (1948–66), but many observers do not realise that the state of emergency declared in Israel in 1948 is still in effect. Although direct military government, which had applied to the Arab areas of Israel, was abolished in 1966, the Defence (Emergency) Regulations, originally enacted by the British Mandatory authorities in 1945, were retained by the Knesset in a special law and the state of emergency has never been lifted completely. These regulations, subject to certain amendments, have remained in force until the present day. Moreover, since the termination of the military administration, Israeli governments have continued legislative and administrative procedures aimed at confiscating lands of the destroyed villages in order to prevent the return of the internally displaced. The Defence (Emergency) Regulations had provided the legal basis for the system of direct military rule imposed on Arab (and only Arab) citizens of Israel from 1948 to 1966; in fact the Military Government existed only in the areas in which the majority of Israel's Arab population resided. Under the Defence (Emergency) Regulations the authorities can still declare closed military areas, confiscate land, close down newspapers, detain people without trial and even expel them.[20] Another Emergency Article for the Exploitation of Uncultivated Land (1948) permitted Israel's Minister of Agriculture to seize Arab property that was uncultivated. Seizures were effected by enclosing an area under the Defence (Emergency) Regulations, thus preventing its cultivation and enabling its expropriation. Lands falling under this category were leased by the Custodian of Absentees' Property to Jewish settlers and farmers, old and new.[21]

The imposition of martial law and Military Government in the period between 1948 and 1966 had an enormous impact on the internally displaced and the remaining Palestinian population in Israel. In 1948 the Israeli Provisional State Council (the forerunner of the Knesset), in search of international recognition for the newly proclaimed state, included in the 'Independence Charter' a promise that the Jewish state would 'uphold the full social and political equality of all its citizens, without distinction of religion, race, and sex'. In fact, what took place was exactly the opposite. After its establishment, Israel treated the Palestinians still remaining within its frontiers almost as foreigners. It swiftly imposed a military administration in the areas inhabited by the Palestinian minority, expropriated over half of the lands of this 'non-Jewish' population, and pursued various policies of demographic containment, political control and systematic discrimination in all spheres of life. Officially the purpose of imposing martial law and military administration on Israel's Palestinian minority was security. However, its establishment was intended to serve a number of both stated and concealed objectives, the second and third of which were specifically aimed at the internally displaced refugees:

1. To prevent the return of the Palestinian refugees ['external refugees'] to their homes, villages and towns in Israel. 'In the process other Arabs who had not infiltrated the country were sometimes driven out as well.'[22]
2. 'To evacuate semi-abandoned [Arab] neighbourhoods and villages as well as some which had not been abandoned – and to transfer their inhabitants to other parts of the country. Some were evacuated from a "security cordon" along the borders, and others were removed in order to make room for Jews.'[23]
3. To reduce the overall number of the internal refugees in the state of Israel.
4. To maintain control and supervision over the Israeli Palestinian citizens, who were separated and isolated from the Jewish population.[24]

To reduce the overall number of the internally displaced persons in the state of Israel in the post-1948 period the military administration carried out many incidents of expulsion, especially from

Galilee and the Little Triangle after the latter's annexation to Israel in May 1949 and following the Rhodes agreement signed with Jordan on 3 April 1949. For instance, in late May or early June 1949, 4,000 'internal refugees' were expelled by the military administration from the Little Triangle across the border into the West Bank. The Military Governor of the central area, Lieutenant-Colonel 'Emmanuel Markovsky, reported to the head of the Military Government, General Elimelech Avner, on 30 June 1949:

> Upon our entry into the area [the Little Triangle] and the proclamation of [Israel's] rule in it, we announced that we will not recognize the ['internal'] refugees as being entitled to reside in the area or any aid and benefit. We prohibited their employment in any work ... we banned organising permanent aid for them. When we received authorisation to transfer them across the border, the action was implemented in full within a week.

Markovsky also added that after the military administration put pressure on 'representatives' of the Little Triangle's villages (possibly certain *mukhtars*), the latter had agreed to assist in the process. In conclusion, Markovsky wrote: 'In retrospect, this action proved that a fair and forceful rule in the [Israeli Arab] villages gives the possibility of implementing tasks in full, and fortifies Israel's rule.'

In the same year (1949), some 1,000 people from the village of Baqa al-Gharbiya in the Little Triangle (presumably many of them 'internal refugees') were expelled by Israel across the border into the West Bank. In early February 1951, the residents of 13 small Arab villages in Wadi 'Ara were expelled over the border. Later, on 17 November of the same year the inhabitants of the village of Khirbat al-Buwayshat in the Little Triangle were also expelled and their houses dynamited by the army. In the same year some 700 people from Kafr Yassif village in Galilee were trucked to the Jordanian border and ordered to cross it. These 'internal refugees' had never left Galilee during the 1948 war, but simply had fled their homes in adjoining villages and moved to Kafr Yassif. In a Knesset debate on 8 March 1949, Communist Knesset Member Tawfiq Tubi strongly protested against this large single expulsion of internally displaced persons. He stated:

> The forced evacuation of Arab villages has also been carried out by the Israeli authorities. Only a few weeks ago 700 people who had

> taken refuge in the village of [Kafr] Yasif [*sic*] during the [1948] war were taken to the Iraqi front [on the northern West Bank border with Israel] in trucks and forced to cross the lines to Abdullah.

In mid-April 1949, the US consul in Jerusalem reported that 'several hundred' Galilee Arabs (some of the 'internal refugees') had been expelled by the Israeli army across the border, together with some Palestinian refugees who had 'infiltrated' back to their villages. Such expulsions often were carried out with brutality, as one Kibbutz woman wrote anonymously to the newspaper *'Al-Hamishmar* of witnessing such 'infiltrators', men, women and children blindfolded, being trucked out:

> Those of us standing nearby had witnessed no bad behaviour on the part of the Arabs, who sat frightened, almost one on top of the other. But the soldiers were quick to teach us what they meant by 'order'. 'The expert' jumped up and began to ... hit [the Arabs] across their blindfolded eyes and when he had finished, he stamped on all of them and then, in the end, laughed uproariously and with satisfaction at his heroism. We were shocked by this despicable act. I ask, does this not remind us exactly of the Nazi acts towards the Jews?

On 31 May 1950 the Israeli army transported about 120 'internal refugees' in two crowded trucks to a point near the edge of Wadi Araba, a hot desert wasteland astride the Israeli–Jordanian frontier between the Dead Sea and the Gulf of Aqaba. The refugees were ordered to cross to Jordan, with the soldiers 'firing bursts over their heads to urge them forward'. While most of the expellees made it, as many as 36 'may be assumed ... [to have] perished from thirst and starvation', the British Minister to Amman, Kirkbride, wrote.[25] The survivors, who were questioned in Jordan, were found to be:

> Members of divided families who infiltrated across the line to find their relatives, or who fled from what is now Israel territory when the Jews arrived there, abandoning money and valuables in their homes; ... Refugees caught *en route* from Gaza to Jordan; ... [and] Arabs living in their homes in Israel, with whom the Jews have become displeased for some reason or other.

The issue of both the internally displaced persons and the 'external refugees' remained a major preoccupation for the military administration, which lasted until 1966. On 24 March 1949 Prime Minister David Ben-Gurion appointed a committee that was directed to submit to him recommendations on whether the military administration should be abolished, or, alternatively, whether any changes in its policies toward the Arab minority and the internally displaced refugees ought to be carried out. By determining the composition of the committee, Ben-Gurion seemed to have ensured the outcome of its investigations. The committee was headed by General Elimelech Avner, who was the head of the military administration, and its two other members were Major Michael Hanegbi, the Military Governor of the Negev, and Yehoshu'a Palmon of the Foreign Ministry. In its report, submitted to the Prime Minister on 3 May 1949, the committee stressed that the continuation of a forceful military administration was essential for security, demographic, and land settlement reasons and for dealing with the question of refugees within Israel. The committee maintained, *inter alia*, that a comprehensive and effective supervision over the Arab population was needed in order:

- to find 'a solution to the problem of the Arab refugees who are present within the boundaries of the state [because the problem of internal refugees] requires the transfer [of Arab communities] from one place to another, the concentration of land for their resettlement, the transfer of [Arab] workers to employment centres, [and] directed [Jewish] settlement policies. ... The implementation of all these requires a regime with military character, which is not subject to the rules of normal procedures';
- '[to facilitate] greatly the implementation of the desired demographic and land policies, and the process of populating [with Jews] the abandoned Arab villages and towns';
- to prevent 'infiltration' of Palestinian [external] refugees back to their homes and villages;
- to prevent the Palestinian minority from becoming a fifth column.[26]

In October 1952, Ben-Gurion asked then Minister-without-portfolio Pinhas Lavon (later Defence Minister) to look into the functioning of the military administration. Lavon's report, which was presented a few weeks later, criticised the military administration as inefficient and as harbouring much corruption. Lavon also attempted to deal with claims he heard from army General Staff representatives, who had asserted that the reason for the difficulties and inefficiency of the military administration was the lack of a consistent policy toward the Arab minority and the internally displaced refugees. This inconsistency, according to the army, was the result of the activities of civilian ministries among the Arab population, in parallel with army activities. The army, Lavon wrote, wanted an exclusive and total authority in dealing with the Arab minority. However, he recommended not accepting the army's demand although he opposed abolition of the Military Government and the Defence (Emergency) Regulations. Lavon's report of 1952 was most telling:

> The claim about the 'lack of a consistent policy' [made by representatives of the General Staff] is based on the demand to [adopt] a policy which would lead to the emigration of the Arab residents from the territory of the State of Israel. ... Such emigration is undoubtedly desirable, but it is doubtful whether it would be possible to achieve that – the emigration of tens of thousands of Arabs – with the means available to a Military Government in time of peace, in a democratic state, which is open to criticism, supervision, and is in need of the world's sympathy. The harm [resulting] from half measures is clear, and their benefit is doubtful. Absolutely effective means [which would bring about the total departure of the Arab minority] cannot be pursued by the state of Israel, without the shaking of its international position.

While describing the idea of a wholesale mass exodus of the Arab minority as 'desirable' but not practicable for international as well as domestic reasons, Lavon, like most Israeli ministers and senior officials, was still in favour of an active policy of encouraging 'voluntary' transfer:

> The above explanation does not come [however] to weaken or belittle the efforts being made in order to obtain the consent of Arab residents [Israeli citizens] to emigrate to foreign countries. Such plans deserve encouragement and full support from the [official] institutions concerned. The required financial investment is certainly worthwhile, and it is desirable that the treasury [Finance Ministry] ought actively to enter into details [of these plans].[27]

The institution of the military administration, together with the imposition of the Defence (Emergency) Regulations, empowered the Military Governors to close off the Arab localities and to restrict entry or exit to those who had been issued permits by the military authorities. These regulations also enabled the Israeli authorities to evict and deport people from their villages and towns; to place individuals under administrative detention for indefinite periods without trial; and to impose fines and penalties without due process.[28] Although the regulations themselves made no distinction between Jew and Arab, there is no doubt that the primary use of most of the powers in these regulations was to impose restrictions on the Arabs in Israel.[29] Regulation 125 in effect legalises the expropriation of Arab land, giving the local military commanders the right to declare any region under their jurisdiction a 'closed area'. (See, for example, the case of Kafr Bir'im below.) As Professor David Kretzmer of the Hebrew University pointed out, 'in the discussion of institutional discrimination [against the Arabs in Israel], during the time of the military government many of the rules applying to closed areas were only applied to Arabs while Jews were allowed to move in and out of the areas freely.'[30] The Military Governors, in particular, were authorised to close Arab areas in order to prevent 'internal refugees' from returning to their homes and lands that had been confiscated by the state and taken over by new and old Jewish settlements.[31] Yehoshu'a Palmon of the Foreign Ministry suggested in a letter to the Custodian of Absentees' Property, Zalman Lifschitz of the Prime Minister's Office, and the attorney-general that 'in the cases in which [internal] refugees want to sell their property in their former place of residence and leave the country, we should encourage them to do that.'[32] Copies of the letter were sent to the foreign minister, the military administration, and Yosef Weitz. A year later, Palmon, then advisor on Arab affairs in the Prime Minister's Office, wrote a letter to Foreign Minister Moshe Sharett in which he expounded his views on the prickly issue of the property of the 'present absentees':

> Arab residents of Israel, who, from a social, religious, or cultural viewpoint, are not inclined to remain in Israel, after they would receive all or a respectable part of the compensation for their property, and their hope for what they had not received [their actual property] was lost, they would look for and find a way to leave the country.[33]

LAND CONFISCATION: THE ABSENTEES' PROPERTY LAW OF 1950

The issue of continuing land expropriation is possibly the most explosive in the relationship between the Palestinian national minority in Israel and the Jewish state. It is an issue that has caused tremendous resentment and bitterness among Israeli Palestinians and has galvanised them into action. This action reached a peak in the 'Land Day' of March 30th, 1976, a day which began as a peaceful general strike and culminated in the confrontation with the Israeli Border Police in the course of which six Palestinians were shot dead.[34] Since 1976, March 30th has become a 'national day' of protest and commemoration of the Palestinian community protests which are mainly directly against the state's policies of land expropriation and land use. A memorandum presented by the late Hanna Nakkara, an Israeli-Palestinian attorney and a leading expert on land matters, to the Arab Popular Congress in Nazareth, held on 17 February 1979, severely criticised Israeli land policies and their impact on the internally displaced:

> Tens of thousands of [Israeli?] Arabs are still far away from their destroyed villages and stolen lands. There is an army of local refugees from Saffuriya, al-Mujaydil, Ma'lul, Hittin, Nimrin, al-Shajara, 'Arab al-Khisas, 'Arab al-Baqqara, al-Kabri, al-Mansura, al-Zib, al-Bassa, 'Amqa, al-Shaykh Dawud, al-Birwa, al-Damun, al-Ruways, al-Ghabisiyya, Iqrit, Kafr Bir'im, 'Anan, al-Farradiya, al-Manshiya, Mi'ar, Sha'b, al-Nahr, al-Sai'ra, Suhmata, Tarbikha, Umm al-Faraj, and others. This army of local refugees was created by the policies of consecutive ethnic governments, existing and working for the eviction of native people and the planting of a new people.[35]

The most recent impact of these land policies was the crisis in Umm al-Fahm, an Arab town in the Wadi 'Ara region, which began in May 1998, when the Israeli government announced that it was expanding a nearby military facility, in the process expropriating 4,500 acres of local Arab agricultural land (one acre equals four dunums). In the three days of rioting that followed the local demonstration of 27 September 1998, over 400 Arab residents were injured in clashes with the Border Police.[36]

Historically, a combination of military-strategic, demographic-land settlement, and Zionist ideological considerations governed Israel's land policies towards the Arab citizens, including the 'internal refugees'. Land and settlement expansion, in particular, have always been at the heart of the conflict between the Zionist immigrants/settlers and the native Palestinians. Until the 1948 *nakba* the Palestinians had been the overwhelming majority in the country and had owned much of the land, while the Jewish community in Palestine (the Yishuv) had been about a third of the total population and had owned about 6 per cent of the land. Hence, the quest for land had underpinned the Zionist project in the pre-1948 period. In a sense, in the post-1948 period the Israeli state's long-lasting battle against the Arab minority was a battle for 'more land'. This battle essentially was dictated by the Jewish state's premises and fundamentals:

- the 'ingathering' of the world's Jews in Israel (*'kibbutz galoyut'*);
- the acquisition, takeover and conquest of land (*'kibbush haadama'*);
- the consolidation of Jewish demography in a state created exclusively for the Jews – who mostly had yet to arrive in Israel – at the expense of the displaced, 'transferred' and internally relocated Palestinians;
- Jewish 'population dispersion' throughout the country (*pezur ochlosiya*);
- Judaisation of Galilee (*yehud hagalil*).

The establishment of Israel in 1948 did not alter Zionism's premises and fundamentals with regard to the Palestinian minority remaining under Israeli control. Indeed, the principal objectives of the Israeli state, as defined in terms of its Zionist ideology, has been the fulfilment of the Jewish majority's aspirations, and those of would-be Jewish immigrants, frequently at the expense of the aspirations of the Palestinian minority (including the internal Arab refugees).

For the remaining Palestinian citizens of Israel, their attachment to the land of their ancestors hardly can be overemphasised. Farming the land was the backbone of the Palestinian economy before 1948. As natives of Palestine, the land for them was a means of livelihood, a symbol of identity, survival and security in the face of the 1948 exodus and dispersal of their compatriots. The question of land use and development has always been crucially important for the survival of the Palestinian Arab minority in Israel. Land expropriation is probably the most significant aspect of the policy of deprivation pursued by Israel against this minority. Predicated on the Zionist premise of more land for the would-be Jewish newcomers and settlers, Israel's policy of land confiscation destroyed the livelihood of many Israeli Arabs, severely curtailed the development of Arab localities and threatened to undermine the very survival of a territorially based Arab national minority in Israel.

The 1948–9 war brought enormous disruption to the economy of the internally displaced and the remaining Palestinian population in Israel. The outcome of the 1948–9 war and the ceasefire agreements between Israel and the Arab countries of 1949 left Israel in control of over 5 million acres of Palestinian land, mostly belonging to the external refugees; the property of the internally displaced Palestinians consisted of about 300,000 dunums of land, which the Israeli state declared to be 'absentee property'.[37] Soon after the 1948 war, the Israeli authorities confiscated nearly 1 million acres of Palestinian refugee land.[38] First the Israeli state took over the land of the 'external refugees', who were barred from returning, while the remaining Palestinian Arab minority (including internally displaced persons) was subsequently subjected to laws and regulations that effectively deprived it of most of its land. The history of expropriation began immediately after 1948. The massive drive to take over Arab land, belonging to 'internal and external refugees', has been conducted according to strict legality. The land was expropriated by the authority of laws passed by the Israeli parliament, and transferred to Jewish control and ownership. Since 1948 Israel has enacted some 30 statutes that transferred land from private Arab to state ownership.[39] In 1955 the then Arab affairs editor for the daily *Haaretz*, Moshe Keren, described this process as 'wholesale robbery in legal guise. Hundreds of thousands of dunams [sic] were taken away from the Arab minority.'[40]

While Israel has used several laws to expropriate land from the Arab citizens or to place restrictions on its use, there is little doubt that major expropriations of lands belonging to Palestinians (internal and external refugees) were carried out under the Absentees' Property Law, 1950. This statute was used to transfer Palestinian properties to Jewish hands via the Custodian of Absentees' Property, who subsequently transferred them to the Israeli Development Authority. The law was proceeded by Defence (Emergency) Regulations dealing with 'absentees' property'. On the face of it, the declared objective of this statute was to 'protect' the property of absentee owners, and to facilitate use of this property for the development of the Israeli economy and the state.[41] The law directs the Finance Minister to appoint a Custodian of Absentees' Property and Section 4(a)(1) provides that

> all absentees' property is hereby vested in the Custodian as from the day of publication of this appointment or the day on which it became absentee's property, whichever is the later date.[42]

The law gives far-reaching powers to the Custodian of Absentees' Property, with severe consequences for the Palestinian landowner whose property was deemed 'absentee property'; it empowers the Custodian to take care of the absentee's property, manage it, and expel occupants who, in the Custodian's opinion, have no right to occupy it. The law does not give the 'absentee' (internal or external refugee) the right to return to his property. Instead it gives the Custodian the power, at his sole discretion, and on the recommendation of a special committee, to release/sell vested property. Where the vested property has been sold 'the property sold becomes released property and passes into the ownership of the purchaser and the consideration which the Custodian has received becomes held property' (Section 28 (c).[43]

The most important provision in the law is the definition of the term 'absentees' property'. Section 1 defines the term 'absentee' as follows:

> (a) 'absentee' means:
> (1) a person who, at any time during the period between the 16th Kislev, 5708 (29 November, 1947) and the day on which a declaration is published, under section 9(d) of the Law and Administration Ordinance, (5708–1948), that the state of emergency declared by the Provisional Council of the State on the 10th of Iyar, 5708 (19th May, 1948) has ceased to exist, was the legal owner of any property situated in the area of Israel or enjoyed or held it, whether by himself or through another, and who at any time during the said period
>
> (i) was a national or citizen of the Lebanon, Egypt, Syria, Saudi-Arabia, Trans-Jordan, Iraq or the Yemen, or
> (ii) was in one of these countries or in any part of Palestine outside the area of Israel or

(iii) was a Palestinian citizen and left his ordinary place of residence in Palestine

(a) for a place outside Palestine before the 27th Av, 5708 (1st September, 1948); or

(b) for a place in Palestine held at the time by forces which sought to prevent the establishment of the State of Israel or which fought against it after its establishment;

(2) a body of persons which, at any time during the period specified in paragraph (1), was a legal owner of any property situated in the area of Israel or enjoyed or held such property, whether by itself or through another, and all the members, partners, shareholders, directors or managers of which are absentees within the meaning of paragraph (1), or the management of the business of which is otherwise decisively controlled by such absentees, or all the capital of which is in the hands of such absentees.[44]

Critical examination of the definition reveals that a person may be an 'absentee' under the law, even though he was present in Israel when his property was deemed to have become 'absentees' property'. In other words, if a person was an 'absentee' at any time between 29 November and 1 September 1948, his property becomes 'absentees' property', whether he is still an absentee or not.[45] While that applied *in absentia* to those Palestinian refugees outside Jewish-occupied Palestine, it also provided for the legal dispossession of those Palestinian citizens of Israel who had never left the newly created state or those Palestinians who were reabsorbed into Israel as a result of the armistice agreements of 1949. Consequently, most of the internally displaced have become 'present absentees' by virtue of the fact that they had properties confiscated; very few of them have ever recovered any property.

In 1948, each Arab village had on average approximately 2,280 acres of arable land; by 1974 this was reduced to 500 acres.[46] Between 1948 and 1990 the Israeli Palestinians (including the 'internal refugees') lost close to 1 million acres of land;[47] during the first four decades of the state 80 per cent of the lands owned by Palestinians living in Israel were confiscated and put at the exclusive disposal of Jewish citizens.[48] Through a series of legal measures, expropriations continue even today, with minimal financial compensation based on undervalued assessments (decided unilaterally and with no relation to market value), which, in any case, many internal refugees refuse.[49] As a result of this massive land seizure and the state's land-use policies within the Green Line, 93 per cent of the land is owned by the state and the Jewish National Fund (JNF);[50] according to a series of laws passed in the early 1960s (especially the Basic Law: Israel Lands and the Israel Lands Authority Law), almost all the land in Israel came to be owned by the state (93 per cent). Yet, when the state assumed control (in the form of the Israel Lands Authority), it agreed to continue to abide by the JNF's mandate for those lands which were once administered by the JNF, whose primary purpose has always been to facilitate the control of land as the 'perpetual property of the Jewish people'.[51] In effect, those lands, originally belonging to Palestinian (external) refugees and 'present absentees', are currently held 'in perpetuity by the Jewish people', not the citizens of Israel, excluding the Arab citizens from ownership and land use.

Furthermore, the Israel Lands Authority continues to transfer lands internally to the JNF – 12,500 acres in 1991, and 10,000 acres in 1998 are but recent examples.[52] In reality, the line between the Israel Lands Authority (ILA) and the JNF is a thin one, as the JNF nominates 6 of the 13 members of the ILA's Board (the rest are government officials). Professor Amnon Rubinstein, writing in *Haaretz* 13 October 1991, critically remarked: 'These transfers present a grave problem, because lands that were intended for use by all Israeli citizens were handed over to an agency that sells and leases land only to Jews.' By self-definition, these lands, whether controlled by the ILA or the JNF, are utilised almost exclusively for the fulfilment of the Zionist goals of Jewish settlement and population dispersion. Inevitably, this land-use policy has resulted in the massive dispossession of the Arab minority, including the 'internal refugees'.[53] According to Right Reverend Riah Abu al-'Assal of Nazareth (enthroned in 1998 as the Anglican Bishop of Jerusalem):

> In 1948, 16.5 dunams were allowed per capita for the Arab minority. Today about 0.5 dunam is allowed. We have no more space to bury our dead. ... I am not exaggerating. I live in a town called Nazareth which has become the most crowded town in the country. ... In the Greek Orthodox Cemetery in Nazareth – and the Greek Orthodox community numbers over 11,000 people –

> they dig up the graves of those who died ten years ago to bury the newly dead.[54]

LEGAL STRUGGLE AND DIRECT ACTION

i. Kafr Bir'im and Iqrit

The most famous case of the internally displaced involved the inhabitants of the two villages Kafr Bir'im and Iqrit, who were forcibly evicted by the Israeli army in November 1948 and never allowed to return. This case also illustrates the strong desire among many of the internally displaced persons to return to their 'original' homes and 'personal' territory. Termed the 'uprooted' (*ha'akurim*) in the Israeli press, the Christian inhabitants of Iqrit and Kafr Bir'im in northern Galilee and their descendants are part of the approximately 250,000 internally displaced Palestinians who were dispossessed by the Israeli army in 1948 and were not allowed to go back to their homes. The villagers of Iqrit and Kafr Bir'im, who did not take up arms in 1948, were 'evicted' by the Israeli army on 6 November 1948 and transferred to various Arab villages in Galilee, including Jish and Ramah. The history of these evicted villagers is one of 'broken promises';[55] initially the Israeli army requested the residents of Iqrit and Kafr Bir'im to leave their villages due to 'security concerns' along the Israeli–Lebanese border (Kafr Biri'm was located about two miles from the Israeli–Lebanese border and nine miles east of Iqrit). In 1948 Iqrit and Kafr Bir'im were considered 'friendly' villages: their inhabitants did not take up arms against Israel. Apparently, their residents complied with the order after receiving explicit assurances from both Galilee District military commander, Elisha' Shultz, and the then Minister for Minorities, Bechor Shitrit, that they would be permitted to return within two weeks.[56] However, this promise, which ran counter to Israel's general policy at the time of creating Arab-free 'security zones' along the borders of the state, was not kept. In *Israel's Border Wars, 1949–1956* (1997), Israeli historian Benny Morris discusses the issue of 'Expelling Border Communities [Israeli Arabs] and Nudging Back the Borders':

> At the end of 1948. ... Israel decided to clear its border areas of Arab villages, to a depth of five or ten kilometres. The motive of the policy – initially implemented at the beginning of November along the Lebanese border – was military: Arab villages along the

> border, just behind IDF positions and patrol roads, constituted a threat. They could receive and assist Arab troops and irregulars should the Arabs renew the war; harbour saboteurs and spies; and serve as way stations for infiltrating returnees [Palestinian refugees], thieves, and smugglers. Partly depopulated villages, such as Tarshiha in Galilee, beckoned infiltrators [returning refugees] bent on resettlement. And some semi-abandoned border villages, such as Zakariya, in the Jerusalem Corridor, were a socio-economic burden on the state since the young adult males were mostly dead, incarcerated, or had fled to Jordan, while the old, the women, and the children of the village lived off government hand-outs. Lastly, the authorities wanted as small an Arab minority as possible in the new Jewish state.
>
> In part, these border-area transfers were designed to hamper infiltration [of Palestinian refugees] into Israel.[57]

On 21 June 1949 the leaders of Kafr Bir'im met with Shitrit, who asked them to be 'patient'. But nothing happened for two years. Having lost faith in the Israeli government, the villagers on 30 August 1951 filed a claim in the High Court of Justice, demanding the government return of their land. The High Court issued a conditional order on 8 October, ordering the government to explain why the villagers had not been allowed to return.[58] In response, in November the army, using the Defence (Emergency) Regulations, declared Kafr Bir'im 'a closed area' for security reasons, requiring a special permit to enter. A month later, in December, while the case of Iqrit was still before the High Court, the army issued retroactive expulsion orders and its sappers systematically blew up every house in the village. The High Court issued its final ruling on the Kafr Bir'im case on 18 January 1952, declaring that in the light of the military actions, the villagers of Kafr Bir'im need to obtain special permits in order to return home – permits which the army refused to issue. On 4 August 1953 the Finance Ministry stepped in, officially confiscating the lands of Kafr Bir'im for the purpose of 'development', using a legal pretext that the lands were 'abandoned and uncultivated by the owners'. Finally on 16 and 17 September the army destroyed the remaining houses of Kafr Bir'im.[59] The lands of the two villages were confiscated, declared 'state lands', and leased to Jewish agricultural and urban settlements. A similar process took place in several Arab villages in Israel.

The villagers of Iqrit and Kafr Bir'im were not permitted to return because, according to Prime Minister Golda Meir in 1972, allowing them to do so might set a precedent for other, similarly uprooted 'internal refugees'.[60] Apparently, monetary compensation was subsequently offered by the Israeli government to the inhabitants of Kafr Bir'im and Iqrit, only to be turned down by the majority of them.[61] When their hopes of return were frustrated, they took action through the Israeli courts, through lobbying and through peaceful demonstrations; their legal and political struggle, and the struggle of their descendants, to return to their homes and original lands have stretched out to more than half a century. There are four main reasons why the case of Iqrit and Kafr Bir'im became a *cause célèbre*:

1. the tenacity of the villagers, their perseverance and direct action, their effective lobbying activities and legal struggle, stretching over half a century; they never gave up hope or ceased their efforts;
2. the mobilisation of Christian churches in the Holy Land and the effective use of their international connections;
3. the formation of grassroots local organisations from an early stage designed to campaign specifically for the rights of the villagers, such as the Committee for the Uprooted of Kafr Bir'im and the Public Committee of Iqrit and Kafr Bir'im;
4. the perception among liberal Zionist-Israelis, who have expressed sympathy for the villagers, that their case was 'unique', and as such would not be taken as a 'precedent' to allow other 'internal refugees' to return to their homes and original lands.

The affair of Kafr Bir'im and Iqrit often burst into the open and provoked controversy inside Israel and soul-searching among Jews and non-Jews in the West. On 23 July 1972, after a long cabinet session discussing whether or not to allow the 'uprooted' of the two villages to return, the Israeli ministers voted against – the government of Golda Meir giving no official reason for its decision.[62] This decision attracted the interest of the Western press, with many articles and editorials sympathetic to the dispossessed villagers and highly critical of the Israeli government appearing in the *New York Times Magazine* (22 October), the *Guardian* (16 August), *Christian Science Monitor* (12 and 26 August), the *New York Times* (4 September). An indication of the impact of the demands of the inhabitants of the two villages on American Jewish opinion was suggested by an article in the American

Jewish Congress journal, the *Congress Bi-weekly*, by Chaim Waxman. Acknowledging that the case of the villagers received some coverage in the United States, and critical of the handling of the case by the Israeli government, Waxman expressed the fear that the government's refusal to allow the villagers to return could become a major weapon in the arsenals of critics of Zionism and Israel.[63] Israeli journalist 'Amos Elon wrote in October 1972: 'The question of the repatriation of a few hundred Israeli Arabs to the now ruined villages [of Kafr Bir'im and Iqrit] has revealed a deep soul-searching ... the passion and occasional viciousness of this last debate surpasses any within recent memory.'[64] Later in the year the Labour government announced the abolition of all closed, security areas laws within the Green Line; a decision which was officially put into effect on 31 December 1972. The next day Defence Minister Moshe Dayan reimposed Defence (Emergency) Regulations on Iqrit and Kafr Bir'im, making them 'closed areas' with the villagers still requiring a permit in order to enter them.[65] Four months later, on 1 April 1973, near Hadera in Israel, some 7,000 Arabs and Jews in Israel took part in an open air meeting of solidarity with the inhabitants of the two villages.[66]

In 1993 (under the pragmatic coalition of Labour-Meretz) a Ministerial Committee under Minister of Justice David Libai was formed to deal with the issue of Kafr Bir'im and Iqrit. Two years later, in December 1995, it announced its recommendations, proposing to settle the case with the residents of the villages on the following conditions:

- partial return: about 600 families to be allowed back; eligibility would be restricted to heads of households who lived in one of the villages and owned a house there on 6 November 1948, as well as two adult descendants per household;
- the land would still be under the control of the Finance Ministry;
- only a small parcel of land would be leased to returning households: only 600 dunums were to be set aside for each village (less than 10 per cent of the two villages' original land);
- they should forgo land and property restitution;
- they should not engage in agriculture.

The Committee declared that solution as representative of the 'generous good-will of the Israeli government'.[67]

These recommendations were never implemented. Although they saw the Committee's recommendations as a step in the right direction, the villagers from Iqrit and Kafr Bir'im, who by then numbered 8,000 persons with claims to thousands of dunums of land, rejected the decision. In 1948 Kafr Bir'im had a population of about 950, while Iqrit had about 500 inhabitants. According to the *Village Statistics, 1945* of the British mandatory government, Kafr Bir'im lands had consisted of 12,244 dunums, while Iqrit had 711 dunums.[68] According to Kamel Ya'aqub, of the Committee for the Uprooted of Kafr Bir'im, there were three problems with the government's decision:

- it limited the number of the villagers who could return;
- the land stayed under state control;
- it did not return all the land which the villagers farmed, land in use by neighbouring Jewish settlements.

As one villager from Bir'im explained: 'How do they expect me to decide which two sons will return with me? What should I say to the other six members of my family?'[69]

The villagers demanded more land (having lost more land through expropriation after 1948) and insisted that all their descendants be allowed back, while Jewish settlements in the area urged that less land be handed back to the Arab villagers.

Another committee of senior Israeli officials, formed in early 1996 in response to the villagers' ongoing campaign, amended the recommendations of December 1995 by removing the 'two descendants' restriction; it also suggested that the government consider expansion of the two villages' boundaries if necessary. No action was taken. A petition filed by the Iqrit villagers in late 1996 was still pending in 1999–2000 before the High Court of Justice: the villagers wanted the Court at least to order that the Ministerial Committee recommendations be implemented. On 2 December 1998, the Knesset defeated a private members' bill, submitted by liberal MK Dedi Tzucker (Meretz), to allow the villagers to return. However, even those liberal Israelis who have supported the villagers' struggle to return to Iqrit and Kafr Bir'im, believe that the case is unique and should not be taken as a precedent to allow other 'internal refugees' to return to their villages and homes. The issue remained unresolved under the governments of Binyamin Netanyahu and Ehud Barak.

On 10 October 2001 the deliberations of the coalition government of Ariel Sharon about whether to respect the 1951 High Court ruling and allow the villagers of Iqrit and Kafr Bir'im to return to their homes and properties finally came to an end, when the 'security cabinet' of Ariel Sharon decided against their return because of 'security concern' and because it 'would set a precedent for other displaced Palestinians who all demand to return to their homes and lands'. The cabinet decision showed that little had changed in Israel's land policies since 1971, when the then Prime Minister Golda Meir issued a similar decision. The official response of the Israeli cabinet to the 1996 petition was to be considered by the High Court in a hearing scheduled for early November 2001, although the prospects of a successful outcome for the residents of Iqrit and Kafr Bir'im in the Israeli legal system appeared to be slim.[70]

ii. The National Committee for the Defence of the Rights of the Internally Displaced and Direct Action

Although the issue of the internal refugees is still conspicuous by its absence from both the international agenda and the Israeli–Palestinian peace negotiations, the early and mid-1990s witnessed a turning point in the struggle of the internally displaced to regain their lands and properties. The 1990s introduced two major factors into the debate over the fate of the internal refugees: (a) the impact of the Madrid and Oslo peace processes on the internal refugees,[71] both positive and negative; (b) the formation, for the first time since 1948, of a nationwide organisation: the National Committee for the Defence of the Rights of the Internally Displaced in Israel (*al-Lajna al-Qutriyya Li-Difai' 'an Huquq al-Muhajjarin fi Israeel*), which has emerged gradually since the early 1990s also under the impact of the Israeli–Palestinian peace process. The National Committee is an umbrella organisation whose three principal aims are:

1. to promote the right of return of the internal refugees to their original villages and to reject compensation as an alternative to return;
2. to unite the efforts and activities of the various local and village committees of the internally displaced within the framework of the National Committee;

3. to conduct public relations campaigns on behalf of the internally displaced directed at Israeli (Jewish and Arab) and international audiences.[72]

The committee was founded in 1992, shortly after the Madrid Peace Conference of October 1991, as according to one of its founders (Ahmad Ashkar), 'the convening of the Madrid Conference convinced us beyond the shadow of a doubt that the PLO and Arab countries had abandoned the Arabs of [19]48 [i.e., Israeli-Palestinians]. Therefore, we decided to take matters into our hands.'[73]

The committee is led by a Galilee-based lawyer, Wakim Wakim, who himself comes from a family of internal refugees originating from the (destroyed) village of al-Bassa in upper-western Galilee. Wakim had this to say in an interview in December 2002:

> We began just after the Madrid Conference. Needless to say, we were very upset with the Palestinian delegation for not raising the issue of the internally displaced, and our fear of exclusion from the PLO's strategy led us to take action by forming a committee to prepare for the peace conference announced by Madrid. Before our initiative, there were already a number of local committees that had been working on their own, representing the inhabitants of specific destroyed villages, such as Iqrit and [Kafr] Biri'm. There was also a committee for Saffuriya (the Committee to Preserve the Heritage of Saffuriya),[74] the Hittin Committee, and a few others.[75]

The beginnings of the National Committee for the Defence of the Rights of the Internally Displaced in Israel were the early 1990s, when a very small number of activists from several local village committees held their first joint meeting at the end of which they announced the establishment of a standing committee for the defence of the rights of the internally displaced. The committee, aiming to unify local efforts and to make its issue a common cause rather than a separate issue of each village, for the next three years organised lectures and panel discussions in various Arab schools and localities around Israel. Then, on 11 March 1995 they held their first nationwide convention (at Qasr al-Salam: near Tamra) in western Galilee with the participation of some 280 delegates representing 39 destroyed villages and various groups of the internally displaced. The conference, which became a major turning point, crucially transformed the standing committee into a nationwide organisation and issued a public statement which rejected 'all alternatives to the right of return'. Significantly, however, it was only in May 2000 that the National Committee was registered as an NGO under the name 'Association for the Defence of the Rights of the Displaced in Israel'.[76] Since then, however, the Association has continued to operate under two slightly different names: one highlighting its delicate legal position in Israel and the other (the National Committee for the Defence of the Rights of the Internally Displaced in Israel), emphasising its national Palestinian character. Interestingly, however, because the overwhelming majority of the internally displaced originated from, and currently live in, the northern part of the country, the activities of the National Committee for the Defence of the Rights of the Internally Displaced are largely concentrated in the north of the country.

iii. *Nakba*, Memory and Commemoration

Since 1948 Israel's refugee strategy towards the internal refugees has consisted of a series of practical measures, including the suppressing of *nakba* memory, the denial of restitution of property and involuntary resettlement. The victims – in this case internally displaced Israeli–Arab citizens – became 'victimisers', a threat to Israel's demographic security and ethnic domination. The struggle of the Palestinian citizens of Israel (including the 'present absentees') for a multicultural, democratic and inclusive state – a state of all its citizens – became a threat to the very central Zionist ethnic project of 'Judaising' Palestine/Israel.

Israel's refugee strategy of turning history on its head has, however, clearly failed. In fact, the more the state policies are focused on suppressing *nakba* memory and dissolving the internal refugee problem, the stronger the indigenous resistance to that policy becomes and the more open *nakba* commemoration and direct action become. Indeed, *nakba* memory and active participation in commemoration, driven by a very real sense of historical injustice, is far stronger among the third generation of 'present absentees' than the first and second. In recent years there has been an awakening of all sorts including the participation of Palestinian communities in Israel in the commemoration of the *nakba* to an extent that was not commemorated in years past. This was largely due to activities of the National Committee for the Defence of the Rights of the Internally Displaced which, since its foundation in the 1990s, has had a number of major successes. It was the first Arab organisation in Israel to articulate successfully the nationwide demands of the internal refugees. To that end it has conducted a widely publicised campaign of direct action. This included commemorative and mass rallies, regular marches to, and cultural activities on the lands of, destroyed villages (such as Saffuriya, Suhmata, al-Ghabisiya, al-Birwa, Ma'lul, Lubya, Hittin) as well as the restoration of holy sites (mosques, churches and cemeteries) in these villages. Moreover, a great number of the activities of the National Committee on the ground are carried out through a non-governmental organisation (NGO) for the protection of holy sites, called 'al-Aqsa'. This body looks after old cemeteries and mosques and campaigns for the release and restoration of mosques existing in abandoned (almost completely destroyed) villages.[77]

Another significant success has been in uniting a large number of Arab mayors, Arab members of the Knesset and practically all Arab political parties and national institutions in Israel (operating under the umbrella of the Higher Arab Monitoring Committee: *Lajnat al-Mutaba'a al-'Ulya*), in support of the demands of the internally displaced.[78] One of the largest and most successful mass rallies to be organised by the National Committee was held on 11 March 2000 in the sports hall of the municipality of Nazareth, the largest Arab town in Israel. It was attended by some 850 participants, including the mayor of Nazareth Ramiz Jarayseh, Muhammad Zaydan, the head of the Higher Arab Monitoring Committee, 'Abdul-Karim al-Zraykhi of the PLO Refugee Department, activists from displaced communities, representatives of Arab political parties and institutions in Israel, as well as solidarity delegations from the occupied Golan Heights and refugee camps in the West Bank. The speakers emphasised two common themes: (1) the determination of Palestinian refugees in general and the internally displaced in particular to continue the struggle for the 'right of return'; (2) the need for united political action towards a solution of the Palestinian refugee problem, based on the implementation of international law and UN resolutions, especially Resolution 194.

Speaking on behalf of the National Committee, Wakim Wakim presented its manifesto with these specific points:

- the National Committee calls for the return of the internally displaced to their homes and property, in accordance with UN Resolution 194. It also calls for the abolition of the Law of Absentees' Property and other laws providing for ethnic discrimination against the Arab citizens of Israel;

- while the National Committee is the representative of the internally displaced in Israel, the PLO is the sole (overall) representative of the Palestinian people, including external and internal refugees;
- The National Committee calls for the maintenance of the sacred sites (mosques, churches and cemeteries) in all destroyed villages and the protection of other Arab sites of historical significance;
- any future political agreement signed by the PLO with Israel that excludes the 'right of return' would be considered null and void by the Palestinian refugees and internally displaced;
- Israel continues to violate the basic rights of its Palestinian citizens: their right to property is denied; some Israeli leaders even question their right to vote to the Knesset and be represented in parliament;
- the National Committee demands broad support for the internally displaced from all Palestinian social and political institutions, for the immediate adoption of the cause of the internally displaced persons in Israel by the Palestinian leadership;
- the National Committee calls for a joint and intensive effort at documentation of Palestinian eviction and displacement during the 1948 *nakba*.[79]

The manifesto of the National Committee and its political activities underline the fact that one of its paramount objectives has been to try to create a linkage between the desire among many of the internally displaced to return to their original villages and regain their land – a desire partly derived from existential and day-to-day problems, including the pressing need for housing among the internal refugees and their descendants – and the wider Palestinian national struggle for the right to return under international law and UN resolutions.[80] A 1986 study of three refugee communities living in Galilee (Shafa'amr, Tarshiha and Kabul) by Majid al-Haj had found that many of the internally displaced had begun to lose hope that their eviction from their homes was temporary.[81] However, many of them continued to demand that their case be resolved in any final settlement reached between Israel and the Palestinians. Since the mid-1990s, however, the internally displaced, as a result of the effective nationwide activities of the National Committee for the Defence of the Rights of the Internally Displaced, have been receiving considerable media attention both inside and outside Israel. Despite constant harassment from, and various restrictions imposed by, the Israeli authorities and police, visits to destroyed villages, public rallies for the commemoration of the Palestinian *nakba*, and protest marches, coordinated by the National Committee, have become a regular event.[82] On 12 May 1997, the 49th anniversary of the creation of the state of Israel, thousands of Arab citizens, including many internal refugees, responded to calls by the National Committee and took part in protest action, processions and commemorations, conducted under the slogan: 'Give the Internal Refugees Back their Lands.'[83] On the 28 March 1998, while Israel was preparing to celebrate its 50th anniversary, thousands of internal refugees held a protest procession from the village of Shaykh Dannun in the foothills of the western Galilee mountains to the ruins of the al-Ghabisiya – a neighbouring abandoned village whose land ownership and use (together with two smaller neighbouring villages) in the mid-1940s was 11,786 dunums.[84] The protesters carried placards with the names of Palestinian villages destroyed in 1948 and called on the Israeli government to let them go back to their villages and lands. These protests turned out to be the start of many events undertaken by the Palestinian citizens of Israel to mark the 50th anniversary of the *nakba*.[85]

Calls to boycott all celebrations of the independence of Israel and replace them by public rallies for the commemoration of the 1948 Palestinian *nakba* have become a regular feature of the tactics of the National Committee in recent years. Success for this tactic came in May 2000 when the Palestinian community in Israel issued, for the first time, a united call for a public boycott of the celebrations of Israel's 'Independence Day' (14 May) – a boycott led by the National Committee in coordination with the Higher Arab Monitoring Committee. When an 'independence celebration' was staged by the Israeli authorities in the Arab town of Shafa'amr on 7 May, it was met by a Palestinian counter-demonstration which led to violent clashes with the Israeli police and resulted in 20 Arab injuries and 30 arrests.[86] A May 2000 statement issued by the National Committee, under the title: 'Their Independence Day – The Day of Our *Nakba*', read:

> We the internally displaced Palestinians suffer a double pain. We have remained near our destroyed villages and towns. With pain we listen to the silent prayers of our mosques and the silent call

> of our church bells – silenced since our eviction and transformed into stables for the settlers' cattle and sites of prostitution and drug abuse. They desecrate the cemeteries of our ancestors who, for 52 years, have not stopped appealing to our conscience and the conscience of humanity.[87]

Direct action and activities organised inside the destroyed villages by the internally displaced were also supported by other Arab NGOs and human rights organisations in Israel. In late October 2001 the Public Committee of Iqrit and Kafr Bir'im organised a mass protest at the church of Iqrit followed by a public rally in the village in which the Catholic Bishop Butrus Mu'alem, the head of the Higher Arab Monitoring Committee, and hundreds of people from Arab towns and villages in Galilee participated.[88] Bishop Mu'alem said that he would present the case of the two villages to the Pope at their meeting in Rome in early November, although he hoped that the Israeli government would begin to tackle the problem, helping the villagers to return to their original land, before the problem becomes an international issue.[89] There are several reasons why the villagers to Kafr Bir'im and Iqrit have been more successful in attracting support and sympathy for their cause, including strong attachment to their personal territory, never giving up hope of returning or ceasing their efforts. It was also the mobilisation of many Christian churches in the Holy Land and abroad in support of their case which made it a *cause célèbre*. Another important factor is that the refugee communities of Kafr Bir'im and Iqrit have become a model for other internally displaced communities to imitate, with their cohesive and distinct village organisations.[90]

EPILOGUE

The data on the internal refugees in Israel and their social and economic conditions have serious shortcomings. Although their situation has remained off the agenda of Israeli–Palestinian negotiations, it is, however, generally viewed as an integral part of the overall Palestine refugee question. Moreover, although they are an integral part of both the Palestinian national minority in Israel and the Palestinian people, their continued existence as a separate social category, and as refugees in their own homeland, make them potential candidates for special concern. Raising awareness of their plight on both local and international levels, therefore, has remained central to the struggle of the internal refugees to bring about the implementation of international resolutions and the fulfilment of their right to return to their destroyed villages. As Israel remains unwilling to concede these rights, support from human rights organisations and the international community will be crucial in the years ahead. Moreover, until the internally displaced are allowed to return to their homes and original lands, it would be difficult to see how the state of Israel can begin to address fundamental issues such as democracy and equality for all citizens irrespective of religious, ethnic or racial affiliation.

The emergence of local Arab organisations, at both village and nationwide levels, have proved to be vitally important; since the early 1990s, the internally displaced have become better organised and more effective politically, mainly through the formation of civil society organisations and NGOs, including the National Committee for the Defence of the Rights of the Internally Displaced in Israel.[91] The emergence of these organisations since the early 1990s, their mass protests and activities inside the destroyed villages, together with the direct action of older, well-established Arab organisations in Israel (such as the Committee for the Uprooted of Kafr Bir'im, the Committee for the Defence of Arab Lands and the Higher Arab Monitoring Committee) have had some impact, attracting attention in the Hebrew press in Israel and, more importantly, support from international human rights organisations. Both the UN Human Rights Committee and the UN Committee on Economic, Social and Cultural Rights severely criticised Israel in 1998 for its land policies and for its treatment of the Arab citizens and 'present absentees'. Israel's policies were described by the Committee on Economic, Social and Cultural Rights as an institutionalised form of discrimination and a serious breach of Israel's obligations under international law, and, more specifically, the International Covenant on Economic, Social and Cultural Rights of 1966. Addressing the issue under articles 16 and 17 of the Covenant, the UN Committee on Economic, Social and Cultural Rights, in its report of December 1998, expressed

> its concern over the plight of an estimated 200,000 uprooted 'present absentees', Palestinian Arab citizens of Israel most of whom were forced to leave their villages during the 1948 war on the understanding that they would be allowed by the Government of Israel to return after the war. Although a few have been given back their property, the vast majority continue to be displaced and

> dispossessed by the State because their lands were confiscated and not returned to them.

On the issue of land use and land policies pursued by semi-official Zionist agencies in Israel

> The Committee expresses concern that excessive emphasis upon the State as a 'Jewish State' encourages discrimination and accords a second-class status to its non-Jewish citizens. The Committee notes with concern that the Government of Israel does not accord equal rights to its Arab citizens, although they comprise over 19 per cent of the total population. ... The Committee notes with grave concern that the Status Law of 1952 authorizes the World Zionist Organization/Jewish Agency and its subsidiaries, including the Jewish National Fund, to control most of the land in Israel, since these institutions are chartered to benefit Jews exclusively. Despite the fact that the institutions are chartered under private law, the State of Israel nevertheless has a decisive influence on their policies and thus remains responsible for their activities. A State party cannot divest itself of its obligations under the Covenant by privatizing governmental functions. The Committee takes the view that property to these agencies constitutes an institutionalized form of discrimination because these agencies by definition would deny the use of these properties to non-Jews. Thus, these practices constitute a breach of Israel's obligations under the Covenant.[92]

The Hebrew daily *Haaretz* of 8 January 2001 published an article entitled: 'Also the Refugees in Israel Want to Return Home':

> Representatives of the 'internal refugees' (the 'displaced') have recently renewed their appeal to the Palestinian leadership. They called on senior [representatives] of the [Palestinian] Authority not to conduct negotiations in their name with regard to their demand to return home.

The Secretary of the National Committee for the Defence of the Rights of the Internally Displaced in Israel, Wakim Wakim, according to *Haaretz*, stated that he and his colleagues were concerned that PA President Yasser 'Arafat would be willing to make far-reaching concessions to Israel with regard to the right of return. Instead of being represented in the final status talks by the PA, the internal refugees were seeking to conduct legal, public and political struggles within the Israeli system. The 'internally displaced', Wakim explained, felt they had a better chance of realising the dream of return than the 1948 external refugees, because, being Israeli citizens, they were better placed to utilise the Israeli legal tools available. Wakim added:

> The government of Israel must remember that, even if it were to succeed in imposing a semblance of settlement on the Palestinian Authority that would dissolve the question of the right of return, it [the government] would have to continue facing our demands – to fulfil our rights as citizens.[93]

Since the early 1990s the struggle against the denial of the *nakba* in Israel has become a major struggle for the Palestinian minority in general and the 'present absentees' in particular. The Palestinian community in Israel has associated, in a way that it did not previously, its collective and individual memories of the 1948 catastrophe with the general Palestinian plight and with its own predicament. This association has been manifested in an array of symbolic events such as memorial services during *nakba* commemoration day, organising tours and marches to abandoned and destroyed Palestinian villages in Israel, regular seminars on the past and extensive interviews with *nakba* survivors in the Arabic press in Israel.[94]

NOTES

1. 'Adalah (the Legal Centre for Arab Minority Rights in Israel), *History of the Arabs in Israel*, at: http://www.adalah.org/histlegal.htm (accessed on 20 November 2000).
2. Hillel Cohen put the figure at 15 per cent. See his work, *Hanifkadim Hanokhahim: Haplitim Hafalastinayyim Beyisrael Meaz 1948* [The Present Absentees: The Palestinian Refugees in Israel Since 1948] (Jerusalem: Centre for the Study of Arab Society in Israel, Van Leer Institute, 2000) (Hebrew); David Grossman, *Nokhahim Nifkadim* [Present Absentees] (Tel Aviv: Kibbutz Meuhad Publications, 1992), p.15. Charles Kamen wrote that in 1948–9 the number was approximately 23,000. Charles S. Kamen, 'After the Catastrophe I: The Arabs in Israel, 1948–51', *Middle Eastern Studies* 23, no.4 (October 1987), pp.468–70.
3. Kamen, 'After the Catastrophe I', p.466.
4. Majid al-Haj, 'The Arab Internal Refugees in Israel: The Emergence of a Minority Within the Minority', *Immigrants and Minorities* 7, no.2

(July 1988), pp.149–65; Majid al-Haj, 'Adjustment Patterns of the Arab Internal Refugees in Israel', *Internal Migration* 24, no.3 (1986), pp.651–73.

5. Riad Beidas, 'The Internally Displaced – Seeking Return Within One's Own Land: An Interview with Wakim Wakim', *Journal of Palestine Studies* 31, no.1 (Autumn 2001), p.33.
6. See, for instance, Cohen, *Hanifkadim Hanokhahim: Haplitim Hafalastinayyim Beyisrael Meaz 1948* [The Present Absentees: The Palestinian Refugees in Israel Since 1948]; David Grossman, *Nokhahim Nifkadim* [Present Absentees] (Tel Aviv: Kibbutz Meuhad Publications, 1992).
7. Kamen, 'After the Catastrophe I', p.466.
8. *Discrimination Diary, 25 May 2000*, The Arab Association for Human Rights, at http://www.arabhra.org/dd/dd225.htm (accessed on 8 December 2001).
9. Although there is no possibility of arriving at a reliable estimate of the number of 'returnees', a study conducted by Majid al-Haj found that 45 per cent of the original 37,500 'internal refugees' first moved to neighbouring Arab countries, before returning to Israel shortly after 1948. Majid Al-Haj, 'The Arab Internal Refugees in Israel: The Emergence of a Minority Within the Minority', in Ian Lustick (ed.), *Palestinians under Israeli Rule* (New York: Garland Publishing Inc., 1994), pp.5–6.
10. Nearly 50 per cent of the marriages of the internally displaced take place within their original community. Majid Al-Haj, 'The Arab Internal Refugees in Israel: The Emergence of a Minority Within the Minority', pp.5–6 and 16. See also Ahmad Ashkar, 'Internal Refugees: Their Inalienable Right to Return', *News From Within* 9, no.8 (August 1995), pp.14–17; Kamen, 'After the Catastrophe I', p.467.
11. Al-Haj, 'The Arab Internal Refugees in Israel: The Emergence of a Minority Within the Minority', p.9.
12. Ibid.
13. Kamen, 'After the Catastrophe I', p.470.
14. Ibid., p.471.
15. Al-Haj, 'The Arab Internal Refugees in Israel: The Emergence of a Minority Within the Minority', pp.5–6.
16. In April 1949, Nazareth, eight months after it was captured, had 5,222 refugees and an additional 7,334 were found in the surrounding villages. Most of the refugees in Nazareth had come from towns or from large villages: one-third came from Haifa, and slightly less than a quarter (or 1,200) came from al-Mujaydil, five kilometres south of Nazareth, whose inhabitants had been expelled to the town after the village had been captured. Ten per cent of the Nazareth refugees were from Tiberias, and a similar proportion (numbering 560 persons) came from 'Illut, a village which lay five kilometres to the west. There were 42 families of refugees from Baysan. Only the refugees from Haifa, 'Illut and Na'ura (six persons) had the possibility of returning to their former localities. Charles S. Kamen, 'After the Catastrophe II: The Arabs in Israel, 1948–51', *Middle Eastern Studies* 24, no.1 (January 1988), pp.78–9.
17. Kamen, 'After the Catastrophe I', p.474.

18. Joseph Schechla, 'The Invisible People Come to Light: Israel's "Internally Displaced" and the "Unrecognized Villages"', *Journal of Palestine Studies* 31, no.1 (Autumn 2001), p.22.
19. Beidas, 'The Internally Displaced – Seeking Return Within One's Own Land', p.34.
20. Ibid., p.36.
21. Simha Flapan, *The Birth of Israel: Myths and Realities* (New York: Pantheon Books, 1997), p.107.
22. Tom Segev, *1949: The First Israelis* (New York: The Free Press, 1986), p.52.
23. Ibid.
24. Ibid.
25. Quoted in Benny Morris, *Israel's Border Wars, 1949–1956* (Oxford: Clarendon Press, Revised edition, 1997), pp. 157–8.
26. See Israeli State Archives (ISA), Foreign Ministry, 2401/19a.
27. For the Lavon's report, see ISA, Foreign Ministry, 2401/19a.
28. Segev, *1949: The First Israelis*, p.51.
29. David Kretzmer, *The Legal Status of the Arabs in Israel* (Boulder, San Francisco: Westview Press, 1990), p.141.
30. Ibid., p.142.
31. See Penny Maddrell, *The Beduin of the Negev* (London: The Minority Rights Group, Report no.81, 1990), p.7.
32. ISA, Foreign Ministry, 2401/21.
33. ISA, Foreign Ministry, 2401/21b.
34. Kretzmer, *The Legal Status of the Arabs in Israel*, pp.50–1.
35. Cited in the manifesto of the National Committee for the Defence of the Internally Displaced Palestinians in Israel, Badil Resource Centre, at: http://www.badil.org/Press/2000/manifesto.htm (accessed on 15 December 2001).
36. *Discrimination Diary, 25 February 2000*, The Arab Association for Human Rights, at: http://www.arabhra.org/dd/dd225.htm (accessed on 8 December 2001).
37. Al-Haj, 'The Arab Internal Refugees in Israel', p.9.
38. David Gilmour, *Dispossessed: The Ordeal of the Palestinians* (London: Sphere Books, 1982), p.101.
39. For selected Israeli laws affecting Arab land ownership, see Oren Yiftachel, *Planning a Mixed Region in Israel* (Aldershot, England: Avebury, 1992), appendix 1, p.313.
40. Quoted in Ian Lustick, *Arabs in the Jewish State* (Austin and London: University of Texas Press, 1980), pp.175–6.
41. See the address of the Chairman of the Knesset Finance Committee, who presented the bill to the Knesset, in *Divrie Haknesset*, 868–70, 27 February 1950.
42. Quoted in Kretzmer, *The Legal Status of the Arabs in Israel*, p.56; Usama Halabi, 'The Impact of the Jewishness of the State of Israel on the Status and Rights of the Arab Citizens in Israel', in Nur Masalha (ed.), *The Palestinians in Israel: Is Israel the State of all its Citizens and 'Absentees'?* (Nazareth: Galilee Centre for Social Research, 1993), pp.22–5.
43. Kretzmer, *The Legal Status of the Arabs in Israel*, p.56.
44. Ibid., pp.56–7.

45. Ibid., p.57.
46. Gilmour, *Dispossessed*, p.108.
47. Benjamin Beit-Hallahmi, *Original Sins* (London: Pluto Press, 1992), p.91.
48. 'Adalah, *History of the Palestinians in Israel*, at: http://www.adalah.org/background.shtml (accessed on 3 November 2001).
49. Al-Haj, 'The Arab Internal Refugees in Israel', p.9; Beidas, 'The Internally Displaced – Seeking Return Within One's Own Land', p.33.
50. *Discrimination Diary, 21 October 1999*, Arab Association for Human Rights, at http://www.arabhra.org/dd/dd10–21.htm (accessed on 8 December 2001). Professor 'Uzi Ornan estimates that 95 per cent of the lands within the Green Line are classified as state land. Cited in Noam Chomsky, *Socialist Revolution* 5 (1975), pp.45–6. For further discussion of land alienation and its effect on Arabs, see Elia Zureik, *The Palestinians in Israel* (London: Routledge & Kegan Paul, 1979), pp.115–22; Ran Kislev, 'Land Expropriations: History of Oppression', *New Outlook* (September–October 1976), pp.23–32.
51. In 1953 the JNF reiterated that its primary mission was to acquire lands 'for the purpose of settling Jews on the said lands and property'. Kretzmer, *The Legal Status of the Arabs in Israel*, pp.61–73.
52. See article by Amnon Rubinstein, in *Haaretz*, 13 October 1999.
53. Henry Rosenfeld, 'The Class Situation of the Arab National Minority in Israel', *Comparative Studies in Society and History* 20, no.3 (July 1978), p.400. Cited in Noam Chomsky, *Socialist Revolution* 5 (1975), pp. 45–6. For further discussion of land alienation and its effect on Arabs, see Elia Zureik, *The Palestinians in Israel* (London: Routledge & Kegan Paul, 1979), pp.115–22; Ran Kislev, 'Land Expropriations: History of Oppression', *New Outlook* (September–October 1976), pp.23–32.
54. Riah Abu Al-Assal, 'Zionism: As It Is in Israel for an Arab', in *Judaism or Zionism?* (London: Zed Books, 1986), p.172.
55. Joseph L. Ryan, 'Refugees Within Israel: The Case of the Villagers of Kafr Iqrit and Bir'im', *Journal of Palestine Studies* II, no.4 (Summer 1993), pp.59–60; *Christian Science Monitor*, 12 August 1972.
56. *Discrimination Diary, 20 December 1999*, the Arab Association for Human Rights, at: http://www.arabhra.org/dd/dd1219.htm (accessed on 8 December 2001).
57. Morris, *Israel's Border Wars*, p.148.
58. *Discrimination Diary, 20 December 1999*, the Arab Association for Human Rights, at: http://www.arabhra.org/dd/dd1219.htm (accessed on 8 December 2001).
59. Ibid.
60. Ibid.
61. Ryan, 'Refugees Within Israel', pp.64–5.
62. *Jerusalem Post*, 24 July 1972.
63. Ryan, 'Refugees Within Israel', p.55.
64. Amos Elon, 'Two Arab Towns that Plumb Israel's Conscience', *New York Times Magazine*, 22 October 1972, p.44.
65. *Discrimination Diary, 20 December 1999*, the Arab Association for Human Rights, at: http://www.arabhra.org/dd/dd1219.htm (accessed on 8 December 2001).

66. Ryan, 'Refugees Within Israel', p.55.
67. *Discrimination Diary, 20 December 1999*, the Arab Association for Human Rights, at: http://www.arabhra.org/dd/dd1219.htm (accessed on 8 December 2001).
68. *Village Statistics, 1945* (Beirut: PLO Research Centre edition, 1970), pp.40, 70.
69. *Discrimination Diary, 20 December 1999*, the Arab Association for Human Rights, at: http://www.arabhra.org/dd/dd1219.htm (accessed on 8 December 2001).
70. 'Israel's Racist Land Policies Remain Unchanged: Government Rejects Return of Internally Displaced Palestinian Villagers of Iqrit and Bir'im', at: Badil Resource Centre, 11 October 2001 (E53/2001).
71. Cohen, *Hanifkadim Hanokhahim*, p.12.
72. Wakim Wakim, *Haq al-'Awda Lemuhajri al-Dahkil Haq Ghair Qabil Littasarrof* [The Right of Return of the Internally Displaced is an Inalienable Right] (Haifa: Initiating Committee for the Defence of the Rights of the Displaced in Israel, 1995), p.2.
73. Ahmad Ashkar, 'Internal Refugees: Their Inalienable Right to Return', *News From Within* 11, no.8 (August 1995), pp.14–17.
74. A destroyed village near Nazareth; there is an entire and very crowded quarter in the city inhabited by displaced people from Saffuriya.
75. Beidas, 'The Internally Displaced – Seeking Return Within One's Own Land', p.35.
76. Ibid., p.36.
77. Cohen, *Hanifkadim Hanokhahim*, p.14.
78. Cohen, *Hanifkadim Hanokhahim*, p.13. See also interview with 'Azmi Bishara, leader of al-Tajamua' al-Watani al-Dimuqrati, in *Haaretz*, 12 June 1996; statements by the Mayor of Umm al-Fahm, Raid Salah, in *Sawt al-Haq Wal-Hurriyya*, 31 March 1995.
79. The manifesto of the National Committee for the Defence of the Internally Displaced Palestinians in Israel, Badil Resource Centre, at: http://www.badil.org/Press/2000/manifesto.htm (accessed on 15 December 2001); Statement by the National Committee for the Defence of Internally Displaced Palestinians in Israel, Badil Resource Centre, 13 March 2000, at: http://www.badil.org/Press/2000/press93-00.htm (accessed on 15 December 2001); *Internally Displaced Palestinians in Israel Reaffirm: We Demand to Return to Our Homes and Property*, Badil Resource Centre, 13 March 2000, at: http://www.badil.org/Press/2000/press93–00.htm (accessed on 15 December 2001).
80. Beidas, 'The Internally Displaced – Seeking Return Within One's Own Land', p.34.
81. Al-Haj, 'The Arab Internal Refugees in Israel: The Emergence of a Minority Within the Minority', p.8.
82. Ashkar, 'Internal Refugees: Their Inalienable Right to Return', pp.14–17; *Al-Ayyam* (Ramallah), 14 May 1997.
83. *Al-Ayyam* (Ramallah), 14 May 1997.
84. Al-Ghabisiya was occupied on 20–21 May 1948. The village surrendered formally and its population were expelled sometime during the following days or weeks. Al-Ghabisiya and two other neighbouring villages, Shaykh

Dannun and Shaykh Dawud, were evacuated. Those inhabitants from al-Ghabisiya who had not sought refuge in Lebanon were joined by other internally displaced from villages such al-Hahr, al-Tall, Umm al-Faraj, 'Amqa, and Kuwaykat and ended up in the repopulated village of Shaykh Dannun which in 1973 had a population of 1,000. The only landmark that remains today in al-Ghabisiyya is the mosque, and the debris of houses, terraces and the village cemetery can be seen amidst a thick forest of cypress trees that was planted on the village site and part of the land. The Jewish population of Netiv Hashayara use the adjacent non-forested land for agriculture. Walid Khalidi (ed.), *All That Remains: The Palestinian Villages Occupied and Depopulated by Israel in 1948* (Washington DC: Institute for Palestine Studies, 1992), pp.13–15; Morris, *The Birth of the Palestinian Refugee Problem*, pp.124–5.

85. *Haaretz*, 29 March 1998.
86. *Palestinians in Israel Boycott Israeli Independence Celebrations: Statement by the National Committee for the Defence of Internally Displaced Palestinians in Israel*, Badil Resource Centre, 9 May 2000, at: http://www.badil.org/Press/2000/press101-00.htm (accessed on 15 December 2001).
87. Ibid.
88. *Fasl al-Maqal*, 26 October 2001.
89. *Al-Ittihad*, 21 October 2001.
90. Al-Haj, 'The Arab Internal Refugees in Israel: The Emergence of a Minority Within the Minority', p.13.
91. Ashkar, 'Internal Refugees: Their Inalienable Right to Return', pp.14–17.
92. *Concluding Observations of the Committee on Economic, Social and Cultural Rights, Israel, UN Economic and Social Council*, General, E/C.12/1/Add.27, 4 December 1998, at: http://www.hri.ca/fortherecord1999/docu.../e-c12-1-add27.ht (accessed on 8 December 2001.) The full text of the International Covenant on Economic, Social and Cultural Rights, at: http://www.tufts.edu/departments/fletcher/multi/texts/BH497.txt11/12/2001.
93. Uri Nir, 'Also the Refugees in Israel Want to Return Home', *Haaretz*, 8 January 2001, pp.1 and 13a.
94. Ilan Pappé, 'Demons of the Nakbah', *Al-Ahram Weekly Online*, no.586, 16–22 May 2002.

6 The 1967 Refugee Exodus

In his study of the 1967 exodus, William Harris found that the exodus from the West Bank involved up to 250,000 people and was by far the largest out-movement of Palestinians caused by the 1967 hostilities. Harris also estimated the population loss of the Gaza Strip between June and December 1967 at 70,000.[1] In total some 320,000 Palestinians fled or were expelled from the West Bank and Gaza in the course of the 1967 hostilities or shortly after.[2] Furthermore, sociologist George Kossaifi pointed to a continuing exodus from the West Bank and Gaza Strip since September 1967, arguing that as many as 655,000 Palestinians were forced from the West Bank and Gaza between June 1967 and December 1986, with an annual average of 33,000 persons. In the category of forced migration he includes those who were deported by Israel, those who left voluntarily but were unable to return because they did not possess a family reunification permit, and those who actually had a valid family reunification permit.[3] In contrast to the large number of books written on the Palestinian refugee exodus of 1948, only meagre historical research has been carried out on the 1967 exodus. In fact, Peter Dodd's and Halim Barakat's *River Without Bridges* (1969)[4] and William Harris's *Taking Root: Israeli Settlement in the West Bank, the Golan and Gaza-Sinai, 1967–1980* (1980) are the only serious scholarly investigations of the 1967 exodus. No comparative work on the two phenomena had ever been attempted. The paucity of published works on the 1967 exodus may be explained by the following: the 1967 exodus was much smaller than the 1948 one and with manifestly different demographic and political consequences for Palestinian society in the West Bank and Gaza Strip; the relevant Israeli state archival sources are still classified; the 1967 exodus is perceived by Israelis and Palestinians alike to be somewhat less controversial than the 1948 one; and the widespread (mis)perception that the 1967 exodus was largely 'voluntary', as opposed to the 'forcible' nature of the 1948 exodus.

An important body of new evidence has been unearthed in recent years, much of it appearing in the form of investigative articles in the Hebrew press, which sheds new light on the events surrounding the 1967 exodus. This chapter is an attempt to examine the causes of the 1967 exodus in the light of this new historical evidence, and more specifically against the background of actual evictions and 'transfer' operations carried out by the Israeli army during and after the 1967 war and their overall impact on the exodus. The Hebrew press has been an important source for the 1967 events. This was supplemented by secondary sources in Hebrew, Arabic and English. However, any definitive conclusions on the 1967 exodus will have to wait until Palestinians produce some good oral history on the 1967 events and Israel declassifies its relevant official documents.

REVIVAL OF 'TRANSFER'

The June war of 1967 marks a decisive turn in the history of Zionism, the Israeli state and the Palestinians, particularly those living in the occupied West Bank and Gaza Strip. Zionism at last had achieved its aim of controlling the whole of Palestine. Moreover, the overwhelming Israeli victory in the war, the seizure of the remainder of Palestine with its large Arab population, the resultant outburst, and later upsurge, of messianic Zionism and the growing Israeli confidence all contributed to the prompt and inevitable revival of the 'transfer' concept. In the wake of the 1967 conquests, the perception of 'Eretz Yisrael' (the 'Land of Israel') as a whole was found not only in the maximalist Revisionist camp of Herut (later Likud), but increasingly gained ground in all mainstream Zionist parties, particularly the traditionally pragmatic ruling Labour Party. Given the fact that ideological/historical and security claims to the occupied areas were to be put forward, action had to be taken to 'redeem the land' – through Jewish settlement without which the 'redemption' process was impossible. At the same time, official and public concern at being faced with what is called 'the demographic problem', that is, the problem of absorbing too many non-Jews within the Jewish state, became manifestly stronger. Although some 320,000 Palestinians fled or were expelled in the course of hostilities or shortly after, the Palestinian inhabitants of the territories – contrary to the 1948 exodus – remained *in situ*.

The number of Palestinians living within the new ceasefire lines – including those who were citizens of Israel – was over 1.3 million in 1967,[5] and given the high Arab birthrate, the prospect of the Palestinians becoming at least 50 per cent of the population – a Zionist/Israeli nightmare – was perceived as a feasible reality. The 'conquest of the land' (*kibbush haadamah*) had always been Zionism's central task. The Zionists needed, as in 1948, to hold the land they had conquered, to people it and 'develop' it, and to 'transfer', or otherwise to keep down, the natives who might oppose them. Indeed, for the Israeli leaders one of the key questions from June 1967 onwards was not whether Israel should maintain a presence in the newly acquired territories, but how it could be maintained without adding over 1 million Palestinians to the Arab minority of Israel. The old Zionist dilemma of non-Jews in a Jewish state had to be resolved. Against this background of Zionist expansionism, transfer ideas were revived in public debates, in popular songs, in articles in the Hebrew press and, most important, in cabinet discussions and government schemes.

A few weeks after the June 1967 war Israel's leading novelist, 'Amos 'Oz, wrote an article in the Hebrew daily *Davar* in which he drew attention to the revival of transfer thoughts in Israel: 'One often hears talk about pushing the Palestinian masses back to rich Kuwait or fertile Iraq.'[6]

'Oz also drew attention to Na'omi Shemer's song 'Jerusalem of Gold', which encapsulated this deep-seated inclination among Israeli Jews to see Palestine as a country without its Arab inhabitants. The song 'Jerusalem of Gold', which came to be defined as a kind of 'national anthem of the Six Day War',[7] was commissioned by the municipality of Jewish Jerusalem, was written for a music festival held on the eve of the war,[8] and became a national hit after the Israeli seizure of Arab East Jerusalem, the West Bank, and Gaza Strip. It is the most popular song ever produced in Israel and in 1967 it swept the country like lightning, genuinely expressing Israeli national aspirations following the new conquests. Na'omi Shemer herself received the Israel Prize for her unique contribution to the Israeli song. The song contains the following passages:

> Jerusalem of Gold ...
> How did the water cisterns dry out, the market-place is empty,
> And no-one visits the Holy Mount [al-Haram al-Sharif] in the Old City.
> And through the cave within the rock winds are whining,
> And no-one descends down to the Dead Sea en route for Jericho.
> .....
> Jerusalem of Gold ...
> We have returned to the water cisterns, to the market-place and the square.

A shofar[9] sounds on the Holy Mount in the Old City.
And in the caves within the rock a thousand suns do glow,
We shall again descend to the Dead Sea en route for
Jericho.[10]

In his *Davar* article, 'Oz offers a liberal Zionist explanation of the connection between the 'land without a people' formula, the popularity of Shemer's song 'Jerusalem of Gold', and the emergence of the transfer 'talk' after the war:

> It seems that the enchantment of 'renewing the days of old' is what gave Zionism its deep-seated inclination to see a country without inhabitants before it ... How fitting would it have been for the Return to Zion to have taken the land from the Roman legions or the nations of Canaan and Philistia. And to come to a completely empty country would have been even better. From there, it is only a short step to the kind of self-induced blindness that consists in disregarding the existence of the country's Arab population, or in discounting it and its importance on the dubious grounds that it 'has created no valuable cultural assets here', as if that would permit us to take no notice of its very existence. (In time, Naomi Shemer would express this state of mind in her song 'Jerusalem of Gold': '... the marketplace is empty/And no-one descends down to the Dead Sea/By way of Jericho.' Meaning, of course, that the marketplace is empty of Jews and that no Jew goes down to the Dead Sea by way of Jericho. A remarkable revelation of a remarkably characteristic way of thinking.)[11]

This 'characteristic way of thinking' echoes strongly the deep-seated formula of 'land without a people' and naturally leads to the revival of the transfer concept, a fact illustrated by the attitude of Na'omi Shemer, the poet laureate of Greater Israel's supporters, toward the indigenous inhabitants of Palestine. In January 1979 one of the famous heroes of the Israeli army, Meir Har-Tzion,[12] who owns a large cattle ranch situated on the lands of the destroyed Arab village of Kawkab al-Hawa in the Baysan valley (the inhabitants of which became refugees in 1948), stated: 'I do not say that we should put them [the Arabs] on trucks and kill them ... We must create a situation in which for them it would not be worth living here, but [to leave] to Jordan or Saudi Arabia or any other Arab state.'[13] Har-Tzion was promptly applauded by Shemer in an article in the Histadrut (Labour-controlled) daily *Davar*: 'Arab emigration from Israel, if it is done with mutual respect and positive will ... is likely to be the right solution ... it is possible that it will be recognised as a most human possibility after much suffering and only after hard and bitter civil war – but talking about it is permitted and must be now'; 'why is the exodus of one million French from Algeria a progressive and human solution and the exodus of one million Arabs from Israel' not?[14] Shemer and Har-Tzion are not marginal figures in Israel. Shemer is Israel's most famous and popular songwriter and Har-Tzion, who was brought up and educated in Kibbutz 'Ein Harod and fought in the Ariel Sharon-commanded 'Unit 101', set up by the army in the 1950s to carry out 'retaliatory' attacks against Arab targets, was described by the late Moshe Dayan as 'the brightest soldier in Jewish history since Bar-Kohkva'.[15]

The argument that the support for the 'transfer' concept does not come only from a fringe group also is illustrated by the fact that other veterans of 'Unit 101' and the paratroops corps, the elite force of the Israeli army which carried out most of the 'retaliatory' operations against Arab targets in the 1950s and the 1960s, have emerged in the 1970s and the 1980s among the most persistent public exponents of Arab 'transfer'. The most important veteran commanders of the paratroopers were Ariel Sharon – Defense Minister 1981–2; Raphael Eitan – Chief of Staff 1978–83; and Colonel Aharon Davidi – a former head of the Paratroops Corps, who became a senior lecturer in Geography at Tel Aviv University. Davidi replied in an interview in the mass-circulation daily *Ma'ariv* how he would solve the Palestinian problem: 'In the simplest and most human manner: the transfer of all the Palestinians from their present locations to the Arab countries'. When interviewer Dov Goldstein remarked that the Arabs would not accept such a solution, Davidi responded:

> They will. The transfer is very important for both the Jews and the Arabs. They will accept it, if they have no choice. The Arab states are spread out over a territory of more than ten million square kilometres. The density of the Arabs is the lowest in the world. Would it be a problem to absorb one million there, and to arrange housing and employment for them, with the help of the great wealth?[16]

Davidi's assertions echoed classical mainstream Zionist argumentation in justification of Arab removal. The argument that the support for the 'transfer' concept does not come only from a fringe minority is also illustrated by the fact that some of the nation's leading authors, novelists, and poets, such as Natan Alterman, Haim Hazaz, Yigal Mossenson, and Moshe Shamir (all of whom supported Israel's retention of all the territories seized in 1967), publicly supported the idea of transfer in the post-1967 era.[17] These leading literary figures also were closely associated with mainstream Labour or left-wing Zionism in the pre-1948 period and the first two decades of the State of Israel.

Natan Alterman (1910–70), whose poetry had a powerful impact on Jewish society during the Yishuv period and the first three decades of the State of Israel, wrote in an article in the mass-circulation daily *Ma'ariv* shortly after the 1967 war, that the transfer 'solution is only possible in an ideal peace situation between us and Arab states, which will agree to cooperate with us in a great project of population transfer'. Alterman had served on the editorial board of the liberal daily *Haaretz* from 1934 to 1943, when he joined the Histadrut daily *Davar*, virtually the mouthpiece of the ruling Mapai Party, and he had been closely associated with the two most important leaders of Mapai, David Ben-Gurion and Berl Katznelson, the founder of *Davar* and the hero of Labour Zionism in the mandatory period.

In justification for his views of the morality of Arab removal in the post-1967 period, Alterman cited statements made by Berl Katznelson in 1943 (the year Alterman joined *Davar*):

> Our contemporary history has known a number of transfers ... [for instance] the U.S.S.R. arranged the transfer of one million Germans living in the Volga region and transferred them to very distant places ... one could assume that this transfer was done against the will of the transferees ... there could be possible situations that would make [Arab] population transfer desirable for both sides ... who is the socialist who is interested in rejecting the very idea before hand and stigmatising it as something unfair? Has Merhavya not been built on transfer? Were it not for many of these transfers Hashomer Hatza'ir [which later in 1948 founded the Mapam Party] would not be residing today in Merhavya, or Mishmar Ha'emek or other places ... and if what has been done for a settlement of Hashomer Hatza'ir is a fair deed, why would it

> not be fair when it would be done on a much larger and greater scale, not just of Hashomer Hatza'ir but for the whole of Israel?[18]

Haim Hazaz (1898–1973) was another example of a leading author who supported the 'transfer' concept in the post-1967 era. As a prolific Hebrew novelist, his works have won him numerous awards, including the Bialik Prize and the Israel Prize, the top prize awarded by the State of Israel. Hazaz, in an article published in *Davar* on 10 November 1967, echoed the Labour Zionist apologia of the pre-1948 period:

> There is the question of Judea and Ephraim [the West Bank], with a large Arab population which must be evacuated to neighbouring Arab states. This is not an exile like the exile of the Jews among the Gentiles. ... They will be coming to their brothers to large and wide and little populated countries. One culture, one language and religion. This is 'transfer' such as that which took place between Turkey and Greece, between India and Pakistan ... putting the world aright in one place through exchanging [the Arab population] to its designated place. We will assume responsibility for this task and assist in planning, organising and financing.[19]

Hazaz repeated his transfer proposal in a simplistic way in an interview in 1968: 'the [1967] war cost us 3 billion [Israeli] pounds – let's take three billion more pounds and give them to the Arabs and tell them to get out.'[20] Hazaz was willing to allow a small Arab minority to remain in Israel provided it 'would not disrupt or change the Jewish character of the Land of Israel'.[21]

The argument that support for the transfer idea does not come only from a fringe also is illustrated by the fact that some of the ideologists, public figures, and veterans of the ruling Mapai party, men such as Eli'ezer Livneh, Dr Haim Yahil, and Tzvi Shiloah, publicly supported the transfer concept in the immediate post-1967 period.[22]

Eli'ezer Livneh (1902–75) had an impressive Labour Zionist record. After emigrating to Palestine in 1920 and joining Kibbutz Ein-Harod, he soon rose from day labourer to labour leader. He held many public offices, including a political job for the Zionist movement in pre-war Nazi Germany. Between 1940 and 1947 he headed the political section of the Haganah, the paramilitary organisation of the Yishuv's leadership. A prominent member of Mapai, Israel's ruling party (later to become the Labour party), he served in the Knesset from 1949 to

1955 and was an editor of *Hador*, an influential Mapai newspaper. In the 1960s and 1970s Livneh was a distinguished columnist for Israel's most respected and influential newspapers and magazines.[23] In the summer of 1967 Livneh co-founded the Whole Land of Israel Movement, an influential movement of territorial maximalism, and put forward a plan for the transfer of 600,000 Palestinian refugees from the West Bank and Gaza Strip. In an article in the mass-circulation daily *Ma'ariv* of 22 June 1967 (less than two weeks after the June war conquests), Livneh wrote: 'They [the refugees] will choose, willingly, resettlement in whatever Arab country, or emigration to countries overseas. The Prime Minister of Australia has already suggested cooperation.' A few weeks later Livneh reiterated the proposal:

> The refugees are now within our boundaries. We could rehabilitate some of them in our country [in Sinai], and transfer others for productive life overseas or resettle them in neighbouring countries with which we will come to an arrangement ... Jordan ... is likely to be the chief beneficiary [to be able] to populate its wide territories.[24]

Livneh developed his proposal further into a fully-fledged plan in an article in the liberal daily *Haaretz* on 28 August 1967 (p. 2). Livneh wrote that in the last 19 years

> tens of thousands of refugees have crossed ... to Saudi Arabia, Kuwait, Bahrain, Qatar, Abu Dhabi, Dubai and the [other] oil principalities. Tens of thousands of their families, who have remained in the camps [in the West Bank and Gaza] have lived off money remitted by their distant relatives. ... Just as half a million Jews immigrated to the Land of Israel from Arab countries ... hundreds of thousands of 'Palestinian' Arabs were crossing to Arab countries. The parallel is amazing. ... What is happening in the refugee camps in a sporadic and limited way without the support of a governmental body [in Arab states] should be widened and developed by us from the side of dimensions and means. This means: a) constructive emigration should be directed to all the countries in need of a workforce including the United States, Canada, Australia and Latin America; b) the emigrants should be entitled to financial support from Israel ...; c) the implementation must be planned for a prolonged time, let us say 18 years; d) the

> number of countries designated for migration and resettlement should be as large as possible.

'If these Arabs [would-be transferees] would want to maintain their Arabness in the United States, Canada, Brazil and Australia', it is up to them, Livneh wrote. Livneh made another little 'concession':

> To the extent that there might be a number of refugees who want, in spite of everything, to experience striking agricultural roots in a landscape close to their spirit and tradition, it is worth offering them settlement in north Sinai ... in the opinion of cautious experts there are there water, land and other conditions for the settlement of tens of thousands (approximately 60,000 persons).

Livneh argued that the 'carrying out of the [transfer] task' depended mainly on Israel and on the conditions it could create:

> a) the allocation of large sums; b) patience. If we spend 5,000 dollars on the emigration of a family of 6–7 persons on average (1500 dollars on the journey, and the rest of the exclusive control of the emigrating family) we would be able to finance every year the emigration of tens of thousands of families, or 60–70,000 persons by 50 million dollars (or 150 million Israeli Lira, 3% of our state budget). There would be no lack of candidates and they would increase when encouraging information from abroad on the settlement of the first ones arrived ... if we placed such encouraging sums ... within 8–9 years about 600,000 persons would be likely to emigrate at this pace, meaning all the refugees from the [Gaza] Strip, the Hebron mountain, the mountains of Ephraim [in the West Bank] and the Jordan valley.

Although in his earlier proposal Livneh had suggested that the world powers should finance the transfer and resettlement, in the August 1967 plan he proposed that Israel and world Jewry should shoulder 'financing the project':

> There is no need to explain its importance from the national, security and propaganda point of view. It should be placed at the top of our national priorities. Insofar as we need for it [financial] means greater than the estimate given here, we are entitled to appeal to the world Jewry. This is more justified and blessed than

> the use of fund-raising to raise the standard of living [of Israelis]. ... The Jews of the diaspora will respond to this in understanding, and even in enthusiasm.

For Livneh, the success of the 'project' would depend on its

> planning in a long breath. In the beginning there will certainly be various difficulties of running it. ... Our reckoning should not be for one month or one season. We will develop the project on our responsibility, without making it conditional upon the participation of other elements. To the extent that we carry it out we will gain the cooperation of others. The United Nations action in the refugee camps (UNRWA) would then assume constructive and purposeful meaning ... the training in the schools of UNRWA would be adjusted to the needs of emigration and resettlement.

From other references it is obvious that Livneh was not content with the removal of 600,000 Palestinian refugees from the West Bank and Gaza, as he put forward his euphemistically termed 'emigration project', but he sought to transform the demographic and political reality of the occupied territories by clearing out other residents as well.[25] What also is noticeable is the absence of any discussion in his plan of the resistance the Palestinians would be likely to put up to foil such a mass removal. Such a deliberate attempt to ignore Palestinian resistance to transfer is – as will be seen again – common to other transfer proposals put forward publicly in the euphoric period following the spectacular conquests of the 1967 war.

Mainstream Zionism rejected the views of a liberal minority – to which 'Amos 'Oz belongs – which argued that Palestine is also the homeland of the Palestinian people. Therefore, one needs to go beyond 'Oz's explanation for understanding the background against which 'transfer' thoughts and debates promptly resurfaced after 1967. This background consists of the standard mainstream Zionist 'solution for the Palestinian problem', which was predicated on the claim for monopolised Zionist/Jewish ownership and Israeli/Jewish domination of *Eretz Yisrael*/Palestine. This being the case, Zionism was bound to base its conception of Jerusalem upon a non-existent entity, Jerusalem of Gold, and to involve abstract historical and ideological rights in the newly acquired territories, as well as resting its claim on territorial expansion and domination and the actual 'redemption of land' through settlement. One implication of the claim for monopolised ownership of a country shared by another people is the 'transfer' solution. Against this background transfer proposals and plans were inevitably put forward by mainstream labour leaders – including ministers – immediately after the 1967 victory.

MOSHE DAYAN'S POLICIES

General Moshe Dayan was appointed Defence Minister on the eve of the 1967 war and retained this powerful post until 1974. He was an exponent of Israeli post-1967 expansionism and the *de facto* integration of the occupied territories into Israel. Dayan instituted a policy of 'creeping annexation', a process by which Israeli administration, jurisdiction, and law were gradually and incrementally imposed on the West Bank and the Gaza Strip. The Dayan-headed Defence Ministry and the Mossad (the Israeli external secret service) resorted, by and large, to discreet 'transfer' activities in the aftermath of the June war. This method of secret transfer activities, as well as transfer discussions at cabinet level, had gradually been revealed by Israeli journalists and researchers as well as politicians. Examples of these revelations are the research of Meir Avidan, published in *Davar* on 2, 5, and 19 June 1987, and the articles published by two Israeli journalists, Yossi Melman and Dan Raviv, who published an article in the *Washington Post* on 7 February 1988 entitled 'Expelling Palestinians'. The same article appeared in the *Guardian Weekly* (London) two weeks later under the title 'A Final Solution of the Palestinian Problem?' and was similar to an article in the Hebrew daily *Davar* by the authors, which appeared around the same time and was entitled 'This is the History of Transfer'.[26]

The product of the June discussions was not a total relocation of the refugee camps' residents to the Sinai desert but rather a 'voluntary' transfer plan, designed to 'thin out' the population of the Old City of Jerusalem, the West Bank and Gaza, which later became known as the Moshe Dayan plan. Immediately after the June 1967 war Dayan consolidated a plan for encouraging Arab emigration from the occupied territories to South America.[27] The scheme began with the formation of a secret unit charged with 'encouraging' the departure of the Palestinians for foreign shores. The secret unit was composed of representatives of the Prime Minister's office, the Defence Ministry and the Israel Defence Forces. Some patchy revelations about the same secret scheme also were made by General

'Uzi Narkiss, Commanding General of the Central Command until 1968 – with responsibility for the West Bank – who told an interviewer in October 1988 that after the June 1967 war

> some of the Mossad men came to me ... and then they offered some [Arab] individuals sums [of money] in exchange for them leaving their property [in the Old City of Jerusalem and the West Bank]. ... These sums were part of the government allocations for this matter. Some agreed, but the experiment failed; it succeeded only with several scores, until one of our daughters was killed – as a revenge – in our embassy in Paraguay, then the operation was stopped.[28]

According to reports in the Israeli press, a total of about 1,000 Palestinians were 'transferred' to South America during the three years the plan continued.[29]

THE DESTRUCTION OF THE AL-MAGHARBEH QUARTER

The June 1967 war began suddenly and ended quickly. In his recent book *Intimate Enemies* (1995), Meron Benvenisti, former deputy mayor of Jerusalem, writes:

> At the end of the 1967 war, there were attempts to implement a forced population transfer. Residents of cities and villages in areas near the cease-fire line were expelled from their homes and their communities destroyed; the Israeli authorities offered financial 'incentives' and free transportation to Palestinians willing to leave.[30]

In fact in the course of hostilities and in the immediate aftermath of the war, with its rapidly changing circumstances, and particularly given the fact that most Western governments applauded the overwhelming Israeli victory, Defence Minister Dayan and other army generals (including 'Uzi Narkiss, Haim Hertzog, and Shlomo Lahat) found an ideal opportunity to drive out tens of thousands of Arabs from their villages, towns and refugee camps in the West Bank and Gaza Strip. In their article in *Davar* of 19 February 1988 entitled 'This is the History of Transfer', the Israeli journalists Yossi Melman and Dan Raviv pointed out that the Israeli conception of 'exploiting opportunities to transfer Arab populations, which was first employed in 1948, resurfaced shortly after the 1967 War: commanders in various ranks of the army believed that the wind blowing from the political echelon was calling for the exploiting of opportunity to thin out the Palestinian population.'

Among the first evictees were the residents of the ancient al-Magharbeh quarter in the Old City of Jerusalem. They were turned out of their homes on 11 June, two days after the capture of East Jerusalem by the Israeli military, with three hours' notice.[31] Apparently, the quarter was completely demolished because it was located immediately adjacent to the southern part of the Wailing Wall, the Western Wall of al-Haram al-Sharif (the Noble Sanctuary). Its inhabitants, about 135 families (or some 650–1,000 persons), were the beneficiaries of an ancient and important Islamic Waqf foundation originally established in 1193 by al-Malik al-Afdal, the son of Salah al-Din. Its obliteration in June 1967 resulted also in the destruction of several historic religious sites (including two mosques, two *zawiyas* and a great number of endowed residences) which the quarter contained.[32]

The Old City of Jerusalem was captured by the Israeli army on 7 June 1967. In his book *Jerusalem: A City Without a Wall*, 'Uzi Benziman, a prominent journalist of the daily *Haaretz*, described in detail the circumstances surrounding the destruction of this Muslim quarter.[33] The story began on 7 June. While Israeli paratroopers were advancing through the alleys of the Old City, an engineering corps officer in the Central Command, Eytan Ben-Moshe, approached Shlomo Lahat, a senior military officer in the Central Command and the designated military governor of Jerusalem (and subsequently mayor of Tel Aviv) and proposed the demolition of a building used as a 'public toilet', which was part of the al-Magharbeh quarter and was adjacent to the Wailing Wall. In fact, Dayan had already requested Lahat, before the latter had arrived in Jerusalem, 'to clear pathways' to the Wailing Wall so that 200,000 Jews would be able to visit the Wailing Wall during the forthcoming feast of Shavuoth (Pentecost).[34] This seemed to suggest that the original idea to level at least part of the quarter came from Dayan. Furthermore, according to Benziman's account, several senior Israeli commanders in the Jerusalem district (including 'Uzi Narkiss, the Commanding General of the Central Command, Shlomo Lahat and Haim Hetrzog) as well as Dayan, the mayor of West Jerusalem Teddy Kollek and former Prime Minister David Ben-Gurion were all involved, one way or another, either in the initial decision or in the actual implementation of the systematic operation to destroy the Arab quarter.

To begin with, Lahat approved of Ben-Moshe's idea and sent the demolition plan to 'Uzi Narkiss (who also gave the orders to bulldoze the three Arab villages: Bayt Nuba, 'Imwas and Yalu, see below). Moreover, on 8 June former premier Ben-Gurion, accompanied by Teddy Kollek and Reserve Colonel Ya'acov Yannai, Director of the National Parks Authority,[35] visited the Wailing Wall. Both Ben-Gurion and Kollek were strongly in favour of the removal of Arab buildings adjacent to the Wailing Wall.[36] Kollek, who had long been closely associated with Ben-Gurion and who had been elected mayor of West Jerusalem in 1965, appeared to have played a central role in the formulation and implementation of the decision to demolish the al-Magharbeh quarter in June 1967. Apparently, he also informed the then Minister of Justice, Ya'acov Shimshon Shapira. The latter replied: 'I am not certain of the legal position, but what should be done – do it quickly, and let the God of Israel be with you.'[37] In addition to Dayan, who represented the civil authority as well as approving and controlling the conduct of the field commanders, and, as we shall see, oversaw the progress of the demolition, Shapira's answer suggests at least some indirect and tacit ministerial approval of the action.

However, the actual order to evict the quarter and destroy its houses was given by Shlomo Lahat, then the Commander of Jerusalem, with the express approval of 'Uzi Narkiss, Commanding General of the Central Command, given at a meeting with Lahat on 9 June.[38] On the following day, Saturday 10 June, Mayor Kollek assembled a group of 'experts' at his apartment to discuss basic information about the Wailing Wall and the al-Magharbeh quarter. The group included Dan 'Max' Tanai, the engineer of the National Parks Authority, the historian and archaeologist professor Michael Avi-Yonah, Ya'acov Yannai, Aryeh Sharon, Chairman of the National Parks Authority, Ya'acov Salman, deputy military governor of East Jerusalem and Lahat's assistant. Kollek explained to the participants the reasons for this urgent meeting:

> The al-Magharbeh quarter adjacent to the Wailing Wall must be demolished. The responsibility for executing the plan will be in the hands of the National Parks Authority in order to give the matter as far as possible an unofficial character. The department of antiquities in the ministry of education and the Israel Defence Forces are not interested in involvement, publicly, in the execution

> of the plan, although they both bless it and will accord it the practical assistance.[39]

Kollek put Tanai in charge of executing the operation, possibly seeking to bestow upon it a civilian legitimacy. Central to the planning and mode of procedure by Kollek and his technical 'experts' was the need to act speedily in order to stave off internal criticism and potential obstruction and avoid attracting too much attention from the foreign media. At noon (10 June) Kollek and his colleagues proceeded to the area of the Wailing Wall and decided on the spot to bulldoze the entire Arab quarter with the aim of creating a vast plaza for the Wailing Wall.[40] Kollek also got in touch with several Jerusalem construction companies and asked them to make earth-moving equipment available and undertake the demolition task as 'a donation to the city'.[41]

While the actual demolition job was partly assigned to a civilian body called the 'guild of builders and contractors', the Israeli army, particularly its Central Command's engineering corps, rendered necessary assistance. At some time during the afternoon or the evening of the same day (10 June) an army officer went from one house to another ordering the residents of the quarter to move out. When many families refused to leave their homes, an army unit moved in and evicted the bulk of the inhabitants by force. Meanwhile two bulldozers and other heavy tools were assembled by the engineering corps and those in charge of the operation sought to complete the whole work on the night of 10–11 June. Commenting on this driven urgency by those responsible for the deed, Benziman explained:

> Those who were presiding over the destruction of the [Arab] neighbourhood assumed that their action was motivated neither by security [considerations] nor by mere town planning. They were driven that night [10–11 June] by an almost mystical feeling: that, in their eyes, they were the representatives of the Jewish people, who came to assert [Jewish] sovereignty over its most sacred site ... the fate of 135 Arab families, who were the victims of these desires, was of no concern to them.[42]

The speed with which the Israeli authorities sought to carry out the levelling of the Arab residential houses was also evident in the fact that in the same evening one demolished wall of a house revealed an unconscious, badly injured, middle-aged Arab women. By midnight she was dead.

The OC Central Command, 'Uzi Narkiss, came to the site in the early morning of Sunday, 11 June and ordered that the levelling be completed speedily. More men and heavy tools were brought in. In the afternoon of the same day Defence Minister Dayan appeared on the site. He also ordered Lahat to complete the levelling as quickly as possible,[43] perhaps in order not to let foreign journalists see the remains of the destroyed Arab quarter. In fact, only muted internal questioning was offered by the minister of religious affairs as well as Prime Minister Levi Eshkol himself, who asked 'Uzi Narkiss on the telephone: 'Why are residential houses being demolished?' The ministry of religious affairs, in particular, appeared to be concerned that the action could tarnish Israel's image abroad.[44] However, backed by a powerful defence minister – who had conducted the June 1967 war almost independently – Narkiss and Lahat managed easily to ignore the criticism and pursued the policy of levelling and forcible evacuation with or without the approval of the civilian authorities. In the case of the al-Magharbeh quarter there was active cooperation with Kollek and other civil authorities. Benziman believed that:

> The policy of evacuation and demolition continued only for several days after the [Israeli army] entrance into the city within the walls. It was executed at the initiative of middle military echelons and with the tacit approval of senior level command. There was lack of communication between the civil authorities and the military government; in practice the latter exercised civilian functions. The military echelons, on its own responsibility, encouraged the Arab residents to get out of Jerusalem and other cities in the West Bank and to go to the East Bank [of Jordan].[45]

The evicted residents of the al-Magharbeh quarter were dispersed in West Bank villages close to Jerusalem (such as Shu'fat, Bayt Hanina, and Silwan) as well as in the Muslim Quarter of the Old City of Jerusalem. None of the Israeli government ministries was prepared to accept responsibility for the demolition of the quarter, and no attempt was made to offer the evictees alternative accommodation.[46] Like the eviction of the large three villages in the Latrun area (see below), this removal should be treated as an internal expulsion rather than a transfer out of the occupied territories. However, it is extremely important to remember that these cases of internal expulsions had a psychological effect on the 1967 exodus from the West Bank to Jordan, helping (almost certainly) to precipitate and encourage further exodus out of the country, especially in the first few weeks following the war.

The evictions and levelling of the al-Magharbeh quarter were only the beginning of the sweeping changes carried out by the Israeli authorities in the Old City of Jerusalem. On 17 June 1967 at 4 a.m. the Israeli army ordered the inhabitants of the former Jewish quarter and the surrounding houses to leave the premises within 24 hours. Apparently this measure affected several hundred Palestinian families who, according to the 1967 Jerusalem Diary of Sister Marie-Therese, could be observed all day carrying their belongings through the alleys of Jerusalem. Some of them were able to find refuge with relatives and friends. But the majority had to leave the town.[47] In the Old City's Jewish quarter and its surrounding districts, some 4,000 Palestinians were evicted to make possible the reconstruction of a vastly enlarged and completely 'Jewish' quarter, excluding its former Arab residents.[48]

The destruction of the al-Magharbeh quarter should be seen as part of a wider internal debate that took place during and after the 1967 war about the future of the Muslim shrines in the Old City of Jerusalem, particularly the third holiest site for Islam: al-Aqsa Mosque and the Dome of the Rock. In this connection a recent revelation made in the Hebrew daily *Haaretz* of 31 December 1997, revealed the details of an extraordinary conversation that took place between General Narkiss and the Israeli army's Chief Rabbi, Shlomo Goren (later to become Ashkenazi Chief Rabbi of Israel from 1973 to 1983), in June 1967. In an interview given to *Haaretz* shortly before his death in late 1997, Narkiss recalled that only a few hours after the Old City was captured by the Israeli army he was urged by Rabbi Goren to blow up the third holiest shrines for Islam. Narkiss had this to say:

> The paratroopers wandered around the plaza [on the Temple Mount] as if in a dream. ... Rabbi Shlomo Goren was among them. I was alone for a moment, lost in thought, when Rabbi Goren approached me. ''Uzi,' Rabbi Goren said. 'Now is the time to put 100kg of explosives into the Mosque of Omar [the Dome of the Rock] so we may rid ourselves of it once and for all.' ... I said to him, 'Rabbi, enough.' He said, 'Uzi, you will go down in history if you do this. ... This is an opportunity that can be taken advantage of now, at this moment. Tomorrow it will be too late.' ... I said,

> 'Rabbi, if you don't stop, I'll take you to jail.' ... He simply walked away silently. He was completely serious.[49]

Also on 31 December 1997 Israel's army radio played a recording of a speech Rabbi Goren made in 1967 to a military convention, in which the army's Chief Rabbi said the following about Dome of the Rock and the al-Aqsa Mosque: 'Certainly we should have blown it up. It is a tragedy that we did not do so.'[50] Whether or not the third holiest shrines for Islam came close to being blown up by Israeli paratroopers immediately after they were captured in June 1967 remains an open question. However, in the 1980s members of a militant Jewish group (*Hamahteret Hayehudit*) were arrested and put on trial for plotting to blow up the shrines. Clearly, the destruction of these shrines remains a most vivid fear for Palestinians and Muslims and an ambition for most extremist Jewish fundamentalists in Israel.

'IMWAS, YALU AND BAYT NUBA

Also among the first to go were the inhabitants of the three ancient villages of 'Imwas (Emmaus of the New Testament), Yalu and Bayt Nuba, situated near the Green Line in the Latrun area north-west of Jerusalem. In 1987 these evicted villagers and their descendants numbered about 11,000 in Amman, Jordan, and 2,000 who lived on the West Bank, near Ramallah.[51] Latrun was on a West Bank salient, 20 miles from Tel Aviv and some 15 from West Jerusalem. It had been the gateway to Jerusalem in 1948, which the Israelis failed repeatedly to capture, and they had had to realign the roadway to bypass it. For many years before 1967 the Israeli army had had plans for taking over the Latrun enclave and straightening the border. According to Israeli military historian Meir Pa'il, there had been a 'minimum plan' which included occupation of the Latrun enclave and the destruction of its Arab villages without moving on beyond the enclave.[52] June 1967 created the opportunity to realise these plans. The Latrun salient was captured by the Israeli army on the morning of 6 June 1967. On orders (not in writing, of course) from Commanding General of the Central Command 'Uzi Narkiss, the army bulldozers moved in and wiped out the three large villages, by reason of their 'strategic location' and in order to 'straighten the [Green Line] border', according to the Israeli officer in charge of the operation.[53] Narkiss (a Labour Party man who later became Director General of the Jewish

Agency's (JA) Department of Immigration and Absorption and was in 1995 chairman of the JA's Department of Information) also commanded the troops who captured Jerusalem and clearly approved of the order to empty the al-Magharbeh quarter.[54]

The demolition of the Latrun villages was carried out by an engineering unit using explosives and bulldozers, and this involved the destruction of 539 houses in Yalu, 375 in 'Imwas and 550 in Bayt Nuba.[55] Some 2,000 families (over 6,000 persons) from the three villages found themselves on 6 June on the road to Ramallah.[56] Those who could, rushed to the East Bank. The rest wandered from village to village in the Ramallah area. 'Amos Kenan, a well-known Israeli journalist, who, as a reservist soldier, took part in the fighting in the Latrun area, revealed, in graphic detail, the story of Bayt Nuba:

> We were ordered to block the entrances of the villages and prevent inhabitants returning to the village from their hideouts after they had heard Israeli broadcasts urging them to go back to their homes. The order was to shoot over their heads and tell them not to enter the village. Beit Nuba [sic] is built of fine quarry stones; some of the houses are magnificent. Every house is surrounded by an orchard, olive trees, apricots, vines and presses. They are well kept. Among the trees there are carefully tended vegetable beds. ... At noon the first bulldozer arrived and pulled down the first house at the edge of the village. Within ten minutes the house was turned into rubble, including its entire contents; the olive trees, cypresses were all uprooted. ... After the destruction of three houses the first column arrived from the direction of Ramallah ... some Arabic-speaking soldiers went over to notify them of the warning. There were old people who could hardly walk, murmuring old women, mothers carrying babies, small children. The children wept and asked for water. They all carried white flags.
>
> We told them to go to Beit Sura. They told us that they were driven out everywhere, forbidden to enter any village, that they were wandering like this for four days, without food, without water, some dying on the road. They asked to return to the village, and said we had better kill them. ... We did not allow them to enter the village, and take anything. ... More and more columns of refugees arrived, until there were hundreds of them. ... The platoon commander decided to go to headquarters and find out if there were any orders about what to do with them, where to send them, and whether it was possible to arrange transport for the women

> and food for the children. He returned saying that there were no orders in writing, simply that they were to be driven out.
>
> We drove them out. They go on wandering in the south like lost cattle. The weak die. In the evening we found that they had not been taken in, for in Beit Sura too bulldozers had begun to destroy the place and they were not allowed to enter. We found out that not only in our sector was the border [the Green Line] straightened out for security reasons but in all other sectors too.[57]

In her 1967 Jerusalem Diary, Sister Marie-Therese wrote:

> And now we see what the Israelis do not want to see: three villages ['Imwas, Yalu and Bayt Nuba] systematically destroyed by dynamite and bulldozers. Alone, in dead silence, donkeys wander among the ruins. Here and there, smashed furniture, a torn cushion protrude from the rubble of stones and cement. A kitchen pot and a blanket abandoned in the middle of the road. They had no time to carry anything away.[58]

According to General Narkiss, the evictees of the 'four [sic] villages of the Latrun area' were evacuated to Ramallah and some of them crossed the river to Jordan.[59] In his book *The Liberation of Jerusalem*, Narkiss wrote: 'I was determined that the Latrun enclave, that years-old thorn in our flesh, would never be returned [to Arab sovereignty].'[60]

Canada Park was created with the help of the Canadian Jewish National Fund on the site of the three bulldozed villages and their 20,000 dunums of agricultural lands.[61] Professor Benjamin Beit-Hallahmi, of Haifa University, commented:

> During most Saturdays every year, hundreds of Israeli families enjoy picnics in the beautiful Canada Park, midway between Tel Aviv and Jerusalem. The park is a popular place even during the week, and offers visitors olive trees, water springs, Roman antiquities, Byzantine churches and sports facilities. ... Canada Park ... has been developed on the site where three Palestinian villages – Bet Nuba, Yalu and Emmaus [sic] stood before June 1967. Immediately after the June War, these villages were bulldozed and their 5000 inhabitants turned into refugees. The Jewish National Fund got to work; millions were spent turning the land into a

> huge park, erasing every trace of the villages but lovingly preserving the antiquities.[62]

More recently plans were announced to plant another section of the same site with trees and name it 'Scharansky Hope Forest' after Nathan Scharansky, the well-known Zionist activist and former Soviet prisoner,[63] who is Minister of Trade and Industry in the current Likud cabinet of Binyamin Netanyahu.

In the same year several other West Bank villages, Bayt Marsam, Bayt 'Awa, Habla, Jiftlik and al-Burj, were cleared and razed to the ground,[64] and only the intervention of a group of liberal Israeli intellectuals and academics saved the West Bank town of Qalqilyah from a similar fate when an order by the army Central Command for the expulsion of the inhabitants and the total destruction of the whole town was cancelled by Dayan.[65] Apparently Zeev Shaham, commander of a force that operated in the area of Qalqilyah-Jenin, had received an order to destroy Qalqilyah from 'Uzi Narkiss, head of the Central Command.[66] Indeed, between 9 June and 18 July 1967 (before the cancellation of the order by Dayan) at least 850 out of 2,000 dwellings in Qalqilyah had been blown up by the Israeli army[67] and dozens of residents were forcibly transported from the town to the Jordan River.[68] At one point Dayan ordered the destruction to stop because the whole operation had become widely known and there was a public outcry.[69] In her Jerusalem Diary, Sister Marie-Therese wrote:

> At Nablus we saw hundreds of families under olive trees; they slept in the open. They told us they were from Qalkilya [sic] and were not allowed to go back. We went to Qalkilya to see what was happening; we received a sinister impression. The city was being blown up by dynamite.[70]

Moreover, on 16 June the Israeli military totally destroyed the two villages of Bayt 'Awa (in the Hebron district) and Bayt Marsam; most of Habla met a similar fate on 27 June 1967; al-Burj was destroyed on 28 June 1967; Jiftlik on 26 November 1967 and the following days.[71] A letter from a resident of Habla, Jamal 'Abdul Hadi al-Qassem, to Defence Minister Moshe Dayan, which was published in the Israeli Arabic-language newspaper *al-Ittihad* of 29 September 1967, read:

> Habla is an Arab village that lies south-east of Qalqilyah [in the West Bank]. Most of its land lies in Israel; it has about 1,000 inhabitants. On Wednesday 27 June 1967 the Israeli army occupied this village. The army turned all the inhabitants, both male and female, out of the village, and drove them to the village of Rafidiya, near Nablus; some of them were sent to the nearby village of Ras 'Atiyya. Hearing that permission had been given for them to return to the village, some of them did so, on Friday 9 July 1967, but the defense army [IDF] confined them in a house and returned them to Nablus on Sunday ,11 July 1967. On Tuesday, 13 July 1967, the Israeli army blew up some of the houses in the village, including the mosque, and a large house of ours, without giving any reason. Meanwhile the said houses were being robbed, plundered and burnt. I own an orchard in the western part of the village, in which there is a dwelling house. All the furniture in this house was looted, as were even water pipes and electric wires. This looting was carried out by the inhabitants of the Samkha colony, over several days, with the full knowledge of the army. I wrote to Your Excellency a letter on this subject on 6 July 1967. This letter explained the matter to you fully, but I have so far received no reply to it. I am therefore writing to you a second time, requesting that you will accord the matter you attention and look into it thoroughly.

Reporting simultaneously in the *New York Times* and *L'Orient* on 3 December 1967, Terence Smith wrote:

> The village of Jiftlik on the Occupied West Bank of Jordan, with about 6,000 refugee inhabitants, has been completely destroyed by the Israeli army. During the last two weeks, army bulldozers have razed about 800 buildings there. ... According to certain information, the Israeli army has also destroyed other villages near Latroun [sic] and Hebron. Since these villages had already been severely damaged during the war, some Israelis are saying that it might have been more sensible to have left half-destroyed the standing houses.

In mid-July 1967 John Reddaway, Deputy Commissioner General of UNRWA, estimated that some 16,000 persons had been left homeless after the Israeli army demolished buildings in West Bank villages.[72]

Attempts to 'thin out' the teeming population of Gaza also were made in the summer of 1967, as a resident of the Strip, Abu Hassan, recalled:

> A few weeks after the Strip had been occupied, the Israelis embarked on a programme of forced deportation. On one occasion, the Israeli army rounded up all the men from my quarter and herded us into Jaffa school. The Israelis had two local *mukhtars* with them who told the officer in charge each man's profession – 'he's a labourer, that one's a teacher' and so on. The Israelis picked out the ones they wanted, put them on trucks and sent them to Jordan. I remember another time the army arrived in trucks early in the morning and grabbed all the young men they could find. Those of us who were around began protesting, but the Israelis told us not to worry because they were only taking the youths for a few hours to help in the disposal of those killed in the Sinai during the war. We never saw those young men again. As soon as the work had been done, their identity papers were confiscated and they were forced to cross the canal into Egypt.[73]

'TRANSFER OF 100,00 WITHOUT ANYBODY SAYING A SINGLE WORD' (JUNE 1967)

Haim Hertzog was the army's first Military Governor of the West Bank after the June 1967 war. He had been a political and military broadcaster during the war and published *Israel's Finest Hour* (1967). He was also a regular radio and television commentator in Israel and abroad and managed to amass honorary doctorates from several universities in Israel and other countries.[74] At a public debate on the Palestinian issue held in Jerusalem on 3 April 1970 this first Military Governor of the West Bank and influential figure in the Labour establishment did not refrain from revealing openly his heart's wishes: 'if we had the possibility of taking one million Arabs [from the territories] and clearing them out, this would be the best.'[75] However, it was only 21 years later in early November 1991, a few days after the Madrid Peace Conference, that President Hertzog revealed publicly and proudly one of Israel's little-known secrets: that he, as the first Military Governor of the West Bank, efficiently organised and carried out, in cooperation with Shlomo Lahat, the commander of Jerusalem, the operation of transferring 200,000 Palestinians from the West Bank in the immediate aftermath of the war. According to a statement confirming that this operation was indeed carried out, the President's office said:

> his [Hertzog's] considerations were that in the departing wave many of the PLO men would leave, and this would make it easier for the military administration. For days and weeks lines of buses ran from the Damascus Gate [in East Jerusalem] to the Allenby Bridge [on the River Jordan]. Altogether during this period 200,000 Palestinians left Judea and Samaria voluntarily, including 100,000 refugees whose camps were in the Jericho valley.[76]

Hertzog claims that he had been prompted to organise this operation during a meeting with Anwar al-Khatib, the former Arab governor of the Jerusalem district, at the Ambassador Hotel in Jerusalem on Friday 9 June 1967. According to Hertzog, al-Khatib raised, *inter alia*, the problem of the families of the staff of Arab consulates stranded in Jerusalem and that of the families of the Jordanian officers who had fled and left their dependents behind, and asked the Israeli Military Governor to allow these families to leave Jerusalem for Jordan via the Allenby Bridge. Hertzog agreed and told al-Khatib that, from the morning of Sunday, 11 June, buses would be waiting near the Damascus Gate to transport any Arab wishing to depart to Jordan, on condition that each departing Arab signed a statement to the effect that he was leaving voluntarily. Hertzog also revealed that Shlomo Lahat, then the commander of Jerusalem and the mayor of Tel Aviv from 1974 until 1993, was put in charge of implementing the operation, and that 'no contrary order was given by [Defence Minister] Moshe Dayan at any stage [to halt the operation].'[77]

In fact, the superior of Hertzog and Lahat, Commanding General of the Central Command 'Uzi Narkiss, told an interviewer in October 1988 that he himself had supervised the implementation of the transfer operation in 1967, which, according to the interviewer, had resulted in the total 'transfer of 100,000 [Palestinians to Jordan] without anybody saying a single word'. Narkiss told the same interviewer in October 1988:

> I placed several buses in Jerusalem and in other cities [of the West Bank], written on them: 'To Amman – Free of Charge'. The bus used to carry them to the [partly] destroyed Allenby Bridge and then they would cross it [to Jordan]. I spread the news about these

> buses through individuals with wide contacts with the inhabitants, such as members of trade unions and chambers of commerce. ... In this [bus] operation between 20 and 25 thousand people got out.[78]

According to the Jerusalem Diary of Sister Marie-Therese, on Sunday, 18 June 1967, Israeli soldiers circulated in east Jerusalem firing shots, while loudspeakers broadcast the following: 'It is forbidden to circulate during curfew, which will last all day tomorrow. Those who wish to go to Amman may do so. Buses are available for them.'[79] One of the extraordinary revelations made by Narkiss in connection with his transfer operation was that of the daily telephone calls he used to receive after the war from the dovish Finance Minister Pinhas Sapir – whose primary concerns were the so-called 'demographic problem' and the question of the maintenance of the Zionist-Jewish character of the Israeli state:[80]

> Pinhas Sapir used to phone me twice a day, to ask: how many [Arabs] got out today? Is the number of the inhabitants of the West Bank diminishing? The number [of those being transported by the buses?] began with 600 and 700 persons a day, and then it began to decline until it reached a few scores, and after two or three months the [bus?] operation stopped.[81]

The statement of the President's office elicited wide publicity in Israel in November 1991 and surprised Israeli historians. Hertzog's claim that Anwar al-Khatib was a partner in such an organised operation of mass 'transfer' was denied by the latter, who promptly convened a press conference at which he said that he had only asked Hertzog at their Ambassador Hotel meeting for the release of the consuls of Egypt, Syria, Lebanon, Iraq, and Saudi Arabia, all of whom had been detained by the Israeli army, and had requested Hertzog to permit 15 Jordanian officials, who had worked in Jerusalem, to reunite with their families living in Jordan. Al-Khatib added that he had been surprised, a few days after his meeting with Hertzog, to find that the military administration had organised buses and trucks for mass transportation of Arabs to the Allenby Bridge.[82]

A former Israeli soldier described the 'voluntary' and 'humane' aspects of this operation in a November 1991 interview with *Kol Ha'ir*:

> My job was to take their [each Palestinian's] thumb and immerse its edge in ink and fingerprint them on the departure statement.

> ... Every day tens of buses arrived. There were days on which it seemed to me that thousands were departing. ... Although there were those departees who were leaving voluntarily, but there were also not a few people who were simply expelled. ... We forced them to sign. I will tell you how exactly this was conducted: [for instance] a bus [carrying men] was arriving and only men were getting off, I emphasise – only men, aged 20 to 70, accompanied by borderguard soldiers. We were told that these were saboteurs, *fedayeen*, and it would be better that they would be outside the state. They [the Arab men] did not want to leave, and were dragged from the buses while being kicked and hit by revolver butts. By the time they arrived to my [signing] stall, they were usually already completely blurred [as a result of beatings] at this stage and did not care much about the signing. It seemed to them part of the process. In many cases the violence used against them was producing desirable results from our point of view. The distance between the border point and the [Allenby] Bridge was about 100 metres and out of fear they were crossing to the other side running; the borderguard men and the paratroopers were all the time in the vicinity. When someone refused to give me his hand [for finger printing] they came and beat him badly. Then I was forcibly taking his thumb, immersing it in ink and finger printing him. This way the refuseniks were removed. ... I have no doubt that tens of thousands of men were removed against their will.[83]

THE JERICHO REFUGEE CAMPS: ('AYN SULTAN, NU'AYMAH AND 'AQBAT JABIR)

Between 1949 and 1967 the Palestinian population in the West Jordan Valley was dominated by three huge refugee camps surrounding the town of Jericho: 'Ayn Sultan, Nu'aymah and 'Aqbat Jabir. The residents of these camps had been driven out from present-day Israel in 1948–9. During the 1967 hostilities or shortly after virtually all residents of these camps, approximately 50,000 people, fled or were expelled to the East Bank, along with more than 50 per cent of the native rural population of the Jordan Valley, reducing the region's total population by 88 per cent – to 10,778.[84] In this context it is worth noting the reactions of two Israeli historians to the 1991 revelations surrounding the 'transfer' operation of Hertzog, Lahat and Narkiss and to the importance of this operation to the almost total depopulation of the three refugee camps near Jericho. Uri Milstein had this to say:

> I remember that 5 days after the Six Day War I was in Jericho. It was empty there and we were told that they [refugee residents 'Ayn Sultan, Nu'aymah and 'Aqbat Jabir] fled. It is more likely that they [the Israeli army] drove them away. In the War of Independence [the 1948 war] there was no organised transfer, people [Israeli commanders] volunteered to carry it out on their own initiative. In the Six Day War there were similar situations. Many thought that we had not completed the job in the War of Independence. It is known that there was a plan to conquer Qalqilyah [town] and destroy it. There was also a plan to carry out transfer in Hebron as a revenge for the massacre [of Jews] in [19]29. I have not read about the evacuation of 200 thousand refugees in buses and I am not aware that this has been published anywhere.

Meir Pa'il stated:

> This story is new to me, but this does not mean that it is incorrect, particularly in the light of the facts that the refugee camps in Jericho ['Ayn Sultan, Nu'aymah and 'Aqbat Jabir] were emptied of their residents in one–two weeks after the Six Day War. The travel route of the buses, which operated as described here, from the Damascus Gate to the Allenby Bridge, had to pass via the Jericho valley and the large refugee camps that were there and this is another confirmation of the story. If one of the four men: President Hertzog, Shlomo Lahat, his deputy Shmuel Albak, or 'Uzi Narkiss, confirms this thing, then this story is true and genuine.[85]

Strafing and firing on refugee columns were in fact reported in the foreign press. According to the *Guardian* of 14 June 1967, 'Israeli aircraft frequently strafed the refugees on the road from Jerusalem to Jericho, destroying and burning.' The London *Times* of 22 June 1967 reported that

> Israeli troops supervising the crossing [of the Jordan River] introduced a dangerous new element today [21 June] by firing their submachine-guns over the heads of the straggling line of refugees. ... This disturbing feature is that there was no obvious point to this display of strength. The refugees were already

> bewildered enough and to risk causing a panic among already frightened people borders on military lunacy.

CONCLUSION

Hundreds of thousands of Palestinians were driven out from the West Bank and Gaza during and after the June 1967 war. In their book *River Without Bridges*, Peter Dodd and Halim Barakat study the 1967 exodus of the Palestinian refugees and attempt to answer the question: why did this exodus take place? The answer, according to them, is that:

> the exodus was a response to the severe situational pressures existing at the time. The situational pressures were generated by the aerial attacks upon a defenseless country, including the extensive use of napalm, the occupation of the West Bank villages by the Israeli army, and the actions of the occupying forces. Certainly the most drastic of these actions was the evictions of civilians and the deliberate destruction of a number of villages ['Imwas, Yalu, Bayt Nuba, Bayt Marsam, Bayt 'Awa, Habla, al-Burj, and Jiftlik]. Other actions, such as threats and the mass detention of male civilians, also created situational pressures.[86]

Dodd and Barakat (who were not aware of the 'transfer' operation of Hertzog, Lahat and Narkiss), added that there were other indirect reasons: the Palestinian villagers were not equipped and were ill-prepared to resist and cope with these situational pressures; they were ill-informed and unfamiliar with the terrifying nature of the aerial attacks. To this the social structure of Arab society should be added: the family-centered social structure diminished attachment to community and nation and some Palestinians left to protect their family, particularly the honour of their womenfolk.

In his investigation of the 1967 exodus, William Wilson Harris (who also made no mention of the 'transfer' activities of Hertzog, Lahat and Narkiss) estimated that, of a pre-war population of approximately 1.4 million, about 430,000 left the territories occupied in the war (including the Golan Heights and Sinai) between June and December 1967. Most of these refugees left in June 1967. He pointed out that the 1967 refugee exodus varied from one region to another: over 90,000 people (almost 90 per cent of the population) fled the Golan Heights, while the Gaza Strip lost less than 20 per cent of its

400,000 residents. There were also local variations in the West Bank and a complex mix of responsible factors. The high population losses in some regions were the result of a 'psychological legacy of pre-war events, a legacy of assorted fears', for instance, in the Hebron district and in the region surrounding the village of Qibya (situated about midway between the Latrun salient and Qalqilyah) in the West Bank, where the Israeli army had carried out a large and infamous massacre in October 1953, in which 65 villagers (mostly women and children) were killed.[87] Another example was in the Latrun salient where the residents of Yalu, 'Imwas, and Bayt Nuba were ordered to leave their villages by the Israeli army and the chain-reaction effect of their movement across the West Bank can be traced in the higher losses from other villages on the Latrun–Ramallah–Jerusalem highway.[88]

In fact, the destruction of the Latrun villages and the al-Magharbeh quarter and the encouragement of Arab departure by the Israeli army were raised in a Knesset debate on 21 June 1967 by two Jewish communist Knesset members, Shmuel Mikunis and Meir Vilner, both strongly protesting against Israeli policy on the treatment of civilians in the newly occupied territories. Vilner stated:

> As regards the Arab inhabitants of the occupied Arab territories, especially on the West Bank of the River Jordan, it has been broadcast over the radio and published in the press that the Military Governor has frequently announced that anyone wishing to cross the river would be welcome to do so; there is no need to comply with any complicated procedure. What does it mean when, in a time of military occupation, we give the inhabitants the choice of leaving their homes? It means that pressure is being exerted on the inhabitants. It is, perhaps, no accident that the other [Arab] side should call on the inhabitants not to leave the places where they live. According to reports in the [Israeli] press 100,000 people have crossed, or been forced to cross the frontier and this number is increasing. ... There have been reports of the blowing up of villages in the Latrun area, for example, for 'strategic, tactical and security reasons'. ... Villages were destroyed not only in the Latrun area after the military operations had ended. ... Old and young, men, women and children, the sick and feeble were moved out of the former Jewish Quarter in the Old City in a horrifying way ... houses have been destroyed in the area around the Western Wall [the al-Magharbeh quarter] and there seems to be general confusion and disorganisation.[89]

However, both Vilner's proposal to debate the subject in the Knesset plenum and Mikunis's proposal to transfer the subject to a parliamentary committee were defeated by a parliamentary majority.[90] In a subsequent parliamentary question another communist member of the Knesset, Tawfiq Tubi, requested that the inhabitants of Yalu, 'Imwas and Bayt Nuba be allowed by Defence Minister Dayan to return to their villages. Once again Dayan rejected this proposal.[91] Since 1967 the evicted inhabitants of 'Imwas, Yalu and Bayt Nuba have been campaigning for the return to, and reconstruction of, their villages,[92] but none of the Israeli ministries has been prepared to take any responsibility for the destruction of these villages. The Israeli government and those army commanders who gave the verbal order to destroy the Latrun villages must have thought that it was possible to rearrange both history and geography: that if they cart away the rubble and rake over the ground and plant seedlings where the homes of thousands of Palestinians had been, they would be able to get away with it.[93]

Encouragement of Arab departure by the Israeli authorities was also reported in the Hebrew press and foreign press. According to the daily *Davar* of 13 June 1967, many of those who had left the West Bank claimed that the Israeli authorities were forcing residents of Jenin, Qalqilyah and Tulkarm (the so-called three towns of 'strategic importance') to leave their homes. The daily *Haaretz* of 20 June 1967 reported that those who had left their homes on the West Bank had not been allowed to return. The *New York Times* of 26 August 1967 reported that each day for the last two weeks some 500 residents had left the Gaza Strip, adding that 'Any reduction in Gaza area's population is a benefit to everyone in Israel's view.' Several months later, the *Observer* (London) reported on 17 December 1967:

> The opportunity of reprisals on security grounds has been taken to hasten the departure of more people from the West Bank and the Gaza Strip and to prevent the return of those who had fled. The Israeli authorities believe that whatever the eventual political status of the Gaza Strip, the refugees there should be moved elsewhere.

The *Observer* of 28 January 1968 also reported: 'It is estimated that between 30,000 and 35,000 people have left the [Gaza] Strip as a result of the measures taken by the Israeli authorities.' The *Guardian* Middle East correspondent Michael Adams wrote: 'No Israeli, when he deals frankly with you (and many do) will deny that he would prefer to accept "the dowry without the bride", meaning that, from Israel's point of view, the ideal solution to the problem of the occupied territories would be their absorption by Israel but without their Arab population.'[94]

In addition to the active encouragement of Arab departure, the Israeli army took tough measures to prevent the return of those who had fled during the war or shortly after. After the war, Israeli troops on the Jordan River apparently routinely shot civilians trying to slip back home on the West Bank.[95] A statement made by an anonymous soldier, who had served in the 5th Reserve Division on the Jordan River, and was issued from the Tel Aviv office of Hebrew magazine *Ha'olam Hazeh* on 10 September 1967, read:

> we fired such shots every night on men, women and children. Even during moonlit nights when we could identify the people, that is – distinguish between men, women and children. In the mornings we searched the area and, by explicit order from the officer on the spot, shot the living, including those who hid, or were wounded (again: including the women and children).[96]

'Uzi Narkiss, the Commanding General of the Central Command, 1965–8, also told an interviewer in October 1988 that after the 1967 war the Israeli troops on the Jordan River killed civilians trying to slip home on the West Bank.[97]

All Palestinian areas conquered by Israel in June 1967 experienced immediate and substantial out-movements of Arab residents, both the native population and those Palestinian refugees who had been driven out from present-day Israel in 1948–9. However, the most distinguishing feature of the 1967 exodus was its 'selective geographical character', with geographical variations in losses of native and refugee populations[98] – as opposed to the wholesale nature of the 1948 exodus.[99] For instance, the Gaza Strip and the West Bank highlands, where most population centres were distant from the 1967 war zone, experienced a comparatively moderate exodus. The Gaza Strip also showed the smallest population reduction, partly due to the fact that the area – in contrast to the West Bank – is furthest from any potential sanctuary.[100] In contrast to the highlands of the West Bank, where population loss was about 20–25 per cent, 88 per cent of the Palestinian population in the West Jordan Valley was driven out from a region 'highly attractive to Israel owing to its strategic attribute'.[101]

Also, both the Hebron district and the Deir Qaddis administrative division, on the western border with Israel, ranked among the highest loss areas.[102]

The policy of eviction, demolition and encouragement of 'transfer' continued for several weeks after the Israeli army occupied the West Bank and Gaza. In fact, some leading Israeli politicians, who were thrilled by the spectacular military victory, were clearly disappointed with the demographic outcome of the war. Indeed Dayan himself was criticised by Deputy Prime Minister Yigal Allon for not driving out all the Palestinian inhabitants of East Jerusalem and Hebron. During the 1948 war Allon had commanded the operation that conquered the twin towns of Lydda and Ramle. According to Israeli historian Benny Morris, on 12 and 13 July 1948, shortly after the two towns were captured, Israeli troops 'carried out their orders, expelling the 50–60,000 remaining inhabitants of and refugees camped in and around the two towns'.[103] Allon's disappointment at the demographic outcome of the 1967 war, which, unlike the 1948 war, did not bring about the evacuation of most of the Palestinian inhabitants of the newly acquired territories, was expressed at a meeting with a delegation of the Whole Land of Israel movement, apparently in November 1967:

> Is this the way to occupy Hebron? A couple of artillery bombardments on Hebron and not a single 'Hebronite' would have remained there. Is this the way to occupy [East] Jerusalem [without driving most of the Arabs out]?[104]

In 1967 evictions and demolitions were evident in numerous geographical locations in the West Bank – the Latrun villages, the al-Magharbeh quarter and the former Jewish quarter in the Old City of Jerusalem, the border towns of Qalqilyah and Tulkarm, the west Jordan Valley and the refugee camps near Jericho and the Hebron district. Young men from several cities and refugee camps were also targeted for deportation.[105] The Palestinian population was still in shock and disarray in the face of Israeli military force, reeling from the military occupation and in no position to resist it.

Evacuation and demolition were executed at the level of middle and senior military echelons with the tacit approval of top-level command and Dayan, who conducted the 1967 war with great confidence and controlled the field commanders during and after the war, managing to shape its immediate consequences. Throughout this process of evacuation and demolition there was some lack of communication between the civil authorities, particularly the Israeli cabinet, and the military commanders;[106] in practice the military exercised civilian functions. The military echelons, backed by Dayan, encouraged Arab residents to get out of East Jerusalem and other cities of the West Bank as well as the refugee camps near Jericho and to go to Jordan.

The forcible eviction of the inhabitants of the Latrun villages, the destruction of the al- Magharbeh quarter and the initial destruction of most of the town of Qalqilyah represented one example of the ideology of force, which reached its apogee between the 1967 war and the October war of 1973. Dayan, who virtually dominated the Labour government's policies in the occupied territories until 1974, in his own style represented that ideology of force, inherited from Ben-Gurion, which was based on the conviction that the defence of Israel depended exclusively on its own strength. The same ideology of force, which helped to reawaken thoughts of transfer during and after 1967, is rooted in the pre-state *Yishuv* and the events that led to the establishment of the State of Israel and the consequent Palestinian exodus of 1948. This ideology of force is predicated on a number of premises: (a) that Palestinians of the occupied territories would resign themselves to their fate, either being kept down or transferred if they dared to oppose Israel; (b) the Arabs only understand the language of force; (c) the Arab world is very divided and Israel can create *faits accomplis*; and (d) it does not matter what the Gentiles say, but what the Jews do – a well-known saying of Ben-Gurion.[107]

In March 1969, two years after the destruction of the Latrun villages, Defence Minister Dayan felt it was necessary to remind his compatriots – including those who were opposed to Jewish settlements in the West Bank and in north Sinai – of what some of them, the younger generation, never knew. Dayan had this to say in a speech to the Technion students in Haifa on 19 March 1969:

> We came here to this country, which was settled by Arabs, and we are building a Jewish State ... Jewish villages arose in the place of Arab villages. You do not even know the names [of these villages], and I do not blame you, because those geography books no longer exist. Not only do the books not exist, the Arab villages are not there either. Nahlal [Dayan's own settlement] arose in the place of Mahlul, Gvat [a kibbutz] in the place of Jibta, Sarid [another

> kibbutz] in the place of Haneifis, and Kfar-Yehoshu'a in the place of Tal-Shaman. There is not one single place built in this country that did not have a former Arab population.[108]

Given this unflinching perception of the uprooting and dispossession of Palestinian communities in the pre-state period, combined with the fact that Zionist objectives had always proceeded against the wishes of the local population, and given the emergence of the ideology of force and its occupation of the centre ground in Israeli policies toward the Palestinians, from there to the massive colonisation and Judaisation of Arab Jerusalem – and Israel's continuing eviction schemes – was only a short step.

NOTES

1. William W. Harris, *Taking Root: Israeli Settlement in the West Bank, the Golan and Gaza-Sinai 1967–1980* (Chichester: Research Studies Press, 1980), pp.7, 16–17.
2. Israeli estimates range from 173,000 to 200,000, while Jordanian and Palestinian estimates range from 250,000 to 408,000 (from June 1967 until the end of 1968). Cited in Walid Salim, 'The [Palestinians] Displaced in 1967: The Problem of Definition and Figures', in *The Palestinians Displaced [in 1967] and the Peace Negotiations* (Ramallah, West Bank: Palestinian Diaspora and Refugee Centre, 1996), p.21. The real figure is probably somewhere around 300,000.
3. George Kossaifi, 'Palestinian Refugees: Their Plight, their Future', in *Beyond Rhetoric: Perspectives on a Negotiated Settlement in Palestine. Part Two. Negotiating Permanent Status: What Price Peace?* (Washington, DC: The Center for Policy Analysis on Palestine, August 1996), pp.36–7. See also Nur Masalha, *A Land Without a People: Israel, Transfer and the Palestinians, 1949–1996* (London: Faber and Faber, 1997); Ghada Karmi and Eugene Cotran (eds), *The Palestinian Exodus, 1948–1998* (Reading: Ithaca Press, 1999).
4. Peter Dodd and Halim Barakat, *River Without Bridges* (Beirut: Institute for Palestine Studies, 1969), p.54.
5. The Palestinian citizens of Israel numbered just below 400,000 in 1967. According to William Harris, the Arab population of the West Bank immediately prior to the 1967 war was approximately 840,000. The 1967 refugee exodus reduced this population by between 200,000 and 250,000. However, by 1977, through a very high natural increase, the number of the West Bankers had recovered to over 820,000. See Harris, *Taking Root*, p.7. The Gaza Strip inhabitants were about 400,000 in 1967.
6. Amos 'Oz, 'The Meaning of Homeland', *New Outlook* 31, no.1 (January 1988), p.22. 'Oz's article was originally published in *Davar* in 1967.
7. Cited from the back cover of 'Jerusalem of Gold', Fontana Records, SRF, 67572, MGF 27572.

8. Tamar Avidar, 'Na'omi Updated her Jerusalem [of Gold]', *Ma'ariv*, 11 June 1967, p.5.
9. The Shofar is a horn used in Jewish high holidays to commemorate events of major significance.
10. Translated from Hebrew, Fontana Records, in Uri Davis and Norton Mezvinsky (eds), *Documents from Israel 1967–1973* (London: Ithaca Press, 1975), p.220.
11. 'Oz, 'The Meaning of Homeland'.
12. Har-Zion became a national hero after serving in 'Unit 101', which, under the command of Ariel Sharon, carried out 'retaliatory' operations against Arab targets in the 1950s. The unit was responsible for the attack on the Arab village of Qibya, to the southwest of Hebron in 1953 in which 63 villagers were slaughtered, and also carried out the expulsion of the al-'Azazmeh tribe from the Negev to Sinai.
13. *Ma'ariv*, supplement, 22 January 1979, p.6; cited also in Meir Kahane, *Lesikim Be'enekhem* [They shall be Strings in Your Eyes] (Jerusalem: Hamakhon Lara'ayon Hayehudi, 1980/81), p.230.
14. *Davar*, 9 February 1979, p.17.
15. Quoted in Zeev Schiff and Eitan Haber (eds), *Leksikon Levitahon Yisrael* [added title: Israel, Army and Defence: A Dictionary] (Tel Aviv: Zmora, Bitan, Modan, 1976), p.178. In his book *Heroes of Israel*, Haim Hertzog (President of Israel from 1983 to 1993) quotes Ariel Sharon's description of Har-Tzion as 'The fighting symbol not only of the paratroopers, but of the entire Israel Defence Forces', Chaim Herzog, *Heroes of Israel: Profiles of Jewish Courage* (London: Weidenfeld and Nicholson, 1989), p.271. See also Moshe Dayan, *Living with the Bible* (London: Weidenfeld and Nicolson, 1978), pp. 96–101. In March 1955 Har-Tzion and his colleagues were involved in a little known massacre of Bedouin in the Negev (see Hanokh Bartov, in *Ma'ariv*, 26 January 1979, p.14). In the wake of those atrocities the then Prime Minister Moshe Sharett entered in his personal diary: 'I am dumbfounded about the essence and fate of this people, which is capable of having a noble soul ... but in addition produces from the ranks of its best youth young men who are capable of murdering human beings in clear mind and cold bloodedness by thrusting knives in the bodies of defenceless young Bedouins' (Moshe Sharett, *Yoman Ishi* [Personal Diary], vol.3, entry for 8 March 1955 (Tel Aviv: Sifriyat Ma'ariv, 1978), p.823.
16. See *Ma'ariv*, 6 December 1974; cited in Yair Kotler, *Heil Kahane* (New York: Adama Books, 1986), pp.89–90.
17. See Mordechai Nisan, *Hamedinah Hayehudit Vehabe'ayah Ha'arvit* [The Jewish State and the Arab Problem] (Tel Aviv: Hadar, 1986), pp.119, 200; Shiloah, *Ashmat Yerushalayim*, p.8; Moshe Shamir, *Hamakom Hayarok* [The Green Place] (Tel Aviv: Dvir Publishing House, 1991), pp.95–9.
18. Quoted in Tzvi Shiloah, *Ashmat Yerushalayim* [The Guilt of Jerusalem] (Tel Aviv: Karni Press, 1989), p.45.
19. Quoted in Aharon Ben-'Ami (ed.), *Sefer Eretz-Yisrael Hashlemah* [The Book of the Whole Land of Israel] (Tel Aviv: Friedman Press, 1977), pp.20–21.

20. Cited in Ephraim Urbach (a professor of Talmud and Midrash at the Hebrew University of Jerusalem), in *Midstream* (a monthly Jewish review), April 1968, p.15. Urbach thought that 'this sort of thing is very harmful and not at all edifying.'
21. Cited in Ben-'Ami , *Sefer Eretz-Yisrael Hashlemah*, pp.20–21.
22. For further discussion of the transfer proposals put forward by Yahil and Shiloah, see Haim Yahil, 'Demography and Israel's Uniqueness', in Ben-'Ami, *Sefer Eretz-Yisrael Hashlemah*, pp.312–13; and Haim Yahil, *Hazon Umaavak: Mivhar Ketavim* [Vision and Struggle: Selected Writings, 1965–74] (Tel Aviv: Karni Press, 1977), p.105; Shiloah, *Ashmat Yerushalayim*, p. 24; Tzvi Shiloah, *Eretz Gdolah Le'am Gadol* [A Great Land for a Great People] (Tel Aviv: Otpaz, 1970), pp.107–8; Tzvi Shiloah in *Moledet*, no.12 (October 1989), p.11.
23. See Ehud Sprinzak, *The Ascendance of Israel's Radical Right* (New York and Oxford: Oxford University Press, 1991), p.57.
24. See Eli'ezer Livneh, in *Moznayim* (literary monthly published by the Hebrew Writers Association in Israel) (July 1967), p.104.
25. See, for instance, Shimon Ballas in *Haumah*, no.2 (November 1967), p.217.
26. Melman and Raviv, 'Expelling Palestinians', *Guardian Weekly* (London), 21 February 1988; *Davar*, 19 February 1988, pp.10–11.
27. *Ma'ariv*, 2 June 1985, p.2; Nisan, *Hamedinah Hayehudit Vehabe'ayah Ha'arvit*, pp.119 and 200.
28. See Gide'on Levi, 'Transfer of 100,000 Without Anybody Saying a Single Word', *Haaretz*, 25 October 1988
29. Melman and Raviv in *Davar*, 19 February 1988.
30. Meron Benvenisti, *Intimate Enemies* (London: University of California Press, 1995), p.191.
31. See Jerusalem Diary of Sister Marie-Therese, in *Cahiers du Temoignage Chrétien* (Paris), 27 July 1967; David Hirst, *The Gun and the Olive Branch* (London: Faber and Faber, 1984), p.225.
32. For further details see Rashid Khalidi, 'The Future of Arab Jerusalem', *British Journal of Middle Eastern Studies* 19, no.2 (1992), pp.139–40; Michael Dumper, *Islam and Israel: Muslim Religious Endowments and the Jewish State* (Washingon, DC: Institute for Palestine Studies, 1994), p.116.
33. 'Uzi Benziman, *Yerushalayim: 'Ir Lelo Homah* (Tel Aviv: Schocken, 1973).
34. Ibid, pp.37–8.
35. Yannai held important functions in the Haganah HQ; formerly, First Commander of the Signal Corps; formerly, Deputy Director General of the Defence Ministry.
36. Benziman, *Yerushalayim*, p.38.
37. Ibid., p.40.
38. See Gide'on Levi, 'Transfer of 100,000 Without Anybody Saying a Single Word', *Haaretz*, 25 October 1988; and Yossi Melman and Dan Raviv in *Davar*, 19 February 1988, pp.10–11.
39. Benziman, *Yerushalayim*, p.41.
40. On the central role played by Kollek in the destruction of the quarter, see ibid., pp.40–41.

41. Cited in M. Ben-Dov, M. Naor and Z. Aner, *The Western Wall* (Jerusalem, Ministry of Defence Publishing House, 1983), p.163.
42. Benziman, *Yerushalayim*, p.42.
43. Ibid., p.43.
44. Ibid., pp.45–6.
45. Ibid., p.45.
46. Dumper, *Islam and Israel*, p.116.
47. Jerusalem Diary of Sister Marie-Therese, in *Cahiers du Temoignage Chrétien*.
48. See Geoffrey Aronson, Geoffrey, *Israel, Palestinians and the Intifada* (London: Kegan Paul International, 1990), p.19. For further discussion of Israel's settlement policies in occupied East Jerusalem, see Michael Dumper, 'Israeli Settlement in the Old City of Jerusalem', *Journal of Palestine Studies* 21, no.4 (Summer 1992), pp.32–53; Dumper, *Islam and Israel*, pp.117–20; Michal Sela' in *Davar*, 30 December 1991, pp.9–10; Robert I. Friedman, *Zealots for Zion* (New York: Random House, 1992), pp.96–100, 113–21. According to 'Uzi Benziman, Shlomo Lahat and his assistant Ya'acov Salman played a key role in the eviction of Arab residents from the Jewish quarter of the Old City of Jerusalem after June 1967. Benziman, *Yerushalayim*, p.45.
49. Quoted in David Sharrock (reporting from Jerusalem), in the *Guardian*, 1 January 1998, p.9. Sharrock's report is based on *Haaretz* of 31 December 1997. See also *Haaretz* of 2 January 1998.
50. Cited by Sharrock, in the *Guardian*, 1 January 1998.
51. These figures were mentioned in a letter by the inhabitants' Committee, cited in *Reconstruct Emmaus* (St-Sulpice, Switzerland: Association for the Reconstruction of Emmaus, December 1987), p.3.
52. Cited in Ehud Maltz and Michal Sela', in *Kol Ha'ir*, 31 August 1984.
53. Cited in George Dib and Fuad Jabber, *Israel's Violation of Human Rights in the Occupied Territories* (Beirut: Institute for Palestine Studies, Third Edn, April 1970), p.xxi; Melman and Raviv in *Davar*, 19 February 1988, pp.10–11.
54. See Levi, 'Transfer of 100,000 Without Anybody Saying a Single Word'; and Melman and Raviv in *Davar*, 19 February 1988, pp.10–11.
55. Cited in Husam 'Izzeddin, 'A Tale of Three Villages', *Jerusalem Times*, 14 June 1996, p.8.
56. Cited in Maltz and Sela' in *Kol Ha'ir*, 31 August 1984.
57. Cited by *Israel Imperial News*, London, March 1968. Kenan's report on the razing of 'Imwas, Yalu and Bayt Nuba was sent to all Knesset members. An English version of the report was also published in *Reconstruct Emmaus*, pp.7–8.
58. Jerusalem Diary of Sister Marie-Therese, in *Cahiers du Temoignage Chrétien*.
59. Levi, 'Transfer of 100,000 Without Anybody Saying a Single Word'.
60. Uzi Narkiss, *The Liberation of Jerusalem* (London: Valentine, Mitchell, 1983), p.199.
61. Aronson, *Israel, Palestinians and the Intifada*, p.19.
62. Benjamin Beit-Hallahmi, *Original Sins: Reflections on the History of Zionism and Israel* (London: Pluto Press, 1992), pp.95–6.

63. Ibid., p.96.
64. Hirst, *The Gun and the Olive Branch*, p.225; Dib and Jabber, *Israel's Violation of Human Rights in the Occupied Territories*, p.xxi.
65. See Yossi Melman and Dan Raviv, 'Expelling Palestinians', the *Washington Post*, Outlook, 7 February 1988. See also 'Oded Lifschitz in *1967–1987: Kovshim 'Atzmam Lada'at* [Added title: A Self-Defeating Conquest] (Tel Aviv: Mapam and 'Al-Hamishmar, 1987), p.77.
66. Cited in Maltz and Sela', in *Kol Ha'ir*.
67. These figures were cited by John Reddaway, Deputy Commissioner General of UNRWA, in the *Daily Star*, 21 July 1967. See also Ian Gilmour and Dennis Walters, in *The Times*, 27 July 1967.
68. Based on personal communication by Dr Anis Kassim, originally a resident of Qalqilyah and currently living in Amman. See also Dib and Jabber, *Israel's Violation of Human Rights in the Occupied Territories*, pp.228 and 235.
69. See Maltz and Sela' in *Kol Ha'ir*, 31 August 1984.
70. Jerusalem Diary of Sister Marie-Therese, in *Cahiers du Temoignage Chrétien*.
71. *The Times* (London), 30 November 1967; Dib and Jabber, *Israel's Violation of Human Rights in the Occupied Territories*, pp.228 and 234–5.
72. Cited in *Daily Star* (Beirut), 21 July 1967.
73. Cited in Paul Cossali and Clive Robson, *Stateless in Gaza* (London: Zed Books, 1986), p.64. See also recollection by the 62-year-old Ibrahim, a construction worker from Gaza, in Lifschitz, *1967–1987*, pp.77–8.
74. The list of universities which awarded him honorary doctorates include: Hebrew University of Jerusalem; Haifa University; Ben-Gurion University of the Negev; Bar-Ilan University; the Technion; Weizmann Institute of Science, Rehovot (Part of the Hebrew University); Georgetown University (Washington, DC); University of Liberia; Yeshiva University, J.T.S.
75. Cited in Nisan, *Hamedinah Hayehudit Vehabe'ayah Ha'arvit*, p.117.
76. Cited by Shmuel Meiri in *Ha'ir* (Tel Aviv), 8 November 1991, p.13; *Kol Ha'ir*, 8 November 1991, p.19.
77. Ibid.
78. Quoted in Levi, 'Transfer of 100,00 Without Anybody Saying a Single Word'. Narkiss also talked about the eviction of the residents of 'four villages in the Latrun area' and the 'flight' of some 60,000 refugees from the three refugee camps near Jericho: 'Ayn Sultan, Nu'aymah, 'Aqbat Jabir.
79. Jerusalem Diary of Sister Marie-Therese, in *Cahiers du Temoignage Chrétien*.
80. A. S. Becker, *Israel and the Palestinian Occupied Territories: Military–Political Issues in the Debate* (Santa Monica, California: The Rand Corporation, December 1971), p.11.
81. Ibid.
82. Cited in *Kol Ha'ir*, 15 November 1991.
83. Ibid.
84. Harris, *Taking Root*, p.9.
85. Cited in *Ha'ir*, 8 November 1991, p.13.

86. Dodd and Barakat, *River Without Bridges*, p.54.
87. Harris, *Taking Root*, p.21. In October 1953, Unit 101, commanded by Ariel Sharon, attacked the village of Qibya in 'reprisal' for the murder of a mother and two children in an Israeli settlement. Jordan had condemned the Arab perpetrators and offered its cooperation to track them down. UN military observers who arrived at the scene two hours after Sharon's commando had completed its operation described what they found:

    > Bullet-riddled bodies near the doorways and multiple bullet hits on the doors of the demolished houses indicated that the inhabitants had been forced to remain inside until their homes were blown up over them. ... Witnesses were uniform in describing their experience as a night of horrors, during which Israeli soldiers moved about in their village blowing the buildings, firing into doorways and windows with automatic weapons and throwing grenades.

    Cited in E.H. Hutchinson, *Violent Truce* (New York: Devin-Adair, 1956), pp.152–8. Commander Hutchinson was an American UN observer. In the biographical sketches of his diary, Meir Har-Tzion describes the attack on Qibya, in which he took part, as follows: 'they [members of Unit 101] stayed [in the village] for three hours, destroyed 42 houses and as a result 70 residents, most of whom hid in the houses, were killed.' Meir Har-Tzion, *Perki Yoman* [Biographical sketches and selections from the diary of Har-Tzion] (Tel Aviv: Lavin-Epstein publication, n.d.), p.165. For further discussion of the Qibya episode, see Benny Morris, *Israel's Border Wars, 1949–1956* (Oxford: Clarendon Press, 1993), pp.225–62.
88. Harris, *Taking Root*, p.22.
89. For Vilner's statement, see *Divrei Haknesset* [Knesset Debates], Sitting 186 of the Sixth Knesset, Second Session, 21 June 1967, pp.2384–5.
90. Ibid.
91. See *al-Ittihad* (Haifa), 6 August 1968.
92. See letter from the inhabitants of 'Imwas, to the Israeli authorities, dated 17 March 1986, published in *al-Bayadir al-Siyasi*, 12 July 1986. On 29 May 1987 a 20-minute film was shown on the Swiss Italian Television, entitled: 'Ritorno a Emmaus', showing the inhabitants of 'Imwas expressing their desire to return to their village. The film also showed two Israelis from the nearby Kibbutz Nachshon stating that they had refused to cultivate the lands of 'Imwas. See *Reconstruct Emmaus*, pp.4–5. For further details on the villagers' campaign, see 'Izzeddin, 'A Tale of Three Villages'.
93. Michael Adams, 'The Road to Emmaus', the *Independent on Sunday*, 16 June 1991.
94. *Guardian*, 19 February 1968.
95. McDowall, *Palestine and Israel*, pp.204 and 302, n.109.
96. Cited in ibid., p.302, n.109.
97. Quoted in Levi, 'Transfer of 100,000'.
98. Harris, *Taking Root*, pp.15 and 17.

99. For further discussion of the 1948 exodus, see Masalha, *Expulsion of the Palestinians*, pp.175–205.
100. Harris, *Taking Root*, pp.15 and 17.
101. Ibid., pp.9, 15 and 21.
102. Ibid., p. 21.
103. Benny Morris, *1948 and After: Israel and the Palestinians* (Oxford: Clarendon Press, 1990), p.2.
104. Cited in Shiloah, *Ashmat Yerushalayim*, pp.53 and 281.
105. Levi, 'Transfer of 100,000'.
106. Benziman, *Yerushalayim*, p.45.
107. For further discussion see Amnon Kapeliouk, *Israel: La Fin Des Mythes* (Paris: Editions Albin Michel, 1975), pp.28 and 183–222.
108. Extracts from the speech were published in *Haaretz*, 4 April 1969, p.15.

7 Israeli Refugee Policies During Negotiations: From Madrid to Taba (October 1991–January 2001)

INTRODUCTION

Any discussion of contemporary Israeli policies towards the Palestinian refugee problem must take into account their Zionist roots and in particular the way in which they are linked to those policies that were instituted in the early years of the Israeli state. After the 1948 refugee exodus the refugees were not repatriated because Israel had no interest in allowing them to return. Since 1948 successive policies adopted by the Jewish state – land, ethnic and demographic, legal and political, military and diplomatic – have been aimed at reinforcing the power and domination of Israel's ruling Jewish majority. A key element in these policies has always been the prevention of the return of Palestinian refugees – residing both inside and outside the borders of the Israeli state – to their ancestral villages and towns. This classic Israeli position against refugee repatriation to the pre-1967 borders has remained unchanged since 1949; Israel's solution to the problem still is the refugees' resettlement in the Arab states or elsewhere. This paramount objective has served until today as a guiding premise underlying successive Israeli policies towards Palestinian refugees, before and throughout the Israeli–Palestinian negotiations.

The refusal to entertain any recognition of culpability for the Palestinian refugee problem runs deep among Israelis of all political persuasions. Throughout the Israeli–Palestinian negotiations Israel has consistently refused to accept moral and legal responsibility for the 1948 refugees and has viewed them as the responsibility of the Arab countries in which they reside – although more recently several Israel 'new/revisionist' historians have raised the issue of Israel's shared accountability for the 1948 exodus.[1] The Zionists continue to deny any wrong-doing.[2] Throughout the negotiations the Israelis argued that the 1948 Palestinian refugees constituted a 'population exchange' with those Jews who left the Arab world in the 1950s. Although Israel's case is as mendacious as it is misleading, Israeli spokesmen have continued to propagate it at home and abroad.[3]

In theory, the decade between 1991 and 2001, from the Madrid peace conference to the Israeli–Palestinian permanent status talks at Taba, Egypt, offered an opportunity to negotiate the Palestinian refugee issue with an intensity not witnessed for four decades. After over four decades of Palestinian dispossession and *nakba*, major changes had occurred in the debate over the future of the Palestinian refugees. In December 1948 the United Nations General Assembly had set up the Palestine Conciliation Commission to deliberate on the status of Palestinian refugees from the 1948 war. The themes of the Commission's deliberations, which began with the Beirut and Lausanne conferences in March and April 1949, included questions of return/repatriation, resettlement, socio-economic rehabilitation of refugees, assessment of lost Palestinian property in Israel and compensation, and family reunification. These issues were still central to the concerns of the Palestinian negotiators during the refugee meetings that were generated by the Madrid Peace conference of October 1991. However, the post-Madrid negotiations and the involvement of the Palestinian team in the Refugee Working Group (RWG) of the multilateral track and in the Quadripartite (Continuing) Committee for the 1967 'displaced persons' took place under completely different circumstances.

In the post-Madrid period the Palestinian refugee question was discussed in five fora:

1. the Refugee Working Group of the Multilateral Track, set up in the wake of the Madrid Conference of 1991;
2. the Continuing or Quadripartite Committee;
3. the Israeli–Palestinian Declaration of Principles of September 1993;
4. the Jordanian–Israeli Peace Treaty of October 1994;
5. the Palestinian–Israeli permanent status negotiations, especially the Camp David Summit of July 2000 and the post-Camp David and Taba negotiations which lasted to the end of January 2001. No Israeli–Palestinian negotiations have taken place since the election of Ariel Sharon as prime minister in early February 2001.

However, few issues in the Israeli–Palestinian negotiations remained as contentious as that of the Palestinian 'right to return'. In reality the Israeli refugee policy throughout the same decade remained strictly tied to its established position vis-à-vis the repatriation of the refugees, with Labour Zionism showing only marginally more flexibility on the issue (especially during the permanent status talks of Taba in January 2001) than the Likud.[4] Israel's rigid position regarding the legal aspects of the refugee problem has recently been reiterated by Ruth Lapidoth, a Professor of International Law at the Hebrew University of Jerusalem, who served as an advisor to the Israeli Ministry of Foreign Affairs throughout the Israeli–Palestinian negotiations:

> neither under the international conventions, nor under the major UN resolutions, nor under the relevant agreements between the parties, do the Palestinian refugees have a right to return to Israel. ... If Israel were to allow all of them to return to its territory, this would be an act of suicide on her part, and no state can be expected to destroy itself.[5]

Other pro-Israeli authors have also claimed that the question of the Palestinian refugees' right to return to their homes is 'ambiguous' in international law.[6] In fact, Israel's rejectionist policies had already been expressed in a Knesset resolution in November 1961:

> The Knesset resolves that the Arab refugees should not be returned to Israeli territory, and that the only solution to the problem is their settlement in the Arab countries.[7]

THE REFUGEE WORKING GROUP OF THE MULTILATERAL TRACK: JANUARY 1992–SEPTEMBER 2000

The Madrid peace process emerged in the wake of the 1991 Gulf War and the US victory over Iraq. The process, beginning with the Madrid conference of October 1991, was based on the formula of a joint Jordanian–Palestinian delegation. Devised to constrain the participation of the PLO, this framework reflected a key demand of the Israeli government, then headed by Likud Prime Minister Yitzhak Shamir, which sought to manage the process very closely. However, after the Madrid conference Israel reluctantly agreed to discuss the refugee question, provided the 'right of return' was not raised. In fact throughout the Madrid and Oslo peace negotiations, Israel strongly opposed recognising the right of 1948 refugees to return, and even stalled on the question of the repatriation to the occupied territories of those Palestinians driven out in 1967. It argued instead for a policy of small-scale 'family reunification' with regard to the 1967 refugees and the creation of an internationally subscribed fund for the compensation and rehabilitation of the 1948 refugees *in situ*. These positions were not altered throughout the permanent status negotiations, although Yossi Beilin's 'Non-Paper' at talks at Taba in January 2001 was an interesting development in terms of accepting a degree of Israeli responsibility for the refugee problem and also for being a partner in its solution (see below).

The multilateral track of the Madrid peace process opened in January 1992 in Moscow. Five working groups were created to complement and support the bilateral process by involving the international community, and by addressing problems of a regional nature such as water, the environment, regional economic development, arms control and regional security, and refugees. The Refugee Working Group (RWG) was one of the five multilateral negotiations in which over 40 states and international organisations discussed the issue of Palestinian refugees and their future in the Middle East peace process. There are six regional parties to the RWG: Egypt, Jordan, Israel, Syria, Lebanon, and the Palestinians (both Syria and Lebanon boycotted the RWG). The mandate of the RWG was to improve the current living conditions of the 1948 Palestinian refugees and the 1967 'displaced persons' without prejudice to their rights and future status; to ease and extend access to family reunification; and to support the process of achieving a viable and comprehensive solution to the refugee issue.[8] In (and after) January 1992 the question of the Palestinian refugees became the subject of the Refugee Working Group. As envisaged by its sponsors, the work of the RWG was basically technical and intended to suggest practical solutions that would feed into future bilateral negotiations. It focused on seven main themes, each with a lead country or 'shepherd'.

1. Data Bases (Norway);
2. Family Reunification (France);
3. Human Resources and Development (the US);
4. Job Creation and Vocational Training (also the US);
5. Public Health (Italy);
6. Child Welfare (Sweden);
7. Economic and Social Infrastructure (the European Union).

In cooperation with the regional parties, the 'shepherds' were responsible for defining needs, developing responses and mobilising resources. Between 1992 and the end of 1995, eight plenary sessions of the RWG were held. The first seven meetings of the RWG were 'gavelled' by Canadian diplomat Marc Perron; he was succeeded by Canadian diplomat Andrew Robinson.

Israel boycotted the first full session of the RWG in Ottawa in May 1992. A month later, in June 1992, the Labour Party coalition came into power and Yitzhak Rabin became Prime Minister. On 1 October 1992 Israeli Foreign Minister Shimon Peres told the United Nations General Assembly, rather vaguely, that the Palestinian refugee problem should be addressed by offering 'a range of possibilities for restoring the dignity of refugees and offering them a good life'.[9] However, at the November 1992 meeting of the RWG in Ottowa Israeli participation was first delayed by a dispute over the participation of Palestinian members of the Palestine National Council, and then cut short by a dispute over the issue of Palestinian 'family reunification'. At the opening of the Ottowa meeting, the Israeli head of delegation, Shlomo Ben-'Ami, representing the new Labour government, stated that the 'Palestinian refugee problem was born as the land was bisected by the sword, not by design, Jewish or Arab'. Palestinian academic Elia Zureik, who took part in many RWG meetings, subsequently argued that Ben-'Ami's statement at Ottowa marked the first official Israeli acknowledgement of at least partial Israeli responsibility for the plight of the Palestinian refugees, a central demand by Palestinian negotiators throughout the RWG meetings.[10] At a subsequent meeting of the RWG, which was held in Tunis on 12 October 1993 (shortly after the signing of the Declaration of Principles (the Oslo Accords), Israeli Deputy Foreign Minister Yossi Beilin had this to say:

> For a whole generation the refugee problem has been perceived as insurmountable. The key to the solution is to understand each others pain and (each) others red lines. In the very near future we will have to tackle sensitive issues left untouched for many decades. We must touch some delicate nerves; the brutalities of past wars, the missed opportunities and the regional 'march of folly'.[11]

Overall, however, Israel's rejectionist stance in the multilateral track on refugees made it difficult to imagine any significant Israeli concessions on the refugee issue in the final status negotiations with the Palestinians. The Palestinian negotiators considered the refugee problem to be the second most important and difficult after Jerusalem; but in formulating their position Palestinian negotiators had to take into account Israeli rejectionism. Although Palestinian negotiators continued to point out that solving the refugee issue remained the key for genuine peace and reconciliation between the Palestinians and Israelis, the refugee issue encountered formidable resistance from the Israeli negotiators and politicians. While some Israeli leaders reconciled themselves to the idea of a mini-Palestinian entity-state in the West Bank and Gaza as a possible outcome of the negotiations, the Israelis generally singled out the return of refugees for a barrage of ideological and political objections. The Israelis were systematic in their rejection of any mention of UN Resolution 194. The return of the refugees to their ancestral villages and towns was singled out as a major security issue and as a prelude to undermining the Zionist-Jewish character of the state. Israeli negotiators even tended to discourage the idea of return of refugees even to the areas that would be under exclusive Palestinian control. The Israeli Labour party in particular attempted to demonstrate a hardline stance on the refugee question in an attempt to appeal to centrist and right-wing voters.[12]

Moreover, throughout the seven plenary meetings of the RWG, the last of which took place in Geneva in December 1995, and the numerous smaller meetings, Israel's approach to the Palestinian refugee problem remained markedly consistent with its policies of the previous 40 years. It favoured projects 'to improve the living conditions' of the Palestinian refugees that were based on the principle of resettlement. Within the RWG, Israel consistently refused to take part in any discussions touching on the final settlement of the refugee issue, arguing that this was to be discussed only in the permanent status talks.

Facing a wide gap between the Israeli and Palestinian approaches, Canada, the lead country in the multilaterals on the Palestinian refugee issue, or 'gavel holder' for the RWG, introduced into discussions the vague term of 'adaptation'. Apparently, this prompted Palestinian negotiators, who were clearly concerned that the introduction of the 'adaptation' rhetoric into the peace process might imply 'resettlement', to insist first that 'adaptation' should be confined to the West Bank and Gaza Strip and should be aimed primarily at Palestinian returnees, and second, that it must not prejudice the rights and future status of the refugees in Arab host countries. Palestinian spokespersons were anxious that, should the rhetoric of 'adaptation' be translated into concrete policies, it could violate the historical rights of the refugees.[13]

The RWG and Family Reunification

Because the issue of the 1967 'displaced persons' (most of them living in Jordan, but some in Lebanon, Syria and Egypt) required a multilateral approach, it was placed on the agenda of both the RWG and the Quadripartite Committee (see also below). Between 1992 and 1996 the RWG was able to show some progress on several fronts, such as funding research and carrying out feasibility studies on various aspects of refugee life, but little was achieved by way of concrete results with regard to the main agenda, that of 'family reunification' of those displaced in 1967.[14] Shortly after the Declaration of Principles of September 1993, Israel agreed to discuss certain categories of the 1967 refugees who might be allowed to return to the West Bank and Gaza Strip within the restricted framework of family reunion. At some stage in the mid-1990s Israel reluctantly agreed to raise the annual ceiling from 1,000 to 2,000 cases and, subsequently, further agreed to increase the quota from 2,000 to 6,000 per year. The Palestinian negotiators, however, contended that there should be a further increase in the quota as well as a relaxation of the criteria, and greater transparency in their application. Moreover, the number of those awaiting family reunion – wives and children unable to live with their husbands and fathers – was estimated at 120,000 by a member of the multilateral Refugee Working Group. There are another estimated 100,000 persons who have been denied re-entry into the West Bank and Gaza on grounds of having stayed abroad for periods longer than the Israeli authorities permitted.[15] However, in practice even within the narrow perspective of family reunion little progress was made in peace talks on the 1967 refugees. There was also the question of the 300,000 people displaced by the 1967 war or expelled shortly afterwards, and their descendants. Although consideration of their case for return is allowed for in Article 12 of the Declaration of Principles, no progress was made on this issue. The parties involved in the talks were unable to reach a consensus on the definition of a 'displaced' Palestinian, the number of refugees, or the means of repatriating the 1967 refugees to the West Bank and Gaza.

There was, however, a certain amount of tripartite cooperation on the 1967 'displaced persons' between the Palestinian Authority, Egypt and Jordan (the three parties which supported the Oslo process and participated actively in the RWG).[16] Moreover, according to *Haaretz* daily, during the years 1993–9 some 40,000 'displaced Palestinians' were allowed to return to the West Bank and Gaza Strip under the 'family reunification' rubric.[17] Some Israeli sources even claimed (with clear exaggeration) that altogether, the number of Palestinians 'returning' to the occupied territories in the aftermath of the Oslo Accord approached 200,000. Overall, however, the multilateral process was supposed to work by consensus,[18] and Israeli objectionism and procrastination ensured that concrete progress in the crucial area of family reunification remained extremely limited.

THE DECLARATION OF PRINCIPLES, SEPTEMBER 1993

The Failure to Establish Linkage with UNGA Resolution 194 and other Fundamental Weaknesses

The 1993 Oslo secret track and the Declaration of Principles (DoP) that emerged from it in September of the same year bypassed the Madrid framework, establishing in its place the principle of direct, bilateral negotiations between Israel and the PLO, who exchanged letters of recognition and initialled the DoP or the Oslo Accords on 13 September 1993. The Oslo Accords established a timetable for the establishment of a self-governing Palestinian Authority in parts of the West Bank and Gaza. Although Oslo's postponement of a resolution of the refugee issue to the 'final status' basket of issues shattered the hope of return for Palestinian refugees,[19] it nevertheless established a timetable for the initiation and completion of 'final status' talks for a resolution of the contested issues between Israel and the Palestinians. Bilateral negotiations to resolve these permanent status issues – refugees, Jerusalem, settlements, security arrangements, and borders – were to commence in 1996.[20]

Throughout the Oslo peace process Israel categorically rejected the Palestinian 'right of return' and was opposed to basing any negotiations with the PLO or neighbouring Arab states on the principles of UNGA Resolution 194. Before and throughout the post-Oslo negotiations Israel consistently rejected the possibility of refugee return to their ancestral homes and villages and even demanded that Palestinians explicitly abandon claims of a 'right of return' to the 1948 areas. Consequently, the greatest weakness of the DoP concerns the status of the Palestinian refugees of both 1948 and 1967: the DoP does not seriously address this issue. Throughout the Israeli–Palestinian negotiations UNGA Resolution 194 remained the cornerstone of the Palestinian position on the 1948 refugees. The 'right of return', both as a basic principle of human rights and as an individual right, was central to the Palestinian position at the Madrid peace conference of 1991 and remained so throughout the post-Oslo negotiations with Israel.[21] At the opening of the Madrid conference, Haydar 'Abdul Shafi, the head of the Palestinian delegation, had spoken about Palestinians coming to Madrid 'to narrate our story'. This story had the theme of dispersal and refugeedom woven into it. 'As we speak', he said, 'the eyes of thousands of Palestinian refugees, deportees, and displaced persons since 1967 are haunting us, for exile is a crucial fate: bring them home. They have the right to return.'[22] The Palestinian position on the refugees was based on the 'right of return', as explained by 'Abdul Shafi and in a paper published in 1995 by the Palestinian Authority's Information Ministry, entitled 'The Palestinian Refugees and the Right of Return'.[23] The paper argued that the Arab countries are economically incapable of absorbing the refugees and that the majority of the refugees, including those in the occupied territories, would prefer to go back to their original homes in Israel.[24] However the Israeli–Palestinian negotiations failed to link UNGA Resolution 194 and the 'right of return' with the Oslo accords. Moreover, both the actual Madrid peace process and the Oslo Accords were anchored in UN Security Council resolutions 242 and 338, adopted following the 1967 and 1973 war respectively. Both resolutions fall short of recognising Palestinian national rights. Most crucially, the fate of the 1948 refugees is particularly handicapped by the absence of any direct reference in the DoP to UNGA Resolution 194.

Furthermore the Israeli–Palestinian negotiations before, during and after Oslo may even have contributed to the dilution of the force of Resolution 194. To begin with the Palestinians entered the Oslo and post-Oslo negotiations with Israel with a series of concessions behind them. Reference to the 'right of return' was ritually made by Palestinian spokespersons in all internal fora, but this right had no concrete expression in any of the agreements signed between Israel and the Palestinians.[25] Under international law the nullification or even dilution of Resolution 194 threatens the rights of Palestinian refugees. The Palestinian Information Ministry's paper of 1995, although reiterating Palestinian adherence to Resolution 194, pointed out the lack of clarity about how the Resolution fitted with the post-

Madrid and post-Oslo negotiations formula. It came to be seen that Palestinian insistence on a reference to Resolution 194 throughout the negotiations resulted in the gradual dilution of the force of the Resolution, and mentioning it eventually became a sort of ritual. Palestinian reference to Resolution 194 in the RWG was routinely accompanied, at the insistence of the United States, and Israel, with qualifications that some members agreed to and others did not.[26] Palestinian negotiators believed that repeated reference to UN resolutions on the Palestinian refugees, particularly Resolution 194 and Security Council Resolution 237 (1967) was futile, even though they did constitute the proper international legal framework in which these issues should be addressed. As Salim Tamari put it, repetition, as a magical refrain, will not have the desired effect. The consensual nature of both the multilateral negotiations and the 'final status' talks required a tactical approach that re-examined these resolutions and made them operational.[27]

At the same time, however, both the Oslo Accords and the Jordanian–Israeli Peace Treaty of 1994 cast the old Palestinian refugee issue in a new light. The official Palestinian position had evolved under new circumstances that distinguished the post-Madrid Palestinian involvement in peace talks from the refugee meetings of the late 1940s and early 1950s. According to Salim Tamari, coordinator of the RWG for the Palestinian Team at the multilateral negotiations and a member of the Quadripartite Committee on the 1967 'displaced persons', the new circumstances involved the recasting of the Palestinians as a people whose cause is no longer an exclusively Arab or Islamic one, but an international cause with concrete territorial claims to a land and sovereignty. More specifically the Palestinian refugee issue was no longer defined as a humanitarian issue, as it was after 1948, but was recast as part of the wider agenda of restoring the right of self-determination to the Palestinian people. While earlier international deliberations on the Palestinian refugee issue focused more or less on exclusively on refugees, the post-Oslo negotiations, both in bilateral and multilateral fora, dealt with Palestinian refugees as part of a complex set of issues that included residencies, family reunification, problems of absorption, compensation and so on. In other words, throughout the post-Madrid, Palestinian–Israeli negotiations, the refugee issue was diluted into various themes of Palestinian national reconstruction.[28]

It was in this framework of bilateral negotiations between Israel and the Palestinians that Israeli policy manifested a slightly modified attitude from the past. In the aftermath of the Oslo Accords the Rabin government had sought to address all issues related to the 'final status' of the occupied territories in a bilateral framework with the PLO. As one of the 'final status' issues, the refugee question was to be negotiated, for the first time in its history, directly between Israel and the Palestinians. This decision had some substantive as well as procedural implications for the content of Labour policies towards the refugees. By accepting the PLO as interlocutor for Palestinian interests, the Rabin government (and subsequent Labour administrations), were acknowledging that the resolution of the refugee issue would take place in the context of the establishment of a Palestinian entity (or mini-state) in the West Bank and Gaza, although Israelis repeatedly emphasised the fact that such an entity could not possibly have the capacity or the space to absorb all or even most of the 1948 refugees. However, the two prevailing assumptions among key (Zionist) Israeli Labour figures involved in the Oslo process diplomacy, such as Yossi Beilin, were:

1. that the resolution of the Palestinian refugee issue would be viewed largely within the context of a Palestinian entity in the West Bank;
2. that the Oslo process would put an end to refugee claims.

Beilin (then Justice Minister in the government of Ehud Barak) had this to say in an interview with the Palestinian newspaper *Al-Quds* on 5 January 2001:

> Since the moment we accepted the resolution on recognising the Palestinians' right to self-determination and their right to set up an independent state ... we practically accepted the resolution on recognising the right to absorb the refugees in this state. In fact, this is the main idea – enabling the Palestinian state to absorb Palestinian refugees, just as the Jewish state absorbs the Jews in places of refuge. Despite all existing differences, the situation is exactly the same. In addition to this – in informal discussions throughout the past years – the Palestinian leadership has told us that it is clear to it that it has to exert great efforts to solve the refugee problem. It is also clear to it that those refugees, in their large masses, will not return to their places of residence, because this is impractical and unrealistic.[29]

THE CONTINUING (OR THE QUADRIPARTITE) COMMITTEE AND THE 1967 'DISPLACED PERSONS'

Article XII of the Declaration of Principles called for negotiations between Israel, the Palestinians, Jordan and Egypt on the 'modalities of admission of persons displaced from the West Bank and Gaza Strip in 1967'. The same article provided for the establishment of the Continuing (or Quadripartite) Committee to address the issue of the 1967 refugees (or 'displaced persons') and to 'decide by agreement on the modalities of admission of persons displaced from the West Bank and Gaza Strip in 1967, together with the necessary measures to prevent disruption and disorder'.[30] In addition to the Oslo Accords, the frame of reference for the Quadripartite Committee included those clauses of the Camp David Accords of 1978 which dealt with 'displaced persons' and the Israeli–Jordanian Peace Treaty of 1994. Subsequently, the Quadripartite Committee, made up of Israel, Jordan, Egypt and the Palestinians, was established to discuss the issue of the 1967 'displaced persons', and 'family reunification' in the West Bank and Gaza Strip. Both Syria and Lebanon had boycotted the whole multilateral process (including the Quadripartite Committee and the RWG) from the beginning. The Quadripartite Committee first met in Amman in May 1995; subsequent meetings were held in Beer Sheba, Cairo, Gaza, Amman and Haifa.

Work within this Quadripartite Committee was extremely slow, with major differences over the definition of a 'displaced person' and hence the number of potential returnees. The Committee failed to overcome these fundamental disagreements between Israel and the Palestinians (backed by Egypt and Jordan) over the definition of a 'displaced person'. While the Israeli representatives stuck to definitions that accepted only 200,000 Palestinians who were displaced in 1967, the three Arab parties insisted on a much larger group of about 1.1 million people which included:

- those who were stranded outside the occupied territories when the 1967 war broke out;
- those who had left the West Bank and Gaza Strip in 1967 but had been refused re-admission by the Israeli authorities;
- the descendants of the 1967 'displaced persons';
- those thousands of Palestinians deported by Israel from the occupied territories in the late 1960s, 1970s and 1980s.[31]

Consequently, being unable to agree on the question of definition, the Quadripartite Committee moved to the questions of 'modalities of admission of displaced persons' and numbers.[32] The Committee made no progress on the questions of modalities or numbers either.

Talks within the Quadripartite Committee broke off in 1997. By then rapid deterioration in the bilateral peace process between Israel and the Palestinians, especially under the Likud government of Binyamin Netanyahu, saw the work of the Committee grind to a halt. In the same year, the Arab League called for a boycott of all the multilaterals in protest over Israeli settlement policies in the West Bank and Gaza Strip. Several months after the coming to power of the Labour coalition of Ehud Barak in February 2000, a ministerial level meeting was held to activate the work of the Quadripartite Committee, but no results were forthcoming. Although low-level work on the multilateral track continued for a while, this ended with the eruption of the 'al-Aqsa Intifada' in later September 2000, which led to the suspension of all the multilateral track activities.

THE ISRAELI–JORDANIAN PEACE TREATY OF OCTOBER 1994

While both the international diplomatic efforts and the Madrid peace process that emerged in the wake of the second Gulf War of 1991 were based on the formula of a joint Jordanian–Palestinian delegation, both the Oslo peace process and the Declaration of Principles that emerged from it in September 1993 bypassed the Madrid framework, establishing in its place the principle of direct, bilateral negotiations between Israel and the PLO. The PLO was recognised by Israel as the principal, if not sole, interlocutor for Palestinian interests, including those of the refugees. Yet, if the Oslo Accords surprised and worried King Hussein of Jordan, they also freed him from the constraints imposed by the desire to maintain a Jordanian–Palestinian consensus. In fact, the day after the Declaration of Principles was signed in Washington DC, Jordan and Israel released the 'Israeli–Jordanian Common Agenda' outlining the framework for a bilateral peace agreement. With regard to 'Refugees and Displaced Persons' the agenda vaguely noted:

> Achieving an agreed just solution to the bilateral aspects of the problem of refugees and displaced persons in accordance with international law.[33]

On 25 July 1994 King Hussein and Prime Minister Yitzhak Rabin signed the 'Washington Declaration', in the presence of US President Bill Clinton, which stated that

1. Jordan and Israel aim at the achievement of just, lasting and comprehensive peace between Israel and its neighbours and at the conclusion of a Treaty of Peace between both countries;
2. The two countries will vigorously continue their negotiations to arrive at a state of peace, based on Security Council Resolutions 242 and 338 in all their aspects, and founded on freedom, equality and justice.[34]

Three months later, on 17 October, Hussein and Rabin initialled a draft of an Israeli–Jordanian Treaty of Peace, again in the presence of President Clinton in Washington. The Treaty was signed by Hussein and Rabin on the Israeli–Jordanian border on 26 October. Jordan became the second Arab state – after Egypt – to conclude a (separate) Peace Treaty with Israel. The Treaty referred not only to bilateral issues between Jordan and Israel, but also to issues such as Jerusalem and refugees that had already been defined in the Israel–PLO Declaration of Principles as part of the agenda for bilateral (Israeli–Palestinian) final status issues set to commence in May 1996. Although Jordan could no longer aspire to represent Palestinian interests on the refugee issue, it still sought to assert its sovereign prerogatives, which derived from the fact that Palestinian refugees who were now Jordanian citizens had a stake, at least individually, in a resolution of the refugee issue.

Article 2 of the Treaty reaffirmed Israeli recognition of Jordan's interest in not becoming a 'dumping ground' for Palestinian refugees from the occupied territories and Lebanon.[35] Most important, Article 8 affirmed Jordan's right to represent the interests of its citizens of Palestinian origins in negotiations with Israel on the resolution of the refugee issue. The same Article acknowledged an Israeli interest in establishing a diplomatic mechanism for supporting Jordanian claims to its sole, sovereign representation of Palestinian refugees residing in Jordan – a position that Jordan impressed upon Israel during the Israeli–Palestinian final status talks of June 2000–January 2001.

Article 8: Refugees and Displaced Persons:

1. Recognising the massive human problems caused to both Parties by the conflict in the Middle East, as well as the

contribution made by them towards the alleviation of human suffering, the Parties seek to further alleviate those problems arising on a bilateral level.

2. Recognising that the above human problems caused by the conflict in the Middle East cannot be fully resolved on a bilateral level, the Parties will seek to resolve them in appropriate forums, in accordance with international law, including the following:

    a. in the case of [1967] displaced persons, in a quadripartite committee together with Egypt and the Palestinians;
    b. in the case of [1948] refugees,

        i. In the framework of the Multilateral Working Group on Refugees;
        ii. In negotiations, in a framework to be agreed, bilateral or otherwise, in conjunction with and at the same time as the permanent status negotiations pertaining to the [occupied] territories referred to in Article 3 of this Treaty;

    c. through the implementation of agreed United Nations programmes and other agreed international economic programmes concerning refugees and displaced persons, including assistance to their resettlement.[36]

Under the Treaty the emergence of the Israeli–Jordanian bilateral avenue for dealing with the refugee issue existed in parallel with and (to some extent) in contradiction to a number of other fora created by the Madrid and Oslo frameworks, most crucially the bilateral Israeli–Palestinian negotiations on final status issues that were high on the agenda at Camp David in July 2002 and at Taba in January 2001. One of the problems of the Treaty was that it established mechanisms for the bilateral (Jordanian–Israeli) treatment of Palestinian refugee-related issues without the necessary reference to an overall, final status resolution of the refugee issue between Israel and the Palestinians or to Palestinian refugee rights under international law.

Interestingly, however, in the wake of the Treaty both countries were obliged to remove any legislation that had the effect of discriminating against the nationals of the country. The Jordanians, for instance, argued that the large body of Israeli legislation relating to lands owned and claimed by Palestinian refugees, who were now citizens of Jordan – a state at peace with Israel – had to be amended in a non-discriminatory fashion. Subsequently, the Israeli Knesset legislated to end discriminatory treatment of Jordanian nationals, but, most crucially, the effective date of legislation was 10 November 1994. All Israeli actions before that, especially the seizure of millions of dunums of Palestinian refugee land, in accordance with the 1950 Absentees' Property Law and other Israeli legislation, were not affected by the 1994 Knesset legislation. Apparently, when then Jordanian ambassador to Israel, Marwan Mu'asher (currently Foreign Minister), wrote to the Israeli government complaining about the fact that Israeli discriminatory legislation still violated the Treaty, he was brushed off by both Labour and Likud administrations.

The Israeli–Jordanian Treaty had reaffirmed Israeli recognition of Jordan's interest in not becoming a 'dumping ground' for Palestinian refugees from the occupied territories and from Lebanon. However shortly after the Taba talks of January 2001 (see below) the daily *Haaretz* published an article entitled: 'The Jordanians Fear Giving Priority to Refugees from Lebanon.' The article highlighted the deep-seated fears among the Jordanians with regard to Zionist designs for an 'alternative Palestinian homeland' in Jordan. *Haaretz* also quoted a document which had been published a few days earlier by the Jordanian daily *al-Rai* (of 31 January 2001), outlining Jordanian attitudes towards the Palestinian refugee question. Jordan, according to *al-Rai*, insisted on:

- the Right of Return: giving every Palestinian refugee the right to choose in line with UNGA Resolution 194;
- compensating both individual refugees in Jordan and the Jordanian state, the latter for the economic costs of looking after the refugees since 1948.[37]

THE 'FINAL STATUS' NEGOTIATIONS, 1999–JANUARY 2001

According to the DoP, bilateral negotiations between Israel and the Palestinians to resolve the permanent status issues – refugees, Jerusalem, settlements, security arrangements, and borders – were scheduled for 1996. The 'final status' bilateral negotiations were formally and ceremonially opened in Taba on 5–6 May 1996. At the start of the negotiations the talks encountered fundamental differences over the refugees' right to repatriation. During the bilateral meeting before the official session, Uri Savir, Director General of the Israeli Foreign Ministry and head of the Israeli delegation, asked Mahmud 'Abbas, head of the Palestinian delegation, not to mention Resolution 194. According to a report by Palestinian Television in Gaza, broadcast on 5 May 1996, Abbas rejected Savir's request.[38] Shortly after the Taba meetings the Likud administration of Binyamin Netanyahu came into power. Under Netanyahu the bilateral peace process between Israel and the Palestinians began deteriorating, and by 1997 had effectively ground to a halt. It was only after the election of the labour coalition of Ehud Barak in 1999 that the permanent status talks were reactivated. From the beginning of the permanent status negotiations in late 1999 to the negotiations at Taba in January 2001 Israel and the Palestinians engaged in intensive bilateral talks, assisted frequently by the United States. However, significantly, the government of Ehud Barak opted for pursuing an exclusively bilateral forum on the refugees with the Palestinians, hoping to achieve an agreement with them that, strangely enough, would be binding not only on the Palestinians but also on Arab countries acting as hosts to refugees. During Barak's intensive talks with Syria the refugee issue was not raised and, throughout the final status talks with the Palestinians, Israeli officials refused to consider the need to expand the final status talks to include the Arab host countries. The prevailing assumptions were that the inclusion of Arab host states in 'final status' talks 'would complicate matters' for Israel and that the host states would acquiesce in a deal reached with the Palestinians.

The Palestinian refugee issue was placed at the heart of the permanent status negotiations in three major fora:

1. at Stockholm in May 2000;
2. at Camp David in July 2000;
3. at Taba in January 2001.

THE CAMP DAVID SUMMIT, JULY 2000

The Camp David summit of July 2000 (the US-sponsored talks between Ehud Barak and Yasser 'Arafat) was basically an exchange of ideas and speeches, which represented the general view of both sides and history as it was seen by both parties. At Camp David, however, Israel refused to entertain any recognition of culpability for the Palestinian refugee problem. The summit was inaugurated by

President Clinton at Camp David, Maryland, on 11 July, in a renewed attempt to reach a framework agreement on a final permanent solution between Israel and the Palestinians. The summit, failing to break the deadlock between the two sides, ended without agreement on 25 July. The main reason for its collapse was the issue of Jerusalem, not the 'right of return'.[39]

At Camp David there was no progress on the refugee issue, in fact no real negotiations on the subject. However, according to Akram Hanieh (the editor of the chief Palestinian daily *al-Ayyam* and a close advisor of 'Arafat; also a member of the Palestinian team at Camp David)

> The greatest failure of the [Camp David] summit was in the refugee committee. This is not surprising, since the refugee file is the 'moment of truth ... the discussion revolved mostly around the past, not the present and future ... the Israeli and Palestinian visions of the past – and more particularly of the root of the conflict, the 1948 Palestinian *nakba* – are in total conflict. ... There is a complete denial of Israeli responsibility for the *nakba*. Instead, the Israeli delegation tried to convince the Palestinians that there had been no massacres or terror campaigns in 1948, that there had been no expulsions or wholesale destruction of villages. So the refugee committee did not move one inch forward. Refusing to take any moral or legal responsibility for what happened, the Israelis were willing only to express sorrow over what befell the Palestinians as a result of the Arab–Israel war of 1948. Because any discussion of the right of return was taboo for Israel – in their eyes tantamount to declaring a war of destruction on the Israeli state – there could be no talk about a timetable for the implementation of return. All that Israel would discuss was compensation for the refugees – not from its pocket, from the pocket of the international community, and part of the funds would be used to compensate Jews who came to Israel from Arab countries. Israel only committed itself to allowing several thousand Palestinians to return over a ten-year period through 'family reunification' and 'humanitarian cases'.[40]

The summit did, however, provide the Palestinians for the first time with the opportunity to present their national narrative and position on the refugee issue directly to the American president without passing through the filter of his advisors. At the summit the

Americans discovered the limits of the Palestinian position on the refugees.[41] After 'a brief summary of the roots of the refugee problem and the Zionist conquest of Palestine', the Palestinians asserted the following points:

- the right of every Palestinian refugee to return home in accordance with UN Resolution 194;
- the need for a mechanism to implement this right, starting with the return of refugees in Lebanon, who would be given priority due to their miserable living conditions and kinship ties with Palestinians in Galilee (illustrated in the dramatic reunion at Fatima Gate following Israel's withdrawal from southern Lebanon). A timetable, including numbers of refugees, would then be established for the return of all those who wished it;
- after the recognition of the right of return and the establishment of the implementation mechanism, the need for a compensation regime;
- the issue of the Jews who left Arab countries and their compensation was not the province of the Palestinian side and would not be discussed.[42]

In his report on the Camp David summit to the Fatah Central Council, Mahmud 'Abbas (Abu Mazen) added to the above demands submitted by the Palestinian delegation: that the host Arab states should be compensated for the cost of burdens they have had to shoulder in looking after the refugees over the last 50 years[43] – a demand which may have been made to counter hostile reactions from disaffected Arab states towards the PLO's conduct in the Oslo process.

The Israelis, for their part, reiterated their classic position: we are not responsible for this problem; we do not recognise the 'right of return'; we are prepared to allow the return of several thousands of persons spread over a number of years under a 'family reunification' programme and for 'humanitarian reasons'; we are ready to discuss international compensation that would also compensate Jews 'expelled' from the Arab countries.[44] In Yossi Beilin's words:

> At Camp David there were real negotiations on the subject. The Israeli view was that Israel was not responsible for the problem, doesn't have to pay for it and the number of refugees who will be admitted will be some hundreds every year and that's it. The

> feeling of the Palestinians was that Israel was not ready to even address the problem.[45]

During the meeting, President Clinton realised that the refugee issue was far more difficult than he had been led to believe by his advisors, who had maintained that progress could be achieved on the basis of compensation, resettlement in the host countries, and a liberal immigration policy for some Western countries.[46]

In December 2000, several months after the eruption of the 'al-Aqsa Intifada', Clinton presented to the Palestinians and Israelis 'bridging' proposals that called on the Palestinian Authority to relinquish the 'right of return' of Palestinian refugees in Arab host countries in exchange for Israeli concessions on the final status issue of Jerusalem.[47] The initial Palestinian response to the proposal seemed to have been slightly confused, however, both Palestinians and Israelis seeking clarification from the White House. By this stage the Palestinian revolt was exhibiting a life of its own, rapidly escalating into armed combat.

Throughout the final status negotiations, especially in the period between July 2000 and January 2001, Palestinian delegates argued that Resolution 194 was the basis for a just settlement of the refugee problem and that the essence of the 'right of return' was choice: refugees should be given the option to choose where they wished to settle, including return to the homes from which they were driven in 1948. Palestinian delegates repeatedly said they were prepared to be flexible and creative about mechanisms for implementing the 'right of return'. In all discussions with the Israelis, they elaborated on mechanisms for implementing the 'right of return' in such a way as to end the refugee status and refugee problem, as well as to accommodate Israeli demographic and security concerns.[48] In contrast, three fundamental assumptions remained central to the Israeli negotiating positions throughout the final status negotiations:

(1) Rejection of the Legal or Moral Responsibility for the Refugee Problem

Throughout the permanent status talks the government of Ehud Barak consistently refused to acknowledge the 1948 Palestinian *nakba* or admit moral responsibility towards the Palestinian refugees. Reflecting the traditional Israeli attitude, Prime Minister Barak, in his inaugural speech to the Knesset on 4 October 1999, stated that he 'recognised the suffering of the Palestinian people' but refrained from any expression of regret or responsibility towards the refugees, echoing earlier statements by Shimon Peres and Yossi Beilin that 'there is no point in settling accounts for historical mistakes.'[49] The same attitude is found in his remarks three months later, stating that Israel 'regret[s] the heavy suffering that the conflict has caused, not only to us but to all the Arab nations that have fought against us, including the Palestinian people'. Israel was prepared to establish relations with the Palestinians

> based on good will, friendship and neighbourliness – but not, under any circumstances, based on a feeling of guilt or responsibility for the emergence of the conflict and its results, a conflict we did not want and which we did much to prevent.[50]

In an address to the 'Peace and Security Council' on 28 June 2000, Barak emphasised that recognition of and regret for Palestinian suffering did not suggest any transformation of Israel's continuing rejection of 'legal or moral responsibility for the refugee problem'.[51] Israeli Attorney-General Elyakim Rubinstein argued in an article entitled: 'The Truth About the 'Right of Return' and Compensation for the Jewish Refugees', published shortly after the Camp David summit of July 2000, that, 'the Israeli position is that legal and moral responsibility for the fate of the Palestinian refugees cannot be recognised even if human empathy can be expressed for the suffering of the people.'[52]

(2) Rejection of the 'Right of Return' as Embodied in UNGA Resolution 194

The Barak government, like all of its predecessors, rejected the principles embodied in the Palestinian 'right of return' because they were inconsistent with the existence of the State of Israel as the 'homeland for Jewish people'. In an address in New York in September 2000, Foreign Minister Shlomo Ben-'Ami reiterated classical Israeli arguments that that it would be 'national suicide' for Israel to agree to accept unlimited numbers of Palestinian refugees. 'We want peace but we are not lunatics.'[53] 'There is no right of return to Israel,' declared Barak after the Taba talks, on the eve of his defeat in February 2001, 'that is a cornerstone.'[54] As Justice Minister Yossi Beilin put in an interview with the Palestinian daily *al-Quds* in January 2001, the Palestinian refugees 'will not return to their places of residence, because this is impractical and unrealistic'. Beilin added that the

Palestinian refugees will be partly absorbed within the context of the emerging Palestinian entity in the West Bank and Gaza, and

> I must admit that raising the refugee issue [in negotiations in 2000] did not surprise me. But what surprised me was raising the right of return. This is because the one who raised it is aware that Israel cannot accept it. Thus, he is perhaps raising it based on his clear expectation that Israel will not accept it and that an agreement will practically not be reached.[55]

(3) Refugee Rehabilitation in Arab Host Countries or Resettlement in Third Countries

For the Barak government most of the refugees would have to be either absorbed *in situ* in Arab host countries or relocated to and resettled in third countries.

The position of the Barak government on the refugee issue was largely endorsed by the Clinton administration. This was clearly reflected in President Bill Clinton's bridging proposals of December 2000 which stated that any final agreement should make it clear that there was no specific 'right of return' to what is now Israel. President Clinton, publicly outlining the American view of the principles of a final status agreement on 7 January 2001, had this to say on the issue of Palestinian refugees:

> A solution will have to be found for the Palestinian refugees who have suffered a great deal – particularly some of them. A solution that allows them to return to a Palestinian state that will provide all Palestinians with a place they can safely and proudly call home. All Palestinian refugees who wish to live in this homeland should have the right to do so. All others who want to find new homes, whether in their current locations or in third countries, should be able to do so, consistent with those countries' sovereign decisions. And that includes Israel. All refugees should receive compensation from the international community for their losses, and assistance in building new lives. You cannot expect Israel to acknowledge an unlimited right of return to present day Israel. We cannot expect Israel to make a decision that would threaten the very foundations of the state of Israel.[56]

The PLO Negotiations Affairs Department remarked on 1 January 2001 that 'the United States proposal reflects a wholesale adoption of the Israeli position that the implementation of the right of return be subject entirely to Israel's discretion.'[57]

TABA, JANUARY 2001: YOSSI BEILIN'S 'NON-PAPER'

The permanent status negotiations between Israeli and Palestinian delegations that took place at Taba from 21 to 27 January 2001 were ultimately unsuccessful. However, for the first time the two sides spoke about the refugee issue seriously and there were real negotiations on the subject. These negotiations were subsequently presented by Israeli Minister of Justice Yossi Beilin, the most senior Israeli delegate in charge of the refugee issue at Taba, as establishing basic elements of a potential agreement for the resolution of the issue. By all accounts the Israeli position on this issue at Taba was an improvement on Barak's totally rejectionist position at Camp David. This was clearly reflected in a draft 'Non-Paper' prepared at Taba by Beilin, initially as a 'private response to the Palestinian refugee paper of 22 January 2001', which was later described by its author as 'an almost complete agreement regarding the principles of an agreement'.[58] The Beilin document became the basis for further negotiations at Taba with a Palestinian team led by Minister of International Cooperation Nabil Sha'ath. The document, which was subsequently published in *Le Monde Diplomatique*, was later presented by its author as offering a conceptual framework of an agreement with the Palestinians that would be acceptable to the then government of Ehud Barak. Both Beilin and some pro-Israeli commentators later described the document as a 'new development' in terms of accepting a degree of Israeli responsibility for the Palestinian refugees and a responsibility to be a partner in its solution.

Central to Beilin's negotiating strategy at Taba was the idea of getting rid of the refugees' historical and legal 'rights', by seeking instead clear, detailed 'practical, mutually acceptable arrangements' between Israel and the Palestinian Authority which would 'end all claims related to the refugee file'.[59] His document, which in many ways echoed Clinton's proposal of December 2002, raises three major issues: the narratives (or the national discourses); the number of refugees to be absorbed in Israel; and an international fund for compensation. The document stated:

- The issue of the Palestinian refugees is central to Israeli–Palestinian relations. Its comprehensive and just resolution is essential to creating a lasting and morally scrupulous peace.

- *Narrative*: The State of Israel solemnly expresses its sorrow for the tragedy of the Palestinian refugees, their suffering and losses, and will be an active partner in ending this terrible chapter that was opened 53 years ago, contributing its part to the attainment of a comprehensive and fair solution to the Palestinian refugee problem.
- For all those parties directly or indirectly responsible for the creation of the status of Palestinian refugeeism, as well as those for whom a just and stable peace in the region is an imperative, it is incumbent to take upon themselves responsibility to assist in resolving the Palestinian refugee problem of 1948.
- Despite accepting the UNGAR 181 of November 1947, the emergent State of Israel became embroiled in the war and bloodshed of 1948–49, that led to victims and suffering on both sides, including the displacement and dispossession of the Palestinian civilian population who became refugees. These refugees spent decades without dignity, citizenship and property ever since.[60]

Explicitly rejecting the Palestinian 'right of return', Beilin was only prepared to recognise a Palestinian 'wish to return':

> Consequently, the solution to the refugee issue must address the needs and aspiration of the refugees, while accounting for the realities since the 1948–49 war. Thus, the wish to return shall be implemented in a manner consistent with the existence of the State of Israel as the homeland for Jewish people, and the establishment of the State of Palestine as the homeland of the Palestinian people.
>
> Since 1948, the Palestinian yearning has been enshrined in the twin principles of the 'Right of Return' and the establishment of an independent Palestinian State deriving the basis from International Law. The realisation of the aspirations of the Palestinian people, as recognised in this agreement, includes the exercise of their right to self-determination and a comprehensive and just solution for the Palestinian refugees, based on UNGAR 194, providing for their return and guaranteeing the future welfare and well being of the refugees, thereby addressing the refugee problem in all its aspects.[61]

Israel had always rejected UN Resolution 194. At Taba, however, Beilin, who was aware that the resolution formed the cornerstone of the Palestinian position on the refugees, came up with a new strategy designed simultaneously to reinterpret the resolution radically and 'empty' it of its legal essence.

Beilin's suggestions were based on the idea that Israel, as a sovereign power, would alone determine the pace and number of returnees in accordance with its own immigration policies. Admission of Palestinian refugees could be accommodated in areas marked for transfer to Palestinian sovereignty as part of a territorial 'swap' or would remain a function of humanitarian considerations to be determined by Israel alone, rather than the implementation of a 'right' recognised by the Israeli state. In his most recent book *Manual for a Wounded Dove* (2001), Beilin had this to say:

> whoever wanted to be absorbed within the sovereign territory of Israel before the Six Day War can do this in neighbourhoods which would be built for them in those areas that Israel would transfer to the Palestinian state, in return for areas of the West Bank that would be annexed to Israel. Israel would not stop giving permits for family reunification and for special humanitarian cases, but it would deal with an extremely limited number of refugees that it would absorb in the course of the coming years.[62]

The 'right of return', unlimited in duration and scope, Beilin suggested, would only be realised in the state of Palestine. This solution, Israel claimed, would satisfy the requirements of UNGAR 194, and thus, within five years, end the saga, claims, and refugee status of Palestinian refugees.[63]

Although the number of refugees that would be admitted to Israel was not specified in the Beilin document, Beilin himself made it clear that it would be extremely limited. According to *Haaretz* of 7 January 2001, since 1967, some 5,000 Palestinians were admitted to Israel for humanitarian reasons. Apparently the numbers discussed publicly by leading members of the Barak government ranged from 'several thousand over several years' (Attorney General Elyakim Rubinstein)[64] to Ben-'Ami's 10–15,000, to 40,000 reportedly proposed by Beilin at Taba,[65] to 100,000 'maximum' noted by Beilin in a 15 June 2001 interview in *Haaretz*. Israel would, in any case, retain its sovereign prerogatives in determining whom to admit and to whom to bar entry. In an interview with *Haaretz* journalist 'Akiva Eldar, Beilin had this to say:

> The second issue [discussed at Taba] was numbers, which, importantly, we negotiated for the first time. From an Israeli point of view, once you speak about numbers, as long as they are not huge, there is no Right of Return but an Israeli decision to accept a certain number of refugees. Not that we solved the problem but I think we got close to a solution which could be satisfactory to both sides. We were speaking about a fifteen year solution in which, in the first three years, 25,000 refugees would be permitted to enter Israel.[66]

Beilin's idea of a 'fifteen-year solution' was neither approved by Barak or made in consultation with him (subsequently Barak stated that Taba was merely an exercise to show Yossi Beilin amd Yossi Sarid, another leading Israeli negotiator, the 'real face of 'Arafat'[67]); but it was accepted by the Palestinian delegation, although the actual numbers were not. Beilin also noted that the maximum number absorbed in Israel would be 75,000;

> but if the experience of the absorption of these refugees is negative, then there is no Israeli commitment to continue this. So that could have solved the problem for both sides and I think had we continued the negotiations at Taba, that could eventually have been the solution. I can't be sure about this because we did not agree on it.[68]

However, the limited admission of Palestinians to Israel was only one of five settlement options devised by negotiators – 'a menu of solutions' Beilin wrote.[69] These options, and the various financial packages that attended each, were to be carefully sequenced and modulated in order to produce the desired outcome.

Regarding 'return, repatriation and relocation of refugees, each refugee may apply to one of the following programs, thus fulfilling the relevant clause of UNGAR 194', the Beilin draft paper claimed, echoing the five options found in Clinton's proposal:

- To Israel: capped to an agreed limit of XX refugees, and with priority being accorded to those Palestinian refugees currently resident in Lebanon. The State of Israel notes its moral commitment to the swift resolution of the plight of the refugee population of the Sabra and Shatila camps.

- To Israeli swapped territory: for this purpose, the infrastructure shall be prepared for the absorption of refugees in the sovereign areas of the State of Israel that shall be turned over to Palestinian sovereignty in the context of an overall development program.
- To the State of Palestine: the Palestinian refugees may exercise their return in an unrestricted manner to the State of Palestine, as the homeland of the Palestinian people, in accordance with its sovereign laws and legislation.
- Rehabilitation within existing Host Countries: where this option is exercised the rehabilitation shall be immediate and extensive.
- Relocation to third countries: voluntary relocation to third countries expressing the willingness and capacity to absorb Palestinian refugees.

Resettlement options and attendant financial compensation were tools that Israel intended to use to achieve certain outcomes:

- to ensure the disappearance of the refugee camps and the removal of UNRWA;
- to build in disincentives for those choosing to return to Israel;
- to assure the economic and political stability of Jordan by sequencing the implementation of the agreement and 'removing economic incentives' to forestall an influx of new refugees; and to 'create incentives' for Palestinians to remain in Lebanon.

Israeli sources estimated that 500,000 refugees would resettle in the state of Palestine. Regarding Jordan, the issue animating Israelis was not how many Palestinians would leave Jordan but how to prevent a new and destabilising influx of refugees into the country. The draft paper gave a priority to refugees in Lebanon: 'Preference in all the above programs shall be accorded to the Palestinian refugee population in Lebanon.' Beilin recognised that the refugees in Lebanon posed the gravest and most immediate problem requiring a solution. The intention of the Israelis was to 'contain' this problem in the following fashion: one-third of the refugees would relocate to

Palestine, another third would resettle in third countries, and the remaining third would stay in Lebanon.

COMPENSATION AND REPARATIONS

In the early 1950s, while rejecting restitution of refugee property, Israel did offer some compensation in lieu of repatriation, although all attempts to work out policy on compensation were tied to a settlement of abandoned Jewish property in Arab states. The question of compensation for Palestinian refugee property in Israel did figure in the post-Madrid peace talks.[70] It seems that, on the question of compensation, both parties came to Taba fairly well-prepared, much more than in Camp David , and they talked about the structures and the methods of assessing the sums of money which would be needed to compensate the Palestinians.[71] Beilin, in his draft paper, rejected the idea of 'restitution' of refugees in Israel, emphasising instead compensation; 'Restitution he [the refugee] will not get, compensation he will.'[72] He suggested the following:

> Each refugee may apply for compensation programs and rehabilitation assistance as shall be detailed in Articles XX. For this purpose an International Commission and an International Fund shall be established (Articles XX below) that shall have full and exclusive responsibility for the implementation of the resolution of the refugee problem in all its aspects, including the gathering and verification of claims, and allocation and disbursement of resources, to be conducted in accordance with the following principles.
>
> - These programs shall address financial and in-kind compensation for displacement (moral suffering – P[alestinian] based position) and material loss, as well as the economic growth of the relevant communities. The dual objectives of individual historic justice and communal economic development shall guide the elaboration of these programs.
> - Programs of a compensatory nature shall be devised on both per-capital and claims based criteria, the former being of a fast-track nature (as detailed in Article XX below), and shall be managed according to a definitive and complete register of property claims to be compiled by an appropriate arm of the International Commission and Fund.

- The Rehabilitation Assistance and Compensation Programs shall form an integral part of efforts to promote economic development and social regeneration of both the individuals concerned and the communities and societies in which they live or resettle, thus incorporating options or baskets of assistance (to be detailed).
- Compensation for Host Countries will be in accordance with Article XX below.
- The international community and the State of Israel shall be the principal contributors to the International Fund up to an agreed ceiling respectively. Israeli fixed assets that will remain in the State of Palestine following the Israeli withdrawal will be transferred to become assets of the International Fund in lieu of an amount of $XX, constituting an integral part of the overall lump-sum of $XX.

With regard to the host countries, the draft paper noted:

- The refugees' host countries shall receive compensation for the significant costs they bore in hosting the refugees. Future rehabilitation costs and investments shall be addressed according to the details of this agreement, via bilateral arrangements between the host countries and the International Commission.

With regard to the International Commission, the paper notes:

- The International Commission shall consist of the Palestinian State, Host Countries, Israel and members of the international community, including the United Nations, the World Bank, The European Union and the G8, as well as other relevant international institutions. The International Commission shall have full and exclusive responsibility for implementing the resolution of the refugee issue in all its aspects. The mandate, structure and mode of operation of the International Commission shall be detailed in this agreement.[73]

Compensation packages to individuals and host countries would complement settlement options, and their structure was to be animated by the same set of priorities. Israel supported the establishment of an international framework for the raising and distribution of compensation and organisation and verification of claims. Such a structure would insulate Israel from direct responsibility to the refugees themselves for the resolution of their status and claims. Israel opposed Palestinian demands that the state of Palestine supervise the distribution of funds, which Israel insisted remain under the control of a commission on which it and the Palestinian state were represented. Israel's own contributions were recognised to be substantial, but its share of the $20 billion amount under discussion at Taba was not specified. A significant part of Israel's contribution would be in real property, including settlements and their infrastructure transferred to Palestinian sovereignty in the West Bank, Gaza Strip, and East Jerusalem.

Apparently the distribution of funds was viewed by Israeli officials as follows: they conceived of a fund of $20 billion, divided evenly between compensation to refugees($10 billion) and development projects($10 billion). The latter would be divided into two parts: host countries' general development programs ($5 billion) and those which focused specifically on refugee rehabilitation ($5 billion). The $5 billion general development budget, to be divided among host countries, would be entirely discretionary, that is, host countries would have total control over the use to which such funds were put. In Israel's view, these funds would be distributed on a per capita basis, both to refugees individually and also for host country development purposes, establishing a powerful financial incentive for host countries to retain their Palestinian populations. One Israeli official highlighted this aspect of the compensation scheme as an instrument for encouraging Lebanon to moderate its opposition to the permanent resettlement of one-third of its Palestinian refugee population. Beilin's paper also contains an article on compensation to 'former Jewish refugees from Arab countries'. Although this issue was not part of the bilateral Israeli–Palestinian agreement, 'in recognition of their suffering and losses, the Parties pledge to cooperate in pursuing an equitable and just resolution to the issue.'[74]

Historically, Israel conditioned its agreement to a negotiated solution to the refugee issue with a demand that such an agreement signify a complete and final resolution of the issue. This demand was also specified in the Taba talks, and it was manifest in certain specific aspects of the agreement. Beilin's draft paper contains specific article entitled: 'End of Claims':

> The Parties agree that the above constitutes a complete and final implementation of Article 11 of UNGAR 194 of 11th December

> 1948, and consider the implementation of the agreed programs and measures as detailed above constitute a full, final and irrevocable settlement of the Palestinian refugee issue in all its dimensions. No additional claims or demands arising from this issue shall be made by either Party. With the implementation of these articles there shall be no individuals qualified for the status of a Palestinian Refugee.[75]

For Beilin end of claims also means that UNRWA, the international expression of the Palestinians' refugee status, would be disbanded within five years. The camps themselves would likewise lose their status as refugee camps as they were amalgamated into the national fabric of the host countries or evacuated. Finally, implementation of the agreement would consign the term 'Palestinian refugee' to the history books, marking a resolution of all personal and communal claims against the state of Israel.

With regard to UNRWA, Beilin's proposal was very much in line with ideas put forward by other Israeli officials in recent negotiations with the Palestinians: to dissolve UNRWA and transfer its assets and responsibilities to the Palestinian National Authority. This, of course, was rejected by Palestinian negotiators who considered UNRWA's existence and registration system to be the main international legal pillar supporting the claims of individual 1948 Palestinian refugees to return and reclaim their properties in Israel.

Beilin's draft paper failed to point out the fact that sums of compensations and reparations were very large, according to the most authoritative recent estimates of property losses alone. Depending on the criteria used, they ranged between $92 billion and $147 billion at 1984 prices, when the Hadawi-Kubursi study was done.[76] The Hadawi-Kubursi study defined refugee compensation in terms of reparations, restitution of property and indemnification. Valuing Palestinian losses in today's dollars by the inclusion of compensation for psychological damage and pain (following the Federal Republic of Germany's compensation schemes to Jews), according to an updated recent study by Kubursi, would double the Hadawi-Kubursi 1984 figures.[77] Some Palestinian negotiators suggested that a fund for compensating Palestinian refugees should be established to which the international community will be required to contribute, and Israel should be a major contributor to this fund. Compensation should be paid on two levels, through a collective fund to be vested with the PA in order to develop the infrastructure of the Palestinian state (which will be, in part, the state of the returnees) and its own facilities destined to assist the absorption of returning refugees and through a family fund that would pay restitution to refugees on the basis of individual claims.[78] However, the availability of tens of billions of dollars for refugee compensation/reparations is uncertain. Israeli negotiators have suggested that the international community should bear the lion's share of any refugee compensation, while other observers have raised questions as to what international financial resources might be available to finance compensation payments, at a time when only $2.5 billion (about a third of it in loans) has been pledged to support the entire Oslo process in the West Bank and Gaza, and when the international community seems unwilling or unable to cover reliably even the budget deficit of the PA.[79]

In conclusion, at Taba Israel again rejected Palestinian 'right of return'. It is, however, evident that at Taba (unlike Camp David) some progress was made over certain aspects of the refugee issue. Beilin, for instance in his 'Non-Paper', accepted a degree of Israeli responsibility for the refugee problem and a responsibility for being a partner in its solution. The Palestinian delegation similarly demonstrated a great deal of flexibility on the issue, demanding that Israel recognise at least some if not full responsibility for the Palestinian *nakba*. However, although the two sides came closer than ever before to discussing the details of an overall settlement on the refugees, for most Palestinian refugees that settlement would not have been seen as a 'just solution'.

THE POST-TABA PERIOD: UNDER ARIEL SHARON

Everyone taking part in the Taba talks knew that, despite the progress made, nothing could protect Ehud Barak from defeat in the prime ministerial elections of 6 February 2001. By this stage Barak had been trailing Likud leader Ariel Sharon in the opinion polls by more than 20 per cent. A few days later Sharon, who had been responsible for the massacres at the refugee camps of Sabra and Shatila in the Lebanon, became prime minister. Shortly after his election, Sharon told Spanish Prime Minister Jose Maria Anzar that the Palestinian refugee exodus of 1948 was due to orders issued by the Arab countries. He added that

> Israel does not bear historical responsibility for the refugee problem and will not under any circumstances agree to their return to Israel, but we will agree to participate in an international aid effort.[80]

At the instigation of a Likud member, on 1 January 2001 the Knesset had enacted legislation echoing the 1961 resolution rejecting the 'right of return'. The contemporary version, which rejected the repatriation of Palestinian refugees unless a majority of Knesset members approved, recorded 61 co-sponsors in the 120-member body and won a majority of 90, attesting to its overwhelming majority across the Israeli political spectrum.

While the Barak government had been responsible for elaborating Israeli refugee policy during the final status negotiations between late 1999 and early 2001, the defeat of Barak by Sharon hardened further Israeli policy towards the Palestinian refugee issue. The election of Sharon, who had always opposed the Oslo process, contributed to the present deadlock in the peace process and brought about a further escalation in the Israeli–Palestinian crisis. Although the current administration of Ariel Sharon had little need to articulate a detailed policy on the Palestinian refugee issue, throughout the 1990s various Likud administrations had clearly stated their position on the Palestinian refugee issue. Their view of a solution to the refugee problem is in line with Israel's classic case of denial, resting upon four basic elements of that denial:

1. no to an assumption of Israeli responsibility for the problem;
2. no to a 'right of return';
3. no to the repatriation of refugees to the West Bank and Gaza – along with the rejection of a sovereign Palestinian state in these territories;
4. no to restitution of property.

The Likud position, which is articulated across the right wing of Israel's political spectrum, is that Jordan, Syria, Lebanon and Egypt should each bear responsibility for resettling Palestinian refugees.

NOTES

1. Israeli allegations regarding the origins of the Palestine refugee question have been examined and discredited as being part of an Israeli disinformation campaign. See also an article in *The Spectator*, 12 May 1961; Benny

Morris, *The Birth of the Palestinian Refugee Problem, 1947–1949* (Cambridge: Cambridge University Press, 1987); Simha Flapan, *The Birth of Israel: Myths and Reality* (London: Croom Helm, 1987); Tom Segev, *1949: The First Israelis* (New York: The Free Press, 1986); Ilan Pappé, *The Making of the Arab–Israeli Conflict, 1947–1951* (London: I. B. Tauris, 1992); Nur Masalha, *Expulsion of the Palestinians: The Concept of 'Transfer' in Zionist Political Thought, 1882–1948* (Washington DC: Institute for Palestine Studies, 1992), pp.173–99.

2. In the 1950s and the early 1960s there was a minority of left-wing and liberal Zionists, represented by the Mapam Party and the small group of Ihud, who were prepared to accept the absorption of a very limited number of refugees in Israel within the framework of an overall peace settlement of the Arab–Israeli conflict. See, for instance, *New Outlook* 4, no.9 (December 1961), p.9.
3. Shimon Peres, *The New Middle East* (Dorset, England: Element Books, 1993), pp.188–9. For further discussion of Israel's position, see Shlomo Gazit, *The Palestinian Refugee Problem* (Tel Aviv: Tel Aviv University, Jaffee Centre for Strategic Studies, 1995), p.10; Rony E. Gabbay, *A Political Study of the Arab–Israeli Conflict: The Arab Refugee Problem* (Geneva and Paris, 1959); 'Opening Remarks for Israel by Shlomo Ben-'Ami at the Multilateral Working Group on Refugees', 11 November 1992, in *Israel–Palestine Journal* II, no.4 (Autumn 1995), pp.115–20.
4. Elia Zureik, *Palestinian Refugees and the Peace Process* (Washington DC: Institute for Palestine Studies, 1996).
5. Ruth Lapidoth, 'Do Palestinian Refugees Have a Right to Return to Israel?, at: http://www.mfa.gov.il/mfa/go.asp?MFAH0j8r0 (accessed on 20 October 2001). See also Ruth Lapidoth, 'The Right of Return in International Law, with Special Reference to the Palestinian Refugees', *Israel Yearbook of Human Rights* 16 (1986), pp.103–25.
6. See, for instance, Kurt Rene Bradley, 'The Palestinian Refugees: The Right to Return in International Law', *American Journal of International Law* 72, no.3 (July 1978), pp.585–614; Don Peretz, *Palestinians, Refugees and the Middle East Peace Process* (Washington DC: United States Institute for Peace Press, 1993), p.70.
7. Simha Flapan, 'The Knesset Votes on the Refugee Problem', *New Outlook* 4, no.9 (December 1961), p.8.
8. Department of Foreign Affairs and International Trade Canada, Introduction to the Refugee Working Group, accessed on 16 April 2001, at: http://www.dfait-maeci.gc.ca/peaceprocess/rwg-e.asp.
9. 'Israel's agenda for Peace', in *Near East Report*, 19 October 1992, p.193, cited in Donna E. Arzt, *Refugees into Citizens: Palestinians and the End of the Arab–Jewish Conflict* (New York: Council on Foreign Relations Press, 1997), p.27.
10. Zureik, *Palestinian Refugees and the Peace Process*, p. 72. Full text of Ben-'Ami's statement in Arzt, *Refugees into Citizens*, pp.208–13.
11. Remarks by Dr Yossi Beilin at a meeting of the Multilateral Refugee Working Group in Tunis, 12 October 1993, par. 14 and 15, cited in Arzt, *Refugees into Citizens*, p.27.

12. Salim Tamari, *Palestinian Refugee Negotiations: From Madrid to Oslo II*, Final Status Issue Paper (Washington, DC: Institute for Palestine Studies, 1996), p.2.
13. Zureik, *Palestinian Refugees and the Peace Process*, p.94.
14. Zureik, *Palestinian Refugees and the Peace Process*.
15. David McDowall, *The Palestinians: The Road to Nationhood* (London: Minority Rights Publications, 1994), pp.148, 192, note no.3.
16. See statement by WAFA (Gaza), (official Palestinian news agency), on the tripartite ministerial committee, Palestinian–Egyptian–Jordanian, which discussed the issue of displaced persons, 27 October 1999.
17. 'Akiva Eldar 'Displaced Yes, Refugees No', *Haaretz*, 5 July 1999, p.36; *Globes*, 17 June 2001.
18. Remarks by Andrew Robinson, Candian gavel holder of the RWG, at a conference in Minster Lovell, England, 27–30 September 1996, at: http://www.arts.mcgill.ca/MEPP/PRRN/docs/gavoxf.html.
19. Adnan Abu Odeh, *Jordanians, Palestinian, and the Hashemite Kingdom in the Middle East Peace Process* (Washington DC: United States Institute of Peace Press, 1999), p.235.
20. Declaration of Principles, Article V. Available online at: http://www.israel-mfa.gov.il.
21. Elia Zureik, 'The Palestinian Refugees and the Right of Return', *Majallat al-Dirasat al-Filastiniyya*, no.19 (Summer 1994), pp.68–81.
22. 'Abdul Shafi, Haydar, 1991. Address delivered to the Madrid Peace Conference, 31 October 199, at: http://www.israel-mfa.gov.il.
23. Palestinian National Authority, *Palestinian Refugees and the Right of Return* (Jerusalem: Ministry of Information, 1995).
24. Tamari, *Palestinian Refugee Negotiations*, p.42.
25. Zureik, *Palestinian Refugees and the Peace Process*, p.94.
26. Ibid., p.92.
27. Tamari, *Palestinian Refugee Negotiations*, p.45.
28. Ibid., p.1.
29. Interview with Israeli Justice Minister Yossi Beilin in *Al-Quds* (Jerusalem), 5 January 2001, p.10.
30. Article XII, Oslo Accords.
31. For discussion of Israel's deportation policies in the West Bank and Gaza, see Nur Masalha, *A Land Without a People: Israel, Transfer and the Palestinians, 1949–1996* (London: Faber and Faber, 1997).
32. Salim Tamari, *Return, Resettlement, Repatriation: The Future of Palestinian Refugees in the Peace Negotiations* (Beirut, Washington and Jerusalem: Institute for Palestine Studies, 1996), p.7. Rex Brynen, *Palestinian Refugees and the Middle East Peace Process*, Lecture to the New Hampshire International Seminar/Yale-Maria Lecture in Middle East Studies, University of New Hampshire, 3 April 1998, p.6, at: http://www.arts.mcgill.ca/MEPP/PRRN/papers/UNH.html. (Accessed on 28 July 2001).
33. Israel-Jordan Common Agenda, 14 September 1993, Washington, DC, at http://www.Israel.org/mfa/go.asp?MFAH00q10.

34. The English and Hebrew texts of the declaration is found in *Divrei Haknesset* [Knesset Debates], 41, Special Session, 3 August 1994 (Jerusalem), pp.10287–90.
35. The text of the treaty is found in *Journal of Palestine Studies* 24, no.2 (Winter 1995), pp.126–46.
36. Ibid.
37. Daniel Sobelman, in *Haaretz*, 2 February 2001, p.5a.
38. See text of report by Palestinian Television in BBC Summary of World Broadcasts, 7 May 1996, p.1.
39. 'Akiva Eldar, 'The Refugee Problem at Taba (interview with Yossi Beilin and Nabil Sha'ath', *Palestine-Israel Journal* 9, no.2 (2002), p.13.
40. Akram Hanieh, 'The Camp David Papers', *Journal of Palestine Studies* 30, no.2 (Winter 2001), p.82.
41. Ibid., p.92.
42. Ibid., p.94.
43. Report published in *Al-Hayat* (London), 11 September 2000.
44. Hanieh, 'The Camp David Papers', p.94.
45. 'Akiva Eldar, 'The Refugee Problem at Taba (interview with Yossi Beilin and Nabil Sha'ath', *Palestine-Israel Journal* 9, no.2 (2002), p.12.
46. Hanieh, 'The Camp David Papers', p.94
47. U.S. Committee for Refugees, *Country Reports: Syria*, at: http://www.refugees.org/world/countryrpt/mideast/syria.htm.
48. PLO Negotiations Affairs Department, 'Remarks and Questions from the Palestinian Negotiating Team Regarding the United States Proposal', 1 January 2001, at: http://www.nad-plo.org/eye/news15.html (accessed on 27 March 2002).
49. Aluf Ben, in *Haaretz*, 5 October 1999, p.1.
50. Ibid.
51. Israeli Government Press Office translation of Prime Minister Barak's address to the 'Peace and Security Council', 28 June 2000.
52. Elyakim Rubinstein, 'The Truth About the "Right of Return" and Compensation for the Jewish Refugees', *Hatzofe*, 25 August 2000, p.4.
53. Quoted in *MidEast Mirror*, 19 September 2000, Israel Section.
54. *Haaretz*, 2 February 2001.
55. *Al-Quds* (Jerusalem), 5 January 2001, p.10. Interview with Israeli Justice Minister Yossi Beilin by Ahmad Mashharawi.
56. William J. Clinton, 'Remarks at Israel Policy Forum Gala', 7 January 2001 cited in Brynen, *Palestinian Refugees and the Middle East Peace Process*, p.2.
57. PLO Negotiations Affairs Department, 'Remarks and Questions from the Palestinian Negotiating Team regarding the United States Proposal', 1 January 2001, at: http://www.nad-plo.org/eye/news15.html (accessed on 27 March 2002).
58. 'Ezra Dalomi, 'The Taba Document', *Yedi'ot Aharanot*, 8 December 2001, Friday supplement, p.5.
59. 'Akiva Eldar, 'The Refugee Problem at Taba (interview with Yossi Beilin and Nabil Sha'ath', *Palestine-Israel Journal* 9, no.2 (2002), p.16.
60. See Israeli 'Non-Paper', Draft 2, 23 January 2001, Taba, published in *Le Monde Diplomatique*, at: http://www.monde-diplomatique.fr/cahier/p.../israelrefugees-e (accessed on 27 March 2002).

61. Israeli 'Non-Paper', Draft 2, 23 January 2001, Taba, published in *Le Monde Diplomatique*, at: http://www.monde-diplomatique.fr/cahier/p.../israelrefugees-e.
62. Yossi Beilin, *Madrich Leyonah Petzo'ah* [*Manual for a Wounded Dove*] (Tel Aviv: Miskal-Yedi'ot Aharonot and Hemed Publications, 2001), p.208. Extracts from the book were published in the daily *Yedi'ot Aharanot* on 8 October 2001, supplement, pp.20–1, 28.
63. Ari Shavit, 'Ish Hakerah' [The Ice Man], *Haaretz*, 15 June 2001, pp.21–6.
64. *Hatzofe*, 25 August 2000.
65. According to Sholomo Ben-'Ami, in *Haaretz*, 14 September 2001.
66. 'Akiva Eldar, 'The Refugee Problem at Taba (interview with Yossi Beilin and Nabil Sha'ath', *Palestine-Israel Journal* 9, no.2 (2002), p.12.
67. Ibid., p.14.
68. Ibid., pp.12–13.
69. Aluf Ben (reporting from Taba) 'Israel and the Palestinians Had Never Been Closer to Achieving Peace', *Haaretz*, 28 January 2001, pp.1 and 10 (Hebrew).
70. See Yerah Tal, 'A Talk with Moshe Zanbar: On the Refugee Problem at the Moscow Talks', *Haaretz*, 29 January 1992, p.2 (Hebrew).
71. 'Akiva Eldar, 'The Refugee Problem at Taba (interview with Yossi Beilin and Nabil Sha'ath', *Palestine-Israel Journal* 9, no.2 (2002), p.13.
72. Ibid., p.16.
73. Israeli 'Non-Paper', Draft 2, 23 January 2001, Taba, published in *Le Monde Diplomatique*, at: http://www.monde-diplomatique.fr/cahier/p.../israelrefugees-e.
74. Israeli 'Non-Paper', Draft 2, 23 January 2001, Taba, published in *Le Monde Diplomatique*, at: http://www.monde-diplomatique.fr/cahier/p.../israelrefugees-e.
75. Israeli 'Non-Paper', Draft 2, 23 January 2001, Taba, published in *Le Monde Diplomatique*, at: http://www.monde-diplomatique.fr/cahier/p.../israelrefugees-e.
76. Sami Hadawi and Atef Kubursi, *Palestinian Rights and Losses in 1948: A Comprehensive Study* (London: Saqi Books, 1988), p.183.
77. Atef Kubursi, 'Valuing Palestinian Losses in Today's Dollars', in Naseer Aruri (ed.), *Palestinian Refugees: The Right of Return* (London: Pluto Press, 2001), pp.217–51.
78. Tamari, *Palestinian Refugee Negotiations*, pp.40 and 47.
79. Rex Brynen, 'The Funding of Palestinian Refugee Compensation', presented to the ISEPME refugee group, Harvard University, February 1996, at: http://www.arts.mcgill.ca/mepp/prrn/papers/brynen1.html.
80. Aluf Ben and Netzan Horowitz, in *Haaretz*, 15 February 2001, p.11a.

Epilogue

The Palestinian refugee problem is the greatest and most enduring refugee problem in the world. Some 70 per cent of Palestinians are refugees; there are nearly 4 million Palestinian refugees in the Middle East and many more worldwide – and they want the right to go home. Resolution of the Arab–Israeli conflict is impossible without addressing their grievances, rights and needs. Will the Palestinian refugees gain their rights? Although the refugees themselves (and a growing number of Palestinian, Israeli and Western historians) have highlighted the coerced nature of the 1948 refugee exodus, Israeli officials continue to deny any Israeli responsibility for the expulsion of Palestinians from what became Israel.

Denial has always been a key component of the Israeli discourse, denial of the existence of a Palestinian people, denial of their ethnic cleansing in 1948, denial of their right to return, denial of their claims to Jerusalem and so on, ad infinitum and ad nauseam. Since the 1948 catastrophe (*nakba*) Israeli policy towards the Palestinian refugees has become a classic case of denial. Denial is a central component in Israel's pre-emptive refugee strategy: after the setting-up of 'transfer committees' (first by the Jewish Agency in 1937–44 and later by the Israeli Cabinet in 1948), and clearing the land in 1948, the Israelis denied any wrongdoing or any historical injustice. They continue to deny any moral responsibility or culpability for the creation of the plight of the Palestinian refugees and to deny restitution of property (i.e. returning the properties to their rightful owners) and reparations – after expropriating the refugees' land and property. The Israeli discourse of denial – with the almost complete unanimity among Israeli writers concerning the inapplicability of the 'right of return' to the Palestinian refugees[1] – was and remains crucial for the success of the Zionist colonial project.[2]

In January 2001 at Taba Yossi Beilin, in his 'Non-Paper', while rejecting both the 'right of return' to Israel and 'restitution' of refugee property, accepted a degree of Israeli responsibility for the refugee problem and with it a responsibility for being a partner in its solution, especially in compensating refugees. Beilin's suggestions, however, were neither approved by Barak nor made in consultation with him;

in fact, subsequently Barak stated that Taba was merely an exercise to show Yossi Beilin the 'real face of Arafat'.[3]

Since 1948 successive Israeli governments have shown little disposition to negotiate the refugee question on a basis acceptable to the Palestinian refugees themselves or to the Arab host countries. Both the Palestinian refugees and the Arab states adhered to UN General Assembly Resolution 194 (III) of December 1948 which stated that 'the refugees wishing to return to their homes and live at peace with their neighbours should be permitted to do so at the earliest practicable date.' UN Resolution 194 – with its emphasis on the 'right of return' – remains the cornerstone of Palestinian refugees' and Arab approaches to the refugee issue. The Resolution, for which members of the United Nations overwhelmingly voted in favour more than five decades ago, affirmed the right of Palestinian refugees to return and repossess their homes and property and receive compensation for damages and losses.

Resolution 194 reflected several international legal and humanitarian considerations:

- a humanitarian approach to the plight of men, women and children, who by no fault of their own, found themselves uprooted from their homeland;
- an international legal approach to the plight of hundreds of thousands of refugees. This approach reflected basic human rights in existing international law and practice, which included the prohibition that people should not be uprooted and expelled from their homeland or arbitrarily deprived of their nationality. Basic human right principles set forth in the Universal Declaration of Human Rights were adopted by the General Assembly one day prior to Resolution 194.[4] Among the 'equal and inalienable rights of all members of the human family' is the right of return and the right to property. Two years prior to the mass expulsions of 1948 the United Nations had affirmed that 'the main task concerning displaced persons is to encourage and assist in every way their early return to their countries of origin';[5]
- the wishes of the Palestinian refugees themselves: 'Every day I say tomorrow will be better, and a hundred times I tell myself we will go back home', a young refugee told international relief workers in Gaza in 1949. 'As you want to live in your house, with your family, so I want to live in mine.' In public hearings

> across the Middle East, American, French and Turkish members of the UN Conciliation Commission for Palestine (UNCCP) took note of the 'unanimous desire' among refugees to return to their homes. 'The Commission was impressed by expressions of these spokesmen for the return of refugees to their homes to live there in peace with their neighbors.'[6]

The Israeli position, on the other hand, has always been that there can be no returning of the refugees to their homes and properties in Israel – a privilege reserved for Jews returning from 2,000 years of exile – and that the only solution to the problem was their resettlement in the Arab host states or elsewhere – something those hosts, with the exception of Jordan, have refused to contemplate. Except for one limited offer in mid-1949 that came to nothing – to take back '100,000' of the refugees to be settled in places of Israel's choosing (an offer which was made under intense American pressure and soon retracted) – Israel has made no significant proposal to repatriate the 1948 refugees. In the 1950s and the early 1960s there was a small minority of left-wing and liberal Zionists, represented by the Mapam Party and the small group of Ihud, who were prepared to accept the absorption of a limited number of refugees within the framework of an overall peace settlement of the Arab–Israeli conflict. For instance, in November 1961 the Mapam Party submitted the following minority resolution to a Knesset debate on the refugee issue:

> Israel is prepared to discuss the refugee problem and to participate in a solution, to a degree and in ways compatible with her ability, of the compensation question, the continuation of the unification of families and the establishment of an international fund for the resettlement of the refugees in the Arab countries. Israel will also be prepared to discuss, within the framework of negotiations for peace with her neighbors, the absorption of a certain and agreed-upon number of refugees in Israel.[7]

The classic Israeli strategy against refugee repatriation to the pre-1967 borders, however, has remained unchanged since 1948. In fact, there is an ideological consensus among the Zionist parties in Israel – from Meretz on the Zionist left through the Labour and Likud parties and on to the extreme right – against the Palestinian 'right of return' to the pre-1967 borders. Israeli journalist Zeev Schiff of *Haaretz* had this to say on 10 October 2000:

> Now it is clear that it would be madness, from a security as well as a demographic point of view, to add to the Arab minority – many of whose members raised the banner of revolt against Israel – tens of thousands of Palestinians who feel cheated and oppressed.

Most recently Yossi Beilin has apparently reached a new 'shadow agreement' with Palestinian Authority officials, based on the Taba understandings, which (according to *Haaretz*) was as follows:

> the new document does not include the right of return for refugees to Israel. French diplomat and journalist Eric Rouleou, who was in Ramallah last weekend [end of January 2003] says [PA] Abu Mazen told him that the entire matter of the right of return was only raised as lip service to the refugees, and emphasised that only a few are actually interested in returning to Palestine. The Palestinian statesman added that the agreement would guarantee that the demographic balance in Israel was not undermined.[8]

Israel's (and Beilin's) refugee approach turns history on its head. It is based on a proactive strategy which consists of pre-emptive measures against such things as 'root causes', justice, restitution, or atonement.[9] The victims, the ethnically-cleansed indigenous Palestinians, become victimisers and the refugees' 'right of return' is a threat to Israel's demographic security and Jewish character. Indeed, the Zionist-Israelis did not want the repatriation of an Arab population that would question the colonial nature of the Zionist project and 'ethnocratic' character of the state of Israel.[10] The case of Israel illustrates the making of an 'ethnocratic' regime, which, as Professor Oren Yiftachel of Ben-Gurion University has shown, centres on the Zionist ethnic project of Judaising Palestine/Israel. Clearly the refugees' 'right of return' touches on the very nature of the state of Israel as an exclusionist 'ethnocracy' and on whether it should become a multicultural democratic state – a state of its all citizens and 'absentees' ('*nifkadim*': to borrow the kafkaesque Israeli terminology).

A recent example of Israel's determination to preserve its ethnocratic character was the decision taken by the Israeli government on 12 May 2002 to approve retroactively an earlier decision by its Interior Ministry to freeze all applications for family reunification between Palestinian citizens of Israel and Palestinian residents of the Palestinian territories occupied in 1967, in order to prevent the latter from acquiring Israeli citizenship. Israeli officials argue that the growth of the non-Jewish population of Israel over the last decade due to Palestinian family reunification (not to mention the large number of non-Jewish immigrants from the former Soviet Union) is a threat to the Jewish character of the state – i.e., the Jewish demographic majority and Jewish control of the land, including land confiscated from Palestinian refugees. Evidently Interior Minister Eli Yeshai also believes that Palestinian family reunification 'is a devious way of getting Arab refugees to return to Israel'.[11]

Israel's pre-emptive refugee strategy also consists of propagating the myth that the Palestinian refugee exodus was a tactic of war on the part of the Arabs who initiated the war against the Jewish Yishuv (settlement) in Palestine. Israel has also argued that the Palestinian refugees constituted a 'population exchange' with those Jews who left the Arab world in the 1950s. Although Israel's case was as mendacious as it was misleading, Israeli representatives continued to propagate it at home and abroad. This politics of denial is most vividly demonstrated by Shimon Peres's book, *The New Middle East* (1993). The author rehashes many of the founding myths of Israel, repeats basic points of Israeli propaganda justifying the rejection of refugee return and refuses to entertain any Israeli recognition of culpability for the Palestinian refugee problem. Peres, a leading member of the Israeli establishment and a key player in the Oslo process, is even trying to suppress the findings of Israel's 'new historiography' and the early buds of Israeli self-awareness and recognition of Israel's role in the Palestinian catastrophe. An official Israeli recognition of the *nakba* would help Israeli citizens to understand better the present deadlock in the peace process.[12]

The mountains of available evidence show that the Palestinian refugee exodus of 1948 was the culmination of over half a century of efforts, secret (Zionist) plans and, ultimately, brute force. The primary responsibility for the displacement and dispossession of 750,000 Palestinian refugees in 1948 lay with the Zionist leadership. Israel was primarily responsible for the 1948 Palestinian catastrophe. In Chapter 1, which is largely based on Hebrew and Israeli archival sources, I have dealt with the evolution of the Zionist concept of 'population transfer' – a euphemism denoting the organised removal of the Arab population of Palestine to neighbouring or distant countries. I have shown that 'ethnic cleansing' (in current terminology) was deeply rooted in Zionism.[13] It was embedded in the Zionist perception that the 'Land of Israel was a Jewish birthright' and belonged exclusively to the Jewish people as a whole, and, consequently, Palestinians were 'strangers' who should either accept Jewish sovereignty over the land or depart. Nearly all the founding fathers advocated transfer in one form or another. However, the 'transfer' solution became central to Zionist strategy in the period between 1936 and 1948. During this period the Zionist leadership pursued transfer schemes almost obsessively. Both the Jewish Agency and the Israeli government set up Transfer Committees and a number of transfer schemes were formulated in secret. Many leading figures justified Arab removal politically, morally, and ethically as the natural and logical continuation of Zionist colonisation in Palestine.

Demography and the land issue were at the heart of the Zionist transfer mind-set and the secret transfer plans of the 1930s and 1940s. In 1947 the Palestinians were the overwhelming majority in the country and owned much of the land, and the Jewish community (mainly consisting of European migrants and settlers) was about a third of the total population and owned about 6 per cent of the land. The general endorsement of 'transfer' during this period was designed to achieve two crucial objectives: (a) to clear the land for Jewish settlers and would-be immigrants; (b) to establish a homogenous Jewish state. Ben-Gurion and other leaders of the Jewish Agency strongly believed that Zionism would not succeed in setting up a Jewish state and fulfilling its imperative of absorbing the expected influx of Jewish immigrants if it allowed the indigenous Palestinians to remain.

With the 1948 war the Zionists succeeded in many of their objectives; above all, they created a vastly enlarged Jewish state on 77 per cent of historic Palestine. From the territory occupied by the Israelis in 1948, about 90 per cent of the Palestinians were driven out – many by psychological warfare and/or military pressure and a very large number at gunpoint. The 1948 war simply provided an opportunity and the necessary background for the creation of a Jewish state largely free of Arabs; it concentrated Zionist-Jewish minds, and provided the security, military and strategic explanations and justifications for purging the Jewish state and dispossessing the Palestinians. The Israeli State Archives and the Zionist Central Archives in Jerusalem contain a large number of official files with extensive information pertaining to Israel's policies towards the Arab minority, including what usually is described in Israel as 'population transfer'. By the end of the 1948 war hundreds of Palestinian villages had been completely depopulated, and their houses blown up or bulldozed, the main objective being to prevent the return of refugees to their homes and villages. The overwhelming evidence shows that the refugee exodus was to a large extent the deliberate creation of Jewish leaders, especially David Ben-Gurion, and military commanders.

Once Palestinians had been driven out of their homes, villages and towns, Israel took steps to prevent their return. Palestinian farms and villages were razed and refugee property seized. Jews, many of them new immigrants, were settled in homes and neighbourhoods belonging to Palestinian refugees. Subsequent policies adopted by the Israeli state were aimed at consolidating the power and domination of the newly created Jewish majority. An essential element in this effort was the prevention of the return of Palestinian refugees. This objective has served until today as a guiding premise underlying Israeli policy concerning refugees.

The outcome of the 1948 war left Israel in control of over 5 million acres of Palestinian land. After the war, the Israeli state took over the land of the 750,000 refugees, who were barred from returning, while the remaining Palestinian minority was subjected to laws and regulations that effectively deprived it of most of its land. These actions were legalised through the enactment of a range of laws reflecting the prevailing Zionist view that Palestinian refugees were not welcome and enshrining their prejudiced position as a matter of state policy. The massive drive to take over Palestinian refugee land was conducted entirely according to strict legality. Between 1948 and the early 1990s Israel enacted some 30 statutes that transferred land from private Arab to state (Jewish) ownership. In the early 1950s Israel did consider some form of restitution of refugee property in lieu of repatriation, although all attempts to work out policy on compensation were tied to a settlement of abandoned Jewish property in Arab states.

The Israeli position towards the refugees has always emphasised their resettlement and rehabilitation in the Arab states, rather than repatriation and/or compensation. This resettlement was designed to prevent refugee return, to 'dissolve' the refugee question and break up the collective identify of the refugees and their perceived militancy, to reduce both international humanitarian, UN and Western diplomatic pressures on Israel and remove a critical problem from the heart of the Arab–Israeli conflict. While the desire among Israeli leaders to resettle the refugees in the Arab states or elsewhere, or, stated baldly, to be rid of the 'Palestinian refugee problem', has remained a constant until the present day, the envisaged modalities of resettlement changed over the years according to circumstances.

Realistic assessments during the 1950s and in the aftermath of the June 1967 conquests necessitated strategies and practical planning that produced a series of specific resettlement plans, generally involving Arab states – such as pre-Qaddafi Libya, Jordan, El 'Arish in Sinai (Egypt) – as well as the Jordan Valley in the West Bank and various Latin American countries. Although the Israeli resettlement schemes of the 1950s, late 1960s, the 1970s and 1980s ended in failure, they are significant in the sense of showing how successive Israeli governments wanted to remove the Palestinian refugee problem from the centre of the Arab–Israeli conflict and eliminate the possibility of refugee return in the future.

In theory the decade between October 1991 and January 2001, from the Madrid peace conference to the Israeli–Palestinian permanent status talks at Taba, Egypt, offered an opportunity to negotiate the Palestinian refugee issue with intensity not witnessed for four decades. In the post-Madrid period the refugee question was discussed in five major fora: (a) the Refugee Working Group of the Multilateral Track; (b) the Continuing or Quadripartite Committee; (c) the Israeli-Palestinian Declaration of Principles of September 1993; (d) the Jordanian-Israeli Peace Treaty of 1993; (e) the Palestinian–Israeli permanent status negotiations, especially the Camp David Summit of July 2000 and the Taba negotiations of January 2001. In reality, however, Israeli refugee policy throughout this decade remained tied to its established position vis-à-vis the repatriation of the refugees. The classical Israeli refugee policies have remained unchanged throughout the Israeli–Palestinian negotiations, including the refusal to entertain any recognition of culpability for the Palestinian refugee problem or of moral and legal responsibility for the refugees. Indeed the politics of denial remained a main feature of the Oslo peace process – a process which important figures of labour Zionism interpreted as putting an end to refugee claims.

After the Madrid Peace Conference of 1991, Israel reluctantly agreed to discuss the refugee question provided the 'right of return' was not raised. Shortly after the Declaration of Principles was issued in September 1993, Israel agreed to discuss certain categories of the 1967 refugees who might be allowed to return to the West Bank and Gaza Strip within the restricted framework of family reunion. Subsequently, Israel also reluctantly announced its willingness to process 2,000 applicants for family reunion annually. However, the number of those awaiting family reunion – wives and children unable to live with their husbands and fathers – is estimated at 120,000.

There are another estimated 100,000 persons who have been denied re-entry into the West Bank and Gaza on grounds of having stayed abroad for periods longer than the Israeli authorities permitted.[14] In practice, however, even within the narrow perspective of family reunion little progress was made in recent peace talks on the 1967 refugees. There is also the question of the 300,000 people displaced by the 1967 war or expelled shortly after and their descendants. Although consideration of their case for return is allowed for in Article 12 of the Declaration of Principles, no progress had been made on this issue as of June 2002. In reality the Israeli refugee policy throughout the last decade remained strictly tied to its established position vis-à-vis the repatriation of the refugees. The classic Israeli refugee policies remained unchanged throughout the Israeli–Palestinian negotiations, including the refusal to entertain any recognition of culpability for the Palestinian refugee problem and to accept moral and legal responsibility for the refugees. In contrast, during the same period Israel has shown a willingness and huge capability to absorb into its territory hundreds of thousands of Russian Jews.

The Palestinian 'right of return' is viewed by Israel's current governing majority (led by General Ariel Sharon) as a strategic, existential problem that retains the capacity to change the nature of the state of Israel. The meaning of the Palestinian right of return, Sharon had noted during the Taba talks of January 2001, 'is the end of the state of Israel'. He pointed out that as a child his parents had already taught him to distinguish between 'the rights over the Land of Israel, which belong *exclusively* to the Jewish people' (*hazchuyot 'al Eretz Yisrael shehem bel'adiyot le'am hayehudi*) and between certain 'rights in the country' which could be given to those 'residing here, including Arabs'.[15] Sharon's view on the right of return was endorsed by an evaluation of Israel's Military Intelligence that Palestinian Authority Yasser Arafat 'remains committed to the right of return and sees it as a key to turning the Jews into a religious minority'.[16] At the instigation of a Likud member, the Knesset, on 1 January 2001, enacted legislation echoing the November 1961 Knesset resolution, which categorically rejected the right of return.[17] The current debate in the Knesset, which rejects the repatriation of Palestinian refugees to their villages and towns, attests to its popularity across Israel's political spectrum.

The Likud view of a solution to the refugee problem rests upon the rejection of three of its basic elements:

- no to a right of return;
- no to an assumption of Israeli responsibility for the problem;
- and no to the repatriation of the 1948 refugees.

The previous Likud government (1996–9) of Binyamin Netanyahu, in which Sharon served as Foreign Minister, did attempt to formulate a position on the refugee issue. The Netanyahu government's views offer instructive guidance on the parameters of policy under Sharon's direction, should the political environment require it. In March 1997 Netanyahu requested the preparation of what one participant in the effort described as an 'inventory of final status issues' including the issue of Palestinian refugees. The confidential 'study' addressed the nature of the problem, suggested guiding principles, offered a range of solutions, and articulated the three 'red lines' mentioned above. Reiterating firmly established positions across the right wing of Israel's political spectrum, Netanyahu's associates raised the idea that Jordan (which many Likud leaders view as a 'Palestinian state') and Egypt should each bear responsibility for resettling Palestinian refugees from Lebanon.[18] In October 1998, before the talks at Wye Plantation that centred on further Israeli redeployment in the West Bank, the then Foreign Minister Sharon had developed an alternative diplomatic approach – based upon an extended interim agreement – to negotiations with the Palestinians that included the establishment of a Palestinian entity in the West Bank and Gaza. In that context Sharon noted that 'Israel will consider the return of the 1967 refugees to the West Bank.'[19] In February 2001, shortly after his election as Prime Minister, Sharon told Spanish Prime Minister Jose Maria Anzar that 'Israel does not bear historical responsibility for the refugee problem and will not under any circumstances agree to their return to Israel.'[20] Sharon's refusal to entertain any recognition of culpability for the Palestinian refugee problem runs deep among Israelis of all political persuasions.[21]

A comprehensive, just and durable settlement will depend on bringing an end to the politics of denial and on addressing the refugee problem seriously. For decades the Palestinian right of return has been central to the Palestinians' struggle against dispossession and expulsion from their ancestral homeland and for national reconstitution. Only by understanding the centrality of the *nakba* and expulsion that the Palestinian people suffered in 1948 is it possible to understand the Palestinians' sense of the right of return. A durable peace in the Middle East is not possible against the desire and right of refugees to return home. The refugees and their descendants are currently demanding to be given a free choice between repatriation and/or compensation, in line with the international consensus enshrined in UN Resolution 194. The trauma of the 1948 catastrophe has remained central to the Palestinian society today (in the same way that the Holocaust has been central to Israeli and Jewish society). Today, the aspirations and hopes of millions of Palestinian refugees are linked to the 1948 catastrophe.

While a catastrophe of these dimensions can never be truly rectified, simple considerations of justice and reconciliation require that the refugees be given the right to return home. Any genuine reconciliation between the two peoples – peace between peoples as opposed to a political settlement achieved by leaders – could only begin by Israel and Israelis taking responsibility for the creation of the Palestinian refugee problem, and the displacement and dispossession of the refugees. Holocaust denial is abhorrent; in some European countries it is a crime. In the same way, acknowledging the Palestinian *nakba* and an official apology by Israel would be very helpful. However, the wrong done to the Palestinians can only be righted, and the disasters ended, through a return to their homeland and restitution of property.

Israel's obligation to compensate Palestinian refugees for land and property formerly owned by them was codified in paragraph 11 of United Nations General Assembly Resolution 194 (III) of 1949.

Resolution 194 affirms two types of compensation: for non-returnees and for damage to property.[22] The question of compensation for Palestinian refugee property in Israel did figure in the final status talks at Camp David and Taba. At Taba, Labour Yossi Beilin, in his private 'Non-Paper', suggested: 'Restitution he [the refugee] will not get, compensation he will.'[23] Beilin, while rejecting repatriation and 'restitution' of property, suggested a fund for compensating refugees should be established to which both the international community and Israel would be required to contribute. Palestinian spokespersons, on the other hand, have rejected the debate over compensation versus return as a false dichotomy and have been careful not to imply that compensation must be in lieu of implementation of the 'right of return' according to Resolution 194.[24] Rather, they view compensation as one of the options delineated by Resolution 194. Palestinians have emphasised compensation, reparations and indemnification: (a) compensation: moneys paid for lost refugee property in Israel; (b) reparations and indemnification:

moneys paid in recognition of the historical injustice which created the refugee problem. Resolution 194 singled out compensation, proposing that 'compensation should be paid for the property of those choosing not to return and for loss of or damage to property which, under principles of international law or in equity, should be made good by the governments or authorities responsible.'

At least part of the strong Palestinian opposition to proposals put forward by Israeli officials during the final status negotiations in favour of dissolving UNRWA and transferring its assets and responsibilities to the Palestinian Authority had to do with the Palestinian perception that UNRWA's existence and registration system is the main international legal pillar supporting the claims of individual Palestinian refugees to return and to reclaim their properties in Israel. Although Palestinians have been reluctant to place a price tag on their historical injustice, Palestinian and Arab estimates of potential compensation/reparations have varied, although they are typically in the tens of billions of dollars. The sums of reparations are very large, according to the most authoritative recent estimates of property losses alone. Depending on the criteria used, they range from \$92 billion to \$147 billion at 1984 prices, when the Hadawi-Kubursi study was done.[25] The Hadawi-Kubursi study defined refugee compensation in terms of reparations, restitution of property and indemnification. Valuing Palestinian losses in today's dollars by the inclusion of compensation for psychological damage and pain (following the Federal Republic of Germany's compensation schemes to Jews), according to an updated recent study by Kubursi, would double the Hadawi-Kubursi 1984 figures.[26]

Will the Palestinian refugees gain restitution? Will Israel ever atone for the *nakba*? Unlike other indigenous people, the Palestinian refugees received neither apology nor acknowledgment of responsibility for displacement, ethnic cleansing, massacres, home demolition and dispossession. Moreover the marginalisation of international law and the corresponding ascendancy of the Israeli role, promoted and protected by the US's global domination and virtual diplomatic monopoly, have combined to create a situation in which culpability for the Palestinian catastrophe is reassigned to the victim.[27]

To expect Israel now (under Ariel Sharon) to acknowledge its wrongdoing in 1948 is a remote prospect. Yet such an acknowledgement remains a precondition for genuine negotiations and reconciliation between Palestinians and Israelis and the achievement of a just and lasting peace in the Middle East. Under principles of international law and UN resolutions the refugee issue is resolvable. Israel must acknowledge its active role in creating the *nakba* and recognise the refugees' 'individual' right to return to both their 'homes' and 'homeland'.[28] For Israel, taking responsibility for the creation of the plight of the refugees also means acknowledging the justice of their claims for monetary compensation, restitution of property and reparation. With acknowledgement and international support, the refugee issue can be resolved on the basis of an historic compromise between Palestinians and Israelis. The Reparations Agreement between Israel and the Federal Republic of Germany of September 1952, which was designed to compensate victims of the Holocaust, could still serve as a model to compensate victims of the *nakba*.[29]

NOTES

1. For a further discussion of Israeli perceptions, see Shimon Peres, *The New Middle East* (Dorset, England: Element Books, 1993), pp.188–9; Itamar Rabinowich, 'Israeli Perceptions of the Right of Return', in *Palestinian Right of Return: Two Views*, Jeffrey Boutwello (ed.) (Cambridge, MA: The American Academy of Arts and Sciences, Paper no.6; Ruth Lapidoth, 'The Right of Return in International Law, with Special Reference to the Palestinian Refugees', *Israel Yearbook on Human Rights* 16 (1986), pp.103–25; Ruth Lapidoth, 'Do Palestinian Refugees Have a Right to Return to Israel?' at: http://www.mfa.gov.il/mfa/go.asp?MFAH0j8r0; Shlomo Gazit, *The Palestinian Refugee Problem*, Final Status Issues-Israel-Palestinians, Study no.2 (Tel Aviv: Tel Aviv University, The Jaffee Centre for Strategic Studies, 1995); Eyal Benvenisti and Eyal Zamir, 'Private Claims to Property Losses in the Future Israeli–Palestinian Settlement', *American Journal of International Law* 89, no.2 (1995), pp.240–340.
2. Naseer Aruri, 'Will Israel Ever Atone? Will the Palestinians Gain Restitutions? at: http://www.tari.org/will_israel_ever_atone.htm (accessed on 28 December 2002).
3. 'Akiva Eldar, 'The Refugee Problem at Taba (interview with Yossi Beilin and Nabil Sha'ath', *Palestine-Israel Journal* 9, no.2 (2002), 14.
4. Badil Resource Centre, '54th Anniversary of UN General Assembly Resolution 194(III): The Road Map Remains Relevant More than 50 Years Later', 11 December 2002 (E/69/02), at: http://www.badil.org/Press/2002/press285-02.htm (accessed on 28 December 2002).
5. (ECOSOC Res. 8/1, 1946), cited in ibid.
6. Ibid. In keeping with these findings, and consistent with international legal obligations, the United States, the primary member of the UNCCP advised that 'We should use our best efforts, through the Conciliation Commission and through diplomatic channels, to insure the implementation of the General Assembly resolution of December 11, 1948; We should endeavor to persuade Israel to accept the return of those refugees who so desire, in the interests of justice and as evidence of its desire to

establish amicable relations with the Arab world; We should furnish advice and guidance to the governments of the Arab states in the task of absorbing into their economic and social structures those refugees who do not wish to return to Israel.' US Department of State, 'Palestine Refugees', Policy paper, 15 March 1949, cited in ibid.

7. Quoted in *New Outlook* 4, no.9 (December 1961), p.9.
8. Cited in 'Akiva Eldar, 'A Time for Testing, and a Testing Time', *Haaretz*, 6 October 2003.
9. Naseer Aruri, 'Will Israel Ever Atone? Will the Palestinians Gain Restitutions?' at: http://www.tari.org/will_israel_ever_atone.htm (accessed on 28 December 2002).
10. For a discussion of Israel's 'ethnocracy' and Judaisation policies see Oren Yiftachel, 'Ethnocracy: The Politics of Judaizing Israel/Palestine', *Constellations* 6, (1999), pp.364–91; Yiftachel, 'Democracy or Ethnocracy: Territory and Settler Politics in Israel/Palestine', *Middle East Report* (Summer 1998), p.3 at: http://www.igc.apc.org/merip/yift.htm; Oren Yiftachel, 'Israeli Society and Jewish–Palestinian Reconciliation: Ethnocracy and its Territorial Boundaries', *Middle East Journal* 51, no.4 (Autumn 1997), pp.506–7.
11. Mazal Mu'alem, 'Yeshai is Working Towards Reducing the Number of Arabs Receiving Israeli Citizenship', *Haaretz*, 9 January 2002, pp.1 and 12a; 'The "Demographic Nightmare": Israel Freezes Family Reunification Process for Palestinian Citizens', Badil Resource Centre (Bethlehem, Palestine), 21 May 2002.
12. Ilan Pappé, 'Demons of the Nakbah', *Al-Ahram Weekly Online*, no.586, 16–22 May 2002.
13. See also my works *Expulsion of the Palestinians: The Concept of 'Transfer' in Zionist Political Thought 1882–1948* (Washington DC: Institute for Palestine Studies, 1992); *A Land Without a People: Israel, Transfer and the Palestinians, 1949–1996* (London: Faber and Faber, 1997), *Imperial Israel and the Palestinians: The Politics of Expansion, 1967–2000* (London: Pluto Press, 2000).
14. McDowall, The Palestinians, pp.148, 192, note no.3.
15. Cited by Nadav Shragai in *Haaretz*, 17 January 2001, p.5a.
16. Meron Benvenisti, 'Zionist or Terrorist', *Haaretz*, 3 January 2002, 1b.
17. The Knesset resolution of November 1961 stated: 'The Knesset resolves that the Arab refugees should not be returned to Israeli territory, and that the only solution to the problem is their settlement in the Arab countries.' See Simha Flapan, 'The Knesset Votes on the Refugee Problem', *New Outlook* 4, no.9 (December 1961), p.8.
18. A similar view was expressed by Rabbi Yoel Bin-Nun, a leader of the settlement movement Gush Emunim who had this to say: 'It must be understood Jews were killed and persecuted for thousands of years because of the Christian claim concerning the injustice we caused them by handing Jesus over to the Romans. If an Israeli government should, God forbid, sign a document taking responsibility for causing injustice to the Palestinians, it could haunt the Jewish people for another few thousand years, and we must not agree to that.' Cited by Yair Sheleg, in *Haaretz*, 27 October 2000, p.4b. See also Tourism Minister Benny Elon

in 'Arutz Sheva News Service, 13 November 2001, at: http://www.IsraelNationalNews.com; Guy Bichor, in *Yedi'ot Aharanot*, 13 July 2000, p.9.

19. 'Akiva Eldar, 'Tochnit Sharon-Ramon', *Haaretz*, 13 March 2000, p.1b.
20. Aluf Ben and Netzan Hurowitz, in *Haaretz*, 15 February 2001, p.11a.
21. Dan Meridor, a senior politician who was a member of the Israeli refugee team at Camp David, in an address at the Washington Institute's Policy Forum on 25 October 2001, stated, 'Israel's priority must be to find a way to maintain the safety and security of its borders while taking into account immutable demographic trends. This imperative – the need to maintain the Zionist ideal of a Jewish majority in a sovereign state – drives the search for a solution to the Palestinian issue. ... The Palestinian claim to a 'right of return' underscores the demographic nightmare for Israel.'
22. Terry Rempel, 'The Ottowa Process: Workshop on Compensation and Palestinian Refugees', *Journal of Palestine Studies* 29, no.1 (Autumn 1991), p.38.
23. 'Akiva Eldar, 'The Refugee Problem at Taba (interview with Yossi Beilin and Nabil Sha'ath', *Palestine-Israel Journal* 9, no.2 (2002), p.16.
24. Tamari, Palestinian Refugee Negotiations, p.38.
25. Sami Hadawi and Atef Kubursi, *Palestinian Rights and Losses in 1948: A Comprehensive Study* (London: Saqi Books, 1988), p.183.
26. Atef Kubursi, 'Valuing Palestinian Losses in Today's Dollars', in Naseer Aruri (ed.), *Palestinian Refugees: The Right of Return* (London: Pluto Press, 2001), pp.217–51.
27. Naseer Aruri, 'Will Israel Ever Atone? Will the Palestinians Gain Restitutions?' at: http://www.tari.org/will_israel_ever_atone.htm (accessed on 28 December 2002).
28. For different legal interpretations of the refugees' right of return to their 'homes' and 'homeland', see John Quigley, 'Family Reunion and the Right of Return to Occupied Territories', *Georgetown Immigration Law Journal* 6 (1992), pp.223–51; John Quigley, 'Displaced Palestinians and a Right of Return', *Harvard International Law Journal* 39, no.1 (1998), pp.171–229; Kathleen Lawand, 'The Right to Return of Palestinians in International Law', *International Journal of Refugee Law* 8, no.4 (October 1996), pp.532–68; Lex Takkenberg, *The Status of Palestinian Refugees in International Law* (Oxford: Clarendon Press, 1998); Antonio Cassese, 'Some Legal Observations on the Palestinian Right to Self-Determination', *Oxford International Review* 4, no.1 (1993), 10–13.
29. Ronald W. Zweig, 'Restitution of Property and Refugee Rehabilitation: Two Case Studies', *Journal of Refugee Studies* 6, no.1 (1993), p.61.

Bibliography

ARCHIVAL SOURCES

Central Zionist Archives (CZA), Jerusalem, Israel, protocols of the meetings of the Jewish Agency Executives; Manuscript notebooks of Yosef Weitz' diary; E. Ben-Horin's file.

Hashomer Hatza'ir Archives, Giva'at Haviva, Israel, papers of Aharon Cohen, papers of Hakibbutz Haartzi and the Mapam Political Committee.

Israel State Archives, Jerusalem, Foreign Ministry files.

Jabotinsky Archives, Tel Aviv, Joseph Schechtman's files.

Public Record Office, Kew, London, British Foreign Office files.

PUBLISHED PRIMARY SOURCES

Ahad Ha'Am, *Complete Works*, (Jerusalem, 1961). (Hebrew).

'Al Darchei Mediniyutenu: Mo'atzah 'Olamit Shel Ihud Po'alei Tzion (c.s.)-Din Vehesbon Male, 21 July–7 August [1938] [A Full Report about the World Convention of Ihud Po'alei Tzion, C.S.] (Tel Aviv: Central Office of Hitahdut Po'alei Tzion Press, 1938).

Ben-Gurion, David, *Michtavim el-Pola Ve el-Hayeladim* [Letters to Pola and the Children] (Tel Aviv, 'Am 'Oved, 1968).

——, *Zichronot* [Memoirs], Vols.1–3 (Tel Aviv: 'Am 'Oved, 1971–1972).

——, *Yoman Hamilhamah* [War Diary] 3 vols. (Tel Aviv: Misrad Habitahon publication, 1982).

Devrei Haknesset [Knesset Debates], (Jerusalem).

Hacongress Hatzioni-Protocol Rishmi [Official Protocols of the Zionist Congresses XIX–XXII: 1935–46] (Jerusalem: Organization Executive Press).

Katznelson, Berl, *Ketavim* [Writings], Vols.1–12 (Te Aviv, Mapai Publication, 1947–59).

Sharett, Moshe, *Yoman Ishi* [Personal Diary], 8 vols. (Tel Aviv: Sifriyat Ma'ariv, 1978).

Weitz, Yosef, *Yomani Veigrotai Lebanim* [My Diary and Letters to the Children], Vols. 3–6 (Tel Aviv: Massada, 1965).

SECONDARY SOURCES

Abu Lughod, Ibrahim (ed.), *The Transformation of Palestine* (Evanston: Northwestern University Press, 1971).

Abu-Lughod, Janet, 'The Demographic War for Palestine', *The Link* 19, no.5 (December 1986), pp.1–14.

Abu Odeh, Adnan, *Jordanians, Palestinian, and the Hashemite Kingdom in the Middle East Peace Process* (Washington DC: United States Institute of Peace Press, 1999).

Abu-Samra, Muhammad, 'Israeli Policy and the Question of the Palestinian Refugees, 1948–1949', *International Problems, Society and Politics* 58, nos.1–2 (1992) (Hebrew).

Abu-Sitta, Salman, 'Right of Return: Sacred, Legal and Feasible', *Al-Dustoor* (Amman), 3 September 1997, p.37 (Arabic).

——, 'Israel Sells Refugees Land and Register Ownership in Jewish Names', *Al-Hayat* (London), 18 June 1998, p.8 (Arabic).

——, *The Palestinian Nakba, 1948: The Register of Depopulated Localities in Palestine* (London: Palestinian Return Centre, 1998).

——, 'War Crimes – Burning Tira (Haifa) Inhabitants Alive in 1948', *Al-Hayat* (London), 5 April 1999, p.8 (Arabic).

——, 'Resettlement of Refugees is a Zionist Doctrine', *Al-Safir*, 24 August 1999 (Arabic).

——, 'Galilee Massacres as an Israeli Policy for Expulsion', *Al-Hayat* (London), 9 January 2000, p.10 (Arabic).

——, 'An end to exile', *Al-Ahram Weekly*, 9–15 March 2000.

Abu Zayyad, Ziad, 'The Palestinian Right of Return: A Realistic Approach', *Palestine-Israel Journal of Politics, Economics and Culture* 2 (Spring 1994), pp.274–8.

——, 'Seeking Justice', *Palestine-Israel Journal of Politics, Economics and Culture* 2, no.4 (Autumn 1995).

Adelman, Howard, 'Refugees: The Right of Return', in *Group Rights*, Judith Baker (ed.) (Toronto: University of Toronto Press, 1994).

——, 'Palestinian Refugees, Economic Integration and Durable Solutions', in *Refugees in the Age of Total War*, Michael R. Marrus and Anna C. Bramwell (eds) (London: Unwin Hyman, 1988).

——, Review of Milton Viorst, 'Reaching for the Olive Branch: UNRWA and Peace in the Middle East', *Middle East Focus* 14, no.2, (1992), pp.11–15.

——, 'Refugees, the Right of Return and the Peace Process', paper presented at a conference on the Economics of Peace in the Middle East at Yarmouk University, Yarmouk, Jordan, 1993.

Agha, Hussein and Robert Malley, 'Camp David and After: An Exchange (2. A Reply to Ehud Barak', *New York Review of Books*, 13 June 2002, pp.46–9.

Al-Aza'r, Khalid Muhammad, 'Guarantees of Refugee Rights and the Current Political Settlement', mimeo,1995 (Arabic).

Al-Haj, Majid, 'Adjustment Patterns of the Arab Internal Refugees in Israel', *Internal Migration* 24, no.3 (1986), pp.651–73.

——, 'The Arab Internal Refugees in Israel: The Emergence of a Minority Within the Minority', *Immigrants and Minorities* 7, no.2 (July 1988), pp.149–65.

Al-Hasan, Bilal, 'Palestinian Refugees', *Majalat al-Dirasat al-Filastiniyya*, no.26 (1996), pp.50–71 (Arabic).

Al-Hur, Munir and T. Al-Musa, *Mashari' al-Taswiya li al-Qadiyya al-Filastiniyya, 1947–1982* [Settlement Plans for the Palestine Question, 1947–1982] (Beirut: al-Muasasa al-'Arabiyya li al-Dirasat wa al-Nashr, 1983) (Arabic).

Al-Maliki, Majdi, *Some Social Consequences of the Intifada for the Jalazoun (Refugee) Camp, Woman, Marriage and the Family* (Ramallah, Palestine: Baysan Centre for Research and Development, 1994) (Arabic).

Al-Qutub, Ishaq, 'Refugee Camp Cities in the Middle East: A Challenge for Urban Development Policies', *International Sociology* 14, no.1, pp.91–108.

Al-Zaru, Nawaf, 'Israeli Plans to Liquidate the Palestinian Camps', *Samid al-Iqtisadi*, no.83 (1991), pp.134–42 (Arabic).

American Society of International Law, 'Human Rights and the Movement of Persons', *Proceeding of the 78th Annual Meeting of the American Society of International Law* (Washington, DC, 1984).

'Amro, Tayseer, 'The Palestinian Refugees in the Context of the Middle East Peace Process and Regional Cooperation', a follow-up to the author's paper presented at the IGCC IIR Conference, Vouliagmeni (Athens), Greece, 4–8 November 1994.

——, 'Displaced Persons: Categories and Numbers Used by the Palestinian Delegation [to the Quadripartite Committee] (not including spouses and descendants)', *Article 74*, no.14 (Jerusalem: Alternative Information Centre for Palestinian Residency and Refugee Rights, 1995).

Aner, Nadav, *Will They be Refugees Forever? Description of Conditions and Suggestions for a Solution* (Jerusalem: Israel Information Office, 1984) (Hebrew).

Ariel, Yehuda, 'Warning Signal in Galilee', *Haaretz*, 23 August 1972 (Hebrew).

Aronson, Geoffrey, *Israel, Palestinians and the Intifada* (London: Kegan Paul International, 1990).

Artz, Donna, 'Negotiating the Last Taboo: Palestinian Refugees', *Jordan Times*, 7 July 1995.

——, *Bibliographical Essay* [on Palestinian Refugees], Electronic Mail, 24 February 1996.

——, *Refugees Into Citizens: Palestinians and the End of the Arab–Israeli Conflict* (New York: Council on Foreign Relations Inc, 1997).

——, and Karen Zughaib, 'Return to the Negotiated Lands: The Likelihood and Legality of a Population Transfer Between Israel and a Future Palestinian State', *New York University Journal of International Law and Politics* 24, no.4 (1993), pp.1399–513.

Aruri, Naseer (ed.), *Palestinian Refugees: The Right of Return* (London: Pluto Press, 2001).

——, 'Will Israel Ever Atone? Will the Palestinians Gain Restitutions?' at: http://www.tari.org/will_israel_ever_atone.htm (accessed on 28 December 2002).

Askhar, Ahmad, 'Internal Refugees: Their Inalienable Right to Return', *News From Within* 11, no.8 (August 1995), pp.14–17.

——, 'The 1948 Palestinian Refugees: "We'll Return to the Village Alive or Dead"', *News From Within* 11, no.9 (September 1995), pp.21–4.

Awartani, Hisham, 'Palestinian–Israeli Economic Relations: Is Cooperation Possible?', in *The Economics of Middle East Peace*, Stanley Fischer, Dani Rodrik and Elias Tuma (eds) (Cambridge, MA: The MIT Press, 1994).

Badil: Resource Centre for Palestinian Residency and Refugee Rights (Bethlehem), 'Palestinian Refugees and the Right of Return: An International Law Analysis', *Palestine-Israel Journal* 9, no.2 (2002), pp.35–42.

Balabkins, Nicholas, *West German Reparations to Israel* (New Brunswick, Rutgers University Press, 1971).

Bar-On, Mordechai, *Sha'arie 'Aza: Mediniut Habitahon Vehahutz Shel Medinat Yisrael* [The Gates of Gaza: Israel's Defence and Foreign Policy] (Tel Aviv: 'Am 'Oved, 1992).

Bar-Zohar, Michael, *Ben-Gurion*, Vol.2 (Tel Aviv: 'Am 'Oved, 1977) (Hebrew).

Beidas, Riad, 'The "Internally Displaced" – Seeking Return Within One's Own Land: An Interview with Wakim Wakim', *Journal of Palestine Studies* 31, no.1 (Autumn 2001), pp.32–8.

Beilin, Yossi, *Madrich Leyonah Petzo'ah* [Manual for a Wounded Dove] (Tel Aviv: Miskal-Yedi'ot Aharonot and Hemed Publications, 2001) (Hebrew).

The Beirut Massacre: The Complete Kahan Commission Report (Princeton and New York: Karz-Cohl, 1983).

Beit-Hallahmi, Benjamin, *Original Sins: Reflections on the History of Zionism and Israel* (London: Pluto Press, 1992).

Ben-Ami, Shlomo, 'Opening Remarks', Official Presentation by the Israeli Delegation to the Refugee Working Group of the Middle East Peace Talks, 11 November 1992, Ottawa, Canada, mimeo.

Ben Porath, Yoram and Emanuel Marx, *Some Sociological and Economical Aspects of Refugee Camps on the West Bank* (Santa Monica, CA: The Rand Corporation, 1971).

Ben Porath, Yoram, Emanuel Marx, and Shimon Shamir, *A Refugee Camp on the Mountain Ridge* (Tel Aviv: Shiloah Institute, Tel Aviv University, 1974) (Hebrew).

Bentwich, Norman, *International Aspects of Restitution and Compensation for Victims of the Nazis* (Oxford: Oxford University Press, 1956).

Benvenisti, Eyal, and Eyal Zamir, 'Private Claims to Property Losses in the Future Israeli–Palestinian Settlement', *American Journal of International Law* 89, no.2 (April 1995), pp.295–340.

Benvenisti, Meron, *The West Bank Data Project: A Survey of Israel's Policies* (Washington: American Enterprise Institute, 1984).

Benziman, Uzi, *Sharon: An Israeli Caesar* (London: Robson Books, 1987).

Bergmann, Carl, *The History of Reparations* (London: Ernest Benn, 1927).

Besson, Yves, 'The Right of Compensation and Return', Conference Paper, Resolving the Palestinian Refugee Problem: What Role for the International Community? The University of Warwick, 23–4 March 1998.

Brand Laurie, *Palestinians in the Arab World* (New York: Columbia University Press, 1988).

——, 'Palestinians and Jordanians: A Crisis of Identity', *Journal of Palestine Studies* 24, no.4 (1995), pp.46–61.

Brynen, Rex, 'The Funding of Palestinian Refugee Compensation', presented to the ISEPME refugee group, Harvard University, February 1996 at: http://www.arts.mcgill.ca/mepp/prrn/papers/brynen1.html.

——, 'Imagining a Solution: Final Status Arrangements and Palestinian Refugees in Lebanon', *Journal of Palestine Studies* 26, no.2 (Winter 1997), pp.42–58.

——, 'Palestinian Refugees and Final Status: Key Issues', at: http://www.arts.mcgill.ca/MEPP/PRRN/prissues.html.

—— and Jill Tansley, 'The Refugee Working Group of the Middle East Multilateral Peace Negotiations', *Palestine-Israel Journal of Politics, Economics and Culture* 2, no.4 (Autumn 1995).

Buber, Martin, 'Statement on the Arab Refugee Problem', *New Outlook* 5, no.1 (January 1962), p.8.

Buseilah, Raja'i, 'The Fall of Lydda: Impressions and Reminiscences', *Arab Studies Quarterly* 3, no.2 (Spring 1981), pp.123–51.

Cahana, Shamay, *The Claim to a 'Right of Return' for the Palestinians and Its Significance for Israel* (Jerusalem: Leonard Davis Institute for International Relations, Hebrew University, 1993) (Hebrew).

Cahnman, Werner J, 'A Program for the Refugees', *New Outlook* 2, no.3 (November–December 1958), pp.15–22.

——, 'Differing and Converging Views on Solving the Palestinian Refugees' Problem', *Davis Papers on Israel's Foreign Policy*, no.51 (Jerusalem: Leonard Davis Institute for International Relations, Hebrew University, 1996).

Caplan, Neil, *Futile Diplomacy: Operation Alpha and the Failure of Anglo-American Coercive Diplomacy in the Arab–Israeli Conflict, 1954–1956*, Vol. 4 (London: Frank Cass, 1997).

Cartin, Amnon, 'Rehabilitation Plans for the Refugees in the Eastern Ghor in Jordan', *Research in the Geography of Israel* 13 (1992), pp.49–62 (Hebrew).

Cassese, Antonio, 'Some Legal Observations on the Palestinian Right to Self-Determination', *Oxford International Review* 4, no.1 (1993), pp.10–13.

Cattan, Henry, *Palestine, the Arabs and Israel* (London: Longmans, 1969).

Cervenak, C.M., 'Promoting Inequality: Gender-Based Discrimination in UNRWA's Approach to Palestine Refugee Status', *Human Rights Quarterly* 16, no.2 (1984), pp.300–74.

Chaudri, Mohammed Ahsen, 'Evacuee Property in India and Pakistan', *Pakistan Horizon* 10, no.2 (June 1957), pp.96–109.

Cheal, Beryl, 'Refugees in the Gaza Strip, December 1948–May 1950', *Journal of Palestine Studies* 8, no.1 (Autumn 1988), pp.138–57.

Childers, Erskine, 'The Other Exodus', *The Spectator*, 12 May 1961, pp.672–5.

——, 'The Wordless Wish: From Citizens to Refugees', in Ibrahim Abu-Lughod (ed.), *The Transformation of Palestine* (Evanston, IL: Northwestern University Press, 1971), pp.165–202.

Chomsky, Noam, *The Fateful Triangle: The United States, Israel and the Palestinians* (Boston: South End Press, 1983).

——, 'A Painful Peace', *Z Magazine* (January 1996), pp.37–50.

Cohen, Aharon, 'Not Too Late to Untangle the Knot', *New Outlook* 3, no.4 (February 1960), pp.22–32.

Cohen, Hillel, *Hanifkadim Hanokhahim: Haplitim Hafalastinayyim Beyisrael Meaz 1948* [The Present Absentees: The Palestinian Refugees in Israel Since 1948], (Jerusalem: Centre for the Study of Arab Society in Israel, Van Leer Institute, 2000) (Hebrew).

——, 'The Internal Refugees in the State of Israel: Israeli Citizens, Palestinian Refugees', *Palestine-Israel Journal* 9, no.2 (2002), pp.43–51.

Coon, Anthony, *Town Planning under Military Occupation: An Examination of the Law and Practice of Town Planning in the Occupied West Bank* (Hants, England: Dartmouth, 1992).

Cygielman, Victor, 'Mutual Recognition of Suffering', *Palestine-Israel Journal of Politics, Economics and Culture* 2, no.2 (Autumn 1995).

Danin, 'Ezra, *Tzioni Bekhol Tnai* [A Zionist in Every Condition], Vol.1 (Jerusalem: Kiddum, 1987) (Hebrew).

Darin-Drabkin, Haim, 'The Refugee Problem', *New Outlook* 4, no.4 (February 1961), pp.31–9.

Davis, Uri, *Citizenship and the State: A Comparative Study of Citizenship Legislation in Israel, Jordan, Palestine, Syria and Lebanon* (Reading: Ithaca Press, 1997).

—— and Norton Mezvinsky (eds), *Documents from Israel 1967–1973* (London: Ithaca Press, 1975).

Dayan, Moshe, *Mapah Hadashah, Yehasim Aherim* [A New Map, Other Relationships] (Tel Aviv: Ma'ariv, 1969) (Hebrew).

——, *Avnie Derekh: Otobiyografya* [Milestones: An Autobiography] (Jerusalem and Tel Aviv: 'Edanim and Dvir, 1976) (Hebrew).

de Azcarate, Pablo, *Mission in Palestine 1948–1953* (Washington DC: Middle East Institute, 1966).

de Zayas, Alfred-Maurice, 'International Law and Mass Population Transfers', *Harvard International Law Journal* 16 (1975), pp.207–58.

——, 'Forced Resettlement', *Encyclopedia of Public International Law* 8 (Amsterdam: North-Holland, 1985), pp.234–7.

——, 'Population, Expulsion and Transfer', *Encyclopedia of Public International Law* 8 (Amsterdam: North-Holland, 1985), pp.438–44.

——, 'A Historical Survey of 20th Century Expulsions', in Anna C. Bramwell (ed.), *Refugees in the Age of Total War* (1988), pp.15–37.

Drori, Moshe, 'The Israeli Settlements in Judea and Samaria', in Daniel Elazar (ed.), *Judea, Samaria, and Gaza: Views on the Present and the Future* (Washington: American Enterprise Institute for Public Policy Research, 1982).

Efrat, Moshe, *The Palestinian Refugees: Economic and Social Research, 1949–1974* (Tel Aviv: David Horowitz Institute, Tel Aviv University, 1976) (Hebrew).

——, *The Palestinian Refugees: The Dynamics of Economic Integration in Their Host Countries* (Tel Aviv: Israeli International Institute for Applied Economic Policy Review, 1993).

El-Jundi, Samir S., 'The Palestinian Refugees' at: http://www.idt.unit.not:80/~isfit/speeches/eljundi.html.

Elmadmad, Khadija, 'An Arab Declaration on the Protection of Refugees and Displaced Persons in the Arab World', *Journal of Refugee Studies* 6, n.2, (1993), pp.173–5.

——, 'Appropriate Solutions for the Palestinian Refugees', paper presented at a Conference on Promoting Regional Cooperation in the Middle East, Vouliagmeni, Greece, 4–8 November 1994.

Elnajjar, Hassan, 'Planned Emigration: The Palestinian Case', *International Migration Review* 27, no.1 (1993), pp.34–50.

Endresen, Lena, and Elia Zureik, *Studies of Palestinian Refugees: A Bibliography*, draft report presented to the Refugee Working Group meeting in Geneva, Switzerland, 12–15 December 1995.

—— and Geir Ovensen, *The Potential of UNRWA Data for Research on Palestinian Refugees: A Study of UNRWA Administrative Data*, 176 (Forskningsstiftelsen: Fafo, 1994).

Erlich, Guy, 'Not only Deir Yassin', *Ha'ir*, 6 May 1992 (Hebrew).

European Union, *Report Presented by the European Commission, Shepherd of the Social and Economic Infrastructure Theme, to the Refugee Working Group*, December 1994.

Eytan, Walter, *The First Ten Years* (New York: Simon & Schuster, 1958).

Falah, Ghazi, 'The 1948 Israeli–Palestinian War and its Aftermath: The Transformation and De-Signification of Palestine's Cultural Landscape', *Annals of the Assoc. of American Geographers 86*, no.2 (June 1996), pp.256–85.

Finkelstein, Norman, Image and Reality of the Israel–Palestine Conflict (London: Verso, 2nd. edn, 2001).

Fischbach, Michael R., 'Who Owns What?', *Le Monde Diplomatique*, English Edn (August–September 1997).

——, 'The United Nations and Palestinian Refugee Property Compensation', *Journal of Palestine Studies* 31, no.2 (Winter 2002), pp.34–50.

Flapan, Simha, 'One More Step is Needed', *New Outlook* 2, no. 5 (January 1959), pp.7–13.

——, 'The Knesset Votes on the Refugee Problem', *New Outlook* 4, no.9 (December 1961), pp.5–13.

——, *Zionism and the Palestinians 1917–1947* (London: Croom Helm, 1979).

——, *The Birth of Israel: Myths and Realities* (New York: Pantheon Books, 1987).

Forsythe, David P., *United Nations Peacemaking: The Conciliation Commission for Palestine* (Baltimore and London: Johns Hopkins University Press, 1972).

——, 'The Palestine Question: Dealing with a Long-Term Refugee Situation', *The Annals of the American Academy of Political and Social Science* (1983).

Frelick, B., 'The Right of Return', *International Journal of Refugee Law* 2, no.3 (1990), pp.442–7.

Fried, Shelly, 'The Refugee Issue at the Peace Conferences, 1949–2000', *Palestine-Israel Journal* 9, no.2 (2002), pp.24–34.

Gabbay, Rony E., *A Political Study of the Arab–Israeli Conflict: The Arab Refugee Problem*, A Case Study (Geneva: Droz, 1959).

Galili, Lily and Ori Nir, 'Refugee Camps in the Heart of Israel', *Haaretz*, 11 December 2000 (Hebrew).

Gazit, Shlomo, 'Fear of the Return', *Yedi'ot Aharonot*, 18 May 1994, p.5 (Hebrew).

——, *The Palestinian Refugee Problem*, Final Status Issues–Israel–Palestinians, Study no.2 (Tel Aviv: The Jaffe Centre for Strategic Studies, 1995).

——, 'Solving the Refugee Problem: A Prerequisite for Peace', *Palestine-Israel Journal of Politics, Economics and Culture* 2, no.4 (Autumn 1995).

Ghabra, Shafeeq, *Palestinians in Kuwait: The Family and the Politics of Survival* (London: Westview Press, 1987).

Gilen, Signe, Are Hovdenak, Rania Maktabi, Jon Pedersen, and Dag Taustad, *Finding Ways: Palestinian Coping Strategies in Changing Environments* (Oslo: Norwegian Institute for Applied Social Science, FAFO Report 177, 1994).

Gilmour, David, *Dispossessed: The Ordeal of the Palestinians* (London: Sphere Books, 1982).

Ginat, Joseph, *A Permanent Settlement Plan for the Palestinian Refugees* (Haifa: University of Haifa, 1994 at: gopher://:gopher-igcc.ucsd.edu).

Goebel, Christopher M., 'A Unified Concept of Population Transfer (Revised)', *Denver Journal of International Law and Policy* 22, no.1 (1993), pp.1–27.

Golani, Motti, *Israel in Search of a War: The Sinai Campaign, 1955–1956* (Brighton: Sussex Academic Press, 1998).

Government of Israel, *The Refugee Issue: A Background Paper* (Jerusalem: Government Press Office, 1994).

——, *Guidelines of the Government of Israel*, 1996 at: http://www.israel-mfa.gov.il.

Hadawi, Sami, *Bitter Harvest: A Modern History of Palestine* (NY: Olive Branch Press, 1990).

—— and Atef Kubursi, *Palestinian Rights and Losses in 1948: A Comprehensive Study* (London: Saqi Books, 1988).

Hagopian, Edward, and A.B. Zahlan, 'Palestine's Arab Population: The Demography of the Palestinians', *Journal of Palestine Studies* 3, no.4 (Summer 1974), pp.32–73.

Hamed, Osama, and Radwan A. Sha'ban, 'One-Sided Customs and Monetary Union: The Case of the West Bank and Gaza under Israeli Occupation', in *The Economics of Middle East Peace*, Stanley Fischer, Dani Rodrik, and Elias Touma (eds) (Cambridge, MA: MIT Press, 1994).

Hamzeh, Fuad Said, *International Conciliation with Special Reference to the Work of the United Nations Conciliation Commission for Palestine* (The Hague: Drukkerij Pasmans, 1964).

Hanafi, Sari, 'Les entrepreneurs en Syrie', *L'Economie de la paix au Proche-Orient*, L. Blin and Phillipe Fargues (eds) (Maisonneuve et Larose: CEDEJ, 1995).

Hanieh, Akram, 'The Camp David Papers', *Journal of Palestine Studies* 30, no.2 (Winter 2001).

Hannum, Hurst, *The Right to Leave and to Return in International Law and Practice* (Dordrecht, The Netherlands: Martinus Nijhoff Publishers, 1987).

Harari, Ishar, 'Making the Wolf a Vegetarian', *New Outlook* 6, no.1 (January 1963), pp.53–6.

Hassassian, Manuel, 'The Evolution of the Palestinian Refugee Problem', *Palestine-Israel Journal of Politics, Economics and Culture* 2, no.4 (Autumn 1995).

——, 'Historical Justice and Compensation for Palestinian refugees', at: http://www.pna.net/peace/historicaljustice.htm.

Hathaway James, 'A Reconsideration of the Underlying Premise of Refugee Law', *Harvard International Law Journal* 31 (1990), pp.129–83.

——, *Law of Refugee Status* (Toronto and Vancouver: Butterworths, 1991).

Hazboun, Norma Masriyeh, 'Refugee Resettlement: The Gaza Strip Experience', *Palestine-Israel Journal of Politics, Economics and Culture* 2, no.4 (Autumn 1995).

——, *Israeli Resettlement Schemes for Palestinian Refugees in the West Bank and Gaza Since 1967* (Ramallah, Palestine: Palestinian Diaspora and Refugee Centre-Shaml, 1996) at: http://www.shaml.org/ publications/monos/ mono4.htm.

Hazboun, Samir, 'A Socio-Economic Study of the Beit-Jibrin Refugee Camp, Bethlehem', *Journal of Arab Affairs* 2, no.1 (1992), pp.54–67.

Heiberg, Marianne, and Geir Ovensen, *Palestinian Society in Gaza, the West Bank and Arab Jerusalem: A Survey of Living Conditions*, FAFO REPORT 115 (Oslo: Norway: Norwegian Institute for Applied Social Science, 1992).

Heller, Mark, and Sari Nusseibeh, *No Trumpets, No Drums: A Two-State Settlement of the Israeli–Palestinian Conflict* (New York: Hill and Wang, 1991).

Henckaerts, J-M, 'Mass Expulsion in Modern International Law and Practice', *International Studies in Human Rights* 41 (The Hague: Kluwer Law International, 1995).

Henry, Marilyn, *The Restitution of Jewish Property in Central and Eastern Europe* (New York: American Jewish Committee, 1997).

Hirst, David, *The Gun and the Olive Branch* (London: Faber and Faber, 1984).

Hoffman, Ranier, 'Refugee-Generating Policies and the Law of State Responsibility', in *Zeitschrift fuer Auslaendiscnes Oeffentliches Recht und Voelkerrecht* 45 (1985), pp.694–713.

Humphrey, M., 'The Political Economy of Population Movements in the Middle East', *Middle East Report*, no.181 (1993), pp.2–9.

Institute of Jewish Affairs, *Compensation to Victims of Nazi Persecution for Property Losses in Expulsion and Similar Areas* (New York: Institute of Jewish Affairs, 1957).

International Law Association, 'Declaration of Principles of International Law on Compensation to Refugees (with Commentary), Including Report and Working Session of the Committee', *International Law Association, 65th Conference Cairo* (April 1992).

International Law Association, 'Declaration of Principles of International Law on Mass Expulsion (with Commentary), Including Report and Working Session of the Committee', *International Law Association, 65th Conference Cairo* (April 1992).

'Israeli–Palestinian Interim Agreement on the West Bank and Gaza Strip, Washington, 28 September 1995', in *Journal of Palestine Studies* 25, no.2 (1996), pp.123–40.

Israel/Palestine Center for Research and Information, *A Review of Literature on the Issue of Palestinian Refugees* at: http://www.ipcri.org/bio.htm.

Jaber, Abdel Tayseer, 'The Situation of the Palestinian Refugees in Jordan' (Amman, Jordan: January 1996, mimeo).

Jerusalem Media and Communications Centre, *Poll: The Year of Autonomy* (Jerusalem: JMCC, 1995).

——, *Israeli Obstacles to Economic Development in the Occupied Palestinian Territories* (Jerusalem: JMCC, 1996).

Jiryis, Sabri, *The Arabs in Israel* (New York: Monthly Review Press, 1976).

Ju'beh, Nazmi, 'The Palestinian Refugee Problem and Final Status Negotiations: A Review of Positions', *Palestine-Israel Journal* 9, no.2 (2002), pp.5–11.

Kadi, Leila S., *Basic Documents of the Armed Palestinian Resistance Movement* (Beirut: PLO Research Centre, 1969), pp.137–42.

Kamal, Chafic, 'Palestinians en Syrie. visa pour l'avenir', *Les Cahiers de l'Orient*, no.35 (1994), pp.113–20.

Kamen, Charles S., 'After the Catastrophe I: The Arabs in Israel, 1948–51', *Middle Eastern Studies* 23, no.4 (October 1987), pp.453–95.

——, 'After the Catastrophe II: The Arabs in Israel, 1948–51', *Middle Eastern Studies* 24, no.1 (January 1988), pp.68–109.

Katzenstien, Liora, 'From Reparations to Rehabilitation: The Origins of Israeli–German Relations, 1948–1953' (Ph.D. Thesis, University of Geneva, 1983).

Kayali Majid, 'Palestinian Intellectuals in Syria Debate Current Palestinian Crisis: Causes, Problems and Questions', *Majallat al-Dirasat al-Filastiniyya*, no.25 (1996), pp.123–54 (Arabic).

Khalidi, Rashid, 'The Palestinian People: Twenty-Two Years After 1967', in *Intifada: The Palestinian Uprising Against Israeli Occupation*, Zachary Lockman and Joel Beinin (eds) (London: I.B Tauris, 1990), pp.113–25.

——, 'Observations on the Palestinian Right of Return', in *The Palestinian Right of Return* (Cambridge, MA: The American Academy of Arts and Sciences, Paper no.6, October 1990).

——, 'Toward a Solution', in *Palestinian Refugees: Their Problem and Future* (Washington, DC: The Center for Policy Analysis on Palestine, October 1994), pp.21–6.

——, 'The Palestinian Refugee Problem: A Possible Solution', *Palestine-Israel Journal of Politics, Economics and Culture* 2, no.4 (Autumn 1995).

Khalidi, Walid (ed.), *From Haven to Conquest* (Beirut: The Institute for Palestine Studies, 1971).

——, 'Plan Dalet: Master Plan for the Conquest of Palestine', *Journal of Palestine Studies* 18, no.1 (Autumn 1988), pp.3–70.

——, (ed.), *All That Remains: The Palestinian Villages Occupied and Depopulated by Israel in 1948* (Washington, DC: Institute for Palestine Studies, 1992).

Khashan, Hilal, 'The Despairing Palestinians', *Journal of South Asian and Middle Eastern Studies* 16, no.1 (Fall 1992).

Khouri, Fred, *The Arab–Israeli Dilemma* (Syracuse, N.Y: Syracuse University Press, Third Edition, 1985).

Kimmerling, Baruch, 'Shaking the Foundations', *Index on Censorship* 24, no.3 (May/June 1995), pp.47–52.

——, 'Between Celebration of Independence and Commemoration of Al-Nakbah: The Controversy Over the Roots of the Israeli State', *Middle East Studies Association Bulletin* 32, no.1 (1998), pp.15–19.

—— and Joel Migdal, *Palestinians: The Making of a People* (New York: The Free Press, 1993).

Kinsella, Kevin, 'Palestinian Population Projections for 16 Countries of the World, 1990 to 2010' (Washington, DC: Bureau of the Census Center for International Research, 1991, mimeo).

Kislev, Ran, 'Land Expropriations: History of Oppression', *New Outlook* 19, no.6 (September–October 1976), pp.23–32.

Klinov, Ruth, 'Compensation and Rehabilitation of Palestinian Refugees: Proposals for Studies Contributing to the Resolution of the Palestinian Refugee Problem', Draft Paper, September–October 1994.

——, 'Reparations and Rehabilitation of Palestinian Refugees', *Palestine-Israel Journal* 9, no.2 (2002), pp.102–8.

Kodmani-Darwish, Basma, 'The Palestinian Question: A Fragmented Solution for a Dispersed People', Ph.D. thesis, Institute d'Etudes Politique, Paris, 1994.

Kossaifi, George, *The Palestinian Refugees' Right of Return* (Amman, Jordan: The United Nations Economic and Social Commission for Western Asia, July 1996).

——, 'Palestinian Refugees: Their Plight, their Future', in *Beyond Rhetoric: Perspectives on a Negotiated Settlement in Palestine. Part Two. Negotiating Permanent Status: What Price Peace?* (Washington, DC: The Center for Policy Analysis on Palestine, August 1996), pp.6–37.

Koussa, Elias, 'How Many Refugees Allowed to Return to Israel?', *New Outlook* 7, no. 9 (October 1964), p.64.

Kretzmer, David, *The Legal Status of the Arabs in Israel* (Boulder: Westview Press, 1990).

Kubursi, Atif, *Palestinian Losses in 1948: The Quest for Precision* (Washington DC: Center for Policy Analysis on Palestine, 1996).

Ladas, Stephen P., *The Exchange of Minorities: Bulgaria, Greece and Turkey* (New York: Macmillan, 1932).

Landman, Lawrence B. 'International Protection for American Indian Land Rights?', *Boston University International Law Journal* 5 (1987), pp.59–90.

Lapidoth, Ruth, 'The Right of Return in International Law, with Special Reference to the Palestinian Refugees', *Israel Yearbook on Human Rights* 16 (1986), pp.103–25.

——, 'Do Palestinian Refugees Have a Right to Return to Israel?', at: http://www.mfa.gov.il/mfa/go.asp?MFAH0j8r0.

Lawand, Kathleen, 'The Right to Return of Palestinians in International Law', *International Journal of Refugee Law* 8, no.4 (October 1996), pp.532–68.

——, 'The Declaration of the Principles of International Law on Compensation to Refugees: Its Significance and Implications', *Journal of Refugee Studies* 6, no.1 (1993), pp.65–70.

Lee, Luke T., 'The Right to Compensation: Refugees and Countries of Asylum', *American Journal of International Law* 80 (1986), pp.532–67.

Lewis, Frank D., 'Agricultural Property and the 1948 Palestinian Refugees: Assessing the Loss', *Exploration in Economic History* 33, no.2 (April 1996), pp.169–94.

Likud, *Likud Party Platform*, at: http://www.israel-mfa.gov.il.

Litani, Yehuda, 'Arafat's Hesitant Step Forward', *Jerusalem Post* (International Edn), 26 November 1988.

Locke, Richard and A. Stewart, *Bantustan Gaza* (London: Zed Books, 1985).

Lorch, Natanel (ed.), *Major Knesset Debates, 1948–1981* (London: University Press of America, 1993).

Luft, Gerda, 'The Refugees Have No Cause for Optimism', *New Outlook* 3, no.4 (February 1960), pp.8–11.

Lustick, Ian, *Arabs in the Jewish State: Israel's Control of a National Minority* (Austin: University of Texas Press, 1980).

Mahmud, Sa'id, 'The Settling in and Integration Process of Internal Refugees in the Arab Sheltering Villages in the North of Israel, 1948–1986', MA thesis, Department of Geography, Hebrew University, Jerusalem, 1990 (Hebrew).

Mallison, Thomas and Sally V. Mallison, 'The Right of Return', *Journal of Palestine Studies*, (Spring 1980), pp.125–36.

——, *The Palestine Problem in International Law and World Politics* (Essex: Longman, 1986).

Mardam-Bey, Farouk, and Elias Sanbar (eds), *Le Droit Au Retour: Le Problème Des Refugiés Palestiniens* (Paris: Sindbad, 2002).

Margalit, Dan, 'The Government Rejects Return of Bir'im and Iqrit Inhabitants Over Opposition of Four Ministers', *Haaretz*, 24 July 1972 (Hebrew).

Marrus, Micahel R., *The Unwanted: European Refugees in the Twentieth Century* (New York: Oxford University Press, 1985).

Marx, Emanuel, 'Changes in the Arab Refugee Camps', *The Jerusalem Quarterly*, no.8 (Summer 1978).

——, 'Rehabilitation of Refugees in the Gaza Strip', *International Problems, Society and State* 5 (1991), pp.64–73 (Hebrew).

——, 'Palestinian Refugee Camps in the West Bank and Gaza Strip', *Middle Eastern Studies* 28, no.2 (April 1992), pp.281–94.

Masalha, Nur, 'On Recent Hebrew and Israeli Sources for the Palestinian Exodus 1948–49', *Journal of Palestine Studies* 18, no.1 (Autumn 1988), pp.121–37.

——, 'Al-Tasawwur al-Suhyuni Le al-Transfer: Nazrah Tarikhiyya 'Amah' [The Zionist Concept of Transfer: An Historical Overview], *Majalat al-Dirasat al-Filastiniyya*, no.7 (Summer 1991), pp.19–45.

——, 'Debate on the 1948 Exodus', *Journal of Palestine Studies* 21, no.1 (Autumn 1991), pp.90–7.

——, *Expulsion of the Palestinians: The Concept of 'Transfer' in Zionist Political Thought 1882–1948* (Washington, DC: Institute for Palestine Studies, 1992).

——, *Tard al-Filastinyyin: Mafhum al 'Transfer' Fi al-Fikr wa al-Takhtit al-Suhyuniyyan* (Beirut: Institute for Palestine Studies, 1992) (Arabic).

—— (ed.), *The Palestinians in Israel* (Nazareth: Galilee Centre for Social Research, 1993).

——, '"1948 and After" Revisited', *Journal of Palestine Studies* 24, no.4 (Summer 1995), pp.90–5.

——, 'A Different Peace', *Index on Censorship*, no.3 (May–June 1996), pp.18–21.

——, *Israeli Plans to Resettle the Palestinian Refugees, 1948–1972* (Ramallah, Palestine: Palestinian Diaspora and Refugee Centre-Shaml, 1996).

——, *Yosef Weitz and Operation Yohanan, 1949–1953*, Occasional Papers Series (Durham: Centre for Middle Eastern and Islamic Studies, University of Durham, 1996).

——, *Akthar Ard wa-Aqal 'Arab* [More Land and Fewer Arabs] (Beirut: Institute for Palestine Studies, 1997) (Arabic).

——, *A Land Without a People: Israel, Transfer and the Palestinians, 1949–1996* (London: Faber and Faber, 1997).

——, 'A Critique on Benny Morris', in Ilan Pappe (ed.), *The Israel/Palestine Question* (London: Routledge, 1999).

——, 'A Galilee Without Christians?', in Anthony O'Mahony (ed.), *Palestinian Christians: Religion, Politics and Society in the Holy Land* (London: Melisende, 1999), pp.190–222.

——, 'The 1967 Palestinian Exodus', in Ghada Karmi and Eugene Cotran (eds), *The Palestinian Exodus, 1948–1998* (Reading: Ithaca Press, 1999), pp.63–109.

——, *Imperial Israel and the Palestinians: The Politics of Expansion* (London: Pluto Press, 2000).

——, 'Le Concept De "Transfer" Dans La Doctrine Et Dans La Pratique Du Mouvement Sioniste', in Farouk Mardam-Bey and Elias Sanbar (eds), *Le Droit Au Retour: Le Probleme Des Refugiés Palestiniens* (Paris: Sindbad, 2002), pp.15–59.

——, 'The PLO, Resolution 194 and the "Right of Return": Evolving Palestinian Attitudes Towards the Refugee Question from the 1948 *Nakba* to the Camp David Summit of July 2002', E. Cotran (ed.), *Yearbook of Islamic and Middle Eastern Law* 7 (2002), pp.127–55.

——, 'Israel y los refugiados', La Vanguardia (Barcelona, Spain), 16 May 2003, at: http://galeon.com/genteaalternativa/triunaoradores/tribuna615.htm.

——, and F. Vivekananda, 'Israeli Revisionist Historiography of the Birth of Israel and its Palestinian Exodus of 1948', *Scandinavian Journal of Development Alternatives* 9, no.1 (March 1990), pp.71–9.

Massis, Alex, 'Biram, Ikrit', *New Outlook* 19, no.2 (February–March 1996), pp.18–24.

McCarthy, Justin, *The Population of Palestine: Population History and Statistics in the Ottoman Period and the Mandate* (New York: Columbia University Press, 1991).

McDowall, David, *Palestine and Israel: The Uprising and Beyond* (London: I.B. Tauris, 1989).

——, *The Palestinians: The Road to Nationhood* (London: Minority Rights Publications, 1994).

Melman, Yossi, and Dan Raviv, 'Expelling Palestinians', *Washington Post*, 7 February 1988.

——, 'A Final Solution to the Palestinian Problem', *Davar*, 19 February 1988 (Hebrew).

Memorandum Submitted by Palestinian Resistance Groups in Lebanon to the Prime Minister of Lebanon (Beirut, Lebanon, 1994).

Morris, Benny, 'Yosef Weitz and the Transfer Committees, 1948–49', *Middle Eastern Studies* 22, no.4 (October 1986), pp.549–50.

——, *The Birth of the Palestinian Refugee Problem 1947–1949* (Cambridge: Cambridge University Press, 1987).

——, 'The New Historiography and the Old Propagandists', *Haaretz*, 9 May 1989 (Hebrew).

——, 'The Eel and History', *Tikkun* (January–February 1990), pp.20–21.

——, *1948 and After: Israel and the Palestinians* (Oxford: Oxford University Press, 1990).

——, 'Falsifying the Record: A Fresh Look at Zionist Documentation of 1948', *Journal of Palestine Studies* 24, no.3 (Spring 1995), pp.44–62.

——, 'Mabat Hadash 'Al Mismachim Tzioniyim Merkaziyim', *Alpayim* 12 (1996), pp.76–7.

——, *Israel's Border Wars, 1949–1956: Arab Infiltration, Israeli Retaliation, and the Countdown to the Suez War* (Oxford: Clarendon Press, rev. edn, 1997).

——, 'Refabricating 1948', *Journal of Palestine Studies* 27, no.2 (Winter 1998), pp.81–95.

——, *Tikkun Ta'ut: Yehudim Ve'aravim Beeretz Yisrael, 1936–1956* [Correcting a Mistake: Jews and Arabs in the Land of Israel] (Tel Aviv: 'Am 'Oved, 2000) (Hebrew).

——, 'Revisiting the Palestinian Exodus of 1948', in Eugene Rogan and Avi Shlaim (eds), *The War for Palestine: Rewriting the History of 1948* (Cambridge: Cambridge University Press, 2001), pp. 37–59.

Mubanga-Chipoya, C.L.C., *Analysis of the Current Trends and Developments Regarding the Right to Leave Any Country Including One's Own and to Return to One's Own Country, and Some Other Rights and Considerations Arising Therefrom* (Geneva: United Nations Subcommission on Prevention of Discrimination and Protection of Minorities (UN doc.E/C N.4/Sub./2/1988/35)).

National Centre for Educational Research and Development, *The Socio-Economic Characteristics of Jordanian Returnees*, Part 1, Statistical Analysis and Indicators (Amman, Jordan, NCERD, 1991).

Natur, Suhayl, *Conditions of the Palestinian People in Lebanon* (Beirut: Dar al-Taqadum al-'Arabi, 1993) (Arabic).

Nazzal, Nafez, *The Palestinian Exodus from Galilee 1948* (Beirut: Institute for Palestine Studies, 1978).

Nedava, Yosef, 'Tochniyot Helufie Ochlosin Lepetron Be'ayat Eretz-Yisrael' [Population Exchange Plans for the Solution of the Problem of the Land of Israel], *Gesher* 24, nos.1–2 (Spring–Summer 1978) (Hebrew).

——, 'British Plans for the Resettlement of Palestinian Arabs', *Haumah*, no.89 (Winter 1987/88) (Hebrew).

Neff, Donald, 'U.S Policy and the Palestinian Refugees', *Journal of Palestine Studies* 18, no.1 (Autumn 1988).

Newton, Nell Jessup, 'Compensation, Reparations, and Restitution: Indian Property Claims in the United States', *Georgia Law Review* 28 (1994), pp.453–80.

Nimrod, Yoram, *Breirat Hashalom Vederech Hamilhamah: Hithavut Defusim Shel Yehasei Yisrael-'Arav, 1947–1950* [War or Peace? The Formation of Patterns in Israeli–Arab Relations, 1947–1950] (Giva'at Haviva, Hamachon Leheker Hashalom, 2000) (Hebrew).

Nir, Ori, 'What is a Refugee? What is a Displaced Person?', *Haaretz*, 7 March 1995, B3 (Hebrew).

Nour, Amer, *Coming Home: A Survey of the Socio-economic Conditions of the West Bank and Gaza* (Jerusalem: Palestine Human Rights Information Centre, 1993).

'Oded, Yitzhak, 'Land Losses Among Israel's Arab Villagers', *New Outlook* 7, no.7 (September 1964), pp.10–25.

Painter, Andrew, 'Property Rights of Returning Displaced Persons: The Guatemalan Experience', *Harvard Human Rights Journal* 9 (Spring 1996), pp.145–83.

Palestinian National Authority, *Palestinian Refugees and the Right of Return* (Jerusalem: Ministry of Information, 1995).

Palestinian Refugee ResearchNet, *Palestinian Refugees and Final Status: Key Issues*, at: http://www.arts.mcgill/ca/MEPP/PRRN/prissues.html.

Palestinian Refugee ResearchNet, *Refugees in the Middle East Peace Process*, at: http://www.arts.mcgill.ac:80/MEPP/PRRN/prmepp.html.

Palumbo, Michael, *The Palestinian Catastrophe* (London: Faber and Faber, 1987).

'Panel Discussion – Arab Refugees, Givat Haviva, September 6, 1967', *New Outlook* 10, no.2 (February 1967), pp.30–44.

Pappé, Ilan, 'Moshe Sharett, David Ben-Gurion and the "Palestinian Option", 1948–1956', *Studies in Zionism* 7, no.1 (1986), pp.77–96.

——, *The Making of the Arab–Israeli Conflict, 1947–1951* (London: I. B. Tauris, 1992).

——, 'Critique and Agenda', *History and Memory* 7, No.1 (1995), pp.60–90.

——, 'The Tantura Case in Israel: The Katz Research and Trial', *Journal of Palestine Studies* 30, no.3 (Spring 2001), pp.19–39.

——, 'Demons of the Nakbah', *Al-Ahram Weekly Online*, no.586, 16–22 May 2002.

Patai, Rephael (ed.), *The Complete Diaries of Theodor Herzl*, Vol.1 (New York: Herzl Press and T. Yoseloff, 1960).

Peres, Shimon, *The New Middle East* (Dorset, England: Elements Book, 1993).

Peretz, Don, 'Problems of Arab Refugee Compensation', *Middle East Journal* 8, no.4 (Autumn 1954), pp.403–16.

——, 'Arab Blocked Bank Accounts in Israel', *Jewish Social Studies* (1956), pp.25–40.

——, *Israel and the Palestine Arabs* (New York: AMS Press, 1958).

——, 'The Situation of the Refugees', *New Outlook* 5, no.6 (July–August 1962), pp.41–4.

——, *The Palestinian Arab Refugee Problem* (The Rand Corporation, October 1969).

——, 'Early State Policy Towards the Arab Population', in *New Perspectives on Israeli History* (New York: New York University Press, 1991).

——, *Palestinians, Refugees and the Middle East Peace Process* (Washington DC: United States Institute for Peace Press, 1993).

——, 'The Question of Compensation', *Palestinian Refugees: Their Problem and Future* (Washington, DC: The Center for Policy Analysis on Palestine October 1994), pp.15–20.

——, *Palestinian Refugee Compensation*, Information Paper no.3 (Washington, DC: The Center for Policy Analysis on Palestine, May 1995).

Peron, Marc, *A Vision Paper of the New Middle East: A Perspective from the Refugee Working Group* (Ottawa, 1995).

Peteet, Julie, 'Identity and Community in Exile', *Journal for Critical Studies of the Middle East*, no.8 (Spring 1996).

——, 'From Refugees to Minority: Palestinians in Post-War Lebanon', *Middle East Report* 200 (July–September 1996).

——, *Lebanon Palestinian Refugees in the Post-War Period* (December 1997), Writenet Country Papers at: http://www.unhcr.ch/refworld/country/writenet/wrilbn.hmt.

Petropulos, John A., 'The Compulsory Exchange of Populations: Greek–Turkish Peacemaking, 1922–1930', in *Byzantine and Modern Greek Studies* 2 (1976), pp.135–60.

Prior, Michael, *The Bible and Colonialism: A Moral Critique* (Sheffield: Sheffield Academic Press, 1997).

——, *Zionism and the State of Israel: A Moral Inquiry* (London and New York: Routledge, 1999).

'The Problem of Arab Refugees from Palestine', in *Senate Committee on Foreign Relations*, U.S. Government Report of the Subcommittee on the Near East and Africa, 24 July 1953.

Quigley, John, 'Family Reunion and the Right of Return to Occupied Territories', *Georgetown Immigration Law Journal* 6 (1992), pp.223–51.

——, 'Displaced Palestinians and a Right of Return', *Harvard International Law Journal* 39, no.1 (1998), 171–229.

Rabinowich, Itamar, 'Israeli Perceptions of the Right of Return', in *Palestinian Right of Return: Two Views*, Jeffrey Boutwello (ed.) (Cambridge, MA: The American Academy of Arts and Sciences, Paper no.6).

Radi, Lamia, 'Les Palestiniens du Koweit en Jordanie', *monde Arabe Maghreb Machrek*, no.144 (avril–juin 1994), pp.55–65.

Radley, Kurt Rene, 'The Palestinian Refugees: The Right of Return in International Law', *American Journal of International Law* 72 (1978), pp.586–614.

Rempel, Terry, 'The Ottowa Process: Workshop on Compensation and Palestinian Refugees', *Journal of Palestine Studies* 29, no.1 (Autumn 1991), pp.36–49.

Results of Public Opinion Polls among Palestinians, 18–20 May 1995 (Nablus: Centre for Palestinian Research and Studies, 1995).

Richmond, Anthony H., *Global Apartheid: Refugees, Racism and the New World Order* (New York and Oxford: Oxford University Press, 1994).

Rogan, Eugene L. and Avi Shlaim (eds), *The War for Palestine: Rewriting the History of 1948* (Cambridge: Cambridge University Press, 2001).

Rolef, Susan Hattis, (ed.), *Political Dictionary of the State of Israel*, 2nd edn (New York: Macmillan Publishing Company, 1993).

Rubinstein, Danny, 'A Material and Spiritual Homeland', *Palestine-Israel Journal of Politics, Economics and Culture* 2, no.4 (Autumn 1995).

Sagi, Naha, *German Reparations: A History of the Negotiations* (Jerusalem: The Magnes Press, The Hebrew University, 1980).

Said, Edward, *The Politics of Dispossession* (London: Chatto & Windus, 1994).

——, *Peace and its Discontents: Gaza–Jericho 1993–1995* (London: Vintage, 1995).

——, *The End of the Peace Process: Oslo and After* (London: Granta, 2000).

—— and Christopher Hitchins (eds), *Blaming the Victims: Spurious Scholarship and the Palestinian Question* (London and New York: Verso, 1988).

——, Ibrahim Abu-Lughod, Janet Abu-Lughod, Muhammad Hallaj, and Elia Zureik, *A Profile of the Palestinian People* (New York and Chicago: Palestinian Human Rights Campaign, 1990).

Said, Maha, 'The Reality of Transfer', *RETURN*, no.2 (March 1990), pp.10–12.

Salam, Nawaf A., 'Between Repatriation and Resettlement: Palestinian Refugees in Lebanon', *Journal of Palestine Studies* 34, no.1 (Autumn 1994), pp.18–27.

Sanbar, Elias, *Palestine 1948* (Beirut: Arab Society for Studies & Publishing 1987) (Arabic).

Savir, Uri, Address delivered on 5 May 1996 in Taba, Egypt, at the opening of the final status talks, at: http://www.israel.mfa.gov.il.

Sayigh, Rosemary, *Palestinians: From Peasants to Revolutionaries* (London: Zed Books, 1979).

——, 'An Uncertain Future for the Palestinian Refugees in Lebanon', *Middle East International*, 13 May 1994.

——, 'Palestinians in Lebanon: Harsh Present, Uncertain Future', *Journal of Palestine Studies* 25, no.1 (1995), pp.37–53.

Sayigh, Yezid, *Armed Struggle and the Search for State: The Palestinian National Movement, 1949–1993* (Oxford: Clarendon Press, 1997).

——, 'Arafat and the Anatomy of a Revolt', *Survival* 43, no.3 (Autumn 2001), pp.47–60.

——, 'The Palestinian Strategic Impasse', *Survival* 40, no.4 (Winter 2002–3), pp.7–21.

Schechla, Joseph, 'The Invisible People Come to Light: Israel's "Internally Displaced" and the "Unrecognized Villages"', *Journal of Palestine Studies* 31, no.1 (Autumn 2001), pp.20–31.

Schechtman, Joseph B., *European Population Transfers 1939–1945* (New York: Oxford University Press, 1946).

——, *Population Transfer in Asia* (New York: Hallsby Press, 1949).

——, *The Arab Refugee Problem* (New York: Philosophical Library, 1952).

——, 'Evacuee Property in India and Pakistan', *India Quarterly* 9, no.1 (January–March 1953), pp.3–35.

——, *Post-War Population Transfers in Europe, 1945–1955* (Liverpool: Charles Birchall and Sons, 1962).

——, *The Refugee in the World: Displacement and Integration* (New York: A.S. Barnes and Company, 1963).

Schiff, Benjamin, 'Between Occupier and Occupied: UNRWA and the West Bank and Gaza', *Journal of Palestinian Studies* 18, no.3 (1989), pp.60–75.

——, 'Assisting the Palestinian Refugees: Progress in Human Rights?', in *Progress in Postwar International Relations*, edited by Emanuel Heller and Beverly Crawford (eds) (New York: Columbia University Press, 1991).

——, *Refugees Unto the Third Generation: UN Aid to Palestinians* (Syracuse, New York: Syracuse University Press, 1995).

Schölch, Alexander (ed.), *Palestinians Over the Green Line* (London: Ithaca, 1983).

Segev, Tom, *1949: The First Israelis* (New York: The Free Press, 1986).

——, *The Seventh Million: The Israelis and the Holocaust* (New York: Hill & Wang, 1993).

Shahak, Israel, 'A History of the Concept of Transfer in Zionism', *Journal of Palestine Studies* 17, no.3 (Spring 1989), pp.22–37.

Shami, Seteney, 'The Social Implications of Population Displacement and Resettlement: An Overview with Focus on the Arab Middle East', *International Migration* 27 (1993), pp.4–32.

Shamir, Shimon, 'The Collapse of Project Alpha', in *Suez 1956: The Crisis and its Consequences*, Wm. Roger Louis and Roger Owen (eds) (Oxford: Clarendon Press, 1989), pp.73–100.

Shamir, Yitzhak, Address delivered on 31 October 1991 at the Madrid Conference at: http://www.israel-mfa.gov.il.

Shapira, Anita, 'Politics and Collective Memory: The Debate over the "New Historians" in Israel', *History and Memory* 7, no.1 (1995), pp.9–10.

Shereshevsky, Simon, 'Peace Without Treaties', *New Outlook* 6, no.2 (February 1963), pp.49–52.

Shuval, Hillel, 'There Can Be No "Return"', *Palestine-Israel Journal* 9, no.2 (2002), pp.74–9.

Silberstein, Laurence J., 'Postzionism: A Critique of Zionist Discourse', *Palestine-Israel Journal* 9, no.2 (2002), pp.84–91.

Singer, Joel, *The West Bank and Gaza Strip: Phase Two*, 1995 at: http://www.israel-mfa.gov.il.

Sharon, Ariel, *Warrior: An Autobiography* (New York: Simon and Schuster, 1989).

Shiblak, Abbas, 'Residency Status and Civil Rights of Palestinian Refugees in Arab Countries', *Journal of Palestine Studies* 25, no.3 (Spring 1996), pp.36–45.

Shlaim, Avi, 'Conflicting Approaches to Israel's Relations with the Arabs: Ben-Gurion and Sharett, 1953–1956', *Middle East Journal* 37, no.2 (1983).

——, 'The Rise and Fall of the All-Palestine Government in Gaza', *Journal of Palestine Studies* 20, no.1 (Autumn 1990), pp.37–53.

Shuckburgh, Evelyn, *Descent to Suez: Diaries 1951–56* (New York: W.W. Norton, 1987).

Simons, Chaim, *International Proposals to Transfer Arabs from Palestine 1895–1947* (New Jersey: Ktav Publishing House, 1988).

Steinboim, Zvit, *The Palestinian Refugees: Portrait and Possible Solutions* (Tel Aviv: Tel Aviv University, March 1993).

Sternhell, Zeev, *The Founding Myths of Israel: Nationalism, Socialism and the Making of the Jewish State* (Princeton: Princeton University Press, 1998).

Sutton, Keith, 'Population Resettlement: The Algerian Experience', *Ekistics*, no.267 (February 1978), pp.59–65.

Tadmor, Yoav, 'The Palestinian Refugees of 1948: The Right to Compensation and Return', *Temple International and Comparative Law Journal* 8, no.2 (1994), pp.403–34.

Takkenberg, Lex, *The Status of Palestinian Refugees in International Law* (Oxford: Clarendon Press, 1998).

Tamari, Salim, 'The Future of Palestinian Refugees in the Peace Negotiations', *Palestine-Israel Journal of Politics, Economics, and Culture* 2, no.4 (Autumn 1995).

——, 'Residency Rights for Returning Palestinians in Oslo II: A Critical Examination', *Palestine Report*, 1 December 1995.

——, *Palestinian Refugee Negotiations: From Madrid to Oslo II*, Final Status Issue Paper (Washington, DC: Institute for Palestine Studies, 1996).

——, *Return, Resettlements, Repatriation: The Future of Palestinian Refugees in the Peace Negotiations*, FOFONET Digest, 22 April 1996.

—— (ed.), *Jerusalem 1948, The Arab Neighbourhoods and Their Fate in the War* (Jerusalem: Institute of Jerusalem Studies and Badil Resource Centre, 1999).

Tansley, Jill, *Adaptation in the West Bank and Gaza: A Discussion Paper* (Ottawa: International Development Research Centre, 1996).

'The Tantura Massacre, 22–23 May 1948', *Journal of Palestine Studies* 30, no.3 (Spring 2001), pp.5–18.

Teveth, Shabtai, *Ben-Gurion and the Palestinian Arabs: From Peace to War* (Oxford: Oxford University Press, 1985).

——, *The Evolution of 'Transfer' in Zionist Thinking* (Tel Aviv: Dayan Centre, 1989).

Tibawi, A.L., 'Visions of the Return: The Palestine Arab Refugees in Arabic Poetry and Art', *Middle East Journal* 17, no.5 (Autumn 1963), pp.507–26.

Tomeh, George (ed.), *United Nations Resolutions on Palestine and the Arab–Israeli Conflict*, Vol.1: 1947–1974 (Washington, DC: Institute for Palestine Studies, 1975).

Turki, Fawaz, *The Disinherited: Journal of a Palestinian Exile* (New York: Monthly Review Press, 1972).

United Nations, *Annual Report of the Director General of UNRWA*, Doc.5224/5223, 25 November 1952.

——, *The Right of Return of the Palestinian People*, published for the Committee on the Exercise of the Inalienable Rights of the Palestinian People (New York: United Nations, 1979).

United Nations Conciliation Commission for Palestine: Report of the UN Economic Survey Mission, 1949, Doc.A/AC.25/6.

United Nations Refugee and Works Agency (UNRWA), *Family and Reunification* (Vienna: UNRWA, October 1992).

——, *Social and Economic Infrastructure* (Vienna: UNRWA, 1992).

——, *Socioeconomic Conditions in the Occupied Territory, Mid-1991–Mid-1992* (Vienna: UNRWA, 1992).

van Boven, Theo, 'The Right to Restitution, Compensation and Rehabilitation for Victims of Gross Violation of Human Rights and Fundamental Freedoms', *The Living Law of Nations: Essays of Refugees, Minorities, Indigenous Peoples and the Human Rights of Other Vulnerable Groups in Memory of Atle Grahl-Madsen* (Kehl: N.P. Engel, 1996), pp.339–54.

Vidal, Dominique, with Joseph Algazy, *Le péché originel d'Israel: L'expulsion des Palestiniens revisitée par les 'nouveaux historiens' israeliens* (Paris: Les Editions de l'Atelier/Les Editions Ouvrières, 1998).

Viorst, Milton, *Reaching for the Olive Branch: UNRWA and Peace in the Middle East* (Washington, DC: Middle East Institute, 1989).

Von Weisl, Wolfgang, 'A New Solution for the Refugee Problem', *New Outlook* 2, no.10 (July–August 1959), pp.30–7.

Weitz, Yehi'am (ed.), *Ben Hazon Le-Revizyah: Meah Shnot Historiyografyah Tziyonit* [Between Vision and Revision: A Hundred Years of Historiography of Zionism] (Jerusalem: Zalman Shazar Centre, 1997).

World Bank, *Developing the Occupied Territories: An Investment in Peace*, 6 vols. (Washington, DC: World Bank, 1993).

World Organization of Jews from Arab Countries, *The Shape of the Arab–Israeli Settlement: Humanitarian and Demographic Issues. The Case of the Jews who Left Arab Countries as Refugees*, paper distributed at a seminar sponsored by the Council on Foreign Relations, 7 February 1994, New York.

Yogev, Shlomo, 'Gaza Without Refugees: The Policy and its Purpose', *New Middle East*, no. 55 (April 1973), pp.26–9.

Yunis, Makram, 'Al-Mashru'at al-Israeliyya li Tawtin al-Lajiin' [Israeli Projects for Resettlement of Refugees, 1967–1978], *Shuun Filastiniyya*, no.86 (January 1979), pp.108–26 (Arabic).

Wakim, Wakim, *Haq al-'Awda Lemuhajri al-Dahkil Haq Ghair Qabil Littasarrof* [The Right of Return of the Internally Displaced is an Inalienable Right] (Haifa: Initiating Committee for the Defence of the Rights of the Displaced in Israel, 1995).

——, 'The Exiled: Refugees in their Homeland', *Palestine-Israel Journal* 9, no.2 (2002), pp.52–7.

Zakay, Dan, Yechiel Klar and Keren Sharvit, 'Jewish Israelis on the "Right of Return"', *Palestine-Israel Journal* 9, no.2 (2002), pp.58–66.

Zakharia, Leila, *The Situation of Palestinian Refugees: The Challenge to a Just, Comprehensive and Durable Peace*, FOFONET Digest, 5–7 July 1996, at: http://www.arts.mcgill.ca:80/mepp/prn/papers/zakharia.html.

Zakin, Dov, 'Rehabilitation of the Refugees', *New Outlook* 15, no.9 (November–December 1972), pp.59–67.

Zarhi, Shaul, 'Economics of Refugee Settlement', *New Outlook* 10, no.9 (December 1967), pp.25–35.

Zaru, Nawaf, 'Mashari' al-Tasfiya al-Israeliyya lil Mukhayamat al-Filastinyya' [Israeli Projects to Eliminate Palestinian Camps], *Samid al-Iqtisadi*, no.83 (January/February/March 1991), pp.134–47.

Zedalis, Rex, 'Right of Return: A Close Look', *Georgetown Immigration Law Journal* 6 (1992), pp.495–517.

Zurayk, Constantine, *The Meaning of Disaster* (Beirut: Khayat College Book Cooperative, 1956).

Zureik, Elia, *The Palestinians in Israel: A Study in Internal Colonialism* (London: Routledge & Kegan Paul, 1979).

——, 'Palestinian Refugees and Peace', *Journal of Palestine Studies* 24, no.1 (Autumn 1994), pp.5–17.

——, 'Palestinian Refugees and the Right of Return', *Palestine-Israel Journal of Politics, Economics and Culture* 2, no.4 (Autumn 1995).

——, *Palestinian Refugees and the Peace Process* (Washington DC: Institute for Palestine Studies, 1996).

——, 'The Trek Back Home: Palestinian Returning Home and the Problems of Adaptation', mimeo, 1996.

——, 'Basic Points that Must be Taken into Consideration in the Final Status Negotiations Regarding the Refugee Issue', *Majallat al-Dirasat al-Filastiniyya*, no.41 (Winter 2000) (Arabic).

——, 'The Palestinian Refugee Problem: Conflicting Interpretations', *Global Dialogue* 4, no.3 (Summer 2002), pp.92–102.

Zweig, Ronald W., *German Reparations and the Jewish World: A History of the Claims Conference* (Boulder: Westview Press, 1987).

——, 'Restitution of Property and Refugee Rehabilitation: Two Case Studies', *Journal of Refugee Studies* 6, no.1/4 (1993), pp.56–64.

NEWSPAPERS AND PERIODICALS

Hebrew

Alpayim
Davar
Gesher
Haaretz
Hadashot
Ha'ir
'Al-Hamishmar

Haumah
Kol Ha'ir
Koteret Rashit
Lamerhav
Ma'ariv
Nekudah
Politikah
Yedi'ot Aharonot

Arabic

Al-Ayyam (Ramallah).
Al-Fajr (Jerusalem)
Fasl al-Maqal (Nazareth)
Al-Hayat (London)
Kol al-'Arab (Haifa)
Majlat al-Dirasat al-Filastiniyya (Beirut)
Al-Midan (Nazareth).
Al-Nahar (Beirut)
Samid al-Iqtisadi
Shaml (Ramallah)
Al-Sinnara (Nazareth)
Shuun Filastiniyya

English and French

Al-Ahram Weekly Online
Christian Science Monitor (Boston)
Foreign Broadcast Information Service, Middle East and Africa Daily Report (FBIS)
Forum (Jerusalem)
The *Guardian* (London)
Holy Land Studies: A Multidisciplinary Journal
Jerusalem Post
Jerusalem Quarterly
Le Monde
Le Monde Diplomatique
Middle East International (London)
Middle East Journal
Middle East Record (Jerusalem)
Mideast Mirror (Beirut)
New Outlook
The *New York Times*
The *Observer* (London)
Palestine-Israel Journal (Jerusalem)
Summary of World Broadcast (SWB), Part 4: The Middle East and Africa (Reading, BBC)
The Times (London)
Washington Post

Index

5011